BASEBALL

A TREASURY OF

ART AND LITERATURE

BASEBALL

A TREASURY OF
ART AND LITERATURE

Edited by Michael Ruscoe

Hugh Lauter Levin Associates, Inc.

Distributed by Macmillan Publishing Company, New York

Copyright © 1993, Hugh Lauter Levin Associates, Inc.
First published in paperback in 1995
Design by Philip Grushkin
Photo Research by Ellin Y. Silberblatt
Type Composition by Ken Scaglia
Printed in China
ISBN 0–88363–700–6

KEY TO SILHOUETTE FIGURES

Introduction: Jackie Robinson. *1st Inning:* Stan Musial. *2nd Inning:* Willie Mays. *3rd Inning:* Joe DiMaggio. *4th Inning:* Ted Williams. *5th Inning:* Pee Wee Reese. *6th Inning:* Satchel Paige. *7th Inning:* Phil Rizzuto. *8th Inning:* Henry Aaron. *9th Inning:* Carl Yastrzemski.
© 1992 Michael A. Schacht.

"Base Ball." Courtesy of the National Baseball Hall of Fame, Cooperstown, N.Y.

"A Challenge." *The Delhi Gazette* (N.Y.), July 13, 1825.

William Clarke. *Boy's and Girl's Book of Sports.* Cory and Daniels, 1835.

"The Knickerbocker Rules." Reprinted from *Baseball (1845–1881) From the Newspaper Accounts.* Preston D. Orem, 1961.

Henry Chadwick. *The Game of Base Ball: How to Learn It, How to Play It, and How to Teach It.* George Munro & Co., New York, 1868.

"New Ball Ground on the North Field at Hoboken." The *New York Clipper*, 1865.

Donald Honig. *Baseball America.* Copyright © 1985 by Donald Honig. Reprinted with permission of Macmillan Publishing Company.

A. G. Spalding. *Base Ball: America's National Game*, 1911.

William K. Zinsser. *Spring Training.* Copyright © 1989 by William K. Zinsser. Reprinted by permission of the author.

Jack Norworth and Albert Von Tilzer. "Take Me Out to the Ball Game." Copyright © 1908 by the York Music Company.

Bruce Anderson. "The National Pastime's Anthem." Reprinted courtesy of *Sports Illustrated* from the April 15, 1991 issue. Copyright © 1991 by Time Inc. All rights reserved.

Ernest L. Thayer. "Casey at the Bat." The *San Francisco Examiner*, 1888.

Franklin P. Adams. "Baseball's Sad Lexicon." The *New York Globe*, 1908.

Satchel Paige. "How to Keep Young." *Collier's* magazine, June 13, 1953.

George Carlin. "Baseball–Football." Copyright © Dead Sea Music. Reprinted by permission of the author.

William Safire. "Out of Left Field." Copyright © 1988 by the New York Times Company. Reprinted by permission.

Terry Cashman. *"Willie, Mickey and the 'Duke' (Talkin' Baseball)".* Copyright © 1981 by Blendingwell Music, Inc.

Mike Sowell. *July 2, 1903.* Copyright © 1992 by Mike Sowell. Reprinted with the permission of Macmillan Publishing Company.

Ty Cobb with Al Stump. *My Life in Baseball.* Copyright © 1961 by Doubleday, a division of Bantam Doubleday Dell Publishing Group, Inc.

Robert W. Creamer. *Babe: The Legend Comes to Life.* Copyright © 1974 by Robert W. Creamer. Published by Simon and Schuster.

John Holway. " 'Cool Papa' Bell." From *Voices from the Great Black Baseball Leagues.* Copyright © 1975, 1992 by John Holway. Published by Da Capo Press, Inc., a subsidiary of Plenum Publishing Corp.

Lawrence S. Ritter. *The Glory of Their Times.* New preface and Chapters 5, 15, 20, and 25. Copyright © 1984 by Lawrence S. Ritter. Remainder copyright © 1966 by Lawrence S. Ritter. By permission of William Morrow & Company, Inc.

Satchel Paige, as told to David Lipman. *Maybe I'll Pitch Forever.* Copyright © 1961 by The Curtis Publishing Company. Copyright © 1962 by David Lipman.

"Dizzy Dean's Day." *The Red Smith Reader*, by Red Smith. Edited by Dave Anderson. Copyright © 1982 by Random House, Inc. Reprinted by permission of Random House, Inc.

Bob Feller with Bill Gilbert. *Now Pitching, Bob Feller.* Copyright © 1990 by Bob Feller and Bill Gilbert. Published by arrangement with Carol Publishing Group. A Birch Lane Press Book.

Alan Courtney and Ben Homer. "Joltin' Joe DiMaggio." Copyright © 1941 by Alan Courtney Music Co.

Gerry Hern. "Spahn and Sain." Copyright © 1948 the *Boston Post.*

Yogi Berra and Thomas N. Horton. *Yogi: It Ain't Over . . .*, Copyright © 1989 by Lawrence Peter Berra and Thomas N. Horton. Published by McGraw-Hill. Reprinted by permission of the author.

Bob Uecker and Mickey Herskowitz. *Catcher in the Wry.* Copyright © 1982 by Bob Uecker and Mickey Herskowitz. Reprinted by permission of The Putnam Publishing Group.

Roger Kahn and Pete Rose. *Pete Rose: My Story.* Copyright © 1989 by Roger Kahn and Pete Rose. Reprinted with the permission of Macmillan Publishing Company.

Thomas Boswell. "Jim Abbott." *The Heart of the Order.* Copyright © 1988. Used by permission of Doubleday, a division of Bantam Doubleday Dell Publishing Group, Inc.

Robert W. Creamer. *Babe: The Legend Comes to Life.* Copyright © 1974 by Robert W. Creamer. Published by Simon and Schuster.

Lou Gehrig. "The Farewell Address at Yankee Stadium." Reprinted from the *Sporting News*, 1939.

Jackie Robinson and Alfred Duckett. *I Never Had It Made.* Copyright © 1972 by Jackie Robinson and Alfred Duckett. Published by G. P. Putnam's Sons.

Bill Veeck and Ed Linn. *Veeck—As In Wreck.* Copyright © 1962 by Bill Veeck and Ed Linn. Reprinted by permission of Sterling Lord Literistic, Inc.

Casey Stengel. From the *Congressional Record*, 1958.

John Updike. "Hub Fans Bid Kid Adieu." From *Assorted Prose.* Copyright © 1960 by John Updike. Reprinted by permission of Alfred A. Knopf, Inc. Originally appeared in the *New Yorker.*

Ed Sullivan. "The Way the Ball Bounces." Copyright © *New York Daily News.* Used with permission.

Henry Aaron with Lonnie Wheeler. Excerpts from *I Had a Hammer.* Copyright © 1991 by Henry Aaron and Lonnie Wheeler. Reprinted by permission of HarperCollins Publishers.

Roger Angell. *Five Seasons.* Copyright © 1975 by Roger Angell. Published by Simon and Schuster. Originally published in the *New Yorker.*

"Reggie Jackson's Three Home Runs." *The Red Smith Reader*, by Red Smith. Edited by Dave Anderson. Copyright © 1982 by Random House, Inc. Reprinted by permission of Random House, Inc.

Dan Shaughnessy. *One Strike Away.* Copyright © 1987 by Dan Shaughnessy. Published by Beaufort Book Publishers. Used by permission of the author.

Nolan Ryan and Jerry Jenkins. *Miracle Man: Nolan Ryan, the Autobiography.* Copyright © 1992 by Nolan Ryan and Jerry Jenkins. Published by Word Books, Dallas, Texas.

"The Chicago Baseball Grounds." Courtesy of the National Baseball Library, Cooperstown, N.Y.

"Ebbets Field Opening Victory for Superbas." Copyright © 1913 by the New York Times Company. Reprinted by permission.

Gay Talese. "Ebbets Field Goes on the Scrap Pile." Copyright © 1960 by the New York Times Company. Reprinted by permission.

Mike Bryan. *Baseball Lives.* Copyright © 1989 by Mike Bryan. Reprinted by permission of Pantheon Books, a division of Random House, Inc.

Bob Wood. *Dodger Dogs to Fenway Franks.* Copyright © 1988 by Bob Wood. Published by McGraw Hill.

Roger Angell. From *Season Ticket.* Copyright © 1988 by Roger Angell. Published by Houghton Mifflin Co.

Jacques Barzun. *God's Country and Mine.* Copyright 1954 by Jacques Barzun. Copyright renewed 1982 by Jacques Barzun. By permission of Little, Brown and Company.

Franklin D. Roosevelt. "The Green Light Letter." Courtesy of the National Baseball Library, Cooperstown, N.Y.

Donald Hall. "Baseball and the Meaning of Life." Copyright © 1981 by *National Review, Inc.*, 150 East 35th Street, New York, N.Y. 10016. Reprinted by permission.

James Cagney. *Cagney by Cagney.* Copyright © 1976. Used by permission of Doubleday, a division of Bantam Doubleday Dell Publishing Group, Inc.

Pete Hamill. "Never Forgive, Never Forget." The *New York Post.*

"Russians Say U.S. Stole 'Beizbol,'" Copyright © 1952 by the New York Times Company. Reprinted by permission.

Robert Whiting. *You Gotta Have Wa.* Copyright © 1989 by Robert Whiting. Reprinted with the permission of Macmillan Publishing Company.

A. Bartlett Giamatti. "Green Fields of the Mind." Estate of A. Bartlett Giamatti; Toni Smith Giamatti, Executrix.

Robert L. Harrison. "The Hellenic League." Reprinted by permission of *Spitball: The Literary Baseball Magazine.*

David E. Brand. "A Batter's Soliloquy." From *Baseball Magazine*, September 1911.

Mark Twain. *A Connecticut Yankee in King Arthur's Court.* Originally published by Charles L. Webster and Co., 1889.

Walter R. Hirsch. "A Coming Fanette." *Baseball Magazine*, June 1912.

Ring Lardner. Excerpt from "Alibi Ike." From *Ring Around the Bases* (New York: Scribners, 1992). First appeared in the *Saturday Evening Post*, July 31, 1915.

Frank Sullivan. "The Cliché Expert Testifies on Baseball." From *The Night Old Nostalgia Burned Down.* Copyright © 1946 by the Curtis Publishing Company. By permission of Little, Brown and Company.

Bernard Malamud. Excerpt from *The Natural.* Copyright © 1952 and copyright renewed © 1980 by Bernard Malamud. Reprinted by permission of Farrar, Straus & Giroux, Inc.

Reprinted from *The Year the Yankees Lost the Pennant*, a novel by Douglass Wallop, by permission of W.W. Norton & Company, Inc. Copyright 1954 by Douglass Wallop. Copyright renewed © 1982 by John Douglass Wallop.

Philip Roth. Excerpt from *The Great American Novel.* Copyright © 1973 by Philip Roth. Reprinted by permission of Farrar, Straus & Giroux, Inc.

Paul Simon. "Night Game." Copyright © 1975 by Paul Simon. Used by permission of the publisher.

"Hard Core Support," by John E. Maxfield. "Season Wish," by Linda Mizejewski. From *Baseball Diamonds*, by Kevin Kerrane & Richard Grossinger, editors. Copyright © 1980 by Richard Grossinger and Kevin Kerrane. Used by permission of Doubleday, a division of Bantam Doubleday Dell Publishing Group, Inc.

William Kennedy. *Ironweed.* Copyright © 1979, 1981, 1983 by William Kennedy. Used by permission of Viking Penguin, a division of Penguin Books USA Inc.

William P. Kinsella. *Shoeless Joe.* Copyright © 1982 by William P. Kinsella. Published by Houghton Mifflin Co.

Robert K. Adair. Excerpts from *The Physics of Baseball.* Copyright © 1990 by Robert K. Adair. Reprinted by permission of HarperCollins Publishers.

Mike Bryan. *Baseball Lives.* Copyright © 1989 by Mike Bryan. Reprinted by permission of Pantheon Books, a division of Random House, Inc.

Richard H. Durbin. From the *Congressional Record*, 1989.

Chester L. Smith. "Uniforms Shouldn't Be—Uniform," 1948. Reprinted by permission of the *Pittsburgh Press.*

Ron Rapoport. "The Pirates Rank No. 1 in the Fashion Parade." Copyright © 1977. Reprinted with permission from the *Chicago Sun-Times.*

Joel Zoss and John S. Bowman. *Diamonds in the Rough: The Untold History of Baseball.* Copyright © 1989 by Joel Zoss and John S. Bowman. Reprinted with the permission of Macmillan Publishing Company.

Ron Luciano and David Fisher. *The Umpire Strikes Back.* Copyright © 1982 by Ron Luciano and David Fisher. Used by permission of Bantam Books, a division of Bantam Doubleday Dell Publishing Group, Inc.

Earl Weaver and Berry Stainback. *It's What You Learn After You Know It All That Counts.* Copyright © 1982 by Earl Weaver. Used by permission of Doubleday, a division of Bantam Doubleday Dell Publishing Group, Inc.

George F. Will. *Men at Work.* Copyright © 1990 by George F. Will. Reprinted with permission of Macmillan Publishing Company.

Joe Gergen. "Expansion." Reprinted by permission of the *Sporting News*, St. Louis, MO.

Leonard Koppett. *The New Thinking Fan's Guide to Baseball.* Copyright © 1991 by Leonard Koppett. Reprinted by permission of Simon and Schuster.

Frank Dolson. *Beating the Bushes.* Copyright © 1982 by Frank Dolson. Originally published by Icarus Press, Inc.

Dan Rea. "Sociology 101 in a Shoe Box." Copyright © 1989 by Dan Rea. Originally published in *Newsweek*, March 27, 1989.

Nicknames of the Major League Clubs. From *The Baseball Encyclopedia*, Eighth Edition. Copyright © 1990 by Macmillan Publishing Company. Reprinted with permission of Macmillan Publishing Company.

J. N. Hook. "How the 26 Major League Baseball Teams Got Their Nicknames." From *All Those Wonderful Names.* Copyright © 1983, 1991 by J. N. Hook. Reprinted by permission of John Wiley & Sons, Inc.

David Nemec. *Great Baseball Feats, Facts & Firsts.* Copyright © 1987 by David Nemec. Used by permission of New American Library, a division of Penguin Books USA Inc.

"Members of the National Baseball Hall of Fame." Courtesy of the National Baseball Hall of Fame, Cooperstown, N.Y.

CONTENTS

This book is dedicated with love and eternal thanks
to Barbara Stockman, who waited all her life to see her
son's name on the spine of a book.

ACKNOWLEDGMENTS

When a ballplayer wins a championship, he usually gets, if he's lucky, between ten and twenty seconds on national television to thank the people who helped with his career—and all this happens while a mob of his teammates pours champagne down his pants. Fortunately, I can be a bit more deliberate.

Many thanks go to Hugh Levin for giving me the opportunity to work on this project at a time that I badly needed it, both financially and spiritually. Also, my sincere thanks go to Ellin Silberblatt. In the language of the game, she gave 110 percent on this book, and kept smiling while this book's editor badgered her with panic attacks and regaled her with his time-honored story of the twenty-five-inning Mets-Cardinals game of 1974.

I'd like to thank Paul Heacock and Ken Samuelson for their highly constructive and much appreciated input and suggestions regarding this book's manuscript. From our first meeting, it was delightfully apparent that our mutual devotion to the game would make working with them both easy and enjoyable. Thanks also to designer Philip Grushkin, whose craftsmanship makes what we authors write look so wonderful. And my thanks go to Ken Scaglia for his assistance with this project.

I thank Jennifer Hanlon for her help in researching this book, and Jim Hanlon for access to his truly impressive baseball card collection. Additional thanks to Craig Hunter for his help in the exploration phase of this project. Also, many thanks to research assistant Beth Anne Ruscoe. I hope I can be of equal help to her when she begins publishing her own books.

Thanks also go to those I encountered while tracking down the various pieces of art and literature included in this project: Bill Deane, Pat Kelley, and Robert Browning of the National Baseball Hall of Fame; William Gladstone, who opened his home and collection to us; Phil Bergen of the Bostonian Society; Glenn Stout of the Boston Public Library; Dick Johnson of the New England Sports Museum; Sydney Waller of Gallery 53 in Cooperstown, New York; Larry Fritsch, whose ability to pull rare baseball cards from out of a hat was both magical and awesome; and Mark Rucker of Transcendental Graphics of Boulder, Colorado. I would also like to thank all the artists and authors who appear in this book. Special thanks to Andy Jurinko and Tom Ross for being baseball fans and nice guys first and foremost.

Finally, my heartfelt thanks to my family, who shared my joy in this project during both happy and mournful times. I thank my father, who took me to my first baseball game; my mother, who let me go on a school night; and my wife, JeriAnn, who puts up with the results.

Introduction:

BASEBALL: A WORK OF ART

Generally, art is recognized as the vast group of creative works that, collectively and individually, reflect the human condition. Art carries within it the evidence of our best aspirations and our worst tendencies; our highest values and our basest cravings. Love and intolerance, greed and philanthropy, violence and tranquility: art carries within it all the qualities that make us human.

This might be why baseball, since its evolution as an American institution, has been so well represented in the world of art; far better represented than any other sport in the history of mankind. Baseball, like art, resonates with the full gamut of human characteristics. I've been watching baseball for more than twenty years, but I never saw this connection between baseball and art until I had the opportunity to edit this book.

To say that I'm a baseball fan is like saying Hank Aaron hit a home run or two during his career. Some of us who follow the game transcend fandom. I measure time by baseball seasons. I see, alongside the personal milestones of my life, the fortunes and failures of my favorite team and the landmark events of the game. I see American history broken into three sections. The first is Before Baseball, in which there was a swirling, amorphous morass of war, farming, invention, and, of course, American politics (our country's second greatest sport). Next came the Early Days of the game, a sort of mythological epoch played out by men with handlebar moustaches, clumsy, oversized bats, peculiar uniforms, loosely organized teams, and crudely sewn baseballs. Finally, there's the Modern Era, in which the game rides the perfect rhythm of the seasons: spring, summer, fall, the dead of winter, and then over again; always there, always constant, a framework for a year, a decade, a lifetime.

I got it bad.

It's nearly impossible to explain it to those who can't find a way to find something of themselves in the game. It's like trying to explain to someone all the reasons you love your husband or wife. In the course of compiling this book, one of the uninitiated asked me about the longest game in baseball history. Easy, I said. Brooklyn Dodgers versus Boston Braves, 1920, twenty-six innings. But, I added, another of the longest games in baseball history was begun on September 11, 1974, at Shea Stadium in New York. The Mets and the St. Louis Cardinals played until 3:15 A.M. in a twenty-five-inning marathon that ended when an errant pickoff throw to first allowed Bake McBride to score what proved to be the winning run for St. Louis. It was three months before my twelfth birthday. My father and I got home from the ballpark at 4:30 in the morning.

"Oh my God," my friend said. "That must have been awful!"

Awful? It's one of the greatest memories of my childhood. The details, so insignificant by themselves, seem magical and impossible to me now. Before the game, while I leaned over the railing and begged for autographs, my father and I had a chance to meet Jerry Cram, a relief pitcher up for a cup of coffee with the Mets. While the team's biggest stars politely signed a few autographs and moved on, Jerry, who would compile a lifetime 0–3 mark in twenty-three games over four years with the Mets and the Kansas City Royals, stood there and chatted with my dad. They talked about men stuff while I stared in awe at his uniform, his cap, his hands. Every now and then he would turn to me and say something funny, or tweak the bill of my cap, or ask me how my hot dog tasted, or what position I played on the ball field at school.

Later, as the game went into extra innings, my father and I moved down into the seats occupied by the season-ticket holders who had decided that it was more important to get a few extra hours' sleep than it was to see baseball history in the making. Soon, we were sitting right behind the Mets dugout. It still wasn't enough for me. Confidently, I made my way toward the prized box at the end of the dugout, the one from which you can look into the dugout and up and down the bench. I was stopped by a New York City police officer.

"Sorry, son," he said. "You can't sit in this box. This is Mrs. Payson's box." Mrs. Payson was the owner of the New York Mets.

The game wore on. The concession stands ran out of hot dog rolls, so they stuck the dogs into paper cups to serve to the few and the proud who remained. Jerry Cram was brought in to pitch, and he threw eight scoreless innings. My father and I cheered ourselves hoarse. The Mets finally blew the game, but that was all right, because that's what they did through most of the 1970s anyway. Dad and I went home exhausted and happy. To this day, that story of that night remains one of our favorites. We gladly rehash it any chance we get, and I have several friends who are frankly sick and tired of hearing about it.

I have other baseball memories. Being in the ballpark the day my childhood hero, Tom

Father and Son Pose with Ball and Bat.
c. 1880. Sepia photograph.
The Gladstone Collection of Baseball Art.

Artist unknown. Boys Playing an Early Form of Baseball on the Boston Common. c. 1840. Wood carving. The Bostonian Society. *This depiction is one of the earliest known illustrations of the sport in America.*

Seaver, returned to the Mets in 1983. Visiting my younger brother in college in Boston and, once again, sneaking down into the good seats during a chilly, perfect night at beautiful Fenway Park. Sitting in the stands at Jack Murphy Stadium in San Diego with my wife during our honeymoon in 1989, looking out over the warm, craggy hillsides of southern California and thinking about how much she must love me. Walking through Monument Park in Yankee Stadium with my father-in-law, who grew up within a couple of blocks of the stadium and who, as a child, actually shook Lou Gehrig's hand.

I saw hundreds of pieces of baseball art while compiling this book, and read dozens and dozens of pieces of writing. All my baseball memories came tumbling out of the recesses of my mind as I sorted through the art and literature contained herein. I saw my life, I saw America, I saw the history we all share as a people. There was love and family. There was fruitless struggle, and there were long, long stretches of hopelessness punctuated by brief, splendid moments of victory that justified the years of hardship. There was humor. There was sudden, inexplicable, unimaginable tragedy. There was life and hope.

Also contained in the art and writing of baseball was the story of America itself, reflected in the game and how generations of artists and authors saw it. Baseball, like America, traces its ancestry through England, although games involving sticks and balls were played as far back as the days of ancient Egypt. As discussed in the first chapter of this book, the basic concept of the game underwent several permutations in America, and elements of it were developed in a variety of games, including Rounders, Town Ball, One Old Cat, Two Old Cats, and Three Old Cats (each "cat" representing a base), Goal Ball, and the Massachusetts Game. Baseball's earliest published references came in the form of instructional booklets and child's books. A short poem appearing in the volume *A Little Pretty Pocket Book* in 1774 is believed to be the first reference to the game in print. William Clarke's *Boy's and Girl's Book of Sports*, published in 1835, also had a brief description of the game of "Base, or Goal Ball."

It was 1845 when Alexander J. Cartwright of the New York Knickerbockers proposed a set of rules that form the basis of the modern game of baseball. Among other innovations set down in the Knickerbocker rules was the establishment of a fixed distance between bases,

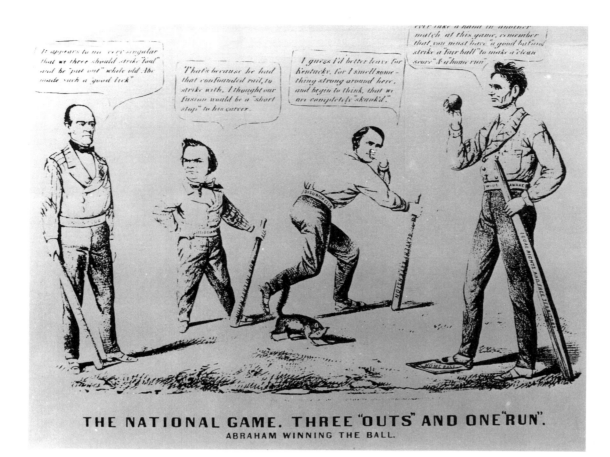

THE NATIONAL GAME. THREE "OUTS" AND ONE "RUN".
ABRAHAM WINNING THE BALL.

CURRIER AND IVES. *The National Game. Three "Outs" and One "Run."* 1860. Lithograph. 10 x 18 in. The National Baseball Library, Cooperstown, New York. *Here, baseball was the motif as the four presidential candidates of the 1860 campaign were caricatured.*

three strikes for an out, and the elimination of the practice of putting a runner out by hitting him with a thrown ball. From 1858 to 1866, the Knickerbocker Club published its by-laws, regulations, and rules, following the tradition of several other organizations that had played under pre-Knickerbocker rules, including the Olympic Ball Club of Philadelphia, the Eagle Ball Club of New York, the Excelsior Ball Club of Brooklyn, and the Takewambait Club of Natick, Massachusetts.

So many baseball teams had formed by 1857 that the Knickerbockers held a convention in New York City to establish their rules as the official guidelines for the game. At this convention, it was decided that a game would be complete at the end of nine innings, rather than the point at which one team scores twenty-one runs. Baseball was still an amateur game when the National Association of Base Ball Players, the first official league, was formed in 1858.

During this first blooming of baseball's popularity, Henry Chadwick of Brooklyn, New York, began earning the title "the Father of Baseball." Chadwick, having emigrated to the United States from England with his family in 1837 at the age of thirteen, began attending matches in the 1850s, and determined that baseball was destined to become America's national game. He became an advocate for the game, not only chronicling what happened on the field, but shaping and guiding baseball's development as an organized sport. He fought against the drinking and gambling that threatened to infest the game, promoted baseball through his writing, and taught the game to the general public with a series of instructional manuals. He also was instrumental in the invention of the box score, a scoring shorthand that is still a vital part of today's sports page.

The Civil War broke out in 1861 while baseball was crawling out of its infancy. As a result of the war, the game spread across the country at a vastly accelerated rate. Baseball was played in camps and prisons among soldiers from both the Union and the Confederacy, as depicted in Otto Boetticher's painting *Union Prisoners at Salisbury, N.C.* (1863). Once the war ended, the game was carried across the length and breadth of North America by soldiers returning home from battle.

As the popularity of the game continued to spread, baseball-related scenes began to permeate American art. Works produced in America still reflected the lush, deep colors and styles of

European art, but artists looking to convey American images were turning to what indeed was becoming the national game. In 1866, Currier and Ives published *The American National Game of Base Ball*, an image of a championship game at the Knickerbockers' Elysian Fields in Hoboken, New Jersey. Later images, such as Thomas Eakins's *Baseball Players Practicing* (1875), William Morris Hunt's *The Ball Players* (1877), and W. P. Snyder's *Collegiate Game of Baseball* (1889), are representative of the genteel, almost bucolic atmosphere associated with baseball by many artists of the era. Douglas Tilden's statue *The Baseball Player* (1888–89) reflects the idealized attributes of the ballplayer of that time: grace, strength, sportsmanship, and sober, steady concentration.

The game also began to show up in works of popular art. For the 1860 presidential election, Currier and Ives published a print titled *The National Game. Three 'Outs' and One 'Run.' Abraham Winning the Ball.* The print caricatured the four presidential candidates in a baseball motif as they discussed the campaign. Also, news of baseball games, along with illustrations, was found to help the sales of periodicals such as *Harper's Weekly* and *Frank Leslie's Illustrated Newspaper.* Art and writing on the game began to reach a baseball-hungry audience through the mass media.

The game enjoyed tremendous postwar popularity, and in 1871, following the lead of the professional and highly successful Cincinnati Red Stockings, ten club representatives met in New York City and formed the National Association of Professional Base Ball Players, the game's first pro league. However, the league was beset by chronic and crippling problems, including the tendency of players to jump from one team to another and public distrust due to interference in the game by gamblers. In 1876, under the leadership of William A. Hulbert of Chicago, the league reorganized, and the National League of Professional Baseball Clubs was born.

The Opening of the 1886 National League Season. 1886. Newspaper illustration. The National Baseball Library, Cooperstown, New York. Frank Leslie's Illustrated Newspaper *celebrated the opening of the 1886 season at the Polo Grounds by publishing this cover for its May 8, 1886 edition.*

Over the years, other leagues were formed, including the Players' League, the Union Association, and the American Association. None could compete with the dominance of the National League, however, and the NL was without competition from 1892 to 1900. *Spalding's Official Baseball Guide,* founded by pioneer player, owner, and league official Albert Goodwill Spalding, began publishing in 1878. It would be released annually until 1939, when it merged for its final two years with the *Reach Baseball Guide.* The *Spalding Guide* would become such a well-known piece of baseball history that fifty years after it ceased publication, broadcasters would criticize major league plays by saying that they weren't made "according to the *Spalding Guide.*" In 1886, *The Sporting News,* then devoted purely to baseball, began publishing in St. Louis. While it includes other sports today, it remains the oldest continuous baseball publication.

Baseball began to express itself in writing from other genres. "Casey at the Bat," one of the best-known American poems ever, was written by Ernest L. Thayer and published in the *San Francisco Examiner* on June 3, 1888. In 1896, the Cincinnati House of Refuge Manual Training School published *In Memoriam: Aaron Burt Champion,* a biographical tribute to the late president of the Red Stockings. *Our Baseball Club,* the first novel devoted exclusively to baseball, was published by E. P. Dutton in 1884, and reissued in 1896. Dime novels, such as *High Hat Harry, the Baseball Detective* and *Double Curve Dan, the Pitcher Detective,* were published in the 1880s. A three-act play titled *A Base Hit* was published in 1888, and a musical-comedy version was released a year later. Baseball also made an appearance in Mark Twain's *A Connecticut Yankee in King Arthur's Court* (1889).

As the public began to follow the careers of star ballplayers, pictorial albums were released featuring the stars of the day. In 1888, the Goodwin Tobacco Company published *Goodwin's Album,* a baseball-shaped booklet containing information and color sketches on the 1887 season. A booklet titled *Art Gallery of Prominent Baseball Players of America* was produced by the National Copper Plate Company in 1898.

In 1901, ex-sportswriter Ban Johnson organized the American League, and after two years of bitter in-fighting, underhanded business moves, court injunctions, and legal entanglements, the two leagues reached a truce in 1903 and agreed to live together in peace. The first World Series, a best-of-nine contest, was played in the fall of that year between the two league champions. The Boston Pilgrims (later to become the Red Sox) beat the Pittsburgh Pirates five games to three.

Baseball prospered in the first decades of the twentieth century, surviving World War I, when America's "Work or Fight" edict saw many star players drafted by the Army. Major league baseball also fended off one more battle from the upstart Federal League, which raided the NL and AL for many of their top players. After losing more than $10 million, though, the Federal League folded after the 1915 season.

Major league baseball faced its most serious threat in 1920 when eight members of the Chicago White Sox were accused of receiving payments from gamblers in exchange for throwing the previous year's World Series against the Cincinnati Reds. Judge Kenesaw Mountain Landis was appointed commissioner of baseball and given the broad authority that allowed him to permanently ban the eight "Black Sox" from the game. Around the same time, Babe Ruth, who had started his major-league career as a pitcher with the Boston Red Sox, was purchased by the New York Yankees. As New York's full-time right fielder, he hit home runs in astonishing numbers. There were fifty-four homers in 1920 for the Babe, ten more than any other team in the league hit as a group. Ruth became a national sensation and a living American legend.

As baseball continued its unprecedented growth in popularity, there was an explosion of baseball art and writing. Songs celebrating the game, most notably "Take Me Out to the Ball Game," were published. *Baseball Magazine,* a monthly publication of articles, photographs, and statistics, began its fifty-seven-year run in 1908. Cards featuring the images of players were released with packs of tobacco, which later gave way to bubble gum. Ballplayers also were featured in newspaper and magazine advertisements. Illustrator Norman Rockwell, who defined Americana with a long series of covers for the *Saturday Evening Post,* on many occasions used baseball as a theme in his work. Other artists began to turn toward more realistic

Buck Leonard At Bat. c. 1940. The National Baseball Library, Cooperstown, New York. *A Hall of Fame first baseman who spent twenty-three years with the Homestead Grays, Leonard was one of the Negro Leagues' greatest players.*

depictions of both the game and American life as urban centers in the United States swelled with immigrants.

Ring Lardner's short story "Alibi Ike" (1915) at once celebrated the game and lampooned the professional athlete, for whom, it seemed, ego was everything. Baseball also found its way into works by pulp writers Gilbert Patten, author of the Dick Merriwell and "Lefty" series; Edward Stratemeyer, author of the "Baseball Joe" books; and Zane Grey, who, while better known for his westerns, wrote three volumes of baseball-related tales. Future Hall of Fame players Christy Mathewson and Frank Chance also lent their names to works of baseball fiction that were ghostwritten by other authors.

Baseball reigned as the undisputed king of all sports in America. The country's devotion to the sport was reflected in the grand architecture of the huge steel-and-concrete stadiums that rose in major league cities. Dynasties began to form. The New York Giants, under the leadership of manager John McGraw, played in nine World Series and won three of them between 1905 and 1924. The New York Yankees began to establish their claim as the world's most successful sports franchise in 1921. Over the next sixty years, they won twenty-two World Series in thirty-three appearances. The St. Louis Cardinals won nine National League pennants and six world championships between 1926 and 1946. Instrumental in this period of domination was general manager Branch Rickey, who formed the first farm system in baseball for the Cardinals after joining the club in 1919. After fueling the success of the Gashouse Gang, Rickey moved to the Brooklyn Dodgers. There, he established an even more important milestone in baseball and American history when he signed Jack Roosevelt Robinson to a Dodgers contract. Jackie Robinson became the first African-American major league ballplayer in modern baseball history when he opened the season at first base for the Dodgers in 1947.

Robinson, however, was not the first black man ever to play in the majors. Moses Walker and his brother Welday, both African-Americans, played for Toledo of the old American Association in 1884. Also in that year, Chicago White Stockings star Cap Anson refused to field his team for an exhibition game against a group of Newark, New Jersey minor leaguers because their pitcher, George Stovey, was black. Anson continued to fight against the admittance of African-American players into the major leagues. In short time, by unspoken agreement, black ballplayers were forbidden by ownership to participate in major league games.

After thirty years of sporadic attempts, the first financially stable Negro Leagues were formed in the 1920s. They collapsed during the Great Depression, but were replaced by the Negro American League and the Negro National League several years later. These leagues featured some of the greatest ballplayers ever to take a field, and their willingness to play the game under conditions deplorably inferior to those of their white counterparts remains a tribute to their love of the game. Because of major league baseball's color barrier, great players such as Josh Gibson, "Cool Papa" Bell, Buck Leonard, Ray Dandridge, Oscar Charleston, Satchel Paige, and many others were denied the opportunity to display their talents in the major leagues. (Paige eventually played in the majors, but long after his best days had passed.) Similarly, most baseball fans never had the chance to see the feats of these athletes. And there are those today who argue persuasively that *all* major league accomplishments prior to the acceptance of the black man into organized baseball must be subject to scrutiny and question, since major league ballplayers didn't face a significant portion of the best available talent of that time.

Meanwhile, proof of the importance of baseball in America's daily life was presented in January 1942, shortly after the United States' entry into the second world war. Judge Landis contacted President Franklin D. Roosevelt and offered to suspend play of the game until the war ended. Roosevelt's response, in which he asked Judge Landis to let the game continue for the good of the country, is included in this book.

By the mid-twentieth century, baseball devotees had a deeply rooted sense of the game's place in the country's ongoing history. On June 12, 1939, the National Baseball Hall of Fame was opened in Cooperstown, New York, baseball's birthplace in legend, if not in fact. *Major First Events in a Century of Baseball,* which included sketches of Hall of Fame members, was published in the same year. *Baseball Digest,* a monthly anthology of newspaper stories, began publishing in August 1942.

Baseball's growth in the twentieth century paralleled social, demographic, economic, and technological changes in America. On August 5, 1921, at Pittsburgh's Forbes Field, announcer Harold Arlin of station KDKA described the first ballgame ever carried on radio. Teams, like the population of America, began to move around the country, pushing their way south and west. The Braves moved from Boston to Milwaukee in 1953, and to Atlanta in 1966. The Athletics moved from Philadelphia to Kansas City in 1955, and finally to Oakland, California, in 1968. The Browns moved from St. Louis in 1954 to Baltimore, where they became the Orioles. The Washington Senators moved to Minnesota and became the Twins; a second group of Senators left the nation's capital in 1972 and became the Texas Rangers. And in 1958, in the two most infamous moves of all, the Giants and Dodgers left Manhattan and Brooklyn for San Francisco and Los Angeles. By autumn 1992 the Giants were poised to move once more, this time to Florida's Tampa Bay–St. Petersburg area.

By this time, baseball had become so strongly fixed in the national consciousness that society responded to it in works ranging from lighthearted to somber. Bernard Malamud's allegorical novel *The Natural,* which explored, among other things, the mortality of the traditional baseball folk hero, was published in 1952. Douglass Wallop's *The Year the Yankees Lost the Pennant* (1954), the story of a Washington Senators fan who sold his soul to the devil for a chance to lead the club to a league championship over the Yankees, was later turned into the Broadway and film musical *Damn Yankees.* Comedians Bud Abbott and Lou Costello performed their classic "Who's on First?" routine for radio, television, and movie audiences. Baseball even found its way into the Pop Art movement of the 1960s, as seen in Andy Warhol's *Baseball* (1962).

As the baby boom thundered across America, major league baseball saw the birth of several new franchises. New York attorney William Shea, under the direction of the city fathers, formulated a plan to bring National League baseball back to New York following the departure of the Dodgers and Giants. He and several investors, including Branch Rickey, announced the formation of the Continental League, effectively threatening major league baseball's monopoly on the sport. Major league baseball, rather than battle the new league, agreed to expand instead. The year 1961 saw the birth of the new Washington Senators and the Los Angeles (later California) Angels of the American League. The New York Mets and the Houston Colt .45's (later to become the Astros) joined the National League a year later. Major league baseball added the San Diego Padres, the Montreal Expos, the Seattle Pilots (who have since become the Milwaukee Brewers), and the Kansas City Royals in 1969; the Seattle Mariners and the Toronto Blue Jays in 1977; and the Colorado Rockies and the Florida Marlins in 1993.

COLORPLATE I

UNIDENTIFIED ARTIST. *Boy with Ball and Bat.* 1844.
Oil on canvas. 23¹/₂ x 19 in. The Gladstone Collection of Baseball Art.

COLORPLATE 2

OTTO BOETTICHER. *Union Prisoners at Salisbury, N.C.* 1863. Colored stone lithograph with buff and blue tints. 21 x 37¹/₂ in. The Gladstone Collection of Baseball Art.

COLORPLATE 3

Currier and Ives. *The American National Game of Base Ball.* 1866.
Colored lithograph. 30¹/₄ x 40¹/₈ in. Yale University Art Gallery. Whitney Collection of Sporting Art.

COLORPLATE 4

WILLIAM MORRIS HUNT. *The Ball Players.* 1877. Oil on canvas. 15 1/8 x 24 in.
© The Detroit Institute of Arts. Gift of Mrs. John L. Gardner.

COLORPLATE 5

THOMAS EAKINS. *Baseball Players Practicing.* 1875. Watercolor. 10⅞ x 12⅞ in.
Museum of Art, Rhode Island School of Design. Jesse Metcalf and Walter H. Kimball Funds.

COLORPLATE 6

Prang Lithography Company Advertising Poster. 1887. 26 x 19 in.
Transcendental Graphics.

COLORPLATE 7

Home Run. 1887. Colored lithograph.
Missouri Historical Society.

COLORPLATE 8

Our National Game. 1887. Colored lithograph.
Missouri Historical Society.

Baseball continued to reflect social attitudes in the 1970s, known as the "Me Decade," and the 1980s, a period characterized by almost uncontrollable greed. The "reserve clause," for generations a traditional part of the standard major league contract that gave teams exclusive rights to individual players for the duration of their careers, was struck down. The result was free agency, in which eligible players were allowed to sign with the team of their choice once a contract expired. The combination of owners desperate for winning teams at any cost and players anxious to add as many zeroes as possible to their paychecks drove major league salaries to dizzying and heretofore unimaginable heights.

During the late twentieth century, baseball art and writing explored almost every genre and artistic category. Philip Roth's comic work *The Great American Novel* (1973) detailed the history of the fictitious Patriot League. William Kennedy won a Pulitzer Prize for *Ironweed* (1979), the melancholy tale of an alcoholic ex-ballplayer trying to make peace with his tragic past. Stand-up comic George Carlin's routine on baseball and football not only compared the two sports, but highlighted the ironies in the language used by each. As a nostalgia craze swept the country, books such as *The Glory of Their Times* by Lawrence S. Ritter (1966) and *The Boys of Summer* by Roger Kahn (1971) exposed younger baseball fans to players of earlier decades. Artist Andy Jurinko began a series of paintings depicting ballparks, many of which, such as Ebbets Field and the Polo Grounds, had fallen before the wrecking ball. Other books, such as Jackie Robinson's autobiography *I Never Had It Made* (1972), took a closer and harder look at some of the problems baseball encountered through its "Golden Age."

Boys Ready for an Early Game.
c. 1880. Sepia photograph.
The Gladstone Collection of Baseball Art.

Baseball attendance figures soared between the 1970s and the 1990s, and the game provided fans with some of its greatest stars and most memorable moments. It also was dogged by social problems that continued to plague America at large. Drugs found their way into the game, as they had in every other walk of life. Players found themselves suspended from the game as baseball struggled to form an antidrug policy to cope with the problem. Also, the average fan bore the brunt of a series of labor disputes that saw the 1981 and 1985 seasons interrupted by player strikes. The opening of the 1991 season was delayed by a spring-training management lockout. In September 1992, Commissioner Fay Vincent resigned following a lengthy battle with several club owners. The threat of another strike or lockout looms in 1993 and 1994 with the renegotiation of the current collective bargaining agreement. The field of play, still green and still perfect, now lies at the center of a forest of television contracts, player representatives, ownership committees, and legal entanglements.

But baseball endures. As this introduction is being written, there are those who say that the game has reached a crossroads. Some argue, as some have since baseball was organized more than a hundred years ago, that major league baseball's financial foundation is crumbling, and that the game as we know it is in jeopardy.

I think these people are wrong. History, as borne out by the works in this book, has proven that the game is stronger than the leagues that are formed to play it. During the baseball strike of 1981, I went to a local park and watched Little League games. I shagged fly balls with my brother and a friend. I recognized that the game of baseball is larger than the corporate scaffolding that surrounds it. It is, in fact, one of our most endearing and durable works of art. Whether it's on a major league field or in your own backyard, every game, every inning, every pitch, and every hit is a small, brightly colored tile in a colossal mosaic that reaches back through the history of our society and forward, endlessly, into our future.

Baseball lends itself so well to the works in this book because it's an outlet, for better or worse, for all that it means to be human: success and failure, tragedy and perseverance, the desire to perform as an individual and the need to be part of a team. Baseball shows us who we are and what we've been. It shows us that one perfect moment of triumph can outweigh weeks, months, and years of adversity. It shows us avarice, and it shows us charity. It shows us bigotry and brotherhood. It shows us Jackie Robinson and Eddie Stanky. Stanky, another member of that 1947 Dodgers club, had told Robinson at the start of the season that he didn't approve of Robinson's being on the team. But early that year, he watched for three days as the Philadelphia Phillies heaped vicious and detestable verbal abuse upon Robinson, who couldn't respond out of concern that he might trigger an incident that would solidify baseball's color line forever. Stanky, enraged at what he heard and no doubt inspired by Robinson's quiet courage, confronted the Phillies dugout single-handedly, screaming, "Listen, you yellow-bellied cowards, why don't you yell at somebody who can answer back!"

Baseball shows us Roberto Clemente, the Pittsburgh Pirates outfielder who was killed in a plane crash in 1973 while on a relief mission to earthquake-stricken Nicaragua, and who remains a more powerful and shining example than all the money-grabbers who have ever invaded the game. Baseball gives us Lou Gehrig, who, while stricken with a fatal illness, notched a win over death and despair when he stood on a field before sixty-two thousand people, counted the blessings he had received over his lifetime, and proclaimed himself the luckiest man on the face of the earth.

Finally, baseball gives us a scene that's played out every day in backyards and parks and lots all over America: a child awkwardly clutching a bat in his hands, while someone who loves him softly pitches a ball, teaching the child how to swing and beginning the child's training in all the skills he'll ever need in life.

MICHAEL RUSCOE
Stratford, Connecticut
October 1992

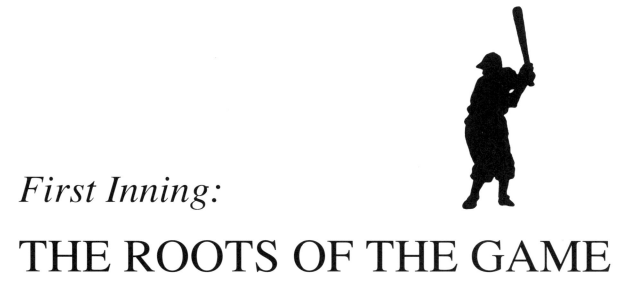

First Inning:

THE ROOTS OF THE GAME

As baseball evolves and spreads throughout America, the game begins to appear in poetry, essays, and newspaper stories.

FROM A LITTLE PRETTY POCKET BOOK

"Base Ball"

Published in 1774, this poem is reputed to be the first mention of the game of baseball in print.

————————

The Ball once struck off,

Away flies the Boy

To the next destin'd Post,

And then Home with Joy.

The Striker.
The National Baseball
Library, Cooperstown,
New York.

FROM *THE DELHI GAZETTE* (N.Y.)
"A Challenge"

This challenge, which appeared in the July 13, 1825, issue of the Delhi (N.Y.) Gazette, is one of the earliest known journalistic references to baseball.

_____

The undersigned, all residents of the new town of Hamden, with the exception of Asa C. Howland, who has recently removed into Delhi, challenge an equal number of persons of any town in the County of Delaware, to meet them at any time at the house of *Edward B. Chace*, in said town, to play the game of BASS-BALL, for the sum of one dollar each per game. If no town can be found that will produce the required number, they have no objection to play against any selection that can be made from the several towns in the county.

ELI BAGLEY, EDWARD B. CHACE, HARRY P. CHACE, IRA PEAK, WALTER C. PEAK, H.B. GOODRICH, R.F. THUMBER, ASA C. HOWLAND, M.L. BOSTWICK.

Hamden, July 12, 1825.

William Clarke
FROM BOY'S AND GIRL'S BOOK OF SPORTS

Baseball, the old adage says, is ultimately a simple game: throw the ball, hit the ball, catch the ball. However, in this piece, published in 1835, the game begins its long-standing tradition of defying simple, more specific description. See also: Casey Stengel.

_____

Base, or Goal Ball.—In Base, the players divide themselves into two equal parties, and chance decides which shall have first innings. Four stones or stakes are placed from twelve to twenty yards asunder, as, *a, b, c, d*, in the margin; another is put at *e*. One of the party, who is out, places himself at c. He tosses the ball gently toward *a*, in front of whom one of the *in-party* places himself, who strikes the ball, if possible, with his bat. If he miss three times, or if the ball, when struck, be caught by any of the players of the opposite side, who are scattered about the field, he is out, and another takes his place. If none of these accidents take place, on striking the ball he drops the bat, and runs toward *b*, or, if he can, to *c, d*, or even to *a*, again. If, however, the boy who stands at *c*, or any of the out-players who may happen to have the ball, strike him with it in his progress from *a* to *b*, *b* to *c*, *c* to *d*, or *d* to *a*, he is out. Supposing he can only get to *b*, one of his partners takes the bat, and strikes at the ball in turn. If the first player can only get to *c*, or *d*, the second runs to *b* only, or *c*, as the case may be, and a third player begins; as they get home, that is, to *a*, they play at the ball by turns, until they all get out. Then, of course, the out-players take their places.

C

B   D

E

A

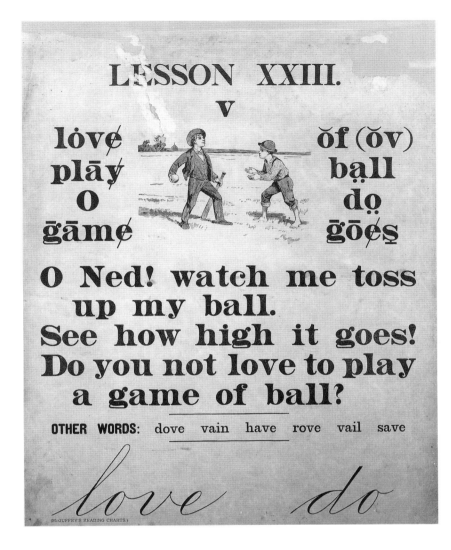

LESSON XXIII.

v

love   ŏf (ŏv)
plāy   ball
o   do
gāme   gōes

O Ned! watch me toss
up my ball.
See how high it goes!
Do you not love to play
a game of ball?

OTHER WORDS: dove vain have rove vail save

love   *do*

(McGUFFEY'S READING CHARTS.)

From *McGuffy's Reader*. c. 1880.
The Gladstone Collection of Baseball Art.

The Knickerbocker Baseball Club

The Knickerbocker Rules

On September 23, 1845, Alexander J. Cartwright and the Knickerbockers of New York adopted these as the rules for their games of baseball. They form the basis of the rules by which the modern game is played.

    1ST. Members must strictly observe the time agreed upon for exercise, and be punctual in their attendance.

    2ND. When assembled for exercise, the President, or in his absence, the Vice-President, shall appoint an Umpire, who shall keep the game in a book provided for that purpose, and note all violations of the By-Laws and Rules during the time of exercise.

    3RD. The presiding officer shall designate two members as Captains, who shall retire and make the match to be played, observing at the same time that the players opposite to each other should be as nearly equal as possible, the choice of sides to be then tossed for, and the first in hand to be decided in like manner.

4TH. The bases shall be from "home" to second base, forty-two paces; from first to third base, forty-two paces, equidistant.

5TH. No stump match shall be played on a regular day of exercise.

6TH. If there should not be a sufficient number of members of the Club present at the time agreed upon to commence exercise, gentlemen not members may be chosen in to make up the match, which shall not be broken up to take in members that may afterwards appear; but in all cases, members shall have the preference, when present, at the making of a match.

7TH. If members appear after the game is commenced, they may be chosen in if mutually agreed upon.

8TH. The game to consist of twenty-one counts, or aces; but at the conclusion an equal number of hands must be played.

9TH. The ball must be pitched, not thrown, for the bat.

10TH. A ball knocked out of the field, or outside the range of the first and third base, is foul.

11TH. Three balls being struck at and missed and the last one caught, is a hand out; if not caught is considered fair, and the striker bound to run.

12TH. If a ball be struck, or tipped, and caught, either flying or on the first bound, it is a hand out.

13TH. A player running the bases shall be out, if the ball is in the hands of an adversary on the base, or the runner is touched with it before he makes his base; it being understood, how-ever, that in no instance is a ball to be thrown at him.

14TH. A player running who shall prevent an adversary from catching or getting the ball before making his base, is a hand out.

15TH. Three hands out, all out.

16TH. Players must take their strike in regular turn.

17TH. All disputes and differences relative to the game, to be decided by the Umpire, from which there is no appeal.

18TH. No ace or base can be made on a foul strike.

19TH. A runner cannot be put out in making one base, when a balk is made on the pitcher.

20TH. But one base allowed when a ball bounds out of the field when struck.

The First Ball Game. The National Baseball Library, Cooperstown, New York. *On June 19, 1846, the first baseball game was played under organized rules.*

Henry Chadwick

FROM THE GAME OF BASE BALL: HOW TO LEARN IT, HOW TO PLAY IT, AND HOW TO TEACH IT

Henry Chadwick, father of sportswriting, inventor of the box score, and a driving force behind baseball's popularity in the nineteenth century, describes the origins of his love of the game.

———————————

Between thirty and forty years ago, my favorite field game was the old school-boy sport of *Rounders*. We used to dig a hole in the ground for the home position, and place four stones in a circle, or nearly so, for the bases, and, choosing up sides, we went in for a lively time at what was the parent game of base ball. When the ball tosser, or "feeder," sent a ball to the bat, and it was hit into the field, the player running round the bases at once became the target of the fielders, their efforts, if the ball was not caught, being directed to hitting him with the ball, in which case he was out, and, failing to do this, they would try and toss the ball into the hole at "home," provided there was no one to take the bat, and, if they were successful, the side at the bat had to retire. When all of the side were put out—each man retiring from play as he was put out—then the field side took the bat, and so the game went on until a certain number of runs were reached—mutually agreed upon—and the party first scoring the required number won the game. Of course the game was merely a source of fun and exercise, but little skill being required to play it, any school-boy being able to learn it in ten minutes. But from this little

The Pitcher. The National Baseball Library, Cooperstown, New York. *In baseball's early days, a pitch was considered legal only if delivered underhand.*

English acorn of Rounders has the giant American oak of Base Ball grown, and just as much difference exists between the British school-boy sport and our American National game, as between the seedling and the full grown king of the forest.

This game, as played by clubs in this country, was called "Town Ball," and one of the oldest of these organizations is the Olympic Club, of Philadelphia, first organized in 1833. Town Ball had more regularity in its rules, but was the same, in principle, as "Rounders." Posts, however, were used as bases in Town Ball, and there were regularly-appointed positions in the field. As usual, with every thing imported, we do not possess it long before we endeavor to improve it, and as our old American edition of base ball, in vogue in New York some twenty-five years ago, was an improvement on Rounders, so is our present National game a great step in advance of the game of base ball as played in 1840 and up to 1857.

About twenty odd years ago I used to frequently visit Hoboken with base ball parties, and, on these occasions, formed one of the contesting sides; and I remember getting some hard hits in the ribs, occasionally, from an accurately thrown ball. Some years afterwards the rule of throwing the ball at the player was superceded by that requiring it to be thrown to the base player, and this was the first step towards our now National game.

In the New England States the old game of Rounders and Town Ball had been replaced by an improved game, which was generally known as the "Massachusetts Game" of base ball, the variation from Town Ball consisting mainly in the fact that the ball was changed in size and weight, and was thrown to the bat instead of being pitched or tossed. For several years this game prevented the introduction, into New England, of our game of base ball, or the "New York game," as it was there called. But the superiority of the National game soon led to a popularity for it in the East which entirely did away with the Massachusetts game, and now the latter, like Town Ball, is rarely played, while base ball clubs have sprung up by hundreds.

It was in 1856, I think, when, on returning from the early close of a cricket match on Fox Hill, I chanced to go through the Elysian Fields during the progress of a contest between the noted Eagle and Gotham Clubs. The game was being sharply played on both sides, and I watched it with deeper interest than any previous ball match between clubs that I had seen. It was not long before I was struck with the idea that base ball was just the game for a national sport for Americans, and, reflecting on the subject, it occurred to me, on my return home, that from this game of ball a powerful lever might be made by which our people could be lifted into a position of more devotion to physical exercise and healthful out-door recreation than they had hitherto, as a people, been noted for. At that period—and it is but eleven years ago—I need not state that out-door recreation was comparatively unknown to the large mass of the American people. In fact, as is well known, we were the regular target for the shafts of raillery and even abuse from our out-door sport-loving cousins of England, in consequence of our national neglect of sports and pastimes, and our too great devotion to business and the "Almighty Dollar." But thanks to Base Ball—the entering wedge of the great reformation which has since taken place—we have been transformed into quite another people, and as we never do things by halves, but generally rush into *furores* and extremes, the chances are that from being too neglectful of out-door sports we shall become too fond of them, and, from being content to play second fiddle to the sportsmen and athletes of England we shall not rest content until we have defeated them in every speciality of games, of which they have, for so many years, been the leading exemplars.

From the time that I first became an admirer of base ball, I have devoted myself to improving and fostering the game in every way I thought likely to promote the main object I had in view, viz: to assist in building up a national game for the country as much so as cricket is for England. At the time I refer to I had been reporting cricket for years, and, in my method of taking notes of contests, I had a plan peculiarly my own. It was not long, therefore, after I had become interested in base ball, before I began to invent a method of giving detailed reports of leading contests at base ball, and, seeing that every thing connected with the game, almost, was new, its rules crude and hastily prepared, with no systematized plan of recording the details of a game, and, in fact, no fixed method of either playing or scoring it, as soon as I became earnestly interested in the subject I began to submit amendments to the rules of the game to the consideration of the fraternity, generally in the form of suggestions through the press, my first

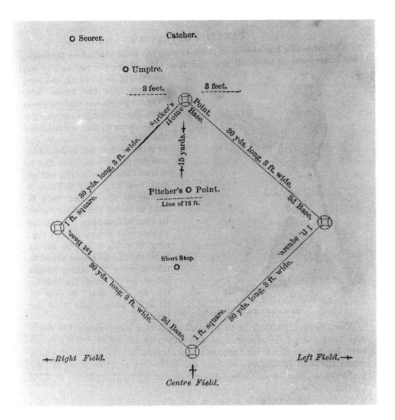

Diagram of a Baseball Field from an Early Manual. The National Baseball Library, Cooperstown, New York.

improvement introduced being an innovation on the simple method of scoring then in vogue. Step by step, little by little, either directly or indirectly, did I succeed in assisting to change the game from the almost simple field exercise it was some twenty years ago up to the manly, scientific game of ball it is now. When I found any special opposition to my views and plans, created by personal prejudice or from any other cause, I induced others to father my ideas, at the cost, sometimes, of a little variation, and, by that means, worked them into being tried on their merits. I did not care for the credit of the suggestion, so long as the idea was carried out and the game improved.

One of the toughest fights I had, in this experience, was in getting the old rule of the bound catch from fair balls abolished, and it was not until I adopted the feint of advocating the rule in one paper and opposing it in others, and had thereby created two influential parties, where but one had before existed, that I fully succeeded in my object. I only asked one season's trial of it at the hands of the Convention, to satisfy the fraternity that the fly rule was the correct one, but it was some years before I could get their consent. From the day that the bound rule was abolished not a single club, of any pretentions to skill as players, have played a game, that I am aware of, under that rule. Even the "muffins"—sensible fellows as they are—have repudiated it, and now, the only surprise is how it remained a rule of the game so long.

There were rules, too, to which custom had given almost a legal sanction, which I found obstacles to an improved condition of the game; among which may be named the old habit of running around the bases without touching them; the facilities which existed for wilfully wild pitching; the great extent of the discretionary power given the umpire; the ill-feeling resulting from unnecessary appeals for judgment; and, above all, the almost total neglect of attention to discipline and training as essential of success. In presenting amendments or suggesting improvements to the game, I have always proved, either by argument or practical demonstration, the correctness of my views, and, in this, I have, of course, been greatly assisted by facts and figures derived from actual observation and from a statistical analysis of the result of each season's play; the system of short-hand reporting for movements made—not words uttered—which I invented several years ago, giving me a correct data, which could not well be gainsaid, except by an equally detailed analysis of matches played.

I have not written this . . . in any egotistical spirit, but simply to place on record the fact, that while many have worked assiduously for the welfare of the game, and devoted themselves to their work as to a labor of love, none have been more strenuous in their efforts to establish base ball as the national pastime, or more solicitous to see the game take a commanding position, as a moral recreation, than I have been. In my capacity as a reporter of the principal contests on the ball fields for the past ten years, and, as the author of the only standard works on base ball, and more recently as editor of the first weekly journal ever published, especially devoted to the interests of base ball, I have naturally possessed greater facilities and more influence in promoting the objects I had in view than others have had, equally as eager as myself to advance the popularity of the game and doubtless possessing more ability. But to no one do I give place in my efforts to bring base ball up to the highest point of excellence, or to rid it of those evil influences, which, of late years, have worked their way into the fraternity, greatly to the injury of that moral reputation the game, in its integrity naturally should possess. . . .

Trusting that this latest of my contributions to the literature of base ball may prove as acceptable to the fraternity as my previous works on the subject, I beg leave to remain, the base ball players' sincere friend,

THE AUTHOR.

FROM *THE NEW YORK CLIPPER*

"The New Ball Ground on the North Field at Hoboken"

THE OPENING GAME BY THE MUTUAL CLUB

Published on June 3, 1865, this piece, possibly written by Henry Chadwick, describes the first day of play on newly laid-out grounds at the Elysian Fields, which had become the home field of the Knickerbockers in 1846.

––––––––––––––

"Everything was lovely and the game was on the fly" on Thursday, May 25th, at Hoboken, and consequently there was a gay gathering of the festive youths of the Mutual Club in particular, and of the admirers of base ball in general, on the gala occasion of the opening game on the newly-laid-out ball ground at the Elysian Fields, which took place on the day in question. Monday, 22d, was the day first named for the opening play on the new grounds, but the rain of that day rendered a postponement necessary, and Thursday being the next practice day of the club, it was proposed to carry out the programme prepared on that day. The weather on Thursday was all that could have been desired, and considering the fact that it was but a week since the old ground was played upon, the new field was in surprisingly good order. A day's rain will beat in the sandy covering which has been placed upon the clay groundwork of the space occupied by the pitcher, striker and catcher, and then, with a good rolling, the surface will be as hard and level as a table.

As the crowd of visitors increased, and the new improvements were duly inspected, terms of praise emanated from every one present, the energetic president of the club, Coroner John Wildey, very properly coming in for the lion's share of the commendation, for to his efforts and liberal expenditure of time, labor and money, are the fraternity indebted for such a fine ball ground—a ground, by-the-way, which in the picturesque character of its surroundings, and the

excellent arrangements made for the comfort and convenience of spectators—especially the fair sex—is not equalled by any other base ball ground in the country. A part of the proceedings of the day was the raising of the new and handsome flag staff presented by President Wildey to the club. An effort was made to place it in its position before the game commenced, but the tackle not being properly prepared, it had to be deferred until later in the afternoon, when the pole was duly raised and planted, and the club colors flung to the breeze from its peak, a ball and bat being the topmast ornaments of the staff.

The Grand Base Ball Match for the Championship, Between the Excelsior and Atlantic Clubs of Brooklyn. July 19, 1860. The Brooklyn Historical Society. *The Excelsiors won, 23 to 4.*

The game played was between a nine—not the nine—and a field side of fifteen, the match, "first nine vs. second" being deferred to Monday, May 29th, on account of the absence of three or four of the contesting players. . . . A full game was played, the score at the close being 25 to 13 in favor of the first nine. The display as a whole was not up to the mark of what the club is capable of by any means, that of the first nine lacking spirit as far as the majority of their players was concerned. Wanzley was lazy, McMahon indifferent, Hunt rather afraid of swift balls, and Harris not in a condition to pitch. Goldie played his position with his usual "vim" and earnestness, and of course did well; Bearman at 2d base made two or three capital stops; Zeller and Pattison marked their fielding with fine fly catches, and Duffy was on hand at 3d base, but on the whole the play of the nine was far below the mark necessary to enter the arena against the Atlantics with any probability of success. . . .

We were several times questioned during the game in reference to the fairness of McSweeny's delivery, some considering it a jerk. This question of jerking a ball is a rather difficult one to decide upon. A jerk, in the ordinary sense of the term, is made when the elbow of the arm, holding the ball, touches the side of the person so delivering it, and we believe this is the definition applied in the case of the rules of the National Association. A ball can be sent with all the swiftness of this style of jerking without the elbow touching the side, but as it is difficult to see the motion, such style of delivery is not considered a jerk according to the rules in question, as we understand them. If McSweeny jerks a ball, so does Pratt, Sprague, and McBride. A jerk, in reference to pitching in base ball, is just as difficult of explanation as that of throwing in round arm bowling at cricket.

While sitting at the scorers' table during the game of Thursday, we were forcibly struck with the propriety of the clubs adopting a rule prohibiting boys, unaccompanied by their parents, from occupying seats on the raised platform. The general class of juveniles who patronize our ball grounds, in the profanity and obscenity of their language, and their propensity for skylarking, are totally unfit to be allowed in the vicinity of any locality occupied by ladies. Besides, adults ought always to have the preference in taking seats, especially when the supply is not equal to the demand. At any rate, keep the boys off the platform seats, if you wish to avoid the annoyances they create.

Donald Honig

FROM BASEBALL AMERICA

Although some misguided cynics attempt to dispute it, many steadfastly adhere to their belief in Santa Claus. So it is also with the legend of Abner Doubleday inventing baseball on a farm in Cooperstown, New York. Donald Honig sets the record straight.

Baseball legends have age and diversity. One of the grand old stories, which once upon a time serious men gave credence to, involved Abraham Lincoln. According to this story, a committee from the Chicago convention, which on May 18, 1860, had nominated Lincoln as the Republican candidate for president, arrived in Springfield, Illinois, to notify him formally of the event. When the distinguished deputation appeared at the Lincoln home they found the candidate not available. A messenger was dispatched to apprise Mr. Lincoln that he had visitors. This particular moment of American history, so the tale goes, found Mr. Lincoln out on the commons engaged in a game of baseball, standing at home plate, bat in hand. When the messenger informed the tall, muscular prairie lawyer that he had a living room full of politicos, Lincoln replied, "Tell the gentlemen that I am glad to know of their coming; but they'll have to wait a few minutes till I make another base hit." (The only thing missing from this little fable is that Lincoln then pointed to the center field chestnut trees and lofted the next pitch over the very spot; but that particular flourish was being reserved for another American original, in the next century.)

Whether Lincoln actually ever struck a pitched ball with a piece of one of those rails he was so famous for splitting is not known, but it is certainly true that baseball was played by the soldiers of North and South during the Civil War. The time spent between the heavy work at places like Chancellorsville, Gettysburg, and Cold Harbor could become tedious. Between battles of terrifying intensity and long marches were months of inactivity. The men lay on cots in Sibley tents or in winter huts and wrote letters, smoked their pipes, read and reread newspapers, or played checkers. They sang songs, encouraged their amateur musicians, cut wood, and had snowball fights. They also burned off the hours by engaging in competitions like foot racing, wrestling, leapfrog, quoits, marbles, and baseball. The last of these, known also as bass ball, was one of the most popular of these diversions.

Wearing their slant-visored forage caps or slouch hats, with a broad X of suspenders crossing their backs, they went to bat, swinging cut-down broomsticks or sawed-off fence planks at balls that may have been so many stockings or so much yarn held together by a piece of stitched leather, sometimes with some rubber from an old boot tucked in to make the ball livelier. Some Confederate boys in Virginia ran the bases after whacking a yarn-wrapped walnut with a roughly trimmed hickory limb.

The game was only recently out of the incubator in those days and there were many variants. One way of playing it saw a base-runner retired if one of the fielders was able to pink him with a thrown ball, implying that the ball was not as hard as the missiles they play with today. Nevertheless, some of those boys could throw even a soggy ball with impact. A soldier from a Texas regiment noted in his diary that "Frank Ezell was ruled out" of the game because "he could throw harder and straighter than any man in the company. He came very near knocking the stuffing out of three or four of the boys, and the boys swore they would not play with him."

The boys in the 1860s knew all about baseball fever. After the war, they scattered to all points of the national compass and, along with tales of cannon fire and bayonet charges, they talked about the new game and showed how it was played. Americans young and old took to it with alacrity, playing it in all its variants, skillfully and clumsily, but with an enthusiasm that guaranteed the contagion would continue to spread. It wasn't long before every community had its team and local rivalries were established. Teams sponsored by merchants or by politicians sniffing a popular craze go back to the 1860s.

The origin of the game is not known, but legends quickly sprang up to fill this gap in our knowledge. The most celebrated story is that Abner Doubleday invented it at Cooperstown, New York, in 1839. This highly varnished fish story received official propagation in 1907, thanks to a distinguished if credulous group known as the Mills Commission. The group was formed at the behest of Albert Spalding, one of the game's pioneer figures and founder of the sporting goods firm that still bears his name, and charged with the task of determining the origin of baseball (or "Base Ball," as they wrote it). The commission included A. G. Mills, described as "an enthusiastic ball player before and during the Civil War," and the third president of the National League; Arthur P. Gorman, a former United States senator from Maryland; Morgan G. Bulkeley, former governor of Connecticut and the first president of the National League; and four other gentlemen of varying distinction and impeccable pedigree.

After sifting through the available evidence, the group came to a unanimous decision, to wit:

> That Base Ball had its origins in the United States.
> That the first scheme for playing it, according to the best evidence obtainable to date, was devised by Abner Doubleday, at Cooperstown, New York, in 1839.

Bingo: instant mythology, particularly in the second assertion, a high bouncer of a story that remained airborne for decades. That the game as we know it today had its origins in the United States is true; but that Doubleday was its originating genius and that Cooperstown was the cradle for all runs, hits, and errors is malarkey of the purest brand. Nobody believes the tale today, but Cooperstown remains the game's symbolic home, and it couldn't have happened to a lovelier, more picturesque American village.

The commission closed its report (signed by Mills) with "evidence" as substantial as a butterfly's wing. In part it reads:

> in the interesting and pertinent testimony for which we are indebted to Mr. A. G.
> Spalding, appears a circumstantial statement by a reputable gentleman, according to
> which the first known diagram of the diamond, indicating positions for the players was
> drawn by Abner Doubleday in Cooperstown, New York, in 1839. Abner Doubleday
> subsequently graduated from West Point and entered the regular army, where, as

Brigadier General Abner Doubleday. c. 1860. The National Baseball Library, Cooperstown, New York. *Doubleday is the man most often and most erroneously credited with inventing the game of baseball.*

Captain of Artillery, he sighted the first gun fired on the Union side (at Fort Sumter) in the Civil War. . . .

> In the days when Abner Doubleday attended school in Cooperstown, it was a common thing for two dozen or more of school boys to join in a game of ball. Doubtless, as in my later experience, collisions between players in attempting to catch the batted ball were frequent, and injury due to this cause, or to the practice of putting out the runner by hitting him with the ball, often occurred.
>
> I can well understand how the orderly mind of the embryo West Pointer would devise a scheme for limiting the contestants on each side and allotting them to field positions, each with a certain amount of territory; also substituting the existing method of putting out the base runner for the old one of "plugging" him with the ball.

And so on and so forth. Doubleday went on to a modestly distinguished military career, rising to the rank of brevet major general. He commanded a division at the battles of Antietam and Fredericksburg and had a moment of glory at Gettysburg when he temporarily assumed command of a corps upon the death in battle of General John Reynolds. However, General George Meade, commander-in-chief of the Army of the Potomac, immediately gave that command to another because Doubleday was not considered aggressive enough. A reputation for deliberateness had earned for Abner the nickname Forty-eight Hours. Today, for those who think baseball is a slow-moving game, that remains Doubleday's only legitimate claim to its invention.

Doubleday died in New Jersey in 1893 at the age of seventy-three, fourteen years before the filing of the Mills Commission concoction, so we will never know what he would have thought about it. No doubt he would have been astounded. As far as anyone knows, he was as removed from the game as a Tibetan lama and didn't know a baseball from a kumquat.

Actually, the game began to take recognizable shape in New York City in the early 1840s. It was around that time that a group of young middle-class gentlemen began playing a very rudimentary game of ball in the open spaces of the Murray Hill area, what is today the East Side around Thirty-second Street. The area was considered uptown then. The heart of New York was still far downtown, with lower Broadway the city's teeming main artery, its pavement stones clattering with horse-drawn omnibuses, hackney cabs, four-wheeled phaetons, two-wheeled tilburies, and private carriages driven by liveried coachmen.

By one conveyance or another, the gentleman players got to the playing ground, and gentlemen they were, for the game as played in the 1840s bore little resemblance to the aggressive, sophisticated, highly competitive baseball of today. The game, an outgrowth of British cricket, was a placid, mannered diversion played purely for recreational purposes. The ladies watching sat on chairs, protected by parasols if the sun was too strong. Bouquets of spectators in their colorful silks and satins and ribbons and tassels, they were attended by their young men in stovepipe hats and grave chin whiskers who bent and gave whispered explication of some nuance of the quietly conducted game before them. The man standing some forty-five or fifty feet away and delivering a one-bounce pitch to a man with a stick? Why, he was the bowler. The man with the stick? He was the striker.

Nothing remained the same for very long in America, and certainly not in that big-shouldered age of growth and expansion. Whatever the country needed seemed to spring miraculously from the creative genius of its citizens. Samuel Morse provided instant communication with the telegraph. Charles Goodyear stumbled upon the secret of vulcanizing rubber. Elias Howe invented and Isaac Singer perfected the sewing machine. Cyrus McCormick constructed reaping machines to harvest the wealth of the prairies. Baseball? Baseball had a luxuriantly whiskered young man named Alexander Joy Cartwright. In the middle of the 1840s this enthusiast came along and began shaping the game into the one we know today. Through observation, calculation, and refining, Cartwright arrived at a design of nine men on a side, four bases, and ninety feet between the bases—those ninety feet being one of the most geometrically perfect concepts in all of sports.

While Abner Doubleday was off in Mexico fighting a war as captain of artillery, Cartwright was formulating the rules of the new game. When the twenty-five-year-old bank

Alexander Joy Cartwright. c. 1845. The National Baseball Library, Cooperstown, New York. *It's been said that his designation of nine men to a side, four bases on the diamond, and ninety feet between bases is as close to perfection as mankind can come.*

teller was finished fine-tuning on the diamond, the game was clearly distinct from any other. With a group of young men from the city's financial district, Cartwright in 1845 organized the Knickerbocker Base Ball Club, whose set of rules was strictly enforced. These included punctuality for the players, the appointment of an umpire whose job included keeping the scorebook, three strikes and out, three outs per side. One of Cartwright's more significant changes was the elimination of "plugging"—throwing the ball at a runner to put him out. "A player running the bases," the rules stated, "shall be out, if the ball is in the hands of an adversary on the base, or the runner is touched with it before he makes his bases; it being understood, however, that in no instance is a ball to be thrown at him."

This was baseball New York style, and it took a while for it to catch on in other parts of the country. It also took a while, a long while, for baseball to catch up with Alexander Cartwright. In 1849 he left New York and eventually ended up in Hawaii, where he spent the rest of his life, dying in 1892 at the age of seventy-two. It wasn't until 1938 that his contributions to the game were duly recognized and he was inducted into the Hall of Fame at Cooperstown.

After the Civil War, the masses took hold of the game and altered it to reflect a much broader common denominator. Baseball as a mere pleasant diversion was soon an obsolete concept, and baseball as a game that was fun, important, and for some, positively essential to win, became the norm. A pungent sense of competitiveness, spurred in part by the increasingly large number of spectators who came out to watch, began communicating itself to the players, leading them to play with more intensity. Professional teams were formed and traveled far and wide to play, representing their cities more than in name alone. As the professional leagues grew in popularity in the 1870s and 1880s, the players were demonstrating greater and more exciting skills, and crowds were responding in larger numbers and more enthusiasm, and civic pride began revealing itself to an ever intensifying degree.

Albert Goodwill Spalding

FROM BASE BALL: AMERICA'S NATIONAL GAME

Why Base Ball Has Become Our National Game—Distinctively American as to Its Nativity, Evolution, Development, Spirit, and Achievements.

Hoist the flag! Strike up the band! Spalding, an early player and founder of the sporting goods company of the same name, believed that baseball was born from creation rather than evolution. He also was among the first of countless writers to equate the game with traditionally American characteristics, as is seen in this excerpt from his 1911 classic.

Have we, of America, a National Game? Is there in our country a form of athletic pastime which is distinctively American? Do our people recognize, among their diversified field sports, one standing apart from every other, outclassing all in its hold upon the interest and affection of the masses? If a negative reply may truthfully be given to all or any of these queries, then this book should never have been published—or written.

To enter upon a deliberate argument to prove that Base Ball is our National Game; that it has all the attributes of American origin, American character and unbounded public favor in America, seems a work of supererogation. It is to undertake the elucidation of a patent fact; the sober demonstration of an axiom; it is like a solemn declaration that two plus two equal four.

Every citizen of this country who is blessed with organs of vision knows that whenever the elements are favorable and wherever grounds are available, the great American game is in progress, whether in city, village or hamlet, east, west, north or south, and that countless thousands of interested spectators gather daily throughout the season to witness contests which are to determine the comparative excellence of competing local organizations or professional league teams.

The statement will not be successfully challenged that the American game of Base Ball attracts more numerous and larger gatherings of spectators than any other form of field sport in any land. It must also be admitted that it is the only game known for which the general public is willing day after day to pay the price of admission. In exciting political campaigns, Presidential candidates and brilliant orators will attract thousands; but let there be a charge of half a dollar imposed, and only Base Ball can stand the test.

I claim that Base Ball owes its prestige as our National Game to the fact that as no other form of sport it is the exponent of American Courage, Confidence, Combativeness; American Dash, Discipline, Determination; American Energy, Eagerness, Enthusiasm; American Pluck, Persistency, Performance; American Spirit, Sagacity, Success; American Vim, Vigor, Virility.

Base Ball is the American Game *par excellence*, because its playing demands Brain and Brawn, and American manhood supplies these ingredients in quantity sufficient to spread over the entire continent.

No man or boy can win distinction on the ball field who is not, as man or boy, an athlete, possessing all the qualifications which an intelligent, effective playing of the game demands. Having these, he has within him the elements of pronounced success in other walks of life. In demonstration of this broad statement of fact, one needs only to note the brilliant array of statesmen, judges, lawyers, preachers, teachers, engineers, physicians, surgeons, merchants, manufacturers, men of eminence in all the professions and in every avenue of commercial and

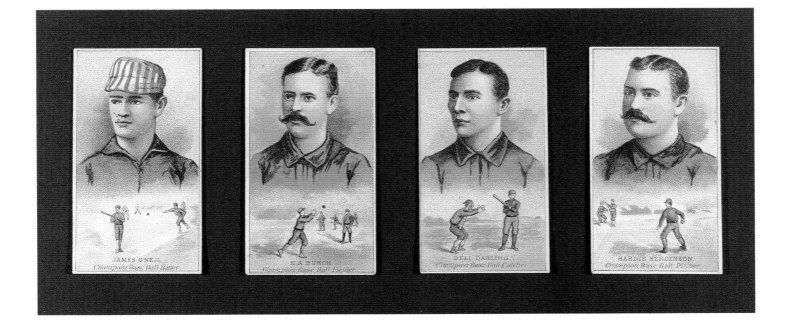

COLORPLATE 9

W.S. Kimball & Co.
Baseball Cards. 1887–88.
Cardboard.
1 1/2 x 2 3/4 in. (each).
The Gladstone Collection
of Baseball Art.

COLORPLATE 10

Woman's Hair Comb with
Baseball Motif. c. 1870.
Horn. 7 1/2 x 7 1/2 in.
The Gladstone Collection
of Baseball Art.

COLORPLATE 11

McLoughlin Baseball Game. c. 1888.
Transcendental Graphics.

COLORPLATE 12 *(opposite)*

HOFFMAN (first name unknown). *Leister's Official Base Ball Score.* 1892–99.
Polychromed wood. 80 x 40 in. The Gladstone Collection of Baseball Art.

COLORPLATE 13

Poster from Albert G. Spalding's Australian Baseball Tour. 1888.
The National Baseball Library and Hall of Fame, Cooperstown, New York.

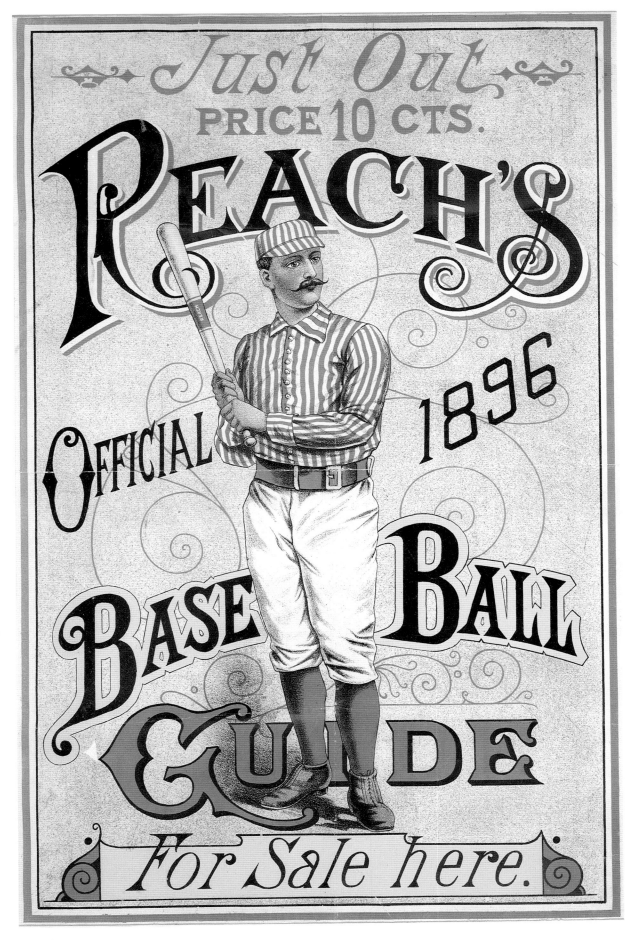

COLORPLATE 14

Advertising Poster for Reach's Official Base Ball Guide. 1896.
Transcendental Graphics.

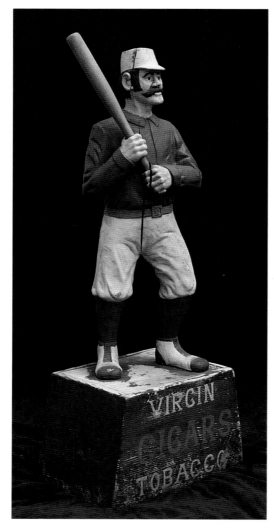

COLORPLATE 15

Cigar Store Figure. 1890s. Wood. 66 in. high.
Transcendental Graphics.

COLORPLATE 16

*"Atta Boy" Amusement Arcade
Baseball Catcher.* Undated.
Wood, metal, cloth, leather.
52 x 26 x 30 in.
The Gladstone Collection of Baseball Art.

46

COLORPLATE 17

Baseball Game Whirligig. Undated. Polychromed wood. 18 x 36 x 10 in.
The Gladstone Collection of Baseball Art.

COLORPLATE 18

Baseball Watch and Watchstand. c. 1900/1910.
Watch: French Niello on silver, 1⅞ in.; Stand: silver, 5½ x 4 x 1½ in.
The Gladstone Collection of Baseball Art.

industrial activity, who have graduated from the ball field to enter upon honorable careers as American citizens of the highest type, each with a sane mind and sound body.

It seems impossible to write on this branch of the subject—to treat Base Ball as our National Game—without referring to Cricket, the national field sport of Great Britain and most of her colonies. Every writer on this theme does so. But, in instituting a comparison between these games of the two foremost nations of earth, I must not be misunderstood. Cricket is a splendid game, for Britons. It is a genteel game, a conventional game—and our cousins across the Atlantic are nothing if not conventional. They play Cricket because it accords with the traditions of their country so to do; because it is easy and does not overtax their energy or their thought. They play it because they like it and it is the proper thing to do. Their sires, and grandsires, and great-grandsires played Cricket—why not they? They play Cricket because it is their National Game, and every Briton is a Patriot. They play it persistently—and they play it well. I have played Cricket and like it. There are some features about that game which I admire more than I do some things about Base Ball.

But Cricket would never do for Americans; it is too slow. It takes two and sometimes three days to complete a first-class Cricket match; but two hours of Base Ball is quite sufficient to exhaust both players and spectators. An Englishman is so constituted by nature that he can wait three days for the result of a Cricket match; while two hours is about as long as an American can wait for the close of a Base Ball game—or anything else, for that matter. The best Cricket team ever organized in America had its home in Philadelphia—and remained there. Cricket does not satisfy the red-blood of Young or Old America.

The genius of our institutions is democratic; Base Ball is a democratic game. The spirit of our national life is combative; Base Ball is a combative game. We are a cosmopolitan people, knowing no arbitrary class distinctions, acknowledging none. The son of a President of the United States would as soon play ball with Patsy Flannigan as with Lawrence Lionel Livingstone, provided only that Patsy could put up the right article. Whether Patsy's dad was a banker or boiler-maker would never enter the mind of the White House lad. It would be quite enough for him to know that Patsy was up in the game. . . .

Cricket is a gentle pastime. Base Ball is War! Cricket is an Athletic Sociable, played and applauded in a conventional, decorous and English manner. Base Ball is an Athletic Turmoil, played and applauded in an unconventional, enthusiastic and American manner.

The founder of our National Game became a Major General in the United States Army! The sport had its baptism when our country was in the preliminary agonies of a fratricidal conflict. Its early evolution was among the men, both North and South, who, during the war of the sixties, played the game to relieve the monotony of camp life in those years of melancholy struggle. It was the medium by which, in the days following the "late unpleasantness," a million warriors and their sons, from both belligerent sections, passed naturally, easily, gracefully, from a state of bitter battling to one of perfect peace.

Base Ball, I repeat, is War! and the playing of the game is a battle in which every contestant is a commanding General, who, having a field of occupation, must defend it; who, having gained an advantage, must hold it by the employment of every faculty of his brain and body, by every resource of his mind and muscle.

But it is a bloodless battle; and when the struggle ends, the foes of the minute past are friends of the minute present, victims congratulating victors, conquerors pointing out the brilliant individual plays of the conquered.

It would be as impossible for a Briton, who had not breathed the air of this free land as a naturalized American citizen; for one who had no part or heritage in the hopes and achievements of our country, to play Base Ball, as it would for an American, free from the trammels of English traditions, customs, conventionalities, to play the national game of Great Britain.

Let such an Englishman stand at the batter's slab on an American Ball field, facing the son of an American President in the pitcher's box, and while he was ruminating upon the propriety of hitting, in his "best form," a ball delivered by the hands of so august a personage, the President's boy would probably shoot three hot ones over the plate, and the Umpire's "Three strikes; you're out," would arouse our British cousin to a realization that we have a game too lively for any but Americans to play.

On the other hand, if one of our cosmopolitan ball artists should visit England, and attempt a game of Cricket, whether it were Cobb, Lajoie, Wagner, or any American batsman of Scandinavian, Irish, French or German antecedents; simply because he was an American, and even though the Cricket ball were to be bowled at his feet by King George himself, he would probably hit the sphere in regular Base Ball style, and smash all conventionalities at the same time, in his eager effort to clear the bases with a three-bagger.

The game of Base Ball is American as to another peculiar feature. It is the only form of field sport known where spectators have an important part and actually participate in the game. Time was, and not long ago, when comparatively few understood the playing rules; but the day has come when nearly every man and boy in the land is versed in all the intricacies of the pastime; thousands of young women have learned it well enough to keep score, and the number of matrons who know the difference between the short-stop and the back-stop is daily increasing.

In every town, village and city is the local wag. He is a Base Ball fan from infancy. He knows every player in the League by sight and by name. He is a veritable encyclopedia of information on the origin, evolution and history of the game. He can tell you when the Knickerbockers were organized, and knows who led the batting list in every team of the National and American Leagues last year. He never misses a game. His witticisms, ever seasoned with spice, hurled at the visitors and now and then at the Umpire, are as thoroughly enjoyed by all who hear them as is any other feature of the sport. His words of encouragement to the home team, his shouts of derision to the opposing players, find sympathetic responses in the hearts of all present.

But it is neither the applause of the women nor the jokes of the wag which make for victory or defeat in comparison with the work of the "Rooter." He is ever present in large numbers. He is there to see the "boys" win. Nothing else will satisfy him. He is bound by no rules of the game, and too often, perhaps, by no laws of decorum. His sole object in life for two mortal hours is to gain victory for the home team, and that he is not overscrupulous as to the amount of racket emanating from his immediate vicinity need not be emphasized here. . . .

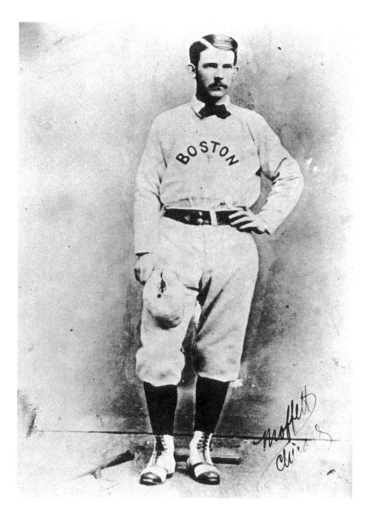

Albert Goodwill Spalding. c. 1870. The National Baseball Library, Cooperstown, New York. *As a player, owner, league official, baseball guide publisher, and equipment manufacturer, Spalding was a pioneer of baseball's early days.*

50

It must be admitted that as the game of Base Ball has become more generally known; that is, as patrons of the sport are coming to be more familiar with its rules and its requirements, their enjoyment has immeasurably increased; because, just in so far as those in attendance understand the features presented in every play, so far are they able to become participators in the game itself. And beyond doubt it is to this growing knowledge on the part of the general public with the pastime that its remarkable popularity is due. For, despite the old adage, familiarity does *not* breed contempt, but fondness, and all America has come to regard Base Ball as its very own, to be known throughout the civilized world as the great American National Game.

Finally, in one other particular Base Ball has won its right to be denominated the American National Game. Ever since its establishment in the hearts of the people as the foremost of field sports, Base Ball has "followed the flag." It followed the flag to the front in the sixties, and received then an impetus which has carried it to half a century of wondrous growth and prosperity. It has followed the flag to Alaska, where, under the midnight sun, it is played on Arctic ice. It has followed the flag to the Hawaiian Islands, and at once supplanted every other form of athletics in popularity. It has followed the flag to the Philippines, to Porto Rico and to Cuba, and wherever a ship floating the Stars and Stripes finds anchorage today, somewhere on nearby shore the American National Game is in progress.

William Zinsser

FROM SPRING TRAINING

"Florida Days"

As baseball expanded as a business, it expanded geographically as well. Here, essayist William Zinsser describes the beginnings of the game's annual ritual of spring training.

On September 19, 1913, the president of the St. Louis Browns, Robert L. Hedges, arrived by train at St. Petersburg, Florida, a fishing town of three thousand people, and was met by a deputation from the local board of trade. The Browns had held their 1912 spring training in Montgomery, Alabama, and had finished seventh; this year they had trained in Waco, Texas, and finished last. Perhaps a spring training camp in Florida was what the club needed. It certainly couldn't hurt.

"Hedges was taken to several possible sites," according to Jabbo Gordon, a former sports editor of the *Bradenton Herald*, who described the visit in a talk to the Manatee County Historical Society in 1970, "and he seemed to like them all. He was particularly impressed when his fishing party captured a nine-foot-long, 500-pound shark. A picture with Hedges and his friends standing by the shark was placed in the St. Louis papers. The people of St. Louis were happy to see that their Browns at least were going to enjoy some good fishing."

The site that Hedges and his board finally selected, announcing their decision at a fractious meeting of stockholders back in St. Louis, was called Coffee Pot Bayou. No reasons for their choice were disclosed, but it's safe to guess that they liked the terms. The twenty-acre lot was offered rent-free for one year, with all holes filled and all stumps removed. At the end of the year the Browns could either give it back to the owners or buy it for $8,000, paying $3,000 down and 8 percent interest for the next five years. A contract was also arranged for the players' room and board, at $2.50 per player per day.

Thus spring training came to Florida as an institution. A wooden grandstand was built, the field was put in shape and presumably destumped, and on February 16, 1914, the Browns' manager, Branch Rickey, arrived in St. Petersburg with twenty players, four reporters and one photographer. The players were so glad to be warm, having left St. Louis in a snowstorm, that they went right out to the ballpark and loosened up. The next day Rickey put them to work in earnest, establishing a schedule that ran from eight-thirty to four-thirty every day except Sunday, with an hour out for lunch, and otherwise applying the principles of Christian abstinence for which, over the next half century, he came to be respected if not necessarily emulated.

"He forbade the playing of poker," Jabbo Gordon noted, "since it would keep the players up late. Liquor and cigarettes were not allowed. Rickey also ordered that no seconds on food would be allowed at meals. Since many boys had come from the farms, where one may eat his fill, they protested but to no avail. The reporters complained and won their point by sitting at a separate table.

"Some of the players were not very happy in St. Petersburg. The movies closed at 9:30 and the one dance a week closed at 10:30. It had recently become a dry town and no saloons were open. Liquor was available at the Elks Club, but only one player was a member of that organization. To enjoy some night life several players visited Tampa, a more lively town across the bay. Unfortunately, they enjoyed Tampa too well occasionally and returned late the next day. This practice was viewed with alarm."

Civic enthusiasm mounted as the players got ready for what was advertised as the first game ever played between major league teams in Florida, the other team being the Cubs. On opening day a half holiday was declared, businesses and schools were closed, and four thousand spectators turned up, some arriving by boat at a dock that had been built just for such waterborne fans. Special trains brought six hundred people from Tarpon Springs and Belleair. As for the game, the Cubs won it, 3–2. Evidently the Browns would need more than sunshine and good fishing.

Strictly, that wasn't the first foray into Florida by a major league club. In the spring of 1888 the Washington Statesmen (later the Senators) went to Jacksonville with fifteen players, including a young catcher named Connie Mack. Mack later recalled that he and his teammates were repeatedly turned away by hotels where they applied for rooms. The one that finally accepted them made the proviso that the players wouldn't mingle with the other guests or eat in the hotel dining room.

But it was the 1914 Browns who started the major leagues' Florida land rush. The baseball fever and the resulting increase in local business that they generated in St. Petersburg were not lost on tourist boards in other towns; maybe they could also get themselves a team. Their lure would be the priceless gift of sunshine, which the clubs were bound to find appealing. They were still stuck for their own spring training in such places as Wilmington, North Carolina; West Baden, West Virginia; Hot Springs, Arkansas; Mobile, Alabama; Augusta, Georgia; Charlottesville, Virginia; and Gulfport, Mississippi.

Every land rush needs a promoter, and the west coast of Florida found one in Al Lang, a Pittsburgh businessman who had moved to St. Petersburg in 1911 and embraced the town with such ardor that he eventually became mayor. Lang made it his mission to attract major league baseball to Florida, proceeding with such zeal that, by 1929, ten of the sixteen clubs had spring training camps there, including three in St. Petersburg—the Browns, the Boston Braves, who came from Galveston in 1922, and the New York Yankees, who came from New Orleans in 1925. The spot where the Yanks trained, Crescent Lake Park, is chiefly remembered because Babe Ruth hit a home run to right field that landed on the front porch of the West Coast Inn. Lang settled the Washington Senators in Tampa, the Brooklyn Dodgers in Clearwater, and the New York Giants in Sarasota, where, according to a contemporary sportswriter, Sam Crane, "nearly the whole team has had to buy real estate in order to get rid of the salesmen long enough to play a little baseball." Lang's reward was to have the new ballpark that was built in St. Petersburg in 1946 named for him, and two generations of fans making a tour of the Grapefruit League have contentedly sat in the sun at Al Lang Field ever since.

Second Inning:

BASEBALL AND THE COMMON CULTURE

One doesn't have to be a baseball fan to have heard of some of these works, or to be familiar with the many facets of the game that have transcended the sport and become part of our shared culture.

Jack Norworth and Albert Von Tilzer

"Take Me Out to the Ball Game"

On any given summer night, the chorus of this hymn, written in 1908, is offered by hundreds of thousands of fans at ballparks all across North America. Most fans, though, are unfamiliar with the verses and the story of diehard hometown rooter Katie Casey.

Katie Casey was baseball mad,
Had the fever and had it bad;
Just to root for the home town crew,
Ev'ry sou Katie blew

On a Saturday her young beau
Called to see if she'd like to go,
To see a show but Miss Katie said
"No, I'll tell you what you can do:"

Take me out to the ball game,
Take me out with the crowd
Buy me some peanuts and cracker jack,
I don't care if I never get back,

Let me root, root, root for the home team,
If they don't win it's a shame
For it's one, two, three strikes you're out,
At the old ball game.

Katie Casey saw all the games,
Knew the players by their first names;
Told the umpire he was wrong,
All along good and strong
When the score was just two to two,
Katie Casey knew what to do,
Just to cheer up the boys she knew,
She made the gang sing this song:

Take me out to the ball game,
Take me out with the crowd
Buy me some peanuts and cracker jack,
I don't care if I never get back,

Let me root, root, root for the home team,
If they don't win it's a shame
For it's one, two, three strikes you're out
At the old ball game.

Bruce Anderson

FROM *SPORTS ILLUSTRATED*

"The National Pastime's Anthem"

If you believed, as many fans do, that Take Me Out to the Ball Game *must have been written in the bleachers between games of a doubleheader, then you were wrong.*

———————————

Many have sung, and many continue to sing *Take Me Out to the Ball Game*. The long roster does not, thank goodness, include Roseanne Barr. But it does have a robot named Johnny-Five, who once hit each note with technical if bloodless precision at Shea Stadium. At the other end of the spectrum (and the subway line) is Metropolitan Opera baritone Robert Merrill, who belts out the tune—in person or on Memorex—at Yankee Stadium.

It's safe to say that no one singing today, neither the mechanical nor the personal, renders the song quite as the supremely unmelodious Harry Caray does. From his perch behind and above Wrigley Field's home plate, the Chicago Cub broadcaster leans forth and croaks out the tune. He starts with a bellowed "Ohhhhhhhh!" and proceeds (a critic might say downhill) from there. The fans love it. Caray's seventh-inning serenade, with a capacity chorus of 38,000-plus Wrigley rooters joining in, was the single most riveting performance at last summer's All-Star Game.

Caray is so identified with *Take Me Out to the Ball Game* that many people think he wrote it. He did not. Jack Norworth, who also wrote *Shine On Harvest Moon*, penned the lyrics, and Albert Von Tilzer put the words to music.

When *Take Me Out to the Ball Game* was published in 1908 it really became that overused oxymoron, the instant classic. Norworth, who was a top vaudeville performer as well as a songwriter, introduced the tune in his act. One night not long afterward he was forced to drop it from his routine because too many performers at Hammerstein's Victoria Theatre in New York City had already used the song in the show.

There have been more than 100 recorded versions of the song. In the 1949 MGM musical *Take Me Out to the Ball Game*, the title song was triple-played by some true all-stars: Frank Sinatra sang it; Gene Kelly tap-danced to it; Esther Williams swam to it. In a 1950 rendition, Roy Campanella and Ralph Branca of the Brooklyn Dodgers and Phil Rizzuto and Tommy Henrich of the Yankees joined Mitch Miller and the Sandpipers, a third team based in New York.

Andy Strasberg, vice-president for public relations with the San Diego Padres and a dedicated collector of baseball memorabilia, has more than 70 different recordings of TMOTTBG. Even his doorbell chimes the familiar strains. "Doesn't everyone's?" he asks. Strasberg's theory about the song's enduring popularity is simple—or, rather, simplicity. "A lot of times I'll find *Take Me Out to the Ball Game* on children's records," he says. "It's so easy to sing. Everyone knows the words to it." Caray agrees. "I would always sing it because I think it's the only song I knew the words to," he says.

The song is so embedded in the American consciousness that people who have never been to a baseball game know the words and music by heart. This is highly appropriate, since neither of the two men who wrote the song saw a game until years after they had composed their classic.

Norworth, who hailed from Philadelphia, was riding the New York subway one day when he looked up and saw a placard: BASEBALL TODAY — POLO GROUNDS. In an interview he gave on the 50th anniversary of the song's publication, he said that the advertisement set him to thinking and, soon, to writing. By the time he reached his destination half an hour later, Norworth had finished the lyrics of his two-stanza, one-chorus ditty. He took it to Von Tilzer, with whom he had collaborated before. Von Tilzer wrote the music, and the rest is sporting and show biz history.

Most of Norworth's inspired verses have long been forgotten; the remains are the cracker-jack chorus. The song, as Norworth originally penned it, tells the story of a young lady—Katie Casey in earlier versions and, for reasons that are unclear, Nelly Kelly in later ones. She is crazy about the game of baseball. A beau who is unaware of her love for the sport calls upon Katie-Nelly and asks her for a date. She accedes, but with the proviso that he, yes, take her out to the ball game.

It was more than 20 years after the song came out that Von Tilzer made it to his first game. Norworth was in even less of a hurry to get to the ballpark. He finally did on June 27, 1940, when the Dodgers had a day for him at Ebbets Field.

How could Norworth, who died in 1959, have written baseball's anthem without having seen a game? He once explained: "A friend of mine, Harry Williams, wrote *In the Shade of the Old Apple Tree*, and he never saw an apple tree."

Ernest L. Thayer
"Casey at the Bat"

One of the best-known American poems ever written, Ernest Thayer's mini-epic will probably outlive anyone who reads it. In it, he captured the essence of a game that's humbled a multitude of Caseys since this classic was published in the San Francisco Chronicle *in 1888.*

The outlook wasn't brilliant for the Mudville nine that day;
The score stood four to two with but one inning more to play;
And then, when Cooney died at first, and Barrows did the same,
A sickly silence fell upon the patrons of the game.

A struggling few got up to go, in deep despair. The rest
Clung to that hope which "springs eternal in the human breast";
They thought, If only Casey could but get a whack at that,
We'd put up even money now, with Casey at the bat.

But Flynn preceded Casey, as did also Jimmy Blake,
And the former was a lulu and the latter was a cake;
So, upon that stricken multitude grim melancholy sat,
For there seemed but little chance of Casey's getting to the bat.

But Flynn let drive a single, to the wonderment of all,
And Blake, the much despised, tore the cover off the ball,
And when the dust had lifted and men saw what had occurred,
There was Jimmy safe at second, and Flynn a-huggin' third.

Paul Nonnast. *The Mighty Casey.* From an article published in the *Saturday Evening Post,* July 3, 1954. © The Curtis Publishing Company.

Then from five thousand throats and more there rose a lusty yell,
It rumbled through the valley; it rattled in the dell;
It knocked upon the mountain and recoiled upon the flat,
For Casey, mighty Casey, was advancing to the bat.

There was ease in Casey's manner as he stepped into his place;
There was pride in Casey's bearing and a smile on Casey's face,
And when, responding to the cheers, he lightly doffed his hat,
No stranger in the crowd could doubt 'twas Casey at the bat.

Ten thousand eyes were on him as he rubbed his hands with dirt;
Five thousand tongues applauded when he wiped them on his shirt.
Then, while the writhing pitcher ground the ball into his hip,
Defiance gleamed in Casey's eye, a sneer curled Casey's lip.

And now the leather-covered sphere came hurtling through the air,
And Casey stood a-watching it in haughty grandeur there,
Close by the sturdy batsman the ball unheeded sped—
"That ain't my style," said Casey. "Strike one," the umpire said.

From the benches, black with people, there went up a muffled roar,
Like the beating of the storm-waves on a stern and distant shore.
"Kill him; kill the umpire!" shouted someone from the stand,—
And it's likely they'd have killed him had not Casey raised his hand.

With a smile of Christian charity great Casey's visage shone;
He stilled the rising tumult; he bade the game go on;
He signaled to the pitcher, and once more the spheroid flew;
But Casey still ignored it, and the umpire said, "Strike two."

"Fraud," cried the maddened thousands, and echo answered "Fraud."
But one scornful look from Casey, and the multitude was awed.
They saw his face grow stern and cold; they saw his muscles strain,
And they knew that Casey wouldn't let that ball go by again.

The sneer is gone from Casey's lip; his teeth are clenched in hate;
He pounds with cruel violence his bat upon the plate.
And now the pitcher holds the ball, and now he lets it go,
And now the air is shattered by the force of Casey's blow.

Oh! somewhere in this favored land the sun is shining bright;
The band is playing somewhere, and somewhere hearts are light.
And somewhere men are laughing, and somewhere children shout;
But there is no joy in Mudville—mighty Casey has Struck Out.

Franklin P. Adams

"Baseball's Sad Lexicon"

By some accounts, Joe Tinker, Johnny Evers, and Frank Chance owe their baseball immortality more to this piece than to their play on the field. Written by Franklin P. Adams, a frustrated New York Giants fan, and published in the New York Globe in 1908, the poem excludes Cubs third baseman Harry Steinfeldt, who had long since passed away when Tinker, Evers, and Chance were inducted to the Hall of Fame together in 1946.

These are the saddest of possible words,
    Tinker-to-Evers-to-Chance.
Trio of Bear Cubs fleeter than birds,
    Tinker-to-Evers-to-Chance.
Ruthlessly pricking our gonfalon bubble,
Making a Giant hit into a double,
Words that are weighty with nothing but
    trouble.
    Tinker-to-Evers-to-Chance.

Harry Steinfeldt, Joe Tinker, Johnny Evers, Frank Chance. c. 1908. The National Baseball Library, Cooperstown, New York. *"These are the saddest of possible words: Tinker to Evers to Chance . . ."*

Satchel Paige
"How to Keep Young"

By following these simple rules, Satchel Paige stayed young longer than anyone else in the game.

---

1. Avoid fried meats which angry up the blood.

2. If your stomach disputes you, lie down and pacify it with cool thoughts.

3. Keep the juices flowing by jangling around gently as you move.

4. Go very light on the vices, such as carrying on in society.
   The social ramble ain't restful.

5. Avoid running at all times.

6. Don't look back. Something might be gaining on you.

LeRoy "Satchel" Paige. c. 1940. The National Baseball Library, Cooperstown, New York. *"Don't look back. Something might be gaining on you."*

George Carlin

"Baseball–Football"

George Carlin, a master of observational humor, captures two sides of America's psychological coin in this classic stand-up routine.

———————————

Baseball is different from any other sport; very different.

For instance, in most sports, you score points or goals; in baseball, you score runs. In most sports, the ball, or object, is put in play by the offensive team; in baseball, the defensive team puts the ball in play, and only the defense is allowed to touch the ball. In fact, in baseball, if an offensive player touches the ball intentionally, he's out; sometimes unintentionally, he's out. In most sports, the team is run by a coach; in baseball, the team is run by a manager; and only in baseball does the manager (or coach) wear the same clothing the players do. If you had ever seen John Madden in his Oakland Raiders football uniform, you would know the reason for this custom.

Now, I've mentioned football as well. Baseball and football are the two most popular spectator sports in this country. And, as such, it seems to me they ought to be able to tell us something about ourselves; about our values or national character, and maybe how those values have changed over the last 150 years. For that reason, I enjoy comparing baseball and football.

Baseball is a nineteenth-century pastoral game.

Football is a twentieth century technological struggle.

Baseball is played on a diamond, in a park! The baseball park!

Football is played on a gridiron, in a stadium, sometimes called Soldier Field, or War Memorial Stadium.

Baseball begins in the spring, the season of new life.

Football begins in the fall, when everything is dying.

In football, you wear a helmet.

In baseball, you wear a cap.

Football is concerned with downs. "What down is it?"

Baseball is concerned with "ups." "Who's up? Are you up? I'm not up. *He's* up!"

In football, you receive a penalty.

In baseball, you make an error. "Whoops!"

In football, the specialist comes in to kick.

In baseball, the specialist comes in to relieve somebody.

Football has hitting, clipping, spearing, piling on, personal fouls, late hitting, and unnecessary roughness.

Baseball has the sacrifice.

Football is played in any kind of weather: Rain, snow, sleet, hail, fog . . . can't see the game, don't know if there is a game going on; mud on the field . . . can't read the uniforms, can't read the yard markers, the struggle will continue!

In baseball, if it rains, we don't go out to play. "I can't go out! It's raining out!"

Baseball has the seventh-inning stretch.

Football has the two-minute warning.

Baseball has no time limit; "We don't know when it's gonna end!"

Football is rigidly timed, and it will end, "even if we have to go to sudden death."

In baseball, during the game, in the stands, there's a kind of picnic feeling. Emotions may run high or low, but there's not that much unpleasantness.

In football, during the game, in the stands, you can be sure that at least twenty-seven times you were perfectly capable of taking the life of a fellow human being.

And finally, the objectives of the two games are completely different. In football, the object is for the quarterback, otherwise known as the field general, to be on target with his aerial assault, riddling the defense by hitting his receivers with deadly accuracy, in spite of the blitz, even if he has to use the shotgun. With short bullet passes and long bombs, he marches his troops into enemy territory, balancing this aerial assault with a sustained ground attack which punches holes in the enemy's defensive line. In baseball, the object is to go home! And to be safe! "I hope I'll be safe at home!"

William Safire

FROM *THE NEW YORK TIMES*
"Out of Left Field"

When considering writers who are best qualified to examine baseball terms that have entered the English language, William Safire's name comes up right off the bat. And while there doesn't seem to be a definitive reason for the origin of the term "out of left field," these explanations seem to be in the ballpark, at least.

Because baseball's third strike has so impoverished the daily reading of the nation's national-pastime junkies, here is a survey from the Hot Stove League of the effect of baseball on the American language.

When a professor of atmospheric science predicted that recent changes in the sun's activity foretold a dry spell of several years in the Northeast, another expert—Robert Harnack, a meteorologist at Rutgers—called that forecast "completely out of left field."

Where in the heavens or on earth is "left field"? How did that area on the baseball field become the metaphoric epitome of far-outedness To come "*from* out *of* left field" is to be rooted in the ridiculous, crackbrained, farfetched; to "*be* out *in* left field" is, according to *American Speech* magazine in 1961, to be "disoriented, out of contact with reality."

When asked for the derivation, members of the Abner Doubleday Lodge of the Lexicographic Irregulars lobbed in these ideas:

"In the older, less symmetrical baseball stadia," writes Robert J. Wilson, Jr., of Riverside, Connecticut, "left field was usually 'deeper' than right, and thus coming from left field was coming from a 'far-out' region."

Our ambassador to the European office of the United Nations, Gerald Helman, writes from Geneva: "Right field was thought of as the most difficult to play because it was the 'sun field,' and required the fielder to have a strong arm for the long throw to third. As a consequence, the good hitting, poor fielding players were put in left. . . . Because of the defensive inadequacies of left fielders, you could expect almost anything to happen when the ball was hit to them."

On the other hand: "The power of a batter in baseball or softball is to his/her 'pull,' or opposite field," posits Thomas Carter of Dayton. "Since some 90 percent of the population is right-handed, this means that many more long hits can be expected to left field. Therefore, the left fielder will usually play farther back than the other outfielders. This then leads to the linking of 'left field' to a person, thing, or idea that is far out." Could be.

"Left field is about as far as one can get from the desirable seats," suggests Morton Brodsky of Lancaster, Pennsylvania. "The home team's bench is generally, if not always, along the first-base line. This makes the preference for hometown fans (1) from home plate to first base, (2) from home plate to third base, (3) right field, (4) left field. Of course, modern stadia have seating all the way around, but I think that 'out in left field' originated in the days when there was nothing out there but a fence."

"Imagine some right-hander of yesteryear (a preponderance of pioneer pitchers were right-handed)," says Jerry Oster of New York City, "with a big sidearm delivery such that the ball, especially to a right-handed batter, seemed to come out of left field."

Since the earliest citation of the phrase appeared in *American Speech*, I queried the editor of that publication, John Algeo, who is one of the heavy hitters in the big league of linguistics today. He assumed it had a least a pseudobaseball origin and appeared early in psychiatric slang; then he tossed himself a fat pitch: "The explanation that the left field was far off from the home base overlooks the fact that the right field is equally far from the home base and the center field is even farther. Why then left field instead of right field or center field?"

Professor Algeo took a hefty cut: "My guess (and it is no more than a guess) is that the expression is a metaphor referring to a baseball field, but was never actually a baseball term. Probably it was coined by someone who watched baseball but was not a player or real aficionado.

"To be in the *outfield* is to be far out. However, the expression *out in the outfield* is uneuphonious, redundant, and too general; it doesn't make a snappy remark. *Center* and *right* both have highly positive connotations that conflict with the sense of isolation that the term was wanted for. . . . *Center* suggests all the virtues of moderation and the golden mean. *Right* suggests correctness, dexterity, and so on (we don't have to go into the political associations). *Left* is certainly the best word for associations—lefties are a minority, they are sinister (etymologically at least) and (at least by pun) they get left behind."

Mr. Algeo concurs with Irregular Carter's observation that balls hit to left field are usually hit harder, causing the fielder to play deeper: "Since the left fielder is farther removed from the center of action in the infield, his position becomes a metaphor for isolation."

In addition, consider the flakiness factor: "Center field would not be appropriate," agrees David Zinman, science editor for *Newsday*, after checking with Stan Isaacs, who used to write a sports column called "Out of Left Field," "because it is the mainstream of the outfield. 'Right' field denotes correctness. . . . On the other hand, 'left' field has overtones of radicalism in politics. Also, left-handers, particularly pitchers, are often thought of as slightly different, sometimes screwy or dizzy individuals."

Like Lucy in the comic strip "Peanuts," Mrs. Melvin Golub of Dunkirk, Maryland, disagrees with everybody; it is her experience that "one rarely hits to left field. The outfielder has little to do; hence, he is lonely. . . . When our company plays softball, my son sends me out to play left field so I can't get into too much trouble." Such an iconoclastic view flies in the face of all statistics about where most hard-hit balls go, and is truly out of left field.

Terry Cashman

"Willie, Mickey and the 'Duke' (Talkin' Baseball)"

This eminently hummable song made the name Kluszewski familiar to millions of nonfans who previously would have had trouble identifying the Reds first baseman, much less spelling his name. After publishing this song in 1981, Terry Cashman, baseball's balladeer, wrote a version for twenty-five of the game's twenty-six major league teams (the Seattle Mariners, who had not yet accumulated enough history, were left out).

The Whiz Kids had won it
Bobby Thomson had done it
And Yogi read the comics all the while

Rock 'n' Roll was bein' born
Marijuana we would scorn
So down on the corner the National
    Pastime went on trial

We're talkin' Baseball
Kluszewski, Campanella
Talkin' Baseball
The Man and Bobby Feller
The Scooter, the Barber and the Newk
They knew 'em all from Boston to Dubuque
Especially Willie, Mickey and the Duke

Well, Casey was winnin'
Hank Aaron was beginnin'
One Robby goin' out, one comin' in
Kiner and midget Gaedel
The Thumper and Mel Parnell
And Ike was the only one winnin'
    down in Washington

We're talkin' Baseball
Kluszewski, Campanella
Talkin' Baseball

The Man and Bobby Feller
The Scooter, the Barber and the Newk
They knew 'em all from Boston to Dubuque
Especially Willie, Mickey and the Duke

Now my old friend the Bachelor
Well, he swore he was the Oklahoma Kid
And Cookie played hookey
To go and see the Duke
And me, I always loved Willie Mays
Those were the days

Well now it's the eighties
And Brett is the greatest
And Bobby Bonds can play for everyone
Rose is at the Vet
And Rusty again is a Met
And the Great Alexander is pitchin' again in Washington

I'm talkin' Baseball
Like Reggie, Quisenberry
Talkin' Baseball
Carew and Gaylord Perry
Seaver, Garvey, Schmidt and Vida Blue
If Cooperstown is callin', it's no fluke
They'll be with Willie, Mickey and the Duke

Mickey Mantle, Willie Mays, Joe DiMaggio, Duke Snider. July 16, 1977. UPI/The Bettmann Archive. *One city, four all-time great center fielders. This reunion took place at a New York Mets Oldtimers' Game.*

Third Inning:

THE PLAYERS

*This lineup features, in their own words and the words of those
who wrote about them, some of baseball's most memorable characters.*

Mike Sowell

FROM JULY 2, 1903

*In his 1992 book investigating the mysterious circumstances surrounding the death of Hall-of-
Famer Big Ed Delahanty, Mike Sowell profiles John J. McGraw, one of baseball's greatest
managers and a dominant figure of the sport in the early twentieth century.*

———————

McGraw was a small man, only five foot seven, who had used his toughness and his cleverness
to succeed in a big man's game. When he arrived on the big-league scene in 1891, he was a
frail, baby-faced kid who weighed barely 130 pounds. His manager, Billy Barnie of the
Baltimore Orioles of the old American Association, stared at his new recruit a full minute
before he could speak.

"Why, you're just a kid," said Barnie. "Can you play ball?"

"If you don't think so, get me out on the field," shot back McGraw. "I'm bigger than I
look."

Johnny McGraw backed up his tough words with his tough play. He was an expert at
finding ways to get on base, whether it required pushing a bunt down the foul line or fouling
off dozens of pitches to wear out the pitcher and work him for a walk. One year, McGraw
reached first base by hit, walk, error, or being hit by a pitch two out of every three times up, a
record that no one ever has approached.

It was McGraw as much as anyone who turned baseball into a science. By the mid-1890s,
he and Hughie Jennings, his roommate, met every night with teammates Wee Willie Keeler,
Joe Kelley, and Wilbert Robinson to scheme up ways to beat the opposition. The Orioles perfected the hit-and-run play to advance runners and they introduced the Baltimore chop, a ball
hit into the ground near home plate so that it bounced high in the air, allowing the batter to
reach first base safely.

In the field, McGraw was a master at trickery. He knew how to discreetly hold on to a runner's belt to keep him from tagging up on a fly ball, and he could discreetly bump a passing baserunner to throw him off stride. The Orioles even went so far as to keep the outfield grass so high in their ballpark that they could keep an extra baseball hidden there to slip into play whenever necessary. This practice ended only after the time left-fielder Joe Kelley threw the spare ball to McGraw at third base in time to retire a runner. To the Orioles' chagrin, a moment later center-fielder Steve Brodie ran down the ball that actually was in play and pegged it back to the infield, also.

When all else failed, the Orioles attempted to bully anyone who got in their way. They fought with opposing players, brawled with fans, and made enemies wherever they went. Umpires were subjected to special abuse, often forced to soak their feet for hours after McGraw and his cronies kicked and stomped them with their spikes.

The Orioles were a perfect fit for Baltimore as the nineteenth century was drawing to a close. H.L. Mencken had written of the city, "Baltimore, by 1890, was fast degenerating, and so was civilization." The same could be said of baseball itself.

The style of ball played by the Orioles became known as "rowdyism," and other teams began to follow their lead. There were protests that baseball was slipping into ruin, but there was no denying the Orioles' success. They won three consecutive pennants from 1894 through 1896 and finished second to Boston the next two years.

McGraw, the captain and ringleader of the Orioles, became a local hero in Baltimore. In 1896, he and Robinson, the Orioles' catcher, became partners in an establishment known as the Diamond Cafe. It featured a dining room in the front and a small bowling alley in the back, and it became the popular meeting place for the city's sports crowd.

The city also provided a lasting nickname for McGraw. When he arrived on the scene, there was a local politician named "Muggsy" McGraw, and it was rumored the young ballplayer was his son. The newspapers began calling the Orioles infielder "Young Muggsy" McGraw, and the name stuck. McGraw hated it, but he never was able to shake his new identity.

Of all the hecklers he faced around the league, the only one who ever got on McGraw's nerves was a fan in Cleveland who picked up on the nickname. Whenever McGraw would make an error or an out, the man would jump from his seat and run back and forth shouting at the top of his voice: "Oh, Muggsy! Oh, Muggsy! Look at your face! Aren't you a beauty! Oh, Muggsy!"

McGraw asked the writers to quit calling him by the name, but to no avail. "You could stop them saying it if you really wanted to," prizefighter Jim Jeffries once told him. "If I was you, I'd stop them quick enough."

"No you wouldn't," said McGraw. "But if I were you, nobody would have the sand to tie a name of that kind on me."

Otherwise, McGraw reveled in the attention he received in Baltimore. And his stature in the city became even greater in 1899 when he took over as manager after Ned Hanlon jumped to Brooklyn and took most of the team's stars with him. McGraw, with Robinson as his right-hand man, led the badly depleted Orioles to a surprising fourth-place finish that year.

But misfortune lay ahead for McGraw. His problems began that summer while his team was in Louisville. He received word his wife, Minnie, had suffered an inflamed appendix, and he rushed back to Baltimore. By the time McGraw's train arrived, his wife had taken a turn for the worse. The appendix had ruptured, and three days later Minnie was dead.

Not long afterward, McGraw learned the National League was cutting back from twelve teams to eight. One of the franchises being dropped was Baltimore. Within a matter of weeks, McGraw lost his wife, his managerial position, and his ball club.

The next setback came early in 1900. McGraw and Robinson were traded to St. Louis, the westernmost outpost in the league. Not wanting to play ball more than eight hundred miles away from their business interests in Baltimore, the two men fought the move. When they finally signed their contracts with the Cardinals, they did so only after the club agreed to drop the "reserve clause." A standard part of all National League contracts, the reserve clause gave the ball club the option to renew its claim on the player, binding him to the team indefinitely.

The season already was three weeks old when McGraw and Robinson arrived in St. Louis.

COLORPLATE 19

W. P. SNYDER. *A Collegiate Game of Baseball.* 1889. Colored woodblock print. $14^{1}/_{2}$ x $20^{1}/_{4}$ in.
The National Baseball Library and Hall of Fame, Cooperstown, New York.

COLORPLATE 20

JONATHAN SCOTT HARTLEY. *The Baseball Player.*
1886. Bronze. 13^1/$_2$ x 6 x 3^1/$_2$ in.
The Gladstone Collection of Baseball Art.

COLORPLATE 21

Baseball Player. c. 1910. Wood. 15 x 6 x 3^1/$_2$ in.
The Gladstone Collection of Baseball Art.

COLORPLATE 22

ORONZO COSENTINO. *Baseball Player (First Baseman)*. c. 1915.
Bronze. 21 x 17 x 10 in. The Gladstone Collection of Baseball Art.

COLORPLATE 23

FRANZ MAYER. *Baseball Stained Glass Window.* c. 1910.
Hand painted, mouth blown antique glass. 54 x 64 in. The Gladstone Collection of Baseball Art.

COLORPLATE 24

JAMES H. DAUGHERTY. *Three Base Hit.* 1914.
Gouache and ink on paper. $12^1/4$ x $17^1/8$ in. Whitney Museum of American Art.

COLORPLATE 25

FRANK HOFFMAN. *Safe at Home.*
Liberty Magazine cover, April 8, 1925. Oil on canvas.
34 x 35 in. Private collection.

THE SATURDAY EVENING POST

An Illustrated Weekly
Founded A.° D.° 1728 by Benj. Franklin

AUGUST 5, 1916   5c. THE COPY

In This Number: Harry Leon Wilson—Samuel G. Blythe—George Lee Burton
Joseph Hergesheimer—Stewart Edward White—Charles E. Van Loan

COLORPLATE 26

NORMAN ROCKWELL. *Gramps and Baseball.*
Saturday Evening Post cover, August 5, 1916.

COLORPLATE 27

LANCE RICHBOURG. *Grover Cleveland Alexander.* 1987. Watercolor. 66 x 51 in.
Norton Center for the Arts, Centre College, Danville, KY. Permanent Collection.

McGraw's salary of ten thousand dollars was said to be the most paid a player in a decade, but because of reporting late he would receive only ninety-five hundred dollars of it. Robinson, on the downside of his career, would be paid five thousand dollars.

Despite the money, the play of the two ex-Orioles was uninspired, and much of their time was spent at the racetrack across the street from the ballpark. When he was injured McGraw did not even bother to show up at the game, preferring instead to attend the races. Finally, Frank de Haas Robison, the St. Louis owner, became so incensed he ordered manager Patsy Tebeau to inform McGraw that he belonged where he drew his pay. So McGraw returned to the ballpark, where he continued to place his wagers on the horses by dispatching couriers to the track between innings.

The turning point for McGraw came in Chicago when he met Ban Johnson. The American League president made a lasting impression on the young ballplayer. While National League owners are fighting each other, McGraw thought to himself, Johnson is fighting for baseball as a game first and for territorial growth next.

After that meeting, McGraw and Robinson talked frequently about Johnson and the American League. For the first time in their lives, McGraw told his friend, they had been privileged to see a blueprint of sound and sincere baseball administration.

That summer, Johnson's agents quietly went about their business, signing up players in every National League city. All of the deals were worked out under the table, and the National League magnates never caught on to what was happening right under their noses.

McGraw was a particularly effective recruiter in his travels around the circuit. He signed underhand pitcher Iron Man Joe McGinnity of Brooklyn to a contract scribbled on the back of a piece of scratch paper. In Chicago, he landed catcher Roger Bresnahan. In Pittsburgh, he got infielder Jimmy Williams. McGraw's St. Louis teammate Turkey Mike Donlin, an outfielder, also agreed to make the jump.

When the season finally ended, McGraw and Robinson were so happy to get out of St. Louis, they tossed their uniforms into the Mississippi River while their train slowly made its way east over the long bridge. As they watched the clothing disappear into the darkness below, the two ballplayers believed they were leaving the National League behind them for good.

Ty Cobb with Al Stump

FROM MY LIFE IN BASEBALL

In this selection from his autobiography, published in 1961 (the year he died), Ty Cobb reveals the intensity, the bitterness, and the anger that became his trademark as a player for the Detroit Tigers from 1905 to 1926. Cobb finished his career with the Philadelphia Athletics in 1927 and 1928.

———————————

If modern players battle fiercely for starting assignments, I have to say that the old-timers were even more wolfish. Over that 1905–6 winter, Detroit acquired Davey Jones, a fleet outfielder and a great lead-off man. That meant that the three outfield jobs were up for grabs among Sam Crawford (a cinch), Matty McIntyre, a light hitter but a good ballhawk, Jones, and Cobb. Who'd sit on the bench? It wouldn't be McIntyre, if a tightly organized clique on the Detroit club could help it. McIntyre and his chums began a systematic, carefully schemed campaign to break my spirit and make me the fellow who picked his teeth with bench splinters while they made the money.

At first, there were no open clashes. McIntyre and his roommate, Twilight Ed Killian, a pitcher, began by locking me out of the hotel bathroom the players shared. I'd stand shivering in a towel or bedsheet while they hogged the tub for hours. At batting practice, I'd be jostled aside and told, "Get out to the outfield, sand-lotter. This is for men only." In restaurants, and there were no hat-check girls then, I'd dine, and find my hat impaled on the rack, minus its crown. It got to the point that I walked up to my tormentors and said, "Whoever did this to my hat, stand up, you————!" They just grinned at me. I could never prove a thing.

It was clear that they intended to razz me off the team and back to the bushes, and that they had endless methods to accomplish it. During Pullman rides, a soggy wad of newspaper would fly down the aisle and smack me in the neck. After wiping off the water, I'd stalk down the aisle, raging mad, and yelling, "Get on your feet, the————who threw that!"

But they wouldn't fight—not quite yet.

It was a war of nerves. My only support came from Wild Bill Donovan, the pitcher, and a few others, who urged me, "Stick up for your rights. If it comes to a showdown, we'll back you up."

Armour, the manager, rightly, saw that it was my personal problem to win or lose and did nothing in particular to stop the hazing. It was a routine hazard in the early century for rookies to be worked over. But usually it was done more in a joshing spirit than with malevolent intent . . . this feud was for keeps.

Social ostracism was introduced. I found myself eating alone, cold-shouldered in the clubhouse and unable to find a permanent roommate. In Detroit, the veterans stayed at a half-hotel, half-burlesque house called the Brunswick, while I roomed at a sedate hostelry a few blocks away. It was a bleak, lonely time for a boy not yet nineteen. For a while, Edgar (Eddie) Willett, a rookie pitcher from Norfolk, Virginia, moved in with me. He was a big, good-looking farm boy with a world of promise. But the high-living McIntyre crowd put pressure on Eddie.

"We're going to run Cobb off the club," they warned him, "and you, too, if you stay friends with him. Either move out and hang around with us, or you're finished."

Eddie told me this. I said, "You're at the crossroads. These men just want to make a beer-drinker out of you, like them. Edgar, they are not driving me off this team. I'd tell them to go to hell, if I were you." But Eddie packed up and left, and soon the sporty life caught up with him. In six seasons he was finished.

My enemies were a sneaky lot, always operating behind a facade of innocence, because, by now, they knew that I always went armed. I kept a weapon of a lethal nature close by me at all times and I had eyes in the back of my head. If they jumped me some dark night, they'd find one Georgia boy who wouldn't hesitate to even the odds with extreme means, if fists failed to save me. One of the most underhanded stunts they pulled was to break my bats. I cherished the fine ash bats I had collected. I found them smashed, and had excellent reason to believe that the man who'd done it was Charlie Schmidt, a powerfully built catcher.

Schmidt—in time—became my good friend. A burly ex-miner from Coal Hill, Arkansas, he was most likable, except when conned by the anti-Cobbs into provoking me into fighting him, which was what the faction wanted. Weighing well over 200, Schmidt once had boxed Jack Johnson, the world's heavyweight champion. For amusement, he'd drive spikes into the clubhouse floor with his fist.

We first clashed during a spring training trip down South, more of a wrestle than a fight. Moving into Mississippi, my tormentors told Charlie, "Cobb is going around claiming he licked you. You going to let him get away with that?"

In Hattiesburg, I had just laced my shoes and was walking toward the field when I heard a voice growl:

"Cobb."

I turned, and Schmidt's punch caught me with both hands at my side, a crushing wallop that knocked me flat and broke my nose. From then on, a terrible anger was in me. Anger, hatred, and humiliation. I hadn't been raised to brawl like this. I could see no reason why ballplayers should lower themselves to an animal level and I felt ashamed of the game and these men who would stop at nothing to ruin a youngster's spirit.

On the field, toward late season of 1906, the thing became so bitter that the Tigers were

Ty Cobb Slides into Third Base. c. 1915. The National Baseball Library, Cooperstown, New York.

dropping games because of it. Davey Jones pulled a Charley horse and I played center field regularly, with McIntyre in left field. Outfielders back each other up on all possible plays, and I obliged whenever McIntyre had a chance to handle, and I could get over behind him. But McIntyre wouldn't back up Cobb. It came to the point in a game with St. Louis that George Stone drove a ball between us—a shot which either of us might catch. I broke for it, and saw that McIntyre hadn't budged. The ball had split our positions and his responsibility to try for it was as great as mine. So I stopped dead-still. The ball bounced between us and on to the fence for a home run.

Pitching that day for our side was Ed Siever, one of the anti-Cobb ring. I'd saved more than one game for Siever with glove and bat, but back in the dugout he cursed me.

I jumped up and stood over him. Where I came from, men had been killed for saying what Siever did. "Get up! Get on your feet!" I shouted at him. Dimly, but almost obliterated by my rage, was the realization that I hadn't been brought up for such hooligan exhibitions, and even as I challenged Siever I felt the shame my parents would have felt had they witnessed the scene.

He didn't get up . . . for I was ready.

But that night at the Planter's Hotel in St. Louis, I came down the staircase and wandered over to the cigar counter, thinking that a smoke would relax me. I was studying the cheroots when Siever edged up close. Wild Bill Donovan put a hand between us. "Let's not have any trouble, boys," he said.

"I want no trouble," I answered.

Siever muttered something and retreated to a corner of the lobby, where he huddled with McIntyre and others. They stood there, talking. Feeling something was up, I eased over behind one of the lobby columns to listen in. But they spotted me.

Suddenly, around the column, and moving fast, came Siever. He was a left-handed puncher, as well as pitcher, and he started one that would have removed my head had it landed. But I smothered the blow and then let go all my pent-up emotion. I hit him a right to the jaw that started him down and connected several times more as he was staggering and falling. Siever went down in a badly damaged condition. Sensible heads, such as Donovan's, broke it up.

"Let's get out of here," urged Donovan. "The police might come."

"Let them come. I'm innocent of anything except defending myself," I said.

"Sure, sure," said Bill, "but you'll land in the cooler, anyway. These guys hate you. They'll prefer charges, or do anything to hurt you."

I didn't run out. I waited a spell, and then I took a long and lonely walk down to the railway station. Only two games remained in the season. I wished I didn't have to play in them. I was sick at heart and disillusioned. I'd dreamed of becoming a part of the Detroit organization, and all I'd known, so far, was jealousy and persecution. I had a hunch that the enemy would expect me to pull out for Georgia and pass up the last two games. But to force an issue that was thrust upon me, and then follow up, had been part of my training as a boy.

I surprised them by showing up for the train leaving St. Louis next morning. I ran into Tom McMahon, our trainer. "You did only one thing wrong," he remarked. "You kicked Siever after you had him down."

"I didn't have to kick him," I replied. "He was well-licked when he went down. Get your facts straight, Tom."

To reach my berth, I had to pass through a narrow aisle, and there, stretched out on a seat, with some players holding beefsteak to his face, was Siever. He was groaning and looked like he'd been in a mangler.

"Siever," I paused to say, "they tell me I kicked you. I don't recall any such thing. But if I did, I apologize for that part of it."

He mumbled something about, "I'll get you . . ."

In bed, I stretched out, but I didn't sleep. It was more than possible that I'd be attacked during the night. If so, I was armed and ready. And I remained ready until the day came when I was established as a Detroit regular and, one by one, my antagonists dropped away.

Readers might be interested in the later-day resolvement of my relationship with these men.

Matty McIntyre died in 1920 without ever shaking my hand and letting bygones be bygones.

Charlie Schmidt died in 1932, and we parted friends. Before then, Charlie would even weep a few tears when he thought of how it had once been with us. The Dutchman was a grand man, and he knew how much I liked him.

Twilight Ed Killian wrote to me one day years after his big league days were ended. He was working in a Studebaker plant in Detroit and thought there might be enough snap left in the old soup-bone to pick up a few dollars in an industrial league. "Ty, it's been tough for me," he wrote. "If I had a pair of shoes and a glove, I could make this team and it would help."

"Ed," I wrote back, "present yourself at the Spalding's sports good store in Detroit and order the best—anything you need. I'll phone them and make sure your order is filled. I hope you win every game."

How small seem these events of the past weighed against the long haul of life . . . yet how large they loomed for me at the time.

It has been widely written that the hazers turned me from a cheerful young fellow into a lone wolf. My rugged style of play is supposed to date from my baptism at Detroit. The fact is that the clique did me a tremendous favor. Although I hated them as much as they hated me, in driving me off by myself, they gave me time to think. I ate alone, roomed alone, and walked alone. In off hours, I couldn't take in a vaudeville show every night. Pool halls, bowling alleys, and saloons didn't interest me. And I wasn't much of a reader in those days. Sitting in my room or taking long hikes, I had only baseball to think about—in particular, pitchers who were handcuffing me at the plate. In an exhibition game, Rube Manning, later of the Highlanders, had fanned me three times. Doc White of the White Sox threw a drop I couldn't fathom—he whiffed me four times running. There were others, mostly left-handers, who threatened to drive me out of the league.

What's more, the attitude of my teammates gave me the extra incentive of becoming a top player in order to show them up. There were a lot of things I couldn't do on the field that even some minor leaguers I'd seen could do. More than ever, I wanted to improve.

Robert W. Creamer

FROM BABE: THE LEGEND COMES TO LIFE
"Kaleidoscope: Personality of the Babe"

In his fascinating biography of the game's first superstar, Robert W. Creamer presents his portrait of the Babe, whose true persona may actually have been more boisterous and exuberant than the legend most are familiar with. Ruth began his career with the Boston Red Sox in 1914 and was sold to the Yankees on January 3, 1920. He finished his career with the Boston Braves in 1935.

On the road he always had a suite, sometimes in a different hotel from the one the team was staying at. He liked to lounge around in red slippers and a red robe, smoking a cigar. Dozens of people streamed in and out of the suite day and night. He always carried a wind-up portable phonograph with him on road trips. He loved to sing. Occasionally he would strum a ukulele. He was always shaved by a barber. ("That's what they're for, aren't they?") In St. Louis he liked to eat at a German restaurant that made barbecued spare ribs. Often, on the day the Yankees were leaving town, he'd go from the ballpark to the restaurant and order a mess of ribs and home brew and take it to the train. He would set up shop in a washroom and sell the ribs to the players for fifty cents a portion. He insisted on being paid too, but he also provided beer, and the players could have all the beer they wanted for their fifty cents.

He was apolitical, although he called himself a Democrat until Franklin D. Roosevelt ran for a third term, and apparently he never cast a vote in a national election until 1944. Yet he created a mild political furor in September 1928, when Herbert Hoover was running for President. Hoover appeared at the ballpark and a publicity man ran down to the Yankee clubhouse to get Ruth to come and pose with the Republican candidate.

"No, sir," said Ruth, "nothing doing on politics." He had been burned a few days earlier by a story saying he was supporting Hoover. He denied it, saying he was for Al Smith, and now he declined to appear with Smith's rival. But, graciously, he said, "Tell him I'll be glad to talk to him if he wants to meet me under the stands." No doubt here as to which was king. . . .

He was so alive, so attractive, like an animal or a child: ingenuous, unself-conscious, appealing. Frank Graham said, "He was a very simple man, in some ways a primitive man. He had little education, and little need for what he had." Tom Meany said he had the supreme self-confidence of the naïve. On a stifling hot day at the Washington ballpark he said to President Harding, "Hot as hell, ain't it, Prez?" He met Marshal Foch when that renowned French hero of World War I was making a tour of the United States early in the 1920s and said politely, "I suppose you were in the war?"

Introduced before a game to a man he had never seen before, Ruth said, "You sound like you have a cold." The man admitted he did. Ruth reached into the hip pocket of his uniform and pulled out a big onion. "Here, gnaw on this," he said. "Raw onions are cold-killers." During a blistering heat wave Ruth brought a cabbage into the dugout and put it in the team's old-fashioned water cooler, and each inning before he went on the field he took a fresh cabbage leaf and put it under his cap to keep himself cool.

Famous for not remembering names (when Waite Hoyt was leaving the Yankees in 1930 after eleven seasons as Babe's teammate in Boston and New York, Ruth shook hands and said solemnly, "Goodbye, Walter"), he had nicknames for other players, not necessarily complimentary nicknames. His teammates were Chicken Neck, Flop Ears, Duck Eye, Horse Nose, Rubber Belly. People he did not know or remember he called Doc or Kid, which he usually pronounced Keed, in the flashy slang pronunciation of the time. He called older men Pop,

NICKOLAS MURAY. Babe Ruth (George Herman Ruth). c. 1927. Gelatin-silver print. 13³/8 x 10⁷/16 in. Collection, The Museum of Modern Art, New York. Gift of Mrs. Nickolas Muray.

older women Mom. Younger women he needed no special name for. He usually called Claire Clara. He himself was called Jidge by the Yankees, a corruption of George that was apparently first used by Dugan.

His appetite was enormous, although accounts of it were often exaggerated. A report of one dinner says he had an entire capon, potatoes, spinach, corn, peas, beans, bread, butter, pie, ice cream and three or four cups of coffee. He was known to have eaten a huge omelet made of eighteen eggs and three big slices of ham, plus half a dozen slices of buttered toast and several cups of coffee. Ty Cobb, no stickler for accuracy in his memoirs of baseball life, said, "I've seen him at midnight, propped up in bed, order six club sandwiches, a platter of pigs' knuckles and a pitcher of beer. He'd down all that while smoking a big black cigar. Next day, if he hit a homer, he'd trot around the bases complaining about gas pains and a bellyache." He belched magnificently and, I was told, could fart at will.

He was, as noted, a sexual athlete. In a St. Louis whorehouse he announced he was going to go to bed with every girl in the house during the night, and did, and after finishing his rounds sat down and had a huge breakfast. In the early 1930s the Yankees signed a superior pitcher named Charlie Devens out of Harvard, who abandoned a promising major league career a year or two later to join his family's banking business in Boston. Devens joined the team in St. Louis, reporting in at the hotel. He was given the key to his room and went up and unpacked. His roommate, some secondary figure on the team, was not around. Just as he finished unpacking, the phone rang and a voice asked, "Devens?"

"Yes."

"Bring your room key with you and come down to the lobby."

Obediently Devens took his key and went downstairs. When the elevator doors opened at the lobby floor, there was Babe Ruth, a girl on each arm.

"You Devens?" Ruth asked.

Devens nodded. Ruth put out his hand. Devens looked at him dumbly.

"The key," Ruth snapped. Devens gave him the key and Babe and his friends swept into the elevator. Later Devens learned that when Mrs. Ruth was with Babe on road trips he occasionally pre-empted teammates' rooms for extracurricular activities. . . .

There is a story, probably apocryphal, about a time he and Meusel were barnstorming together. They shared a hotel suite. Meusel was half asleep when Ruth came in with a girl, went into his room and made love to her in his usual noisy fashion. Afterwards he came out to the living room of the suite, lit a cigar and sat in a chair by the window, smoking it contemplatively. When he finished the cigar he went back into the bedroom and made love again. And then came out and smoked another cigar. In the morning Meusel asked, "How many times did you lay that girl last night?" Ruth glanced at the ashtray, and so did Meusel. There were seven butts in the tray. "Count the cigars," said Ruth. . . .

Everything about him reflected sexuality—the restless, roving energy; the aggressive skills; fastball pitching; home run hitting; the speed with which he drove cars; the loud, rich voice; the insatiable appetite; the constant need to placate his mouth with food, drink, a cigar, chewing gum, anything. When he played poker, he liked to raise even when his cards did not justify a raise, and when he lucked into a pot he chortled happily. He was a fairly skillful bridge player, but he wanted to play every hand himself and often outbid his partner as well as their opponents. In retirement his favorite sports were golf and bowling; he liked to hit a golf ball a long way, and in bowling to keep track of the total number of pins he knocked down rather than his average score. He loved to win in whatever he did. He received absolute physical joy from cards, baseball, golf, bowling, punching the bag, sex. . . .

Physically he was a paradox. He was big, strong, muscular, exceptionally well coordinated, yet he was often injured and he suffered from a surprising number of colds and infections. This would indicate a low resistance to disease, yet he had an amazing ability to recover quickly. He dramatized injuries; no player in big league history was carried off the field on his shield as often as the massive Bambino. But he could ignore both illness and injury and play superlatively well despite them. . . .

Many stories about Ruth were turned into legend by the encrustations of time. . . . The story of Johnny Sylvester is one of the most famous in Ruth lore. The simplest version says that Johnny, a young boy, lay dying in a hospital. Ruth came to visit him and promised him he would hit a home run for him that afternoon. And he did, which so filled Johnny with the will to live that he miraculously recovered. The facts are parallel, if not so melodramatic. In 1926 eleven-year-old Johnny Sylvester was badly hurt in a fall from a horse and was hospitalized. To cheer him up, a friend of Johnny's father brought him baseballs autographed by players on the Yankees and the Cardinals just before the World Series that year, as well as a promise from Ruth that he would hit a home run for him. Ruth hit four homers in the Series, and after it was over paid a visit to Johnny in the hospital, which thrilled the boy. The visit was given the tears-and-lump-in-the-throat treatment in the press, and the legend was born. After that, few writers reviewing Ruth's career failed to mention a dying boy and the home run that saved his life.

The following spring Ruth was sitting with a couple of baseball writers when a man came up to him and said, "Mr. Ruth, I'm Johnny Sylvester's uncle. I just want to thank you again for what you did for him."

"That's all right," Ruth said, "glad to do it. How is Johnny?"

"He's fine. He's home, and everything looks okay."

"That's good," said Ruth. "Give him my regards."

The man left. Ruth watched him walk away and said, "Now who the hell is Johnny Sylvester?". . .

Yet his affection for children was genuine, and it remained with him all his life. In 1943 he played a round of golf in the rain at the Commonwealth Country Club near Boston. As he was teeing up on the first hole he noticed two boys staring through a chain-link fence.

"Hey," he called to them. "You want to follow me around? It won't be any drier but it'll be more fun. You want to?"

The kids nodded. "Show them how to get into this joint," Ruth said to Russ Hale, the club pro. He waited until the boys reached the tee before he hit his drive, and he walked down the fairway with one arm around each, talking. He played nine holes in the rain, most of the time laughing and joking with the other men in his foursome but always returning to the kids to make sure they were enjoying themselves. . . .

He liked seeing children the best. He enjoyed them. He was comfortable with them. "He's just a big kid" was a common description of him, and perhaps the only time he was truly at ease was when he was with children. With them there were no rules, no authority, no need to apologize, to explain, to explode, to drink, to fuck, to prove himself over and over. Without thinking about it, he knew who they were and they knew who he was. They got along. Like a child, he did not like to wait or plan for the right moment. He did not like to wait for anything. "It might rain tomorrow," he would say.

He did things impulsively, the way a child does. Children are emotionally neutral to things that deeply affect adults. Without malice, they casually hurt the feelings of a close friend. Without love, they do an act of exceptional thoughtfulness for a casual acquaintance. In his novel *Stop-Time* Frank Conroy wrote, "Like all children, I was unsentimental." Hoyt said of Ruth, "Babe was not a sentimentalist and generally made no outward demonstration of affection either by word or action."

This may explain a curious thing that Paul Carey, his great friend, said when he was asked about Ruth's feelings toward Claire. "I don't think the Babe really loved Clair," Carey said. "I don't think he really loved anybody."

John Holway

FROM VOICES FROM THE GREAT BLACK BASEBALL LEAGUES

" 'Cool Papa' Bell"

Hall-of-Famer James "Cool Papa" Bell's speed was legendary, even though he was never allowed to exhibit it in the major leagues. Satchel Paige once said that Bell was so fast he could turn off the lights and be in bed before the room got dark. In this passage from John Holway's 1975 collection of reminiscences of the Negro Leagues, Bell talks about his speed on the diamond.

———————————

I've scored from first base on singles lots of times. Sometimes I could even score on a bunt. The last time I did that was against Bob Lemon's all-stars when I was forty-five years old. I was playing winter ball in California in 1948. Satchel Paige picked me as a reserve outfielder on his team. I had about quit playing ball, but Satchel wanted someone out there with experience. Some of those young boys just coming up, they would seem like they had a fear of those major leaguers. They'd say, "I'm not as good as the major leaguers, I don't know whether I can hit them or not."

Satchel said, "When I pitch, I want Bell to play."

I said, "Satchel, I'm not in condition, I'm just halfway in condition. I've been managing this farm team and I don't play every day." I could hit the ball, catch it, but by not being in condition, I said, "Don't let me lead off. I don't want to be coming to bat too often, get on base often."

Satchel said, "Oh, you'll be in condition. I've told all the guys what you can do and they don't believe it. And I told them you're older than me and they don't believe *that!*" I said, "I

James "Cool Papa" Bell. c. 1930. The National Baseball Library, Cooperstown, New York. *Bell's legendary speed even intimidated Olympian Jesse Owens: "They wanted us to run once in Cleveland, and [Owens] saw me running bases and came out on the field and praised my running and said, 'I don't want to run today. I didn't bring my track shoes.'"*

don't want to lead off, I'm not in condition." He said, "I'll pitch five innings, you play five innings, then you can come out."

So this time I was hitting eighth and I got on base, and Satchel came up and sacrificed me to second. Well, Bob Lemon came off the mound to field it and I saw that third base was open, because the third baseman had also charged in to field it. Roy Partee, the catcher, saw me going to third, so he went down the line to cover third and I just came on home past him. Partee called "Time, time!" But the umpire said, "I can't call time, the ball's still in play," so I scored.

Satchel Paige says I would have made Jesse Owens look like he was walking. Jesse Owens ran 100 yards in nine-something, and I could circle the bases—120 yards, plus—in twelve flat. So, comparing his time and mine, they said I was faster than Owens. . . .

I don't know if Maury Wills ever saw me play or not. I was playing with the Washington Homestead Grays when he was a kid in Washington. I only met Wills once, here in St. Louis the year he broke Ty Cobb's record. I said, "I have noticed that you're running bases and some guy fouls the pitch off." I knew Junior Gilliam was a team man, Gilliam would probably take a strike in order to give him a chance to steal. I said, "Do you have anyone else behind Gilliam who can do that?" He said no. I said, "I'm going to tell you when I was running bases, I had about three guys behind me, and I had a signal when I was going to steal a base, on the first pitch or the second pitch. So if I'm going to steal a base, they had a chance to help me, they wouldn't hit that ball." I said, "If you had cooperation, you could steal more bases. Tell them to get back in the box, and hold the bat back. You don't have to swing as long as you hold that bat back here. If you're back here in the box, you give the catcher less room to throw. That gives you a couple of steps. And then if you don't get a good lead, he can swing at the ball."

He said, "I hadn't thought of that."

I said, "Well, that's the kind of ball we played." You don't have those kinds of players today. These players today, they don't think of things like that. When we came up we played different baseball than they do in the major leagues. We played "tricky" baseball.

I would be alert on the bases. A lot of fellows could do the same things I did if they were alert. A guy drops the ball and *then* they run. I was always looking for a break. It wasn't that I was that much faster than the other guys, it was just the way I played. They said, "You're faster than those guys." I said, "I don't know, they're just slow in thinking."

The best year I ever had on the bases was 1933. I stole 175 in about 180 or 200 ball games.

They once timed me circling the bases in twelve seconds flat. One guy said, "If you can do it in twelve, you can do it in eleven." So he had a field day, and I was supposed to run against Tuck Stainback, who played center field for the Yankees. The major league record was :13.3 by a guy named Swanson with Cincinnati. We were going to try to break it. Well, it rained and it was muddy and Stainback wouldn't run. He said he had a cold. But the fans kept hollering, so I ran alone in :13.1 on a wet ground.

Back then Fats Jenkins of the Lincolns was supposed to be the fastest guy out East. A white fellow had seen Fats Jenkins run but when he saw me, he said I was the fastest man he'd ever seen. He asked me, "Bell, do you want to make some money? I can take you overseas running on tracks and nobody would beat you running." But I never did. I don't know how I would have done.

I scored from first base on singles lots of times. If the ball isn't hit straight at the outfielder, I'd score. You have to be heads up and watch those things.

Lawrence S. Ritter

FROM THE GLORY OF THEIR TIMES
"Hank Greenberg"

In his extraordinary oral history of the game's early days, Lawrence S. Ritter introduces the reader to Hall of Fame first baseman Hank Greenberg, who towered over the opposition both literally and figuratively. Greenberg played for the Detroit Tigers in 1930, from 1933 until he was drafted early in the 1941 season, and then from 1945 to 1946. He also played for the Pittsburgh Pirates in 1947. Here, he tells in his own words the story of his life before and after his illustrious career.

We lived in the East Tremont section of the Bronx on Crotona Park North, which is another name for East 174th Street, just across the street from Crotona Park and only a block from the park's baseball field. That's where I spent most of my time, practicing, practicing, practicing. Someone once said I didn't *play* ball when I was a kid, I *worked* at it, and I guess they were right. I'd play pepper by the hour, for example, to improve my fielding. Guys would hit or bunt the ball to me and I'd catch it. Over and over again. I'd count how many balls I'd fielded without an error, and then after I missed one I'd start counting all over again.

To improve my hitting, I'd get friends and kids hanging around the park to pitch to me and to shag balls for me. Usually there would be three or four of them—one pitching and two or three shagging in the outfield. Sometimes I'd have a couple of infielders, too. There was no backstop in Crotona Park, which meant I had to hit the ball, because if it got past me I was the one who had to chase it. The idea was to hit fly balls to the guys shagging and get a fly ball to each of them often enough so they didn't get bored and quit. But you couldn't hit the ball too far away from them so they had to do too much running, because then they'd quit not because they were bored, but because they were tired. You also had to be careful not to hit the ball hard straight back at the pitcher, because if he got hit with a batted ball, he'd quit and go home, too.

I got so I was able to hit fly balls within 10 or 15 feet of where I wanted in the outfield, or hit ground balls within a few feet of where I was aiming for in the infield, and whenever a bad pitch came in, I could successfully throw my bat at it and stop it from getting by me. You do this all day long, every day, day after day, and sooner or later you're bound to get pretty good.

I know I spent a lot of time in Crotona Park because I wanted to make myself a better ballplayer, but in all frankness I suspect it was also more complicated than that. I'm no psychologist, but I think one reason I spent so much time there was related to the fact that I was 6 feet 3 inches tall when I was only thirteen. I was awkward and clumsy and had a bad case of adolescent acne and felt out of place. At school, I'd squeeze behind one of those tiny desks, and if I had to go to the blackboard it would be the event of the day: all the kids would titter 'cause I'd tower way above the teacher. Everybody always teased me. "How's the air up there?" I heard that a dozen times a day. At home, if company was at the house they'd be astounded: "My God, look how much he's grown! He's grown two feet in a week!"

I began to think I was a freak. I felt that everybody was laughing at me. It was embarrassing. I was always slouching around, more or less hiding, never standing up straight.

Sports was my escape from all that. Many of the very things that were liabilities socially were assets in sports. I felt more comfortable with athletics, and I think that had a lot to do with why I spent most of my time in Crotona Park. . . .

After I finished playing, I had a whole second career on the management level. I met Bill Veeck at the 1947 World Series, found a kindred spirit, and joined him in the Cleveland Indians' front office in 1948. In my opinion, Bill Veeck is the smartest and most innovative baseball executive of all time. Except for Branch Rickey, he doesn't even have any competition.

Veeck converted me. I was a ballplayer, you see, and the game was everything. What happened aside from the game was irrelevant to me. Bill taught me that baseball was more than just balls and strikes, hits and errors. You have to get people into the ball park, and to do that you have to attract them with a good time as well as a good team. I finally recognized that baseball is part entertainment and show business. I think that Veeck's genius of drawing more than two and a half million fans in Cleveland in 1948, a town that typically drew less than a million, was as big an accomplishment in its own way as Ted Williams hitting .406.

First I was farm director and then general manager at Cleveland, and afterwards vice-president of the White Sox when Veeck took over that club. I was part owner of each franchise as well, I guess one of the few who went from the sandlots through the players' ranks to the front office and eventually an ownership position.

When Veeck became ill and had to sell the White Sox in 1961, I had an opportunity to increase my stock ownership and acquire a majority interest in the club. After a lot of thought, I finally decided against it. What tipped the scales against buying was the other owners: I recognized then that there was a lot of prejudice against me. I'd have had my life savings tied up in the club, and I realized that if I ever needed any help, I sure wouldn't get it from my fellow owners. It would be closed ranks against me.

Strangely enough, that was the first time anti-Semitism really affected me adversely in baseball. As a player, I often had fans and opposing players taunting me, calling me names. For at least ten years I hardly played in a ball park where there wasn't some loud-mouthed fan popping off with anti-Jewish remarks. In the minors—the Piedmont League, the Texas League—and for many years in the majors, too, my religion was seen as an appropriate topic for ridicule.

However, I think that *helped* me more than it hurt. I was a very sensitive, fired-up ballplayer, and when they got on me that way, it brought out the best in me. I played all the harder.

In my mind, by the way, players belong in a different category than fans. It was considered fair game to try to probe for a guy's weak spot so you could catch his attention and destroy his concentration. Joe McCarthy used to have two third-stringers on the Yankee bench—we called them bench jockeys—whose main job was to ride the opposition and try to get their goat.

When opposing bench jockeys taunted me, was it really anti-Semitism or just a psychological ploy to distract me? Probably some of both, but in my opinion it was mostly a psychological ploy. After all, Al Simmons heard similar insults about his Polish ancestry and Joe DiMaggio about his Italian heritage. Babe Ruth was called a "big baboon," and much worse, and Zeke Bonura "banana nose." In all honesty, I couldn't then and I can't now single out the insults aimed at me as any different from all the others. I think they were all the same kind of thing.

You want to talk about real bigotry, that was what Jackie Robinson had to contend with in 1947. Teammates asking to be traded rather than play with him, opponents threatening to

Hank Greenberg. c. 1940. The National Baseball Library, Cooperstown, New York. *Baseball's first Hammerin' Hank (Aaron was the second), Greenberg hit a grand-slam home run in the bottom of the ninth of the season's last game to win the 1945 pennant for the Detroit Tigers.*

strike rather than play against him; in many places he couldn't eat or sleep with the rest of the team. I never encountered anything like that.

I was with Pittsburgh in the National League that year, so I saw it close up. Brooklyn was leading the league and we were in last place, they were beating our brains out, and here's some of our guys having a good time yelling insults at Jackie! I had to put up with little more than a mild hazing compared with what he went through.

Sometimes it could get pretty bad for me too, of course. The Chicago Cubs were especially vicious in the 1935 World Series. They got on me from the first pitch with some really rough stuff. George Moriarty was umpiring behind home plate, and it bothered him so much he went over to quiet them down. They told Moriarty to mind his own business; they weren't getting on him, they were getting on me. I broke my wrist in the second game of the Series and couldn't play anymore, so that ended that. They had a rough crew, but we had the last laugh: we won the Series.

I realize now, more than I used to, how important a part I played in the lives of a generation of Jewish kids who grew up in the thirties. I never thought about it then. But in recent years, men I meet often tell me how much I meant to them when they were growing up. It's almost the first thing a lot of them say to me. It still surprises me to hear it, but I think I'm finally starting to believe it.

They all remember that I didn't play on Yom Kippur, the Jewish holiday. They remember it as every year, but in fact the situation arose only once, in 1934. Both Rosh Hashanah and Yom Kippur came in September that year, and since we were in the thick of the pennant race, the first for Detroit in many years, it became a national issue whether or not I should play on those days. The press made a big thing out of it.

The question was put before Detroit's leading rabbi, Rabbi Leo Franklin. He consulted the Talmud, a basic source for Jewish morality, and announced that I could play on Rosh Hashanah, the Jewish New Year, because that was a happy occasion on which Jews used to play ball in the streets long ago. However, I could not play on Yom Kippur, the Day of Atonement, because that day should be spent in prayer.

So I played on Rosh Hashanah and, believe it or not, I hit two home runs off Boston's Dusty Rhodes. We beat the Red Sox, 2–1, with my second homer winning the game in the tenth inning. Just like in the movies, right? . . .

It's a strange thing. When I was playing, I used to resent being singled out as a Jewish ballplayer. I wanted to be known as a great ballplayer, period. I'm not sure why or when I changed, because I'm still not a particularly religious person. Lately, though, I find myself wanting to be remembered not only as a great ballplayer, but even more as a great *Jewish* ballplayer.

Probably Bill Veeck's fault, right? After all, he's the one started me thinking maybe there are other things in life besides balls and strikes. Back in good old Crotona Park, I never would have believed a word of it!

Satchel Paige, as told to David Lipman
FROM MAYBE I'LL PITCH FOREVER

Satchel Paige may very well have pitched forever, but because most of that time was spent in the Negro Leagues, his statistics are lost to history. Paige finally broke into the majors in 1948 with the Cleveland Indians. He pitched for the St. Louis Browns from 1951 to 1953, and appeared in one game for the Kansas City Athletics in 1965 when his age was estimated at fifty-nine.

The next day I went looking for work, but those who knew where I'd been turned me down and those who didn't know didn't seem to have any steady work. Or maybe I wasn't really looking.

That afternoon I ended up over at Eureka Gardens, where the semi-pro Mobile Tigers still played, just like they did before I went up. My brother, Wilson, pitched and caught for them.

I sat down in the stands and leaned back to watch. The Tigers were getting ready for the regular 1924 season and were still trying out some guys for the club.

I looked all over but couldn't spot Wilson. He must not have come out that day.

The Tigers worked out about an hour and the longer I watched them the worse that itch to play got. Finally all the players except the catcher and the guy who'd been running the practice session left.

After the field was clear, a kid who'd been sitting down on the first row walked out on the field.

The kid went to the pitcher's mound and threw a few warmup pitches to the catcher. Then the Tigers' manager picked up a bat and stepped into the batting box. The kid started pitching again.

The Tigers' manager cracked those pitches all over the park.

He'd bat two thousand if he could come up against that kid every day, I thought.

One thing I was sure of was if that kid could try out for the Tigers, I sure could.

Then I got excited. Why not?

I looked close at that kid again.

I knew I could throw better than that shuffler.

Down I went, fast.

I waited at the side of the field until the kid walked off. I guess the manager had figured like me. That kid wouldn't cut it.

I walked up to the manager.

"You still looking for a pitcher?" I asked.

He just looked at me. "Go home, boy," he said. "I'm tired."

But when I told him I was Wilson's brother, he decided to let me pitch. He flipped a ball to me.

"Where've you been pitching?" he asked.

"Oh, around," I said.

He just nodded.

I felt good out on the mound. I whistled in a few of my fast ones, not bothering to wind up. They popped against the catcher's glove like they was firecrackers.

They never heard anything like that, I thought.

"I'm ready for you, mistah," I called to the manager.

He stepped into the box.

I threw. Ten times I threw. Ten times he swung. Ten times he missed.

I grinned. I stuck my foot up in his face and then tore the catcher's hand off with my blazer. He didn't have a chance against me.

The manager was grinning too.

"Do you throw that fast consistently?" he asked me.

"No, sir, I do it all the time."

That's the day I learned a new word.

The manager gave me a dollar and told me to come back with Wilson for the next game. I felt like that dollar was a thousand.

That was the point where I gave up kid's baseball—baseball just for fun—and started baseball as a career, started doing what I'd been thinking about doing off and on since my coach at the Mount'd told me about getting somewhere in the world if I concentrated on baseball.

And getting somewhere in the world is what I wanted most. Baseball had to be the way, too. I didn't know anything else.

Wilson, they called him Paddlefoot, and I were real tough for the Tigers. Actually, Wilson could throw about as hard as I could and we would have made one of the best two-man staffs you ever saw if he'd stuck with baseball, but he didn't.

First of all, he didn't want to leave Mobile then, and Wilson didn't love baseball like me. I'd do anything—practice for hours, watch and study for hours—just to get a little better.

While we were with the Tigers, though, we made a lot of people talk about us.

Wilson already was a big man around Eureka Gardens when I joined the team. It only took

Satchel Paige's Windup. c. 1940. The National Baseball Library, Cooperstown, New York. *Included in the repertoire of the immortal Paige was his famous "hesitation" pitch, which still drove batters to distraction when Paige finally reached the major leagues in 1948.*

me a few games to become another hero. All the guys wanted to buy me drinks. All the gals just wanted to be around, squealing and hanging on my arms.

That's a mighty comforting feeling.

It's funny what a few no-hitters do for a body.

But those no-hitters don't make you rich. Not in semi-pro ball. I'd get about a buck a game when enough fans came out so we made some money after paying for expenses. When there wasn't enough money, they gave me a keg of lemonade.

I got to laugh at that now. Back in 1924, I'd get a keg of lemonade to pitch and just a few years later I was getting as much as $500 for pitching those same nine innings.

I won just about all the games I pitched for the Tigers. We had a pretty good club and one of our best players was my old buddy, Julius Andrews. He played first base.

Sometimes I pitched for other teams. I jumped whenever there was some green waved.

The Tigers didn't like it too much, but my pocketbook did.

And I don't like to be tied down. Never have. I like to fly free.

'Course playing for a semi-pro club ain't a job, so I had to get me some work too. I landed a job over at the Mobile Bears' stadium. That was the white team, a minor-league club. Pretty soon those guys over there started hearing about Ol' Satch.

They heard good.

But all of them weren't buying what they heard. One day about four of them came up to me and told me how they had been told I was some pitcher.

"We made a bet you couldn't throw as good as all of them say," one of them told me.

He offered me a dollar to show them.

That's the easiest dollar I ever made.

We went down on the field and one of them grabbed a bat and another a glove to catch me. I threw four or five real easy like, just to warm up. Then the batter headed for the plate.

"No need for you to tote that wood up there," I yelled at him. "It's just weight. You ain't gonna need it 'cause I'm gonna throw you nothin' but my trouble ball."

I threw. Them little muscles all around me tingled. They knew what we were doing. The first guy up there swung and missed three fast ones.

Another tried it. He just caused a breeze.

"We sure could use you," one of them finally told me. "If you were only white . . ."

That was the first time I heard it.

For an eighteen-year-old kid, the cheers I got were mighty pleasing. I got plenty of laughs, too. But that was just by luck. I was a serious pitcher.

But when you're as tall and skinny as I am and when you got feet that are feet, maybe you look a little funny. And I like walking slow. Moving that way got them to laughing, too.

Laughing is a pretty sound and soon I was reaching for more laughs. But I never joked when I was pitching. Between pitches, okay. But that ball I threw was thoughtful stuff. It knew just what it had to do.

It did it.

In the 1924 season, I won about thirty games. I lost once. That was the start of a long string of winning streaks for me. I don't know which one was the longest. They were all long. I went by the years without losing a game.

By the next year, every team around town wanted me. And the best team was the team I was on.

But I still was a poor man. I still lived in that shotgun house on South Franklin and we still had to struggle to get money for all the food we needed. That don't sit well when you've found out there is dancing and hunting and fishing, with the fine rods and reels and all the equipment.

That was the fishing I wanted.

So you just keep scratching and trying to get a dollar. Sometimes you do and sometimes you don't. Sometimes you forget you got to go hungry. Sometimes you forget how you can't buy clothes. Sometimes you forget, but usually you don't.

I didn't forget and the more times I remembered how poor I was, the more I wanted to have something better. And the only way I knew how to get something better was with pitching.

That meant I had to get a professional ball club interested in me.

I pitched harder. About halfway through the 1926 season I had me a twenty-five game winning streak going. I was going for number twenty-six when suddenly it looked like that winning streak was going to go up in smoke.

I was pitching for the Down the Bay Boys and we were playing some other Mobile semi-pro club. I slid through the first eight innings of the game without any trouble. The first two guys up in the ninth also were easy outs. Then the troubles began. My infield fell apart.

There were three straight errors and the other team had the bases loaded. Since I only had a one to nothing lead, a hit would tie the game or lose it for me.

I was burning. I walked off the mound and kicked the dirt. I was so mad my stomach felt it. Then I heard the crowd. They sounded like someone was twisting their tail. They were booing to beat all blue, not really booing me, but just booing.

Hearing that booing made me even madder.

Somebody was going to have to be showed up for that.

I looked around and then I waved in my outfielders. When they got in around me, I said, "Sit down there on the grass right behind me. I'm pitching this last guy without an outfield."

"What?" one of them said.

The other two started screaming, too. You'd have thought I'd declared war on the government.

But finally I talked them into sitting down.

The crowd went crazy. They weren't booing now. They were watching me and only me.

I heard the roar all around. Everybody was yelling. I took my time, then pumped back and forth and threw.

It was strike one, but you couldn't hear the umpire for all the yelling. He just waved his arm.

He waved strike two and you couldn't even hear yourself.

Back I leaned and then I threw. The batter swung but my quickie hopped right over the wood into the catcher's glove.

The crowd really went crazy. You wouldn't think a few hundred could make that much noise. But they did.

My outfielders danced around like they'd sat on hot coals.

My infielders just walked off the field, but not before I wagged my nose at them.

Red Smith
"Dizzy Dean's Day"

Red Smith, who was to sportswriting what Mays and DiMaggio were to baseball, published this piece in the St. Louis Star *in 1934. Dean, later to achieve immortality once more as a broadcaster, pitched for the St. Louis Cardinals from 1930 to 1937, for the Chicago Cubs from 1938 to 1941, and briefly for the St. Louis Browns in 1947.*

St. Louis, 1934

Through the murk of cigarette smoke and liniment fumes in the Cardinals' clubhouse a radio announcer babbled into a microphone.

"And now," he read with fine spontaneity from a typewritten sheet prepared hours in advance, "and now let's have a word from the Man of the Hour, Manager Frank Frisch."

COLORPLATE 28

Major League Indoor Base Ball Game. Made by the Philadelphia Game Manufacturing Co. c. 1911.
13 x 19 in. The Gladstone Collection of Baseball Art. *The cover depicts sixteen major league players.*
More than half eventually were inducted to the Hall of Fame.

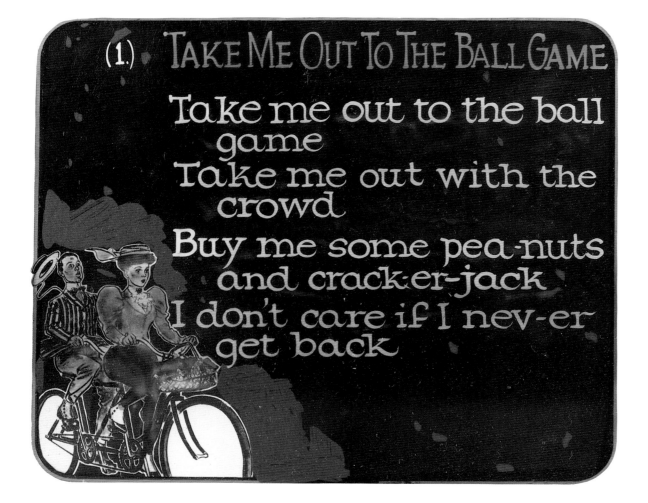

(1.) TAKE ME OUT TO THE BALL GAME

Take me out to the ball
game
Take me out with the
crowd
Buy me some pea-nuts
and crack-er-jack
I don't care if I nev-er
get back

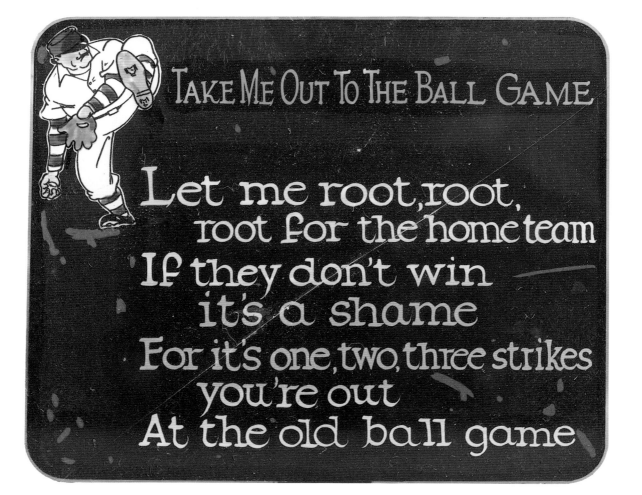

TAKE ME OUT TO THE BALL GAME

Let me root, root,
root for the home team
If they don't win
it's a shame
For it's one, two, three strikes
you're out
At the old ball game

COLORPLATE 30

Beech Nut 1926 World Series Display Advertising.
Transcendental Graphics.

COLORPLATE 29 *(opposite)*

Take Me Out to the Ballgame movie theatre glass slides. Made by the Kansas City Slide Company.
c. 1930. 3 x 3³/₄ in. each. The Gladstone Collection of Baseball Art.

COLORPLATE 31

ROBERT THOM. *Ruth's Called Shot.* 1976. Oil on canvas. 32 x 40 in.
The National Baseball Library and Hall of Fame, Cooperstown, New York.

COLORPLATE 32

MIGUEL COVARRUBIAS. *Babe Ruth.*
Vanity Fair cover, September 1933.

COLORPLATE 33

Vaclav Vytlacil. *Baseball Player.* 1932.
Tempera on canvas. 21 x 25¹/₄ in. The Gladstone Collection of Baseball Art.

COLORPLATE 34

EDWARD LANING. *Saturday Afternoon at Sportsman's Park.* 1944.
Oil on canvas. 36 x 32 in. The Gladstone Collection of Baseball Art.

COLORPLATE 35

MORRIS KANTOR. *Baseball at Night.* 1934. Oil on linen. 37 x 47¹⁄₄ in.
National Museum of American Art, Washington, D.C.

The Man of the Hour shuffled forward. He had started changing clothes. His shirttail hung limply over bare thighs. The Man of the Hour's pants had slipped down and they dragged about his ankles. You could have planted petunias in the loam on his face. The Man of the Hour looked as though he had spent his hour in somebody's coal mine.

Beside him, already scrubbed and combed and natty in civilian clothes, awaiting his turn to confide to a nationwide audience that "the Cardinals are the greatest team I ever played with and I sure am glad we won the champeenship today and I sure hope we can win the World Series from Detroit," stood Dizzy Dean, destiny's child.

There was a conscious air of grandeur about the man. He seemed perfectly aware of and not at all surprised at the fact that just outside the clubhouse five thousand persons were pressing against police lines, waiting to catch a glimpse of him, perhaps even to touch the hem of his garment.

He couldn't have known that in that crowd one woman was weeping into the silver fox fur collar of her black cloth coat, sobbing, "I'm so happy! I can't stand it!" She was Mrs. Dizzy Dean.

All afternoon Dizzy Dean had seemed surrounded by an aura of greatness. A crowd of 37,402 persons jammed Sportsman's Park to see the game that would decide the National League pennant race. To this reporter it did not appear that they had come to see the Cardinals win the championship. Rather, they were there to see Dizzy come to glory.

It was Dean's ball game. He, more than anyone else, had kept the Cardinals in the pennant race throughout the summer. He had won two games in the last five days to help bring the Red Birds to the top of the league. Here, with the championship apparently hinging upon the outcome of this game, was his chance to add the brightest jewel to his crown, and at the same time to achieve the personal triumph of becoming the first National League pitcher since 1917 to win 30 games in a season.

And it was Dizzy's crowd. Although the game was a box office "natural," it is doubtful that, had it not been announced that Dean would pitch, fans would have been thronged before the Dodier Street gate when the doors were opened at 9:30 A.M. They were, and from then until game time they came in increasing numbers. Eventually, some had to be turned away from lack of space.

Packed in the aisles, standing on the ramps and clinging to the grandstand girders, the fans followed Dizzy with their eyes, cheered his every move.

They whooped when he rubbed resin on his hands. They yowled when he fired a strike past a batter. They stood and yelled when he lounged to the plate, trailing his bat in the dust. And when, in the seventh inning, with the game already won by eight runs, he hit a meaningless single, the roar that thundered from the stands was as though he had accomplished the twelve labors of Hercules.

The fact was, the fans were hungry for drama, and that was the one ingredient lacking. With such a stage setting as that crowd provided, with such a buildup as the National League race, with such a hero as Dizzy, Mr. Cecil B. DeMille would have ordered things better.

He would have had the New York Giants beat Brooklyn and thus make a victory essential to the Cards' pennant prospects. He would have had Cincinnati leading St. Louis until the eighth inning, when a rally would have put the Red Birds one run ahead. Then Mr. DeMille would have sent ex–St. Louis Hero Jim Bottomley, now one of the enemy, to bat against Hero Dean, with Cincinnati runners on every base. And he would have had Dizzy pour across three blinding strikes to win the ball game.

In the real game there was no suspense. Cincinnati tried, but the Cards couldn't be stopped. They just up and won the game, 9–0, and the pennant, and to blazes with drama.

Still, drama is where you find it. The crowd seemed to find it in the gawky frame of Mr. Dean, and in the figures on the scoreboard which showed Brooklyn slowly overhauling the Giants in their game in the east.

Dean was warming up in front of the Cardinal dugout when the first-inning score of the New York–Brooklyn game was posted, showing four runs for the Giants and none for the Dodgers. As an apprehensive "Oooooh!" from the fans greeted the score, Dizzy glanced toward the scoreboard. Watching through field glasses, this reporter saw his eyes narrow slightly. That was all. A moment later he strolled to the plate, entirely at ease, to accept a diamond ring donated by his admirers.

Then the game started, and for a few minutes the customers' attention was diverted from their hero by the exploits of some of his mates.

In the first inning Ernie Orsatti, chasing a low drive to right center by Mark Koenig, raced far to his left, dived forward, somersaulted, and came up with the ball. To everyone except the fans in the right field seats it seemed a miraculous catch. The spectators closest to the play were sure they saw Orsatti drop the ball and recover it while his back was toward the plate. But everyone screamed approbation.

Magnificent plays, one after another, whipped the stands into a turmoil of pleasure. In Cincinnati's second inning, after Bottomley had singled, Leo Durocher scooted far to his right to nail a grounder by Pool and, in one astonishingly swift motion, he pivoted and whipped the ball to Frisch for a forceout of Bottomley.

Again in the fourth inning, there was a play that brought the fans whooping to their feet. This time Frisch scooped up a bounder from Pool's bat and beat Koenig to second base, Durocher hurdling Frisch's prostrate body in order to avoid ruining the play. A few minutes earlier Frisch had brought gasps and cheers from the stands by stretching an ordinary single into a two-base hit, reaching second only by the grace of a breakneck headfirst slide.

Play by play, inning by inning, the crowd was growing noisier, more jubilant. Cheer followed exultant cheer on almost every play.

Meanwhile the Cards were piling up a lead. Meanwhile, too, Brooklyn was chiseling runs off New York's lead, and the scoreboard became a magnet for all eyes. When Brooklyn scored two runs in the eighth inning to tie the Giants, Announcer Kelly didn't wait for the scoreboard to flash the news. He shouted it through his megaphone, and as fans in each succeeding section of seats heard his words, waves of applause echoed through the stands.

Shadows were stretching across the field when Cincinnati came to bat in the ninth inning. The National League season was within minutes of its end. The scoreboard long since had registered the final tallies for all other games. Only the tied battle in New York and the contest on this field remained unfinished.

Dean lounged to the pitching mound. The man was completing his third game in six days. He was within three putouts of his second shutout in those six days. He didn't seem tired. He hardly seemed interested. He was magnificently in his element, completely at ease in the knowledge that every eye was on him.

The first two Cincinnati batters made hits. Dizzy was pitching to Adam Comorosky when a wild yell from the stands caused him to glance at the scoreboard. The Dodgers had scored three runs in the tenth. New York's score for the inning had not been posted.

Seen through field glasses, Dean's face was expressionless. He walked Comorosky. The bases were filled with no one out. Was Dizzy tiring, or was he deliberately setting the stage for the perfect melodramatic finish?

The scoreboard boy hung up a zero for the Giants. The pennant belonged to the Cardinals. Most pitchers would have said, "the hell with it," and taken the course of least resistance, leaving it to the fielders to make the putouts.

But this was Dean's ball game. Seen through a haze of fluttering paper, cushions and torn scorecards, he seemed to grow taller. He fanned Clyde Manion. A low roar rumbled through the stands. The fans saw what was coming. Dizzy was going to handle the last three batters himself.

Methodically, unhurriedly, he rifled three blinding strikes past Pinch-Hitter Petoskey. Was that a faint grin on Dizzy's face? The roar from the stands had become rolling thunder. The outfielders foresaw what was coming. They started in from their positions as Dizzy began pitching to Sparky Adams.

They were almost on the field when Adams, in hopeless desperation, swung at a pitch too fast for him to judge. His bat just tipped the ball, sending it straight upward in a wobbly, puny foul fly to DeLancey.

Dean didn't laugh. He didn't shout or caper. The man who has been at times a gross clown was in this greatest moment a figure of quiet dignity. Surrounded by his players he walked slowly to the dugout, a mad, exultant thunder drumming in his ears.

Bob Feller with Bill Gilbert

FROM NOW PITCHING, BOB FELLER

"The Iowa Farm Boy vs. 'The Gas House Gang'"

Bob Feller, whose fastballs once outraced motorcycles and who, in his seventies, still possesses a deep, resonant voice and a grip of iron, accumulated 266 victories against only 162 losses. Those numbers are even more impressive when one considers that Feller, like many stars of the 1940s, lost some of his best years to the service in World War II. He pitched for the Cleveland Indians from 1936 to 1941 and from 1945 to 1956.

It has always seemed such a natural marriage—baseball and me. I've been pitching at every age, as a major league rookie who broke in when Joe DiMaggio did, 1936, when I was 17, to today as a 71-year-old still pitching in Old Timers Games. From the day Dad gave me a real baseball uniform from a mail order house in Chicago back in 1928, I've never wanted to do anything else, whether I was seven or 70 or in between.

You have to love baseball to play as much of it as I always have. Imagine pitching over 300 innings a year for the Cleveland Indians and then between three and seven innings every day on a barnstorming tour of 35 cities in 30 days after the major league season ended, plus 25 or 30 innings in spring training. Imagine logging over 500 innings a year that way.

Imagine yourself in your 71st year of life and your 54th year of baseball, pitching almost 100 innings that summer, more than 50 years after some baseball people and writers said you would ruin your arm because you're pitching too much.

Through all those balls and strikes, imagine pitching against your boyhood heroes like Lou Gehrig and Rogers Hornsby and having Babe Ruth hold your bat in that classic picture as he says farewell at Yankee Stadium in 1948.

Imagine yourself embroiled in one of the most controversial plays in the history of the World Series, or being called a hero in 1941 because you joined the Navy two days after the United States entered World War II and a villain in 1947 because you were injured and had to pass up the All-Star Game. Imagine being blessed enough to have a Hall of Fame career, but never realizing your lifelong dream of winning a game in the World Series.

Imagine being lucky enough to win 266 games and pitch three no-hitters and 12 one-hitters while playing with and against the greatest stars of your time—DiMag, Ted Williams, Hank Greenberg, Joe Cronin, Jimmie Foxx, Larry Doby, Lou Boudreau, and so many others.... And imagine playing with the real characters of the game—Satchel Paige with his warning never to look back because there's a man back there and he might be gaining on you, Rollickin' Rollie Hemsley and his alcohol-inspired Superman feats like tip-toeing along hotel ledges ten floors above downtown streets, Bill Veeck and his Barnum-like genius for attracting people to his show, and the first major league hitter I ever struck out, Leo "The Lip" Durocher.

If you can't imagine being lucky enough to be a starting pitcher in the majors while on a high school vacation and being allowed to live a life that had all this and much more, I can't either. But I have....

Maybe a pitcher's first strikeout is like your first kiss—they say you never forget it. My first strikeout as a major league pitcher was in an exhibition game against the St. Louis Cardinals on July 6, 1936, four months before my 18th birthday and less than one month after finishing my junior year at Van Meter High School in Iowa.

Over 12,000 fans came to Cleveland's old League Park, even though it was an exhibition game. The score was 1–1 when our manager, Steve O'Neill, waved me in from the bullpen to start the fourth inning. As a quiet kid who wasn't even shaving yet, I was facing a bunch of grizzly, hell-raising veterans on the famous "Gas House Gang" team that included Dizzy Dean, Pepper Martin, Ducky Medwick, Johnny Mize, Rip Collins and their fiery manager, Frankie Frisch, "The Fordham Flash."

The Cardinals in those years, in fact, the Cardinals in most years, were one of the best examples of the greater emphasis on team play compared to today. The Brooklyn Dodgers of the 1940s and '50s and our own Indians of that same period were two other excellent examples of the "team attitude" which you and your teammates displayed and which management encouraged.

The Cardinals had some great talent, and they also had players who were completely willing to give themselves up by bunting their teammate from second to third, even though they knew they'd get charged with a time at bat without a hit. They were willing to hit the ball on the ground to the right side to advance their teammate to third, again knowing they would be thrown out and charged with another time at bat without a hit—but their teammate would be on third with only one out and able to score after a fly ball and get the Cards another run.

They had hitters willing to punch the ball to the opposite field for a hit to start a rally in the late innings, instead of trying to knock it out of the park just because "singles hitters drive Fords—home run hitters drive Cadillacs." They had base runners willing to make it difficult for the opposing second baseman to turn a forceout at second into a double play, and starting pitchers willing to come into a game in relief if their team needed them.

You have individual players today with those same team values, but how many teams as a whole play the game that way? Some of them claim to have "a good team attitude," but you have to wonder. The 1979 Pittsburgh Pirates talked a lot about "family." When they won the National League pennant and then defeated the Baltimore Orioles in the World Series, there was so much talk along those lines that the Pirates became the most famous "family" since the Kennedys. But when they took the annual team picture that year, their two biggest stars refused to be included because it might represent a conflict between the sponsor of the photo and some of the sponsors they represented. So much for that "family."

The St. Louis Cardinals of 1936 never talked about "family"—they just played like one. I knew all about them. Dad and I saw them in the 1934 World Series, and we could pull in the Cubs games on our radio back home on the farm, especially if we put the headsets in a metal dishpan on the living room table to amplify the sound. We strung copper wiring in the trees and the barn to pick up the signal. We couldn't listen to any of the games during the week— this was before night baseball—because I was either in school or doing my chores, but on Sunday, Dad and I would sit in the living room in the afternoon if we weren't playing catch, and listen to the Cubs and their announcer, Bob Elson. Later, a sportscaster came to WHO in Des Moines and did re-creations of the Cubs games. His name was Ronald Reagan.

Since the Cards were a National League team, I knew about them from those Cubs broadcasts and from one of my biggest treats as a kid, a trip to the 1934 World Series in St. Louis when the Cardinals defeated the Detroit Tigers in seven games. I was only 15, but I remember thinking to myself while I sat there in Sportsman's Park, "I can do that." I told Dad the same thing on our drive back home, and he didn't jump on me for sounding cocky. He said he agreed with me, that I had the ability to make it in the big leagues.

I remember something else from that Series—the sight of Dizzy Dean getting hit right between the eyes going into second base to break up a double play. He made the mistake of going in standing up, and Bill Rogell wasn't going to use valuable time to get out of his way. He did exactly what the pivot man should do in that case. He stood his ground and made his throw.

Dizzy was examined at the hospital, and the announcement was made: "X-rays of Dizzy Dean's head showed nothing." This was 25 years before the same story went around about Yogi Berra.

Now it was less than two years later, and I was pitching against those same stars I saw in the World Series. Scared? Never. Not in my entire pitching career was I ever scared of any hitter or any situation. That's a luxury you can't afford if you're going to make it as a pitcher. Challenges and crises are what pitching is. If that's a problem for you, then you'd better take up another line of work.

Dizzy Dean. c. 1938. The National Baseball Library, Cooperstown, New York. *Dean was traded from the St. Louis Cardinals to the Chicago Cubs following the 1937 season, when a broken toe sustained in that year's All-Star Game triggered the slow demise of the right-hander's brilliant career.*

It also doesn't hurt for a pitcher to have a mean streak in him or at least an attitude that sometimes borders on defiance. It may sound melodramatic, like a line from a B movie, but it's true that the hitter is up there trying to take bread out of your mouth so he'll have some for his. You simply can't let him do that to you, and to your teammates.

That doesn't mean you have to be dirty about it. You don't have to hit batters intentionally and otherwise be a dirty player, but you sure as heck have to be tough out there or the hitter will have you right where he wants you. Pitching is like hitting in that respect—you have to believe you can do it. You have to have the talent, but if you're out there with any question in your mind at all about your ability to win and your ability to defeat every single hitter who stands up there as a threat against you, then you're going to be a failure.

I wasn't about to let that happen to me. As I stood out there on the mound, I knew I was on the verge of achieving something that dreams are made of, and I was determined in my own high school student's mind not to let the St. Louis Cardinals or anybody else keep me from becoming a successful major league pitcher.

That was my attitude as I prepared to pitch to the first major league hitter of my life, Brusie Ogrodowski, the Cards' backup catcher, in the fourth inning. You've never heard of him because he couldn't hit much, so he played only that year and the next. But there he was, the first man I faced in the majors, even if it was an exhibition game.

O'Neill did a smart thing. Frankie Pytlak, Joe Becker, and Billy Sullivan were our catchers that year, but O'Neill put himself behind the plate when I came into the game. He wanted to handle me himself, with his 17 years of experience as a big league catcher. He hadn't played in eight seasons, but he wanted to give me his personal treatment because he thought I had the potential to make it big.

I knew my fast ball always had an intimidating effect on hitters, but that was in amateur ball. I was about to find out what the major leaguers thought of it, and of me.

My first pitch to Ogrodowski was a called strike, and it made that smacking sound as it hit

O'Neill's mitt, the sound that is so sweet to a pitcher and his catcher. Ogrodowski turned to O'Neill and said, "Let me out of here in one piece."

He was serious. He laid the next pitch down, bunting down the third base line to Sammy Hale. He was an easy out, but he achieved his purpose—he got out of there in one piece.

That brought up Durocher. He was a shortstop in the majors for 17 years and he was having an excellent season. He led the National League in fielding that year and hit a respectable .286. In addition to his ability, he was an intimidator. He broke in with the Yankees in 1925, and the stories started going around both leagues in a hurry about this brash kid who quickly took on Babe Ruth and Ty Cobb in separate confrontations. He never backed down from anybody, and he wasn't above starting a nice little riot every now and then if it helped his cause. . . .

I was still throwing nothing but fast balls, and each one seemed faster than the one before. One of them sailed over Durocher's head, one went behind his back, and Cal Hubbard, the umpire, called two other strikes. I was wild, which was frequently the case in my early years, and I had a big windmill windup and a habit of glancing into left field and then flashing my eyes past third base as I turned toward the plate. It scared the hitters even more.

I had Leo's attention. I was the intimida*tor*, and he was the intimida*tee*. After one of my pitches, he stepped out of the batter's box, turned toward Hubbard, and said, "I feel like a clay pigeon in a shooting gallery."

After the second strike, with the count two and two, Durocher bolted into the Cardinals' dugout and pretended to hide behind the water cooler. Hubbard, a giant of a man who had starred in pro football before becoming an umpire, lumbered over toward the dugout and ordered Leo to get back up there. He said, "You've got another strike coming, Leo."

He went back, but only long enough to take a feeble swing, just going through the motions of swinging while not getting within shouting distance of home plate. He didn't want to have anything at all to do with those fast balls. Strike three swinging, sort of. I had my first strikeout as a major league pitcher.

Cleveland isn't that far from Iowa, but it seemed like a long way from those times back on the farm and the Norman Rockwell life we led, where every day could have been one of his *Saturday Evening Post* covers.

Still, baseball was a big part of everything I did there, so much that folks on the other farms and around town in Van Meter used to shake their heads and chuckle about Bill Feller wasting all that time with his boy Bob when he could be planting more corn. When he switched from corn to wheat because that requires less time to harvest and leaves more time for baseball, they were sure he'd lost his mind completely.

One of my favorite baseball memories, in fact, came not in the big leagues but back in Iowa in 1928, when I was nine years old. *Both* Babe Ruth and Lou Gehrig were coming to town. Well, they weren't exactly coming to town because Van Meter had only a few hundred people, but they were coming to Des Moines, and that was less than 25 miles away, to play an exhibition game. The major league season was over, so Ruth and Gehrig had put together two barnstorming teams—the Bustin' Babes and the Larrupin' Lous—and they were touring minor league cities by train and car all during October.

They were going to play at the Des Moines Demons' park, and each of them would come to bat every inning. The thought of a nine-year-old farm boy named Bob Feller getting to see Babe Ruth and Lou Gehrig—and nine times at bat for each of them, plus a pre-game batting show and Babe pitching one inning—was making me jump out of my skin. But there was even more exciting news than that. A hospital in Des Moines was selling baseballs autographed by the Babe and Lou for five dollars, and I came up with my own plan for being able to buy one of those balls.

Our country had a serious problem with gophers in those days, so the county government had a program which gave you a bounty of ten cents a pair for the front claws of any gopher you killed. The little varmints were more than just pests—they were damaging the crops, and the farmers wanted to get rid of them.

So I recruited my pal and neighbor, Paul Atkins, and gave him a gunny sack and told him to hold it over the gopher holes in our alfalfa field. Then I ran a hose from the gopher's mound to the exhaust of Dad's 1922 Dodge truck, turned the engine on and pulled the choke knob out all the way. I was careful not to use up all the gas. After all, it cost Dad six cents a gallon—nine cents minus a three-cent tax rebate if you used it for agricultural purposes.

Paul and I smoked out 50 gophers from those holes in two hours, all of them the victims of smoke inhalation and asphyxiation. Dad drove me to the Dallas county courthouse the next day in Adel. We went straight to the treasurer's office and I proudly presented my 50 sets of gopher claws and collected my $5.00. Later that week we drove down to the Demons' ballpark on Sixth Avenue at the Des Moines River in Dad's '27 four-door Rickenbacker Brougham sedan, and I bought myself one of those baseballs autographed by Babe Ruth and Lou Gehrig themselves—my first gopher ball.

I still have that ball.

I would have been crazy even to dream that I would meet up with both Ruth and Gehrig later, but that's what happened. I pitched against Lou several times . . . and I was able to be of some help to Babe on his last day in his Yankees uniform.

It happened 20 years later, in June 1948. It was Babe Ruth Day at Yankee Stadium, a chance for all of us to pay one final salute to the Babe for all he had done in bringing so much enjoyment to all of us, and for rescuing baseball after the Chicago "Black Sox" scandal in 1920. The Babe was wasted away by this point, losing a long struggle against cancer. He was dying, and all of us knew it.

I was the starting pitcher against the Yankees that day, and as I warmed up before the game with our bullpen catcher, Bill Lobe, Ruth walked through the Cleveland dugout on the third base side of Yankee Stadium—"the house that Ruth built"—on his way to home plate for pre-game ceremonies. Because of his drained condition, he was unsteady on his feet, so Eddie Robinson, our first baseman, alertly reached into the bat rack and pulled out the first bat he could put his hands on so the Babe would have something to lean on as he strolled onto the field and stood at home plate during the ceremonies. Ruth took the bat into his hands and said to Eddie, "It feels good." Robinson told him, "It's a Babe Ruth model that Bob Feller uses." My name was on the bat.

The contrast between the two baseball players must have been a stunning one. There was our muscular first baseman, the very picture of health and strength, six feet three inches, 210 pounds, with black wavy hair and a real Ladies Day favorite, who hit 172 home runs of his own, next to the emaciated, once robust home run king.

As the Babe stood at home plate—head bowed, in those familiar pin stripes and his immortal Number 3 on his back, cap in one hand, bat in the other—a photographer snapped the emotional sight from behind. The picture became a classic overnight.

When my first turn at bat came in the second or third inning, I couldn't find my bat. I sent the bat boy into the clubhouse to get another one. It wasn't until 34 years later, in 1982, that I found out what happened to my bat. It was the one Eddie Robinson gave to the Babe that day. After the ceremonies, Ruth brought my bat back to the dugout. Then Eddie did something understandable: He kept the bat. He couldn't bear giving up something so precious. I've never blamed him. I would have done the same thing.

The only time since 1948 that I've seen my Babe Ruth model bat is in Babe Ruth's hands in that picture.

But at this moment in 1936, I couldn't be thinking about the past or the future, even if they involved Babe Ruth. The only thing I could be thinking about were the St. Louis Cardinals.

Leo Durocher had some company that day. I pitched three innings and struck out eight batters. Dizzy Dean, who spoke in an Arkansas twang and baseball clichés, told me after the game, "You sure poured that ol' pea through there today, fellows." The Cleveland papers called me "Master Feller." I signed a contract with the Indians the next day.

Steve O'Neill must have liked what he saw. Despite my wildness, or maybe because of it, he began working me into action whenever he could, usually in games already decided, to test me in real competition, not just an exhibition game like the one against the Cardinals. These were real games and the results counted. . . .

One month after my debut, my personal stats added up to six appearances, eight innings, five runs, eleven hits, six strikeouts, eight walks, no wins, but no losses either. I was doing all right, and some people had trouble believing that a kid could hold his own as a major league pitcher in the same year he was playing for his high school team.

I was sure of one thing: When I went back to school in September and the teacher asked us how we spent our summer vacations, I was going to have the best answer in the whole school.

Alan Courtney and Ben Homer
"Joltin' Joe DiMaggio"

In ancient times, heroes and their greatest accomplishments were celebrated in song. This one was penned in 1941 for Joe DiMaggio, who patrolled center field for the New York Yankees from 1936 to 1942 and from 1946 to 1951.

He started baseball's famous streak,
That's got us all aglow.
He's just a man and not a freak;
Joltin' Joe DiMaggio.

Joe, Joe, DiMaggio
We want you on our side.

He tied the mark at forty-four,
July the first you know,
Since then he's hit a good twelve more;
Joltin' Joe DiMaggio.

Joe, Joe, DiMaggio
We want you on our side.

From coast to coast that's all you hear,
Of Joe the one-man show,
He's glorified the horsehide sphere,
Joltin' Joe DiMaggio.

Joe, Joe, DiMaggio
We want you on our side.

He'll live in baseball's Hall of Fame,
He got there blow by blow,
Our kids will tell their kids his name,
Joltin' Joe DiMaggio.

We dream of Joey with the light brown bat.
Joe, Joe, DiMaggio,
We want you on our side.

And now they speak in whispers low,
Of how they stopped our Joe,
One night in Cleveland, oh-oh-oh,
Goodbye streak, DiMaggio.

Joe, Joe, DiMaggio,
We want you on our side.

Joe DiMaggio. June 26, 1941. UPI/The Bettmann Archive. *The Yankee Clipper belts one against the Washington Senators as part of his record 56-game hitting streak.*

Warren Spahn. c. 1950. The National Baseball Library, Cooperstown, New York. *Spahn, who pitched for twenty-one seasons, was the game's winningest southpaw.*

Gerry Hern

"Spahn and Sain"

Published by the Boston Post *in 1948 and inspired by the Braves' lack of pitching depth, this poem spawned the Boston rallying cry of "Spahn and Sain and pray for rain." Forty years later, the poem was still being paraphrased as Red Sox fans said of their pitching staff, "(Roger) Clemens and (Bruce) Hurst and expect the worst." Hall-of-Famer Warren Spahn pitched for the Boston and Milwaukee Braves in 1942 and from 1946 to 1964. He also pitched briefly for the New York Mets and the San Francisco Giants in 1965. Johnny Sain pitched for the Boston Braves in 1942 and from 1946 to 1951. He was traded to the New York Yankees late in 1951 and remained with them until 1955, his final season, which he finished with the Kansas City Athletics.*

First we'll use Spahn, then we'll use Sain,

Then an off day, followed by rain.

Back will come Spahn, followed by Sain

And followed, we hope, by two days of rain.

Yogi Berra and Thomas Horton

FROM YOGI: IT AIN'T OVER . . .

What did he say and what did he mean? Only Yogi knows for sure. Berra, one of the game's greatest catchers and most beloved characters, played for the New York Yankees from 1946 to 1963 and briefly for the New York Mets in 1965. He has managed both the Yankees and the Mets and has served as a coach for the Houston Astros.

———————————

"It ain't over until it's over" is supposed to be the best thing I ever said. I hope not. (And I try to say: "It *isn't* over until it's over.") . . .

I said it in 1973. The way the Mets were bouncing around in the standings that year, it was true. We won the National League East division by winning 82 games and losing 79. That was a 50.9% average, and it meant it isn't over until it is over, or until the team is in first place after the last game.

Sometimes it is over before it begins—if I fought Joe Louis in his prime, it would be over before it began. But in 1973 what I said made sense. When I think back on that year, I get a little mad. . . . A lot of writers said it was awful that the Mets won with such a lousy percentage. But when the Yankees later would clinch their division by September 1, those same guys would say, "Break up the Yankees."

You have to give 100 percent in the first half of the game. If that isn't enough, in the second half, you have to give what is left. The first time I said that is right here.

When I was watching a Steve McQueen movie on TV, I said that he "must have made that before he died." I said the same thing about Jeff Chandler and some other actors, too, I am sure. It seemed to make sense at the time.

When I went to the mayor's mansion in New York City on a hot day, Mayor Lindsay's wife, Mary, said to me, "You look nice and cool, Yogi." I answered, "You don't look so hot yourself." I didn't mean for it to sound that way, and Mrs. Lindsay knew what I meant. . . .

Another one I did say, and am sort of proud of, was when some of the guys wanted me to see a dirty movie. I didn't want to go. I really didn't want to go, but I have never been good at saying no. I kept saying, "I want to see *Airport*." (This all happened before I got the movie critic job; now I could say, "I have to see *Airport*.") Anyway, I got tired of saying "No, let's go see *Airport*," so I said, "Okay, who's in it?" People seem to think that response is great, and it may be. I am just happy that they know I don't like going to dirty movies.

"Baseball is 90 percent mental; the other half is physical." I have seen this written as: "Baseball is 50 percent mental and the other 90 percent is physical." Either way, the writer will say something like: "Yogi may think fine, but he can't add." It may be 95 percent or it may be only 80, but anybody who plays golf, tennis, or any other sport knows what I mean. . . .

"If you come to a fork in the road, take it." I really don't know about that one. The commencement speaker at Arizona State used that in his speech last year. Somebody sent me the student newspaper. The Dartmouth College student newspaper called a big meeting on campus "A Yogi Berra Affair." The reason I thought it was funny is that I didn't finish high school, and now college people use something I said, or maybe never said, to make a point. The Dartmouth story was about a long meeting. That was not a cheap shot, but I don't think it was a good shot. Maybe I should say it this way. If the Dartmouth reporter wants to use my name in the headline of a story about a long meeting, that's fine. I think it is like reaching for a pitch out of the strike zone. But it was sort of fun to see it, and they didn't try to make me look bad.

A writer for the *Wall Street Journal* once said, "Yogi Berra, on the other hand, is a figure of mirth, or—to use the technical term—a dummy." I thought that was a bad and cheap shot. The story had a good headline, "You can hear a lotta Yogi-isms just by listening." I thought that was nice. . . .

So many people claim that they have asked me what time it was and I said, "Do you mean now?" that if I listed them all, this would be a very fat book. Not many people ask me what time it is anymore, and if they do, I don't answer. I thought my answer made sense when I said it. I will admit that when the waitress asked if I wanted my pizza cut into four or eight slices and I said, "Four, I don't think I can eat eight," I knew she was going to laugh and write it down. I was with my son Tim. He knew what I meant, but I know why she didn't.

Twenty questions is a game. If you know it, I don't need to explain it; and if you don't it really isn't worth it. One time when we were playing on a train trip, I asked the question, "Is he living?" Then, without thinking, I asked, "Is he living now?" I got a lot of heat about that one. . . .

I am not going to say I didn't ask, "What kind of bird is a cyst?" I asked that question of Joe Page when he told me he had been hunting with Enos Slaughter, and Enos had been jumping in and out of the bushes so much looking for quail that he got a cyst on his back. I don't hunt, and I thought it was a good question. People have asked me dumber questions. Lots dumber.

When Carmen and I went to see the opera *Tosca* at La Scala, I really liked it. I told somebody I did and added, "Even the music was nice." That was true, and so was a story I still think is funny—a story about Venetian blinds. We were going to have some of ours repaired, only I didn't know it. I was upstairs when our son Larry called out, "The man is here for the Venetian blinds." I told him to look in my pants pocket and give him five bucks. Numbers are not big with me. That may come as a surprise to some people, but when somebody asked me if I take a nap before a night game, I said, "I usually take a two-hour nap from one to four."

When I said, "He is a big clog in their machine," like Tony Perez with the Reds, or Ted Williams, I meant to say "cog." But it didn't come out right, and they didn't let me forget it. Other times I don't understand as much as I would like. . . .

"Contract lens" is easy for anybody to say, and I hope you have, or something like it. One of my friends calls those low-slung German dogs "Datsuns." I can't prove it, but I bet he tells people he got it from me. I know some people say I told them, "When I was young and green behind the ears . . ." and "Never answer an anonymous letter." I didn't, but the anonymous letter idea is a good one.

"Why buy good luggage? You only use it when you travel." I did say that. I thought that made sense when I said it, but I don't think so any more. The good stuff lasts longer and looks better, too.

I didn't say about a sick friend that he was in "Mt. Sinus Hospital," but I could have.

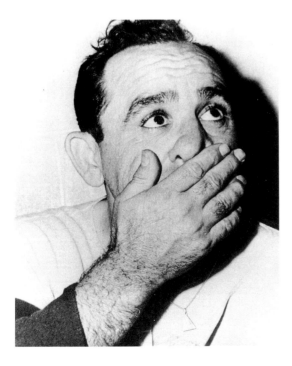

Yogi Berra. c. 1960. AP/Wide World Photos.
Did he say it or didn't he? Ninety percent
of all Yogi-speak is attributed accurately:
the other half isn't.

I could also have said, "We've had enough trowles and tribulation," if I knew what it meant. I don't, but it has been written that I said it.

I did say "It gets late early out there." I said that when I missed a ball in the sun. I was playing left field in the World Series. It was 1961, against the Reds. What I meant was that because of the shadows in Yankee Stadium at that time of year, it was tough to see the ball even early in the game. Baseball parks are all very different. I played right field, left field, and third base. Once a reporter asked me which field I liked the best. I said, "Chicago." He thought it was funny, but I thought I answered his question. . . .

Another . . . story that came back to haunt me is one that Frank Scott, an old friend, likes to tell. He can make it last 15 or 20 minutes. Frank came to our house once with a big dog in the back of his car. He said, "What do you think of my daughter's Afghan?" I said, "Looks nice. I am thinking about a Vega." I have seen several versions of that story. The name of the dog is the same in all of them, but the name of the car changes. . . .

Not listening can make you look bad. One time I came out of the dressing room. I think it was during spring training with the Yankees. During that time you could have forty or fifty or even sixty players in camp. . . . Anyway, I came out into the parking lot and saw this kid. I knew he was on the team and I said, "Who ya waiting for?" He said, "Bo Derek." I said, "I haven't seen him." He was kidding me and I ended up getting kidded.

Another time in spring training I was that young player, and the clubhouse man asked me what size hat I wore. I told him I was not in shape yet. . . .

When I said that a nickel wasn't worth a dime anymore, it was true. It's not anymore. I didn't say, "It's déjà vu all over again," and I didn't say, "Always go to other people's funerals; otherwise, they won't go to yours." But I did get a phone call from William Safire, the *New York Times* columnist, asking if I had. He didn't seem disappointed when I told him no. That made me like him even though we had never met. Carmen got on the upstairs phone and they had a nice chat. She told him some things I had said and maybe some more for all I know. I didn't listen to all of it. I was watching the Giants and the Redskins.

By the time Johnny Bench broke my record, most home runs by a catcher, I had the reputation I have now. They sent him a telegram and said, "Congratulations. I knew the record would stand until it was broken." I don't know who the "they" was, but it was signed Yogi Berra. It was a public relations stunt. . . .

I have said a lot of times that I don't mind people making up things I said and didn't say. It has helped keep my name in the public. That is not all bad. It is not all good, but it is not all bad.

Bob Uecker and Mickey Herskowitz

FROM CATCHER IN THE WRY

"A Funny Thing Happened on My Way to Cooperstown"

Bob Uecker told an interviewer that he had played a pivotal role when his St. Louis Cardinals won the World Series in 1946—he contracted hepatitis. "How did you catch it?" the interviewer asked. Uecker replied, "The trainer injected me with it." Here are some more reflections from baseball's most successful lifetime .200 hitter, who also played for the Philadelphia Phillies as well as the Milwaukee and Atlanta Braves.

In June and July of every year I go through the same ritual—an ordeal, really—of waiting for the telephone to ring. I am waiting to be told that the dream of my lifetime has come true.

I am waiting to be told that I, Robert George Uecker, known as "Mr. Baseball" to a generation that never saw me play, have been elected to baseball's Hall of Fame.

But the call doesn't come. And I realize there is no point in getting nervous or uptight. My record speaks for itself, and the fans, at least, haven't forgotten me. I go to the Old-Timers' games now and I know I haven't lost a thing. I sit in the bullpen and let people throw garbage at me, just like in the old days.

Actually, given the way things work now in our National Pastime, and were I just a few years younger, I too could be the object of a bidding war. I would play out my option, declare myself a free agent and twenty-six teams would be drooling. I would probably have to take my phone off the hook. Can you imagine what the market would be today for a defensive catcher who had a career lifetime average of .200?

And I mean on the nose. Not .201 or .199. A cool .200, lifetime. A lot of retired players joke about being a career .200 hitter, but I was the real article. Modestly, I'd say I could command a salary today of one hundred fifty thousand dollars per annum as a backup playing sixty games. Of course, if the team I signed with was deep in catching and only needed me for thirty games, I'd be worth two hundred thousand. The fewer games they needed me for, the higher the minimum bidding would go.

Of course I'm not a few years younger, and bidding wars or not, I can't but feel a warm glow of nostalgia when I think back over my years in the big leagues. I played with three teams, in four cities, under six managers. My teammates included four Hall of Famers: Henry Aaron, Eddie Mathews, Warren Spahn, Bob Gibson.

In my heart of hearts, I believe my accomplishments were as great as theirs. What did it mean for Aaron or Mathews to hit their .350 or their forty homers? Anybody with ability can play in the big leagues. To last as long as I did with the skills I had, with the numbers I produced, was a triumph of the human spirit. I played thirteen years of pro ball, and remember all but the last six clearly. Up to the very end of my career, I was still being judged on my "potential."

Many times I have been asked how a player knows when he is washed up, through, at the end of the line. Willie Pep, the former boxing champion, once said that you could look for three signs: "First your legs go. Then your reflexes go. Then your friends go." My friends went first.

In baseball the clues were more subtle. In my case, I began to get the hint when my bubble gum card came out and there was a blank space where the picture was supposed to be. Sporting goods companies offered to pay me *not* to endorse their products. I got to the park for what the manager had announced would be a night game, and found out they'd started at 1:00 P.M. I came to bat in the bottom of the ninth, two out, the bases loaded, my team trailing by a run, and looked over at the other dugout and saw them already in their street clothes.

When a player is sold or traded, he may feel a certain rejection. But when he gets cut, well, the news is traumatic. He is face to face with that moment of final truth, that he will never put on a big league uniform again. Nor is it easy on the manager who has to break the news. How do you tell a man that his career is over, that the only life he had ever known is behind him?

I'll never forget how it happened to me. I went to spring training with Atlanta in 1968. The manager was Luman Harris. I opened the door to the clubhouse and Luman looked up and said calmly, "No visitors allowed."

I suppose it is safe to say that my sense of humor caused me to reach the big leagues at least a year late, and my sense of mischief drove me out a few years too soon. But I hung around long enough to prove that my first manager was wrong, the one who sent me back to the minors with the warning, "There is no room in this game for a clown."

There was, and is, a place for Bob Uecker, it pleases me to report. Actually, I still have the view I always had—from behind home plate. Today I'm just a few tiers higher than field level, as a broadcaster for the Milwaukee Brewers. . . . I enjoy my job. It's a lot safer up there, and I don't get booed as much as I did when I was catching. As a matter of fact, my career might have been prolonged if Clete Boyer had hit one less home run in 1967.

That year a Honda dealer in Atlanta had a promotion going at the ball park. Any player who hit a homer or pitched a shutout in the month of September received a free Honda. Boyer hit one the last day of the season. The next morning I dropped by his apartment to road-test it. I was shoeless and shirtless when I roared off down the street in front of Clete's place.

A pack of dogs, excited by the noise, began chasing me. Feeling for the brake, my feet got tangled, I hit the gas instead, jumped a curb and tipped over. I was lucky to get away with a broken right arm and a pair of badly slashed feet.

The cast was removed three weeks before I was to report to camp the following spring. When a trainer tried to "work out" the adhesions by yanking and twisting my arm, he rebroke it. My arm was back in a cast when I got to Florida, and the Braves put me on the roster as a player-coach.

My luck continued pretty much in that vein. One day the club went to Orlando to play the Minnesota Twins, and I stayed behind because of my arm. Billy Martin was the manager of the Twins then. Billy had been with the Braves at the end of his career, and was still friendly with Clete Boyer and Deron Johnson. He gave them a jug of martinis to take back on the bus. I was to meet them that night at the Cock 'n Bull restaurant in West Palm Beach. I had been waiting maybe a half hour when they appeared. They were loaded when they got off the bus.

The three of us were sitting at the bar, when the next thing I knew some drunk had jerked Boyer off his stool. I spun around, got to my feet and slugged him. He skidded through the dance floor area. The bartender jumped across the bar and yelled, "Bob, dammit, no more, that's all!"

I didn't want any more problems, but as I got up a friend of the first guy hit me across the head with a full beer bottle. Busted my head wide open. When I reached up and felt the blood I thought, "Oh, jeezus." I knew it wasn't beer. Not even light beer. Beer isn't red and sticky. The wound later took forty-eight stitches to close.

A terrific fight was breaking out all around me, like a scene from a "B" western. But at that point I had one goal in life: to get the hell away from that bar. I staggered out the nearest door and found myself looking at a dead-end alley, so I had to go back in and walk the length of the place to the front door. The cops were just pulling up to the curb as I fell into my car. Jim Britton, one of our pitchers, drove me to the hospital. I had my head sewn and paid the bill, $175. I went back to my hotel room, expecting to find Boyer. He wasn't there. I called the Cock 'n Bull and whoever answered said, "Yeah, he's still here. They're both here."

The doctor had wrapped my head in one of those white bandages piled up like a turban. I put on an old fishing hat and went back to the bar. Deron and Clete were sitting right where I had left them. They were so drunk they had never moved. Deron looked up and said, "Hot damn, look who's back. Uke's here. Give us another round."

I wasn't worried about Deron. His wife was in town and she could do the worrying. But Clete was rooming with me and it was past curfew and I had to get them out of there. I finally did. I dropped off Deron at his bungalow and half-carried Clete back to the room.

The next morning my head was killing me. I felt like I had the hangover they were saving for Judas, and no matter how hard I tried, I couldn't get Boyer out of bed. At ten I went to the ball park and told Luman Harris what had happened. He said, "Okay, go back to your room and if any of the writers call tell 'em you were in a car wreck."

I finally got Clete awake and he left for the park. At one o'clock he was back. Luman had found him asleep under the stands. After the game that day, I drove to the hospital to have my bandage changed. Now the news comes over the radio: *Three Atlanta players involved in a brawl.*

A week later the Braves released me. I guess they thought I had been a bad influence, but since I was so good at getting into trouble, they offered me a job in public relations, which is how I wound up making speeches and doing the game color on television.

I am able to look back on my career now with few illusions. The highest salary I ever drew, twenty-three thousand dollars, came after my best season . . . that's right, the one in which I played the fewest games. But I had my share of thrills. Probably the biggest was when I started my first game for the Braves, in my hometown of Milwaukee, in April 1962. My folks, my friends, my old schoolmates were there. And they were all cheering.

We were playing the Giants that day and Juan Marichal was pitching. I had his bubble gum card and that told me all I wanted to know about Marichal.

Before the game, Birdie Tebbetts, our manager, said he knew a lot of my relatives were in the park, but he didn't want me to be nervous or uptight. I assured him I was fine. I had been in the minors six years waiting to get here and I was ready to play.

As I walked toward the batting cage, he hollered after me: "Kid, you're doing good, except that up here in the big leagues most of us wear our athletic supporters on the inside of our uniforms."

I hit my only home run that year—the first of fourteen in my career—off Diomedes Olivo, a forty-two-year-old rookie relief pitcher for the Pittsburgh Pirates. When the ball landed in the seats, the fan who caught it threw it back. Years later, someone turned up a tape of that home run and put together a strip for a roast-and-toast, with a staff announcer giving it the H. V. Kaltenborn treatment:

"The great power hitters of days gone by recall their first home runs in the major leagues, their eyes filled with tears and their voices shaking with excitement, every detail of their first round-tripper as clear as if it had happened yesterday. It's the same for all the great ones . . . Steve Bilko, Harry Hannebrink, Clint Courtney, big Albie Pearson, Curt Blefary and Ed Bouchee.

"And so it is for Robert Uecker. He remembers that first looping line drive and so do all his fans. Recall with us now that thrilling day when Bob stepped to the plate still looking for Number One. Here's the play-by-play, as it happened, with Earl Gillespie at the microphone:

"'. . . oh and one, the pitch swung on and a drive [voice rising] INTO DEEP LEFT FIELD . . . GOING BACK TOWARD THE WALL . . . IT MAY BE . . . IT'S BACK AT THE WALL . . . HOME RUN FOR BOB UECKER!!! Well, Bob Uecker . . . quite a thrill . . . '"

Gillespie's description was followed by five minutes of the kind of laugh track you hear at a carnival fun house, interrupted by a wailing siren and Earl's voice repeating, over and over, "Well, Bob Uecker . . ."

Actually, a home run I remember even better than my first was a grand slam I delivered a few seasons later off Ron Herbel of the San Francisco Giants. After I connected, the manager, Herman Franks, came out of their dugout to remove the pitcher, and he was carrying Herbel's suitcase. For some reason, other teams took me lightly.

Pete Rose and Roger Kahn
FROM PETE ROSE: MY STORY
"Fathers and Sons"

During the investigation into gambling that eventually led to his banishment from baseball, Pete Rose repeatedly told reporters that he would eventually tell "his story." While this 1989 work left some questions unanswered in terms of Rose's alleged misdeeds, it did reveal another side of the man who was best known for his head-first slides and his dirty-uniform style of play. Rose began his career with the Cincinnati Reds in 1963, and later served as the Reds manager. In between, he played for the Philadelphia Phillies and the Montreal Expos.

When Pete and I began voyaging together in what now seems so very long ago, we did not really know each other well. He recognized who I was, knew my Brooklyn roots and that some of my books had sold well. For myself, I had observed Rose, surely underestimated his

Pete Rose Slides Home. August 2, 1974. UPI/The Bettmann Archive. *Rose's hard-nosed image on the field belied a gentler heart, according to author Roger Kahn.*

measure in the early seasons, heard his chatter, seen his headfirst slides, and, like so many others, come to accept him as an American institution, but somewhat remote. We had not talked much one-on-one. We were no more than genial strangers. Then suddenly we found ourselves thrust into the intimacy of a collaboration which, to be worth our time or the time of readers, would have to go beyond such matters as pickoff plays and into sometimes painful details of Rose's extraordinary life.

So much has happened in these several years. Pete Rose stopped playing major league baseball. Pete Rose, Jr., began playing minor-league baseball. Pete has been suspended from the game.

As I started the book I had three children. Two survive. Whatever the adversity, one tries to prevail.

Now of Pete I remember lines composed by John Kieran to help a great Yankee team say farewell to Lou Gehrig, who was young and strong and dying:

We've been to the wars together,
We took our luck as it came.

Pete and I know each other well; I feel considerable admiration for him. He is indeed an American institution. On the whole, he deserves to be one.

Rose's tough, competitive core is rough-hewn granite that will always be, as today, the stuff of legend. Quite apart from that, on a scale that may seem smaller but surely is no less important, shines his compassion.

One day, during the 1986 season, Buddy Bell, who played third base for the Reds before the arrival of young, fiery Chris Sabo, knocked at the door of Rose's office. Bell is a soft-voiced man, handsome, fair haired, and restrained. A year earlier Bell's wife Gloria gave birth to their fifth child, a girl the Bells named Traci. Traci Bell was born suffering from Down's syndrome.

Bell mentioned that doctors had just discovered a dysfunction in the infant's heart. The next day Traci would undergo open-heart surgery. Bell was asking if he could miss a game. Would it be all right with the skipper if he took tomorrow off?

COLORPLATE 36

NELSON ROSENBERG. *Out at Third*. Undated. Watercolor and gouache on paper. 15 x 21 7/8 in.
© The Phillips Collection, Washington, D.C.

COLORPLATE 37

JEFF CORNELL. *Ted Williams.* 1986. Graphite, watercolor, and pastel. 8 x 10 in.
Collection of Mr. and Mrs. Joseph Caput IIIrd. *Captured here is Ted Williams' distinctive
and graceful swing. Williams was widely recognized as the best pure hitter in the history
of the game.*

COLORPLATE 38

ROBERT THOM. *The Gashouse Gang.* 1976. Oil on canvas. 32 x 40 in.
The National Baseball Library and Hall of Fame, Cooperstown, New York.

COLORPLATE 39

PAOLO CORVINO. *Old Yankee Stadium. The First Night Game, May 28, 1946.*
Painted from memory, 1969. Oil on canvas. 30 x 40 in. The Museum of the City of New York.

COLORPLATE 40

ARNOLD FRIEDMAN. *World Series.* Undated.
Oil on canvas. 20^{1}/$_{8}$ x 24^{1}/$_{8}$ in. © The Phillips Collection, Washington, D.C.

COLORPLATE 41

UTZ. *World Series Scores.* Undated. Gouache. 27 x 21 in.
The National Baseball Library and Hall of Fame, Cooperstown, New York.

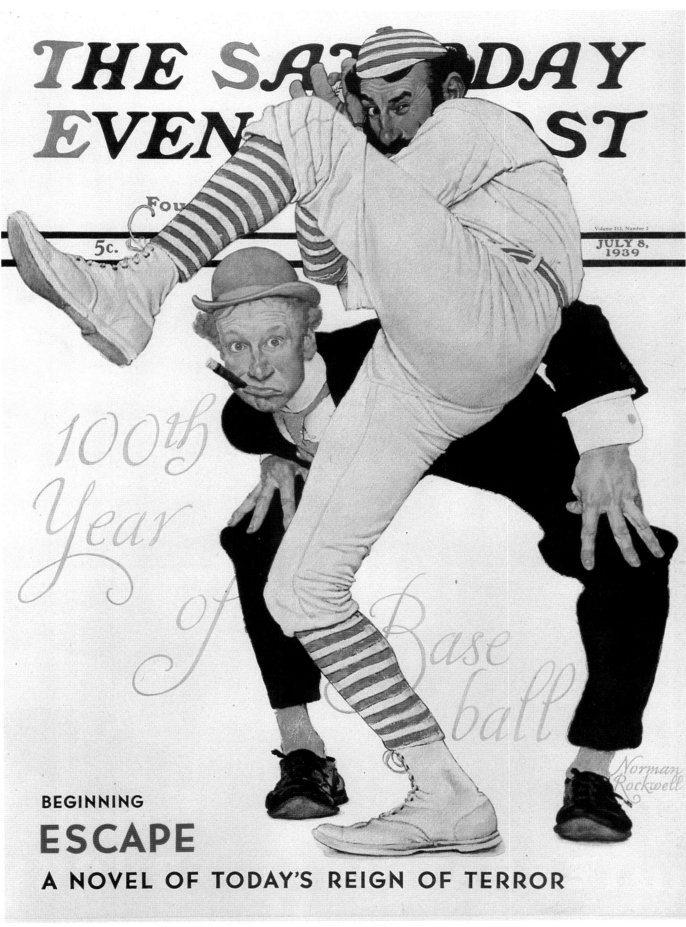

COLORPLATE 42

Norman Rockwell. *100 Years of Baseball.*
Saturday Evening Post cover, July 8, 1939.
The National Baseball Library and Hall of Fame, Cooperstown, New York.

COLORPLATE 43

CLYDE SINGER. *Minor League.* 1946. Oil on canvas. 40 x 50 in.
The Butler Institute of American Art, Youngstown, Ohio.

"Buddy," Pete said, "you don't have tomorrow off. You have off for as long as you want. You look after your little girl. I'll worry about the pennant race." Rose's look, not quite a smile, was alive with concern. He reached across his desk and patted Bell's arm.

Two days later Bell was back in the clubhouse. "The surgery went well," he said. "Traci's going to be all right."

"Long operation?" I asked.

"Five hours," Bell said. He puffed air through his cheeks. "Gloria and I were out there waiting for five hours before we got word."

"Well, the doctors came through for you and Pete came through for you."

Pete had met my second son, Roger Laurence Kahn, in the spring of that year, 1986. Or Roger had met Pete Rose. Roger was a good high-school baseball player and a high-scoring lineman in hockey until he discovered Topanga Canyon and California girls. By 1986, he was a junior at UCLA.

The Reds were still training in Tampa and Roger followed me onto the field at Redsland, under a hot spring sky, wearing a sweatshirt that proclaimed: Prop. UCLA Athletic Department. Rose was chattering near the batting cage. "This your boy?" he said. "How you doing, son?" Rose poked a finger at Roger's stout chest and said, "UCLA. That's the University of California at Los Angeles, am I right?"

"Right," Roger said. He was twenty. His tone sounded patronizing.

"Miller, Jackson, Haley, Hatcher, and Richardson," Rose said. "If I'm not mistaken, that's the starting five, the UCLA basketball team."

He was dead right. Roger looked startled. He had underestimated Pete Rose. Later Roger said to his mother, in a youthful inversion, "I don't think he was too impressed with me."

In fact, Pete enjoyed bantering with Roger and asked me later what kind of athlete Roger was, what kind of student. I mentioned Roger's academic achievements and his hockey. Pete was indeed impressed. He wondered why anyone who liked playing hockey that much would move to southern California. I wondered the same thing myself.

Now, in August, the telephone rang at a small apartment I had taken in Cincinnati, and Roger began a confusing story. He was in Westwood Hospital for drug rehabilitation, he said.

I had not known Roger was using drugs. "Heroin," he said. "You know I sniff it. I play in this fast-pitch softball league and one of the Los Angeles Lakers turned me on."

"You sniff heroin?" Incredulity!

"Sure, but I'm in rehab. I turned in this pusher. He got away from the police. He's coming after me with a gun. And this hospital says that unless you give them $7,000 for me right now, they're throwing me out into the street. If that happens, I'm a dead man. If that happens, you have a dead son."

Some of what Roger said was so. The insurance company behind the UCLA health plan insisted that Roger's heroin use was a long-standing condition. Lone Star Insurance refused to meet his hospital bill. The story about the pusher was probably fiction. Whatever, Roger was in a dangerous situation and I had better fly to California to help him.

In the Reds locker room, I stopped for moment to talk to Dave Parker, the 230-pound right fielder who had spent time himself in drug rehabilitation. "Can you actually sniff heroin?" I asked.

Parker took the question as an accusation and began blabbering in anger.

"Not to write, Dave. It's in my family."

"Oh, sorry," said this gigantic, wounded man. "Yeah, you can sniff that stuff. It's the worst there is. You get a quick high. It makes your nose go crazy. I got a T-shirt here. Dave Parker: Say no to drugs. Give it to the kid. But I'll be straight with you. Kicking heroin is tougher than kicking cocaine."

Into the lime-green office, closing the door behind me. Rose was making out a lineup card. "I'll have to leave you for a little while, Pete. Roger's in drug rehab. I better go to California."

Rose continued to work on the lineup. He did not look up as he said, "Tell him to get off the pot and get high on your books."

"This seems serious, Pete. The kid has been messing with heroin."

Rose put down his pen and I saw the same sad, almost smiling look—concern, perhaps alarm—that had touched Buddy Bell.

"Sure," Pete said. "Go out there, then, and tell him I said hello, if that'll help. Fly well. You can handle this. You're strong. Whenever you get back here, I'll do everything I can to make the book easy for you."

And so Pete did.

Roger rallied through rehabilitation. "What's the prognosis?" I asked a young California psychiatrist named Greg Sawyer.

"I don't envy you the next two years."

Greg Sawyer, who was wearing sneakers and an open-collared shirt, was accurate as a sharpshooter's bullet.

On July 7, 1987, in the intensive-care room at Los Robles Hospital in Thousand Oaks, California, Roger died. He had these strong hockey player's hands, graced by a braiding of dark hair. Even as he died, the hands looked strong. Strong, well-remembered, motionless.

Roger felt he had been driven hopelessly into debt by heroin. He wrote me a farewell letter which began: "After twenty-two years in the amusement park, this roller coaster isn't fun any more, so I'm getting off the ride."

I don't believe I'd wept for thirty years. Lose a son and you discover your own tears. Poor Roger. Sweet bloody Roger. I had bought a coffin for my father. Now I would have to bury my tortured son.

The funeral service on Martha's Vineyard was presided over by a Roman Catholic priest. Roger's mother said the priest was wonderful with children and she would ask him to recite the Twenty-third Psalm.

> *The Lord is my shepherd;*
> *I shall not want.*
> *He maketh me to lie down in green pastures.*

Those words start this towering psalm, as most of us have known it. I heard each word throughout the porches of my brain and thought, or fantasized, Good. Sufficient. Surely the blood of King David coursed through Roger when he was quick and warm.

The gentle priest recited:

> *Yahweh is my shepherd,*
> *I lack nothing.*
> *In grassy meadows*
> *He lets me lie.*

Indignation tore my heart. Who dares edit the King James version of a psalm of David? But the spirit, the spirit, that was what to take away. My boy was gone now. Soon he was laid in sandy soil, above a windblown wetland, to lie unmoving there, silent for eternity.

I flew home and the telephone rang at 12:30 that night. "Rog, this is Pete. I heard. I'm sorry. That the boy I met?"

"Yes. The boy you met in spring training."

"I'll tell you this. You haven't lost him. He's up there in the sky right now and he's playing catch with my dad."

Pete Rose's consolation overwhelmed me. I wept and then apologized for weeping.

"What are you apologizing for?" said gruff and mighty Peter Edward Rose. "When my dad died I sat in my room and I cried for three days."

There would be a memorial service in Manhattan at the meeting house of the Society of Friends. Roger's mother came from generations of Pennsylvania Quakers. "I'll be there," Rose said. "I don't know how I'll get there, but I'll come."

When Pete arrived at the meeting house, I explained a Quaker service. "Anybody here may speak. You just stand and say whatever is in your heart."

Pete wore a dark suit. He looked stricken. "I wouldn't know what to say." Rose can talk to presidents and all the swarming press. That is a special pride of his, like his bat speed. I had never before heard him suggest, much less come out and state, that he wouldn't know what to say at any time.

"You can talk about whatever you want. Youth. Drugs. Baseball. Anything."

Pete looked pained. "Is it all right if I just sit in the back and be quiet?"

A pianist played a poignant work by Schubert. Someone read the Twenty-third Psalm in the version we remember. Peter Malkin, the Israeli warrior who captured Adolf Eichmann, spoke Kaddish, the ancient Hebrew monotheistic prayer for the dead. Some others talked and then, since Roger was a child of the twentieth century, the pianist played a stirring work by Shostakovich.

Only two people from baseball came on that warm July morning to comfort our stricken family. One was Mrs. Jackie Robinson. The other was Peter Edward Rose.

Baseball's representatives were not numerous. But we had the very best.

Thomas Boswell

FROM THE HEART OF THE ORDER
"One-Handed Pitcher: Jim Abbott"

When he broke into the majors with the California Angels in 1989, Jim Abbott insisted that he didn't want to be known as "the one-handed pitcher." By 1991, he had established himself as one of the American League's most prominent young stars, and his 18–11 record and 2.89 ERA that year proved that he was simply a pitcher first and foremost. This piece was written while Abbott, now an inspirational figure to millions of fans, was still a member of the U.S. Olympic baseball team.

HAGERSTOWN, Maryland, July 1988—Face it. A kid born with one hand is never going to pitch in the big leagues. It was a nice fantasy. Everybody loved Jim Abbott when he won the '87 Sullivan Trophy as America's top amateur athlete. But now he's pitching to grown men.

Obviously, international competition bothers Abbott a lot. Take him out of the small pond of college baseball—where he was 26–8 at Michigan (3.03 career earned run average) and, last month, became a no. 1 draft choice of the California Angels—and the truth starts to come out. When he's facing Cuba, Japan and Taiwan—average age about twenty-eight—we've seen a much different Abbott for two summers.

Last year, he had an ERA of 0.00 in three appearances in the Pan American Games. He also became the first U.S. pitcher to beat Cuba in Havana in twenty-five years.

This summer, the U.S. national team—collegiates headed to the Olympics—are barnstorming. And, as usual, Abbott is getting his ears pinned back. His ERA is 0.00 again. He's given up four hits already—in three games.

Just when you think Abbott has surpassed all rational expectations, he moves up a level—and gets better.

Olympic coach Mark Marquess, whose Stanford team has won back-to-back NCAA titles, said, "As a person, they told me Abbott was the All-American boy—almost too good to be true. But he's surprised me. He's better than that, if a person can be . . . As a pitcher, he didn't have a great junior year [this season]. I expected him to be a polished left-hander. What I didn't know is that, right now, he's the hardest thrower on my staff . . . The Japanese [hitters] aren't going to be divin' in on him. He brings it too hard."

Once upon a time, being America's best Olympic pitcher meant little. Now, after the '84 Olympic team sent Will Clark, Mark McGwire, Cory Snyder, Barry Larkin, B. J. Surhoff, Mike Dunne and others to the majors in a hurry, the Olympic team is a Grade A pedigree. This year, Abbott and second baseman Ty Griffin of Georgia Tech have been the showstoppers so far for a nice 13–3 squad.

To understand Abbott, it helps to watch him on a 102-degree day in a small Maryland town in the foothills of the Shenandoah Mountains when he's not even scheduled to pitch. The grandstand is standing room only—that's 6,500 in Hagerstown—and the PA system plays "Some Kinda Wonderful." Abbott heads to the bullpen to do some work. Others think he's almost the finished product. He thinks he's only halfway there.

"You develop to your [level of] competition. You learn to do what they force you to learn," said Abbott. "When I went to Michigan, I just had a fastball. Then a curve. I added a cut fastball, which is my slider. Now I'm working on a straight change-up and slow curve. And I know I have to learn to pitch inside. That's the big thing."

In college, with aluminum bats, low and away is the key location. In pro ball, with wooden bats and a generation of Jose Cansecos who feed off any pitch that lets them extend their huge arms, the inside corner, especially for a left-handed pitcher, is the heart and soul of success.

"It's totally different," says Abbott. "You gotta hit some people. In Japan [on a five-game tour], I hit a guy flat in the face. I'd never done that before. But I have to get over it. It's part of the game."

In the bullpen, the dust hangs heavy in the air, the catchers don't want to crouch and even the billboards seem to shimmer with a wavering desert-heat quality. Abbott works through his entire repertoire, throwing almost machine-gun fast. Fastballs and sliders—in, down and in,

Jim Abbott. c. 1990.
Courtesy California Angels.

and then far enough inside that you can see imaginary hitters skipping rope, sucking in their guts, diving under the low bridge. Jim Abbott has had to overcome a lot; if hitters have to overcome some heat in their kitchens, the six-foot-three, 200-pound kid with the choirboy face might not mind as much as you'd think.

Abbott's glove stays on his stump of a right hand, just six inches from where his left hand ends his balanced follow-through. If a batter were at the plate, he would pluck it off and put it on his left hand in one motion after every pitch; Abbott has done it so quickly and smoothly for so long that some fans barely notice his handicap. "He's an average fielder. I expected below-average," says Marquess. "They bunt on him. He throws them out. Next case."

It's the line drives through the box that scouts worry about. "That question grinds at you," Abbott said. "I'll try to do the best I can. I can talk till I'm blue. That doesn't prove anything. But I think I can [protect myself]."

Is it possible that the worst danger is actually almost behind him—the lethal aluminum bats that create liners faster than any in the major leagues? "That's possible," he said, grinning.

Finally, pouring sweat, Abbott switches to straight change-ups. They're raw. Some bounce. But they're all low; and his motion is almost the same. Already it could be a waste pitch.

These days, Abbott is a twenty-year-old in a sweatbox laboratory. The U.S. national team plays a schedule that would exhaust any minor league team. Six-hour bus rides, twelve-hour flight to and from Japan, seldom two nights in one town and never three. The minors can't be this hard, not with 4:15 A.M. wake-up calls and big-time media in every town. After a 6 A.M. flight, they got to Durham, North Carolina, at 9 A.M. only to find their hotel rooms would not be vacated for several hours. "Is this how the U.S. Olympic basketball team travels?" asked Abbott.

Even when they got to the Durham Bulls park—yes, where the movie was made—they found out that, as Abbott said, "The Bull is really in foul territory." Another Hollywood trick.

Abbott and his teammates are meeting real baseball this summer, not college ball with training tables and more days off than games. The question isn't Can You Play, it's Can You Play Every Day? Play exhausted. Play depressed. Manage your body, your mind, your time. Some are chewed up. Some eat it up.

So far, and it's early, Abbott seems to like the learning process. He's fascinated to face an entire Japanese team—the defending Olympic champions who beat the United States in the finals in Dodger Stadium in '84—full of high-fastball guess hitters. He and Andy Benes, the no. 1 pick in the whole draft, marvel at a team so disciplined that players will "start swinging while you're in your windup so they can get out in front of your best fastball," even though they may look ridiculous—fooled by ten feet—on a change-up.

This summer will seem interminable, and sometimes demoralizing. Those seven straight games in August with Cuba, then the World Championships in Italy (with Cuba on hand again), will be man-sized work. "Cuba is better than some major league teams. No question," said Marquess.

By deep September, when the United States plays the first of five games that could win it an Olympic exhibition-sport title, this team—and Abbott—will be either worn to a frazzle or partway to grown-up.

Many questions will be asked about this Olympic team. But no one will face as many as Abbott, who has fascinated baseball fans with his unique personality and his unique liability. For now, why not look at it this way: some athletes seem followed by a special destiny that seeks them even as they pursue it. For example, Abbott has the inside track on the first-game Olympic starting assignment. Circle the date. September 19. Abbott has until then to finish becoming a man at his game.

September 19 is also Abbott's twenty-first birthday.

P.S.: The U. S. Olympic baseball team won first prize at Seoul, Korea. Abbott won the championship game. In fact, he saved the game—and the Olympics—with a great defensive play. One-handed.

Fourth Inning:

GREAT MOMENTS

To the devout baseball fan, these memorable events aren't just milestones in the history of the game, they're defining moments in a lifetime. Where were you when Bobby Thomson hit his classic home run, when Carlton Fisk waved the ball around the foul pole, or when Mookie Wilson's grounder eluded Bill Buckner and found the freedom of the right-field grass?

Robert W. Creamer

FROM BABE: THE LEGEND COMES TO LIFE

"The Magnificent Moment: The Called-Shot Home Run"

Always remembered, often parodied, but never duplicated in the tens of thousands of ball games to follow, Babe Ruth's "called" home run at Wrigley Field in the 1932 World Series is a moment so burned into the national consciousness that people who weren't born at the time and have little interest in baseball today are familiar with the image of the Bambino pointing his huge arm toward the center-field wall. Whether or not it happened precisely according to the legend is addressed in this passage.

————————

There was considerable doubt that he would be able to play in the Series, but he was in the Yankee lineup for the last five games of the year (he had only three hits in sixteen at bats), and when the Cubs faced the Yankees on Wednesday, September 28, there was Ruth in right field, batting third. This was the World Series that is remembered for Ruth's called home run, the single most famous facet of his legend, yet it was really Gehrig's series. . . . Gehrig had nine hits in the four games, including three home runs and a double, and he scored nine runs and batted in eight as the Yankees won, 12–6, 5–2, 7–5 and 13–6.

Yet Gehrig's exploits were obscured, as they so often were during his career, by a brighter sun, meaning Ruth. Along with being the highest scoring Series ever played, it probably had the most bench jockeying, and the Babe was in the forefront of it. . . .

The jockeying continued . . . as the Yankees won the first two games in New York. Then the Series shifted to Chicago, where thousands of people crammed into La Salle Street Station to see the ball clubs arrive. Ruth, accompanied by Claire, fought his way through the not unfriendly crowd to a freight elevator and then out to a cab. Motorcycle cops had to clear the way for the Yankees, and as Ruth and his wife entered their hotel a woman spat on them.

Such anti-Yankee feeling was isolated on the streets, but it was overwhelmingly evident at Wrigley Field before and during the third game of the Series. . . .

Almost 50,000 people were jammed into every part of Wrigley Field, and most of them were yelling at Ruth. Whenever a ball was lofted his way in pregame practice, a lemon or two would come flying out of the bleachers. Each time, Babe picked up the lemons and threw them back. He was in a good mood. There was a strong wind blowing toward right field, and during batting practice he and Gehrig put on an awesome show. . . . Babe hit nine balls into the stands, Gehrig seven. Ruth yelled at the Cubs, "I'd play for half my salary if I could hit in this dump all the time." . . .

The jockeying between the two teams, or, to be more accurate, between Ruth and the Cubs, became more intense as the game began. Charlie Root was the starting pitcher for Chicago, but Bush and Grimes and Malone were on the top step of the Cub dugout, leading the verbal barrage on Ruth. Andy Lotshaw, the Cubs' trainer, yelled, "If I had you, I'd hitch you to a wagon, you potbelly." Ruth said afterwards, "I didn't mind no ballplayers yelling at me, but the trainer cutting in—that made me sore." As he waited to bat in the first inning, according to Richards Vidmer in the *New York Herald Tribune*, "He paused to jest with the raging Cubs, pointed to the right field bleachers and grinned." . . .

[I]t was 4–4 in a rowdy game as the Yankees came to bat in the fifth. Another lemon bounced toward Ruth as he waited in the on-deck circle while Sewell went out. Boos and hoots rose to a crescendo as he stepped into the batter's box. The Cubs were on the top of the dugout steps, Bush cupping his hands around his mouth as he taunted Ruth. Babe grinned, then stepped in to face Root. The pitcher threw. It was a called strike. The crowd cheered, and the Cubs razzed Ruth louder than ever. Still grinning, holding his bat loosely in his left hand, he looked over at the Cubs and raised one finger of his right hand. Root pitched again, in close, for ball one. He pitched again, this time outside, and it was ball two. The crowd stirred in disappointment, and the razzing from the Cubs let up slightly. Again Root pitched, and it was called strike two. The crowd roared, and the Cubs yammered with renewed vigor. Bush was so excited he ran a step or two onto the grass in front of the dugout, yelling at Ruth. Grimes was shouting something. Ruth waved the exultant Cubs back toward their dugout and held up two fingers. Gabby Hartnett, the Chicago catcher, heard him say, "It only takes one to hit it." Root said something from the mound, and Ruth said something back. Gehrig, who was in the on-deck circle, said, "Babe was jawing with Root and what he said was, 'I'm going to knock the next pitch right down your goddamned throat.'"

Root threw again, a changeup curve, low and away. Ruth swung and hit a tremendous line-drive home run deep into the bleachers in center field. Johnny Moore, the center fielder, ran back and stood there looking up as it went far over his head into the stands. It was the longest home run that had ever been hit in Wrigley Field. Ruth ran down the first base line laughing. "You lucky bum," he said to himself. "You lucky, lucky bum." He said something to Charlie Grimm, the Cubs' player-manager first baseman. He said something to second baseman Billy Herman. He shook his clasped hands over his head like a victorious fighter. . . . In a box near home plate Franklin D. Roosevelt, who was running for President against Herbert Hoover, put his head back and laughed, and after the Babe crossed home plate Roosevelt's eyes followed him all the way into the dugout, where he was mauled and pounded by his gleeful Yankee teammates.

Gehrig stepped to the plate, Root threw one pitch and Gehrig hit a home run. Two pitches, two home runs; the Yankees led, 6–4, all their runs coming on homers by Ruth and Gehrig. Root was taken out of the game, and it ended with the Yankees winning, 7–5.

The Babe. August 7, 1943. The National Baseball Library, Cooperstown, New York. *Eleven years after his famous "called" home-run shot and eight years after his retirement, Babe Ruth knocks one out during a War Bond Drive exhibition game.*

The New York clubhouse roared with noise afterwards. Ruth yelled, "Did Mr. Ruth chase those guys back into the dugout? Mr. Ruth sure did!" . . .

Now. What about the legend? What about the story, often affirmed, often denied, that Babe pointed to a spot in center field and then hit the ball precisely to that spot? It is an argument over nothing, and the fact that Ruth did not point to center field before his home run does not diminish in the least what he did. He did challenge the Cubs before 50,000 people, did indicate he was going to hit a home run and did hit a home run. What more could you ask?

The legend grew, obviously, because people gild lilies and because sometimes we remember vividly seeing things we did not see. . . . Any lawyer will concede that honest witnesses see the same things differently.

Here are what some witnesses said about it.

Charlie Root: "Ruth did not point at the fence before he swung. If he had made a gesture like that, well, anybody who knows me knows that Ruth would have ended up on his ass. The legend didn't get started until later. I fed him a changeup curve. It wasn't a foot off the ground and it was three or four inches outside, certainly not a good pitch to hit. But that was the one he smacked. He told me the next day that if I'd have thrown him a fastball he would have struck out. 'I was guessing with you,' he said."

Gabby Hartnett, the Chicago catcher: "Babe came up in the fifth and took two called strikes. After each one the Cub bench gave him the business, stuff like he was choking and he was washed up. Babe waved his hand across the plate toward our bench on the third base side. One finger was up. At the same time he said softly, and I think only the umpire and I heard him, 'It only takes one to hit it.' Root came in with a fast one and it went into the center field seats. Babe didn't say a word when he passed me after the home run. If he had pointed out at the bleachers, I'd be the first to say so."

Doc Painter, the Yankee trainer: "Before taking his stance he swept his left arm full length and pointed to the center field fence. When he got back to the bench, Herb Pennock said, 'Suppose you missed? You would have looked like an awful bum.' Ruth was taking a drink from the water cooler, and he lifted his head and laughed. 'I never thought of that,' he said."

Joe McCarthy, the Yankee manager: "I'm not going to say he didn't do it. Maybe I didn't see it. Maybe I was looking the other way. Anyway, I'm not going to say he didn't do it."

Jimmy Isaminger, Philadelphia sportswriter: "He made a satiric gesture to the Cub bench and followed it with a resounding belt that had so much force behind it that it landed in the bleachers in dead center."

The *San Francisco Examiner*, October 2, 1932: "He called his shot theatrically, with derisive gestures towards the Cubs' dugout."

The *Reach Guide*, covering the 1932 season: "Ruth hit the ball over the center field fence, a tremendous drive, after indicating in pantomime to his hostile admirers what he proposed to do, and did."

Warren Brown, Chicago sportswriter: "The Babe indicated he had one strike, the big one, left. The vituperative Cub bench knew what he meant. Hartnett heard Ruth growl that this was what he meant. Ruth, for a long while, had no other version, nor was any other sought from him."

Ford Frick, who was not at the game, tried to pin Ruth down on the subject when the two were talking about the Series some time later.

"Did you really point to the bleachers?" Frick asked.

Ruth, always honest, shrugged. "It's in the papers, isn't it?" he said.

"Yeah," Frick said. "It's in the papers. But did you really point to the stands?"

"Why don't you read the papers? It's all right there in the papers."

Which, Frick said, means he never said he did and he never said he didn't.

Lou Gehrig

THE FAREWELL ADDRESS AT YANKEE STADIUM

While many are more familiar with the speech Gary Cooper gave as Lou Gehrig in the classic film Pride of the Yankees, *Gehrig's actual address—which differs considerably from the Cooper version—seems simpler, more honest, and more straightforward, and thus probably gives a more accurate insight into baseball's Iron Horse. Gehrig was fatally ill at the time this speech was made before more than sixty-two thousand fans at Yankee Stadium on July 4, 1939. He had played in a remarkable 2,130 consecutive games at first base for the Yankees in a career that spanned from 1923 to 1939. He died on June 2, 1941.*

_____

Fans, for the past two weeks you have been reading about the bad break I got. Yet today I consider myself the luckiest man on the face of the earth. I have been in ballparks for seventeen years, and have never received anything but kindness and encouragement from you fans. Look at these grand men. Which of you wouldn't consider it the highlight of his career just to associate with them for even one day? Sure I'm lucky. Who wouldn't consider it an honor to have known Jacob Ruppert? Also, the builder of baseball's greatest empire, Ed Barrow? To have spent six years with that wonderful little fellow, Miller Huggins? Then to have spent the next nine years with that outstanding leader, that smart student of psychology, the best manager in baseball today, Joe McCarthy? Sure I'm lucky. When the New York Giants, a team you would give your right arm to beat, and vice versa, sends you a gift—that's something. When everybody down to the groundskeepers and those boys in white coats remember you with trophies— that's something. When you have a wonderful mother-in-law who takes sides with you in

Lou Gehrig Day. July 4, 1939. AP/Wide World Photos. *During ceremonies at Yankee Stadium, the terminally ill Iron Horse tells more than 62,000 fans that he still has "an awful lot to live for."*

squabbles with her own daughter—that's something. When you have a father and a mother who work all their lives so you can have an education and build your body—it's a blessing. When you have a wife who has been a tower of strength and shown more courage than you dreamed existed—that's the finest I know. So I close in saying that I may have had a tough break, but I have an awful lot to live for.

Jackie Robinson and Alfred Duckett

FROM I NEVER HAD IT MADE

"The Noble Experiment"

Baseball's most significant moment on or off the field came in 1945 when Jackie Robinson signed a contract to play with the Montreal Royals, the top farm team of the Brooklyn Dodgers. That contract doomed the "gentleman's agreement" among baseball's ownership that had, until that time, barred African-American players from the major leagues. In this passage from his 1972 autobiography, Robinson discusses the two men who made it possible: himself, and Dodgers boss Branch Rickey.

In 1910 Branch Rickey was a coach for Ohio Wesleyan. The team went to South Bend, Indiana, for a game. The hotel management registered the coach and team but refused to assign a room to a black player named Charley Thomas. . . . Mr. Rickey took the manager aside and said he would move the entire team to another hotel unless the black athlete was accepted. The threat was a bluff because he knew the other hotels also would have refused accommodations to a black man. While the hotel manager was thinking about the threat, Mr. Rickey came up with a compromise. He suggested a cot be put in his own room, which he would share with the unwanted guest. The hotel manager wasn't happy about the idea, but he gave in.

Years later Branch Rickey told the story of the misery of that black player to whom he had given a place to sleep. He remembered that Thomas couldn't sleep.

"He sat on that cot," Mr. Rickey said, "and was silent for a long time. Then he began to cry, tears he couldn't hold back. His whole body shook with emotion. I sat and watched him, not knowing what to do until he began tearing at one hand with the other—just as if he were trying to scratch the skin off his hands with his fingernails. I was alarmed. I asked him what he was trying to do to himself.

"'It's my hands,' he sobbed, 'They're black. If only they were white, I'd be as good as anybody then, wouldn't I, Mr. Rickey? If only they were white.'"

"Charley," Mr. Rickey said, "the day will come when they won't have to be white."

Thirty-five years later, while I was lying awake nights, frustrated, unable to see a future, Mr. Rickey by now the president of the Dodgers was also lying awake at night, trying to make up his mind about a new experiment.

He had never forgotten the agony of that black athlete. When he became a front office executive in St. Louis, he had fought, behind the scenes, against the custom that consigned black spectators to the Jim Crow section of the Sportsman's Park, later to become Busch

1947 World Series Program Cover.
The Brooklyn Historical Society.

Stadium. His pleas to change the rules were in vain. Those in power argued that if blacks were allowed a free choice of seating, white business would suffer.

Branch Rickey lost that fight, but when he became the boss of the Brooklyn Dodgers in 1943, he felt the time for equality in baseball had come. He knew that achieving it would be terribly difficult. There would be deep resentment, determined opposition, and perhaps even racial violence. He was convinced he was morally right, and he shrewdly sensed that making the game a truly national one would have healthy financial results. He took his case before the startled directors of the club, and using persuasive eloquence, he won the first battle in what would be a long and bitter campaign. He was voted permission to make the Brooklyn club the pioneer in bringing blacks into baseball.

Winning his directors' approval was almost insignificant in contrast to the task which now lay ahead of the Dodger president. He made certain that word of his plans did not leak out, particularly to the press. Next, he had to find the ideal player for his project, which came to be called "Rickey's noble experiment." . . .

Unknown to most people and certainly to me, after launching a major scouting program, Branch Rickey had picked me as that player. . . . The manhunt had to be camouflaged. If it became known he was looking for a black recruit for the Dodgers, all hell would have broken loose. The gimmick he used as a cover-up was to make the world believe that he was about to establish a new Negro league. In the spring of 1945 he called a press conference and announced that the Dodgers were organizing the United States League, composed of all black teams. This, of course, made blacks and prointegration whites indignant. He was accused of trying to uphold the existing segregation and, at the same time, capitalize on black players. Cleverly, Mr. Rickey replied that his league would be better organized than the current ones. He said its main purpose, eventually, was to be absorbed into the majors. It is ironic that by coming very close to telling the truth, he was able to conceal that truth from the enemies of integrated baseball. Most people assumed that when he spoke of some distant goal of integration, Mr. Rickey was being a hypocrite on this issue as so many of baseball's leaders had been.

In August, 1945, at Comiskey Park in Chicago, I was approached by Clyde Sukeforth, the Dodger scout. . . . I was out on the field when Sukeforth called my name and beckoned. He told me the Brown Dodgers were looking for top ballplayers, that Branch Rickey had heard about me and sent him to watch me. . . .

Sukeforth said he'd like to talk with me. . . . He asked me to come to see him after the game at the Stevens Hotel. . . .

Sukeforth looked like a sincere person and I thought I might as well listen. I agreed to meet him that night. When we met, Sukeforth got right to the point. Mr. Rickey wanted to talk to me about the possibility of becoming a Brown Dodger. If I could get a few days off and go to Brooklyn, my fare and expenses would be paid. At first I said that I couldn't leave my team and go to Brooklyn just like that. Sukeforth wouldn't take no for an answer. . . .

I continued to hold out and demanded to know what would happen if the Monarchs fired me. The Dodger scout replied quietly that he didn't believe that would happen.

I shrugged and said I'd make the trip. I figured I had nothing to lose.

Branch Rickey was an impressive-looking man. He had a classic face, an air of command, a deep, booming voice, and a way of cutting through red tape and getting down to basics. He shook my hand vigorously and, after a brief conversation, sprang the first question.

"You got a girl?" he demanded.

It was a hell of a question. I had two reactions: why should he be concerned about my relationship with a girl; and, second, while I thought, hoped, and prayed I had a girl, the way things had been going, I was afraid she might have begun to consider me a hopeless case. I explained this to Mr. Rickey and Clyde.

Mr. Rickey wanted to know all about Rachel. I told him of our hopes and plans.

"You know, you *have* a girl," he said heartily. "When we get through today you may want to call her up because there are times when a man needs a woman by his side."

My heart began racing a little faster again as I sat there speculating. First he asked me if I really understood why he had sent for me. I told him what Clyde Sukeforth had told me.

"That's what he was supposed to tell you," Mr. Rickey said. "The truth is you are not a

Jackie Robinson and Branch Rickey. 1947. The
National Baseball Library, Cooperstown, New York.
*Robinson and Rickey shattered baseball's color barrier
when Robinson signed with the Dodgers in 1947.*

candidate for the Brooklyn Brown Dodgers. I've sent for you because I'm interested in you as
a candidate for the Brooklyn National League Club. I think you can play in the major leagues.
How do you feel about it?"

My reactions seemed like some kind of weird mixture churning in a blender. I was
thrilled, scared, and excited. I was incredulous. Most of all, I was speechless.

"You think you can play for Montreal?" he demanded.

I got my tongue back. "Yes," I answered.

Montreal was the Brooklyn Dodgers' top farm club. The players who went there and made
it had an excellent chance at the big time.

I was busy reorganizing my thoughts while Mr. Rickey and Clyde Sukeforth discussed me
briefly, almost as if I weren't there. Mr. Rickey was questioning Clyde. Could I make the
grade?

Abruptly, Mr. Rickey swung his swivel chair in my direction. He was a man who conducted himself with great drama. He pointed a finger at me.

"I know you're a good ballplayer," he barked. "What I don't know is whether you have
the guts."

I knew it was all too good to be true. Here was a guy questioning my courage. That virtually amounted to him asking me if I was a coward. Mr. Rickey or no Mr. Rickey, that was an
insinuation hard to take. I felt the heat coming up into my cheeks.

Before I could react to what he had said, he leaned forward in his chair and explained.

I wasn't just another athlete being hired by a ball club. We were playing for big stakes.
This was the reason Branch Rickey's search had been so exhaustive. The search had spanned
the globe and narrowed down to a few candidates, then finally to me. When it looked as
though I might be the number-one choice, the investigation of my life, my habits, my reputation, and my character had become an intensified study. . . .

One of the results of this thorough screening were reports from California athletic circles that I had been a "racial agitator" at UCLA. Mr. Rickey had not accepted these criticisms on face value. He had demanded and received more information and came to the conclusion that, if I had been white, people would have said, "Here's a guy who's a contender, a competitor."

After that he had some grim words of warning. "We can't fight our way through this, Robinson. We've got no army. There's virtually nobody on our side. No owners, no umpires, very few newspapermen. And I'm afraid that many fans will be hostile. We'll be in a tough position. We can win only if we can convince the world that I'm doing this because you're a great ballplayer and a fine gentleman."

He had me transfixed as he spoke. I could feel his sincerity, and I began to get a sense of how much this major step meant to him. Because of his nature and his passion for justice, he had to do what he was doing. He continued. The rumbling voice, the theatrical gestures, were gone. He was speaking from a deep, quiet strength.

"So there's more than just playing," he said. "I wish it meant only hits, runs, and errors—only the things they put in the box score. Because you know-yes, you would know, Robinson, that a baseball box score is a democratic thing. It doesn't tell how big you are, what church you attend, what color you are, or how your father voted in the last election. It just tells what kind of baseball player you were on that particular day."

I interrupted. "But it's the box score that really counts—that and that alone, isn't it?"

It's all that *ought* to count," he replied. "But it isn't. Maybe one of these days it *will* be all that counts. That is one of the reasons I've got you here, Robinson. If you're a good enough man, we can make this a start in the right direction. But let me tell you, it's going to take an awful lot of courage."

He was back to the crossroads question that made me start to get angry minutes earlier. He asked it slowly and with great care.

"Have you got the guts to play the game no matter what happens?"

"I think I can play the game, Mr. Rickey," I said.

The next few minutes were tough. Branch Rickey had to make absolutely sure that I knew what I would face. Beanballs would be thrown at me. I would be called the kind of names which would hurt and infuriate any man. I would be physically attacked. Could I take all of this and control my temper, remain steadfastly loyal to our ultimate aim?

He knew I would have terrible problems and wanted me to know the extent of them before I agreed to the plan. I was twenty-six years old, and all my life back to the age of eight when a little neighbor girl called me a nigger—I had believed in payback, retaliation. The most luxurious possession, the richest treasure anybody has, is his personal dignity. I looked at Mr. Rickey guardedly, and in that second I was looking at him not as a partner in a great experiment, but as the enemy—a white man. I had a question and it was the age-old one about whether or not you sell your birthright.

"Mr. Rickey," I asked, "are you looking for a Negro who is afraid to fight back?"

I never will forget the way he exploded.

"Robinson," he said, "I'm looking for a ballplayer with guts enough not to fight back."

After that, Mr. Rickey continued his lecture on the kind of thing I'd be facing.

He not only told me about it, but he acted out the part of a white player charging into me, blaming me for the "accident" and calling me all kinds of foul racial names. He talked about my race, my parents, in language that was almost unendurable.

"They'll taunt and goad you," Mr. Rickey said. "They'll do anything to make you react. They'll try to provoke a race riot in the ball park. This is the way to prove to the public that a Negro should not be allowed in the major league. This is the way to frighten the fans and make them afraid to attend the games."

If hundreds of black people wanted to come to the ball park to watch me play and Mr. Rickey tried to discourage them, would I understand that he was doing it because the emotional enthusiasm of my people could harm the experiment? That kind of enthusiasm would be as bad as the emotional opposition of prejudiced white fans.

Suppose I was at shortstop. Another player comes down from first, stealing, flying in with spikes high, and cuts me on the leg. As I feel the blood running down my leg, the white player laughs in my face.

"How do you like that, nigger boy?" he sneers.

Could I turn the other cheek? I didn't know how I would do it. Yet I knew that I must. I had to do it for so many reasons. For black youth, for my mother, for Rae, for myself. I had already begun to feel I had to do it for Branch Rickey.

Bill Veeck with Ed Linn

FROM VEECK—AS IN WRECK

"A Can of Beer, A Slice of Cake—and Thou, Eddie Gaedel"

Baseball has always carried within it a struggle between two opposing factions: the Purists, who would sooner condone a deletion from the Scriptures than the designated hitter rule; and those who simply want to have fun. Leading the pack for the Hedonists is Bill Veeck, the late maverick owner and showman whose other "great moments" included a quartet of gold-plated midgets (Eddie Gaedel among them) who dropped to the Comisky Park infield by helicopter and made "honorary Martians" of shortstop Luis Aparicio and second baseman Nellie Fox. Here, Veeck gives a behind-the-scenes account of his most famous stunt: the day he sent Gaedel—all three feet, seven inches of him—up to bat as a full-fledged member of the St. Louis Browns.

Eddie came to us in a moment of desperation. Not his desperation, ours. After a month or so in St. Louis, we were looking around desperately for a way to draw a few people into the ball park, it being perfectly clear by that time that the ball club wasn't going to do it unaided. The best bet seemed to be to call upon the resources of our radio sponsors, Falstaff Brewery. For although Falstaff only broadcast our games locally, they had distributors and dealers all over the state.

It happened that 1951 was the Fiftieth Anniversary of the American League, an event the league was exploiting with its usual burst of inspiration by sewing special emblems on the uniforms of all the players. It seemed to me that a birthday party was clearly called for. It seemed to me, further, that if I could throw a party to celebrate the birthdays of both the American League and Falstaff Brewery, the sponsors would be getting a nice little tie-in and we would have their distributors and dealers hustling tickets for us all over the state. Nobody at Falstaff's seemed to know exactly when their birthday was, but that was no great problem. If we couldn't prove it fell on the day we chose, neither could anyone prove that it didn't. The day we chose was a Sunday doubleheader against the last-place Detroit Tigers, a struggle which did not threaten to set the pulses of the city beating madly.

Rudie Schaffer, the Browns' business manager, and I met with the Falstaff people—Mr. Griesedieck Sr., the head of the company, Bud and Joe Griesedieck and their various department heads—to romance our project. "In addition to the regular party, the acts and so on," I told Bud, "I'll do something for you that I have never done before. Something so original and spectacular that it will get you national publicity." . . .

The Falstaff people, romantics all, went for it. They were so anxious to find out what I was going to do that they could hardly bear to wait out the two weeks. I was rather anxious to find out what I was going to do, too. The real reason I had not been willing to let them in on my top-secret plan was that I didn't have any plan.

What can I do, I asked myself, that is so spectacular that *no one* will be able to say he had seen it before? The answer was perfectly obvious. I would send a midget up to bat. . . .

I put in a call to Marty Caine, the booking agent from whom I had hired all my acts when I was operating in Cleveland, and asked him to find me a midget who was somewhat athletic and game for anything. "And Marty," I said, "I want this to be a secret." . . .

Marty Caine found Eddie Gaedel in Chicago and sent him down to be looked over. He was a nice little guy, in his mid-twenties. Like all midgets, he had sad little eyes, and like all midgets, he had a squeaky little voice that sounded as if it were on the wrong speed of a record player.

"Eddie," I said, "how would you like to be a big-league ballplayer?"

When he first heard what I wanted him to do, he was a little dubious. I had to give him a sales pitch. I said, "Eddie, you'll be the only midget in the history of the game. You'll be appearing before thousands of people. Your name will go into the record books for all time. You'll be famous, Eddie," I said. "Eddie," I said, "you'll be immortal."

Well, Eddie Gaedel had more than a little ham in him. The more I talked, the braver he became. By the time I was finished, little Eddie was ready to charge through a machine-gun nest to get to the plate.

I asked him how much he knew about baseball. "Well," he said, "I know you're supposed to hit the white ball with the bat. And then you run somewhere."

Obviously, he was well schooled in the fundamentals. "I'll show you what I want you to do," I told him.

I picked up a little toy bat and crouched over as far as I could, my front elbow resting on my front knee. The rules of the game say that the strike zone is between the batter's armpits and the top of his knees "when he assumes his natural stance." Since Gaedel would bat only once in his life, whatever stance he took was, by definition, his natural one.

When Eddie went into that crouch, his strike zone was just about visible to the naked eye. I picked up a ruler and measured it for posterity. It was 1 1/2 inches. Marvelous.

Eddie practiced that crouch for awhile, up and down, up and down, while I cheered him on lustily from the sidelines. After a while, he began to test the heft of the bat and glare out toward an imaginary pitcher. He sprang out of his crouch and took an awkward, lunging swing.

"No, no," I said. "You just stay in that crouch. All you have to do is stand there and take four balls. Then you'll trot down to first base and we'll send someone in to run for you."

His face collapsed. You could see his visions of glory leaking out of him. . . .

"Eddie," I said gently, "I'm going to be up on the roof with a high-powered rifle watching every move you make. If you so much as look as if you're going to swing, I'm going to shoot you dead." . . .

On Sunday morning, we smuggled Eddie up to the office for further instruction on the fine art of crouching. That was a little dangerous. I have always taken the doors off my office and encouraged people to walk right in to see me. We posted a lookout and from time to time either Mary Frances or Bob or Rudie would have to hustle Eddie out to the farm-system offices in the back. Always they'd come back with the same story. As soon as Eddie got out of my sight he'd turn tiger and start swinging his little bat. "He's going to foul it up," they all told me. "If you saw him back there you'd know he's going to swing."

"Don't worry," I'd tell them, worrying furiously. "I've got the situation well in hand." . . .

We went all out in our between-games Birthday Celebration. We had a parade of old-fashioned cars circling the field. We had two men and two women, dressed in Gay Ninety costumes, pedaling around the park on a bicycle-built-for-four. Troubadours roamed through the stands to entertain the customers. Our own band, featuring Satchel Paige on the drums, performed at home plate. Satch, who is good enough to be a professional, stopped the show cold. . . .

Eddie Gaedel had remained up in the office during the game, under the care of big Bill

COLORPLATE 44

NORMAN ROCKWELL *A Tough Call.* 1949. Oil on canvas. 43 x 41 in.
The National Baseball Library and Hall of Fame, Cooperstown, New York.

COLORPLATE 45

JAMES CHAPIN. *Veteran Bush League Catcher.* 1948.
Oil on canvas. 50 x 40 in. Collection of Dale C. Bullough.

138

COLORPLATE 46

JAMES CHAPIN. *Man on First.* 1948.
Oil on canvas. 28 x 24 in. The Gladstone Collection of Baseball Art.

COLORPLATE 47

JOHN GROTH. *Dem Bums Abroad;
The Brooklyn Dodgers at Havana
Training Camp.* 1947. Watercolor, ink.
29 x 39 in. The National Art Museum
of Sport, Indianapolis.

COLORPLATE 49

ANDY JURINKO. *Miracle at Coogan's Bluff (The Polo Grounds, New York)*. 1992.
Oil on canvas. 56 x 112 in. Private collection.

COLORPLATE 48 *(opposite)*

RICK McCOLLUM. *Shot Heard Round the World*. 1985. Oil on canvas. 17 x 22 in. Collection of the artist.
Bobby Thomson's "shot heard 'round the world," struck October 3, 1951, might be baseball's most
dramatic and memorable moment. Thomson's home run in the bottom of the ninth inning of the third and
decisive National League playoff game lifted the New York Giants over the Brooklyn Dodgers, who had
led the Giants by 13 1/2 games in the standings as late as August 7.

COLORPLATE 50

UNIDENTIFIED ARTIST. *Untitled (Black Baseball Players)*. Undated.
Oil on canvas. 16 x 23¹/₂ in. The Gladstone Collection of Baseball Art.

Durney. Between games, Durney was to bring him down under the stands, in full uniform, and put him into a huge 7-foot birthday cake we had stashed away under the ramp. There was a hollowed-out section in the middle of the cake, complete with a board slab for Eddie to sit on. For we had a walk-on role written in for Eddie during the celebration; we were really getting our $100 worth out of him. As a matter of fact, the cake cost us a darn sight more than Eddie did. . . .

Up on the roof behind home plate, we had a special box with a connecting bar and restaurant for the care and feeding of visiting dignitaries. By the time I got up there to join Bud Griesedieck and the rest of the Falstaff executive force, the cake had already been rolled out onto the infield grass. Along with the cake came Sir John Falstaff or, at any rate, a hefty actor dressed in Elizabethan clothes. *There* was a touch to warm the cockles and hops of the Falstaff crowd.

"Watch this," I chuckled.

Our announcer, Bernie Ebert, boomed: "Ladies and gentlemen, as a special birthday present to manager Zack Taylor, the management is presenting him with a brand-new Brownie."

Sir John tapped the cake with his gleaming cutlass and, right on cue, out through the paper popped Eddie Gaedel.

There was a smattering of applause from the stands and a light ripple of laughter.

In the Falstaff box, there was nothing but stunned silence.

"Holy smokes," Bud said, "this is what your big thing is? A little midget jumps out of a cake and he's wearing a baseball uniform and he's a bat boy or something?"

"Don't you understand?" I said. "He's a real live Brownie." . . .

Karl Vollmer, their advertising manager, was plainly disgusted. "Aw, this is lousy, Bill," he said. "Even the cake gimmick, you've used that before in Milwaukee and Cleveland. You haven't given us anything new at all."

I begged them not to be too unhappy. "Maybe it isn't the best gag in the world," I said, "but the rest of the show was good and everybody seems happy. It will be all right."

They were determined to be unhappy, though. The gloom in that box was so thick that our Falstaff could have come up and carved it into loaves with his cutlass. (That didn't seem like a very good idea at the moment, however, because Vollmer looked as if he was just about ready to grab the cutlass and cut my throat.) "This is the explosive thing you couldn't tell us about," Vollmer muttered. "A midget jumps out of a cake and, what do you know, he's a real live Brownie."

I did my best to look ashamed of myself.

In the second game, we started Frank Saucier in place of our regular center fielder, Jim Delsing. This is the only part of the gag I've ever felt bad about. Saucier was a great kid whom I had personally talked back into the game when I bought the Browns. Everything went wrong for Frank, and all he has to show for his great promise is that he was the only guy a midget ever batted for.

For as we came up for our half of the first inning, Eddie Gaedel emerged from the dugout waving three little bats. "For the Browns," said Bernie Ebert over the loudspeaker system, "number one-eighth, Eddie Gaedel, batting for Saucier."

Suddenly, the whole park came alive. Suddenly, my honored guests sat upright in their seats. Suddenly, the sun was shining. Eddie Hurley, the umpire behind the plate, took one look at Gaedel and started toward our bench. "Hey," he shouted out to Taylor, "what's going on here?"

Zack came out with a sheaf of papers. He showed Hurley Gaedel's contract. He showed him the telegram to headquarters, duly promulgated with a time stamp. He even showed him a copy of our active list to prove that we did have room to add another player.

Hurley returned to home plate, shooed away the photographers who had rushed out to take Eddie's picture and motioned the midget into the batter's box. The place went wild. Bobby Cain, the Detroit pitcher, and Bob Swift, their catcher, had been standing by peacefully for about 15 minutes, thinking unsolemn thoughts about that jerk Veeck and his gags. I will never forget the look of utter disbelief that came over Cain's face as he finally realized that this was for real.

Eddie Gaedel of the St. Louis Browns. August 19, 1951. UPI/The Bettmann Archive. *Gaedel carved himself a small niche in baseball history when he batted for the St. Louis Browns during a game against the Detroit Tigers.*

Bob Swift rose to the occasion like a real trouper. If I had set out to use the opposing catcher to help build up the tension, I could not have improved one whit upon his performance. Bob, bless his heart, did just what I was hoping he would do. He went out to the mound to discuss the intricacies of pitching to a midget with Cain. And when he came back, he did something I had never even dreamed of. To complete the sheer incongruity of the scene—and make the newspaper pictures of the event more memorable—he got down on both knees to offer his pitcher a target.

By now, the whole park was rocking, and nowhere were there seven more delirious people than my guests in the rooftop box. Veeck the jerk had become Willie the wizard. The only unhappy person in that box was me, good old Willie the wizard. The only unhappy person in that box was me, good old Willie the wizard. Gaedel, little ham that he was, had not gone into the crouch I had spent so many hours teaching him. He was standing straight up, his little bat held high, his feet spraddled wide in a fair approximation of Joe DiMaggio's classic style. While the Falstaff people were whacking me on the back and letting their joy flow unrestrained, I was thinking: *I should have brought that gun up here. I'll kill him if he swings. I'll kill him, I'll kill him.*

Fortunately, Cain started out by really trying to pitch to him. The first two deliveries came whizzing past Eddie's head before he had time to swing. By the third pitch, Cain was laughing so hard that he could barely throw. Ball three and ball four came floating up about three feet over Eddie's head.

Eddie trotted down to first base to the happy tune of snapping cameras. He waited for the runner, one foot holding to the bag like a pro, and he patted Delsing on the butt in good professional exhortation before he surrendered the base. He shook hands with our first-base coach and he waved to the cheering throng. . . .

Nothing remained but to wait for the expected blasts from league headquarters and, more particularly, from the deacons of the press, those old-timers who look upon baseball not as a game or a business but as a solemn ritual, almost a holy calling.

The press, for the most part, took the sane attitude that Gaedel had provided a bright moment in what could easily have been a deadly dull doubleheader between a 7th and an 8th place ball club. Vincent X. Flaherty of Los Angeles pretty much summed up the general reaction when he wrote, "I do not advocate baseball burlesque. Such practices do not redound to the better interests of the game—but I claim it was the funniest thing that has happened to baseball in years."

It's fine to be appreciated for a day; I recommend it highly for the soul. It's better for the box office, though, to be attacked for a full week. I was counting on the deacons to turn Gaedel into a full week's story by attacking me for spitting in their Cathedral. They didn't let me down, although I did feel the words "cheap and tawdry" and "travesty" and "mockery" were badly overworked. The spirit was willing, but I'm afraid the rhetoric was weak. . . .

The battle with league headquarters had begun before Eddie stepped into the batter's box. Will Harridge, the league president—for reasons best known to himself—had gone to his office that Sunday and had seen the report come over the Western Union teletype that I was trying to send a midget up to bat. While Hurley was still looking over the papers, our switchboard operator, Ada Ireland, sent word to me that Harridge was on the phone threatening to blow a fuse unless someone in authority came out to talk to him. I sent back word that we had all disappeared from the face of the earth. . . .

The next day, Harridge issued an executive order barring Gaedel from baseball. A new rule was promptly passed making it mandatory that all player contracts be filed with and *approved* by the president.

Naturally, I was bewildered and alarmed and shocked. I was a few other things too: "I'm puzzled, baffled and grieved by Mr. Harridge's ruling," I announced. "Why, we're paying a lot of guys on the Browns' roster good money to get on base and even though they don't do it, nobody sympathizes with us. But when this little guy goes up to the plate and draws a walk on his only time at bat, they call it 'conduct detrimental to baseball.'"

If baseball wanted to discriminate against the little people, I said, why didn't we have the courage to be honest about it, write a minimum height into the rules and submit ourselves to the terrible wrath of all right-thinking Americans. "I think," I said, "that further clarification is called for. Should the height of a player be 3 feet 6 inches, 4 feet 6 inches, 6 feet 6 inches, or 9 feet 6 inches?" Now that midgets had been so arbitrarily barred, I asked, were we to assume that giants were also barred? I made dark references to the stature of Phil Rizzuto, who is not much over five feet tall, and I implied very strongly that I was going to demand an official ruling on whether he was a short ballplayer or a tall midget. . . .

In the end I had to agree, reluctantly, to bow to superior authority. "As much as it grieves

THOM ROSS. *Thomson Triptych: The Agony of Ralph Branca.* 1989. Pastel on paper. 32 x 40 in. Private collection. *Bobby Thomson's "Shot Heard 'Round the World," fired October 3, 1951, was a perfect melding of bitter rivals and impossible heroics. Thomson's home run off the Brooklyn Dodgers' Ralph Branca gave the 1951 National League Pennant to the New York Giants, who had trailed the Dodgers by thirteen and a half games in August. Thomson struck with one out in the bottom of the ninth inning of the third and final play-off game for the championship.*

me," I said, "I will have to go along with this odd ruling." I thought that was rather big of me, especially since I had only hired Gaedel for one day. . . .

I did not recognize at the time that Gaedel's moment was my moment too. . . .

I have done a few other things in baseball, you know. I've won pennants and finished dead last; I've set attendance records and been close to bankruptcy. . . .

But no one has to tell me that if I returned to baseball tomorrow, won ten straight pennants and left all the old attendance records moldering in the dust, I would still be remembered, in the end, as the man who sent a midget up to bat. It is not the identification I would have chosen for myself when I came into baseball. My ambitions were grander than that. And yet I cannot deny that it is an accurate one. I have always found humor in the incongruous, I have always tried to entertain. And I have always found a stuffed-shirt the most irresistible of all targets.

I'm Bill Veeck, the guy who sent a midget up to bat?

Fair enough.

Casey Stengel

FROM *THE CONGRESSIONAL RECORD*

When Casey Stengel became the first manager of the New York Mets in 1962, his third base-man at the start of the season was a journeyman infielder named Don Zimmer. Over the next thirty years, the Mets used more than eighty players at third base, leading some to speculate that Zimmer had screwed up the position so badly that no one could ever play there again. Perhaps Stengel, who gave this testimony on baseball antitrust legislation before a Senate committee in 1958, had a similar effect on Congress. Stengel played outfield for the Brooklyn Dodgers from 1912 to 1917. He also played for the Pittsburgh Pirates, the Philadelphia Phillies, the New York Giants, and the Boston Braves in a career that ended in 1925. In addi-tion to managing the Mets for almost four years, he also managed the Brooklyn Dodgers and the Boston Braves, and as manager of the New York Yankees from 1949 to 1960, Stengel won ten pennants and seven World Series titles.

———————————

Senator Kefauver. Mr. Stengel, will you come around and sit down?

Mr. Stengel. Is this where I sit down?

Senator Kefauver. Mr. Stengel, you are the manager of the New York Yankees. Will you give us very briefly your background and your views about this legislation?

Mr. Stengel. Well, I started in professional ball in 1910. I have been in professional ball, I would say, for 48 years. I have been employed by numerous ball clubs in the majors and in the minor leagues.

I started in the minor leagues with Kansas City. I played as low as class D ball, which was at Shelbyville, Ky., and also class C ball, and class A ball, and I have advanced in baseball as a ballplayer.

I had many years that I was not so successful as a ballplayer, as it is a game of skill. And then I was no doubt discharged by baseball in which I had to go back to the minor leagues as a manager, and after being in the minor leagues as a manager, I became a major league manager in several cities and was discharged, we call it "discharged," because there is no question I had to leave. [Laughter.]

And I returned to the minor leagues at Milwaukee, Kansas City, and Oakland, Calif., and then returned to the major leagues.

In the last 10 years, naturally, in major league baseball with the New York Yankees, the New York Yankees have had tremendous success and while I am not the ballplayer who does the work, I have no doubt worked for a ball club that is very capable in the office. I . . . I must have splendid ownership, I must have very capable men who are in radio and television, which no doubt you know that we have mentioned the three names—you will say they are very great.

We have a wonderful press that follows us. Anybody should in New York City, where you have so many million people.

Our ball club has been successful because we have it, and we have the spirit of 1776.

We put it into the ball field and if you are not capable of becoming a great ballplayer since I have been in as the manager, in 10 years, you are notified that if you don't produce on the ball field, the salary that you receive, we will allow you to be traded to play and give your services to other clubs.

The great proof of that was yesterday. Three of the young men that were stars and picked by the players in the American League to be in the all-star game were Mr. Cerv, who is at Kansas City; Mr. Jensen who was at Boston, and I might say Mr. Triandos that caught for the Baltimore ball club, all three of those players were my members and to show you I was not such a brilliant manager they got away from me and were chosen by the players and I was fortunate enough to have them come back to play where I was successful as a manager.

If I have been in baseball for 48 years there must be some good in it. I was capable and strong enough at one time to do any kind of work but I came back to baseball and I have been in baseball ever since.

I have been up and down the ladder. I know there are some things in baseball, 35 to 50 years ago that are better now than they were in those days. In those days, my goodness, you could not transfer a ball club in the minor leagues, class D, class C ball, class A ball.

How could you transfer a ball club when you did not have a high-way? How could you

The Catch. September 29, 1954. AP/Wide World Photos. *In one of the few World Series contests of the 1950s that didn't feature the New York Yankees, Willie Mays of the New York Giants made this impossible catch an estimated 460 feet from home plate at the Polo Grounds. The unfortunate batter was Vic Wertz of the Cleveland Indians.*

transfer a ball club when the railroads then would take you to a town you got off and then you had to wait and sit up 5 hours to go to another ball club?

How could you run baseball then without night ball?

You had to have night ball to improve the proceeds, to pay larger salaries and I went to work, the first year I received $135 a month.

I thought that was amazing. I had to put away enough money to go to dental college. I found out it was not better in dentistry, I stayed in baseball.

Any other questions you would like to ask me?

I want to let you know that as to the legislative end of baseball you men will have to consider that what you are here for. I am a bench manager.

I will speak about anything from the playing end—in the major or minor leagues—and do anything I can to help you.

SENATOR KEFAUVER. Mr. Stengel, are you prepared to answer particularly why baseball wants this bill passed?

MR. STENGEL. Well, I would have to say at the present time, I think that baseball has advanced in this respect for the player help. That is an amazing statement for me to make, because you can retire with an annuity at 50 and what organization in America allows you to retire at 50 and receive money?

I want to further state that I am not a ballplayer, that is, put into that pension fund committee. At my age, and I have been in baseball, well, I will say I am possibly the oldest man who is working in baseball. I would say that when they start an annuity for the ballplayers to better their conditions, it should have been done, and I think it has been done.

I think it should be the way they have done it, which is a very good thing.

The reason they possibly did not take the managers in at that time was because radio and television or the income to ball clubs was not large enough that you could have put in a pension plan.

Now I am not a member of the pension plan. You have young men here who are, who represent the ball clubs.

They represent them as players and since I am not a member and don't receive pension from a fund which you think, my goodness, he ought to be declared in that too but I would say that is a great thing for the ballplayers.

That is one thing I will say for the ballplayers they have an advanced pension fund. I should think it was gained by radio and television or you could not have enough money to pay anything of that type.

Now the second thing about baseball that I think is very interesting to the public or to all of us that it is the owner's own fault if he does not improve his club, along with the officials in the ball club and the players.

Now what causes that?

If I am going to go on the road and we are a traveling ball club and you know the cost of transportation now—we travel sometimes with three pullman coaches, the New York Yankees and remember I am just a salaried man and do not own stock in the New York Yankees, I found out that in traveling with the New York Yankees on the road and all, that it is the best, and we have broken records in Washington this year, we have broken them in every city but New York and we have lost two clubs that have gone out of the city of New York.

Of course we have had some bad weather, I would say that they are mad at us in Chicago, we fill the parks.

They have come out to see good material. I will say they are mad at us in Kansas City, but we broke their attendance record.

Now on the road we only get possibly 27 cents. I am not positive of these figures, as I am not an official.

If you go back 15 years or if I owned stock in the club I would give them to you.

SENATOR KEFAUVER. Mr. Stengel, I am not sure that I made my question clear. [Laughter.]

MR. STENGEL. Yes, sir. Well that is all right. I am not sure I am going to answer yours perfectly either. [Laughter.]

SENATOR KEFAUVER. I was asking you, sir, why it is that baseball wants this bill passed.

Casey Stengel. c. 1955. The National Baseball Library, Cooperstown, New York. *Stengel, who baffled Congress during his 1958 testimony before a subcommittee on antitrust and monopoly, baffled the American League for a dozen years as manager of the powerful New York Yankees.*

MR. STENGEL. I would say I would not know, but I would say the reason why they would want it passed is to keep baseball going as the highest paid ball sport that has gone into baseball and from the baseball angle, I am not going to speak of any other sport.

I am not in here to argue about other sports, I am in the baseball business. It has been run cleaner than any business that was ever put out in the 100 years at the present time. . . .

SENATOR O'MAHONEY. Did I understand you to say, Mr. Stengel, at the beginning of your statement that you have been in baseball for 48 years?

MR. STENGEL. Yes, sir; the oldest man in the service.

SENATOR O'MAHONEY. How many major league teams were there in the United States when you entered baseball?

MR. STENGEL. Well, there was in 1910—there were 16 major league baseball teams.

SENATOR O'MAHONEY. How many are there now?

MR. STENGEL. There are 16 major league clubs but there was 1 year that they brought in the Federal League which was brought in by Mr. Ward and Mr. Sinclair and others after a war, and it is a very odd thing to tell you that during tough times it is hard to study baseball. I have been through 2 or 3 depressions in baseball and out of it.

The First World War we had good baseball in August.

The Second World War we kept on and made more money because everybody was around going to the services, the larger the war, the more they come to the ball park, and that was an amazing thing to me.

When you were looking for tough times why it changed for different wars.

SENATOR O'MAHONEY. How many minor leagues were there in baseball when you began?

MR. STENGEL. Well, there were not so many at that time because of this fact: Anybody to go into baseball at that time with the educational schools that we had were small, while you were probably thoroughly educated at school, you had to be—we had only small cities that you could put a team in and they would go defunct.

Why, I remember the first year I was at Kankakee, Ill., and a bank offered me $550 if I would let them have a little notice. I left there and took a uniform because they owed me 2 weeks' pay. But I either had to quit but I did not have enough money to go to dental college so I had to go with the manager down to Kentucky.

What happened there was if you got by July, that was the big date. You did not play night ball and you did not play Sundays in half of the cities on account of a Sunday observance, so in those days when things were tough, and all of it was, I mean to say, why they just closed up July 4 and there you were sitting there in the depot.

You could go to work some place else but that was it.

So I got out of Kankakee, Ill., and I just go there for the visit now. [Laughter.] . . .

SENATOR O'MAHONEY. Mr. Chairman, I think the witness is the best entertainment we have had around here for a long time and it is a great temptation to keep asking him questions but I think I had better desist.

Thank you.

SENATOR KEFAUVER. Senator Carroll.

SENATOR CARROLL. Mr. Stengel, I am an old Yankee fan and I come from a city where I think we have made some contribution to your success—from Denver. I think you have many Yankee players from Denver.

The question Senator Kefauver asked you was what, in your honest opinion, with your 48 years of experience, is the need for this legislation in view of the fact that baseball has not been subject to antitrust laws?

MR. STENGEL. No. . . .

SENATOR KEFAUVER. Thank you very much, Mr. Stengel. We appreciate your presence here. . . .

Mr. Mickey Mantle, will you come around? Mr. Mantle, do you have any observations with reference to the applicability of the antitrust laws to baseball?

MR. MANTLE. My views are just about the same as Casey's.

John Updike

FROM ASSORTED PROSE

"Hub Fans Bid Kid Adieu"

What makes this John Updike essay unique is the immediacy of its characters: the old Boston ballpark, the fans sitting in the drizzle in what otherwise would have been a meaningless game, and Ted Williams himself, the greatest hitter who ever lived, as he wrapped up his tremendous and tumultuous career.

Fenway Park, in Boston, is a lyric little bandbox of a ballpark. Everything is painted green and seems in curiously sharp focus, like the inside of an old-fashioned peeping-type Easter egg. It was built in 1912 and rebuilt in 1934, and offers, as do most Boston artifacts, a compromise between Man's Euclidean determinations and Nature's beguiling irregularities. Its right field is one of the deepest in the American League, while its left field is the shortest; the high left-field wall, 315 feet from home plate along the foul line, virtually thrusts its surface at right-handed hitters. On the afternoon of Wednesday, September 28, as I took a seat behind third base, a uniformed groundkeeper was treading the top of this wall, picking batting-practice home runs out of the screen, like a mushroom gatherer seen in Wordsworthian perspective on the verge of a cliff. The day was overcast, chill, and uninspirational. The Boston team was the worst in twenty-seven seasons. A jangling medley of incompetent youth and aging competence, the Red Sox were finishing in seventh place only because the Kansas City Athletics had locked them out of the cellar. They were scheduled to play the Baltimore Orioles, a much nimbler blend of May and December, who had been dumped from pennant contention a week before by the insatiable Yankees. I, and 10,453 others, had shown up primarily because this was the Red Sox's last home game of the season, and therefore the last time in all eternity that their regular left fielder, known to the headlines as TED, KID, SPLINTER, THUMPER, TW, and, most cloyingly, MISTER WONDERFUL, would play in Boston. "WHAT WILL WE DO WITHOUT TED? HUB FANS ASK" ran the headline on a newspaper being read by a bulb-nosed cigar smoker a few rows away. Williams' retirement had been announced, doubted (he had been threatening retirement for years), confirmed by Tom Yawkey, the Red Sox owner, and at last widely accepted as the sad but probable truth. He was forty-two and had redeemed his abysmal season of 1959 with a—considering his advanced age—fine one. He had been giving away his gloves and bats and had grudgingly consented to a sentimental ceremony today. This was not necessarily his last game; the Red Sox were scheduled to travel to New York and wind up the season with three games there.

I arrived early. The Orioles were hitting fungoes on the field. The day before, they had spitefully smothered the Red Sox, 17–4, and neither their faces nor their drab gray visiting-team uniforms seemed very gracious. I wondered who had invited them to the party. Between our heads and the lowering clouds a frenzied organ was thundering through, with an appositeness perhaps accidental, "You *maaaade* me love you, I didn't wanna do it, I didn't wanna do it . . ."

. . . The batting cage was trundled away. The Orioles fluttered to the sidelines. Diagonally across the field, by the Red Sox dugout, a cluster of men in overcoats were festering like maggots. I could see a splinter of white uniform, and Williams' head, held at a self-deprecating and evasive tilt. Williams' conversational stance is that of a six-foot-three-inch man under a six-foot ceiling. He moved away to the patter of flash bulbs, and began playing catch with a young Negro outfielder named Willie Tasby. His arm, never very powerful, had grown lax with the years, and his throwing motion was a kind of muscular drawl. To catch the ball, he flicked his glove onto his left shoulder (he batted left but threw right, as every schoolboy ought to know) and let the ball plop into it comically. This catch session with Tasby was the only time all afternoon I saw him grin.

A tight little flock of human sparrows who, from the lambent and pampered pink of their faces, could only have been Boston politicians moved toward the plate. The loudspeakers mammothly coughed as someone huffed on the microphone. The ceremonies began. Curt Gowdy, the Red Sox radio and television announcer, who sounds like everybody's brother-in-law, delivered a brief sermon, taking the two words "pride" and "champion" as his text. It began, "Twenty-one years ago, a skinny kid from San Diego, California . . ." and ended, "I don't think we'll ever see another like him." Robert Tibolt, chairman of the board of the Greater Boston Chamber of Commerce, presented Williams with a big Paul Revere silver bowl. Harry Carlson, a member of the sports committee of the Boston Chamber, gave him a plaque, whose inscription he did not read in its entirety, out of deference to Williams' distaste for this sort of fuss. Mayor Collins presented the Jimmy Fund with a thousand-dollar check.

Then the occasion himself stooped to the microphone, and his voice sounded, after the others, very Californian; it seemed to be coming, excellently amplified, from a great distance, adolescently young and as smooth as a butternut. His thanks for the gifts had not died from our ears before he glided, as if helplessly, into "In spite of all the terrible things that have been said about me by the maestros of the keyboard up there . . ." He glanced up at the press rows suspended above home plate. (All the Boston reporters, incidentally, reported the phrase as "knights of the keyboard," but I heard it as "maestros" and prefer it that way.) The crowd tittered, appalled. A frightful vision flashed upon me, of the press gallery pelting Williams with erasers, of Williams clambering up the foul screen to slug journalists, of a riot, of Mayor Collins being crushed. ". . . And they were terrible things," Williams insisted, with level melancholy, into the mike. "I'd like to forget them, but I can't." He paused, swallowed his memories, and went on, "I want to say that my years in Boston have been the greatest thing in my life." The crowd, like an immense sail going limp in a change of wind, sighed with relief. Taking all the parts himself, Williams then acted out a vivacious little morality drama in which an imaginary tempter came to him at the beginning of his career and said, "Ted, you can play anywhere you like." Leaping nimbly into the role of his younger self (who in biographical actuality had yearned to be a Yankee), Williams gallantly chose Boston over all the other cities, and told us that Tom Yawkey was the greatest owner in baseball and we were the greatest fans. We applauded ourselves heartily. The umpire came out and dusted the plate. The voice of doom announced over the loudspeakers that after Williams' retirement his uniform number, 9, would be permanently retired—the first time the Red Sox had so honored a player. We cheered. The national anthem was played. We cheered. The game began.

Williams was third in the batting order, so he came up in the bottom of the first inning, and Steve Barber, a young pitcher who was not yet born when Williams began playing for the Red Sox, offered him four pitches, at all of which he disdained to swing, since none of them were within the strike zone. This demonstrated simultaneously that Williams' eyes were razor-sharp and that Barber's control wasn't. Shortly, the bases were full, with Williams on second. "Oh, I hope he gets held up at third! That would be wonderful," the girl beside me moaned, and, sure enough, the man at bat walked and Williams was delivered into our foreground. He struck the pose of Donatello's David, the third-base bag being Goliath's head. Fiddling with his cap, swapping small talk with the Oriole third baseman (who seemed delighted to have him drop in), swinging his arms with a sort of prancing nervousness, he looked fine—flexible, hard, and not unbecomingly substantial through the middle. The long neck, the small head, the knickers whose cuffs were worn down near his ankles—all these points, often observed by caricaturists, were visible in the flesh.

One of the collegiate voices behind me said, "He looks old, doesn't he, old; big deep wrinkles in his face . . ."

"Yeah," the other voice said, "but he looks like an old hawk, doesn't he?"

With each pitch, Williams danced down the base line, waving his arms and stirring dust, ponderous but menacing, like an attacking goose. It occurred to about a dozen humorists at once to shout, "Steal home! Go, go!" Williams' speed afoot was never legendary. Lou Clinton, a young Sox outfielder, hit a fairly deep fly to center field. Williams tagged up and ran home. As he slid across the plate, the ball, thrown with unusual heft by Jackie Brandt, the Oriole center fielder, hit him on the back.

"Boy, he was really loafing, wasn't he?" one of the boys behind me said.

"It's cold," the other explained. "He doesn't play well when it's cold. He likes heat. He's a hedonist."

The run that Williams scored was the second and last of the inning. Gus Triandos, of the Orioles, quickly evened the score by plunking a home run over the handy left-field wall. Williams, who had had this wall at his back for twenty years, played the ball flawlessly. He didn't budge. He just stood there, in the center of the little patch of grass that his patient footsteps had worn brown, and, limp with lack of interest, watched the ball pass overhead. It was not a very interesting game. Mike Higgins, the Red Sox manager, with nothing to lose, had restricted his major-league players to the left-field line—along with Williams, Frank Malzone, a first-rate third baseman, played the game—and had peopled the rest of the terrain with unpredictable youngsters fresh, or not so fresh, off the farms. Other than Williams' recurrent appearances at the plate, the *maladresse* of the Sox infield was the sole focus of suspense; the second baseman turned every grounder into a juggling act while the shortstop did a breathtaking impersonation of an open window. With this sort of assistance, the Orioles wheedled their way into a 4–2 lead. They had early replaced Barber with another young pitcher, Jack Fisher. Fortunately (as it turned out), Fisher is no cutie; he is willing to burn the ball through the strike zone, and inning after inning this tactic punctured Higgins' string of test balloons.

Whenever Williams appeared at the plate—pounding the dirt from his cleats, gouging a pit in the batter's box with his left foot, wringing resin out of the bat handle with his vehement grip, switching the stick at the pitcher with an electric ferocity—it was like having a familiar Leonardo appear in a shuffle of *Saturday Evening Post* covers. This man, you realized—and here, perhaps, was the difference, greater than the difference in gifts—really intended to hit the ball. In the third inning, he hoisted a high fly to deep center. In the fifth, we thought he had it; he smacked the ball hard and high into the heart of his power zone, but the deep right field in Fenway and the heavy air and a casual east wind defeated him. The ball died. Al Pilarcik leaned his back against the big "380" painted on the right-field wall and caught it. On another day, in another park, it would have been gone. (After the game, Williams said, "I didn't think I could hit one any harder than that. The conditions weren't good.")

The afternoon grew so glowering that in the sixth inning the arc lights were turned on—always a wan sight in the daytime, like the burning headlights of a funeral procession. Aided by the gloom, Fisher was slicing through the Sox rookies, and Williams did not come to bat in the seventh. He was second up in the eighth. This was almost certainly his last time to come to the plate in Fenway Park, and instead of merely cheering, as we had at his three previous appearances, we stood, all of us—stood and applauded. Have you ever heard applause in a ball park? Just applause—no calling, no whistling, just an ocean of handclaps, minute after minute, burst after burst, crowding and running together in continuous succession like the pushes of surf at the edge of the sand. It was a somber and considered tumult. There was not a boo in it. It seemed to renew itself out of a shifting set of memories as the kid, the Marine, the veteran of feuds and failures and injuries, the friend of children, and the enduring old pro evolved down the bright tunnel of twenty-one summers toward this moment. At last, the umpire signaled for Fisher to pitch; with the other players, he had been frozen in position. Only Williams had moved during the ovation, switching his bat impatiently, ignoring everything except his cherished task. Fisher wound up, and the applause sank into a hush.

Understand that we were a crowd of rational people. We knew that a home run cannot be produced at will; the right pitch must be perfectly met and luck must ride with the ball. Three innings before, we had seen a brave effort fail. The air was soggy; the season was exhausted. Nevertheless, there will always lurk, around a corner in a pocket of our knowledge of the odds,

Ted Williams.
September 28, 1960.
AP/Wide World Photos.
An uncharacteristic handshake from Ted Williams just after the Splendid Splinter homered during the last at-bat of his career.

an indefensible hope, and this was one of the times, which you now and then find in sports, when a density of expectation hangs in the air and plucks an event out of the future.

Fisher, after his unsettling wait, was wide with the first pitch. He put the second one over, and Williams swung mightily and missed. The crowd grunted, seeing that classic swing, so long and smooth and quick, exposed, naked in its failure. Fisher threw the third time, Williams swung again, and there it was. The ball climbed on a diagonal line into the vast volume of air over center field. From my angle, behind third base, the ball seemed less an object in flight than the tip of a towering, motionless construct, like the Eiffel Tower or the Tappan Zee Bridge. It was in the books while it was still in the sky. Brandt ran back to the deepest corner of the outfield grass; the ball descended beyond his reach and struck in the crotch where the bullpen met the wall, bounced chunkily, and, as far as I could see, vanished.

Like a feather caught in a vortex, Williams ran around the square of bases at the center of our beseeching screaming. He ran as he always ran out home runs—hurriedly, unsmiling, head down, as if our praise were a storm of rain to get out of. He didn't tip his cap. Though we thumped, wept, and chanted, "We want Ted," for minutes after he hid in the dugout, he did not come back. Our noise for some seconds passed beyond excitement into a kind of immense open anguish, a wailing, a cry to be saved. But immortality is nontransferable. The papers said that the other players, and even the umpires on the field, begged him to come out and acknowledge us in some way, but he never had and did not now. Gods do not answer letters.

Ed Sullivan

FROM *THE NEW YORK DAILY NEWS*
"The Way the Ball Bounces"

Only once in the history of the game has anyone lived every boy's fantasy of hitting a game-winning home run in the bottom of the ninth inning in the last game of a World Series. That distinction goes to Bill Mazeroski, Pittsburgh Pirates second baseman, who did it in 1960 against the New York Yankees. In one of the most unusual series ever, the Pirates lost games by scores of 16–3, 10–0, and 12–0. The losing team set World Series records for highest batting average, most runs, most hits, most total bases, and most runs batted in. Yankees shortstop Tony Kubek caught a bad-hop grounder in the throat. Here's how Ed Sullivan saw the series in his Little Old New York column in The New York Daily News.

It was the toughest of all possible breaks for veteran Casey Stengel; it was the most amazing of bad breaks for Tony Kubek but there is no disputing the fact that the Pittsburgh Pirates are the fightingest team that ever stuck it out for seven games of a World Series. Groat, Hoak, Virdon and Mazeroski formed the spearhead of resolution that finally paid off. Beaten three times by the Yankees in games in which the Yankees rolled up 38 runs, these Pirates continued to charge back into action. Other teams would have been demoralized by the three lacings the Pirates absorbed. Not these guys! The one you feel sorriest for is Casey Stengel, who ends his baseball career now. Had anyone told Casey that he'd lose a series that meant so much to him because a ground ball would bound up and disable Kubek, Casey would have thought it an insane prediction. But that's what happened in the most unusual World Series this reporter ever has seen.

Bill Mazeroski Wins the 1960 Championship for Pittsburgh. October 13, 1960. AP/Wide World Photos. *Mazeroski is greeted at home plate after his ninth-inning home run beat the Yankees in Game Seven of the 1960 World Series.*

Henry Aaron with Lonnie Wheeler
FROM I HAD A HAMMER

A crown is never easily taken from one king by another. In his 1991 autobiography, Henry Aaron, baseball's all-time home-run champ, describes the tremendous pressures of approaching and finally surpassing Babe Ruth's record. Aaron played for the Milwaukee and Atlanta Braves from 1954 to 1974, and for the Milwaukee Brewers from 1975 to 1976.

A righthander named Clay Kirby pitched for the Reds on Sunday. Kirby was not one of the best pitchers in the National League, but he had one of the best sliders, which was a pitch that consistently gave me more trouble than any other because it was hard to identify as it came toward the plate. I struck out twice against Kirby and grounded out a third time. By then we had a good lead and Mathews sent somebody in for me. I couldn't believe it after the game when the writers suggested, and later wrote, that I might have deliberately struck out against Kirby. The last thing I wanted to do was to look bad in that situation, or, worse yet, ruin my reputation by going into the tank. If I was going to do something crooked, I sure as hell wouldn't do it with 250 reporters watching every move I made. I had always taken a strong stand against anything that wasn't within the spirit and rules of the game—like spitballs. I believed in the integrity of the game as strongly as anybody, and it irked me to have my own integrity assaulted. The fact is, on both strikeouts I was called out by John McSherry, and one of them was a bad call that I argued. Even Kirby said that he thought the pitch was a ball.

I was in a foul mood when we got back to Atlanta, but Atlanta was in a good mood. The annual Dogwood Festival was going on, and the Braves had planned a big Hank Aaron Night for the home opener on Monday. There were almost 54,000 people at the ballpark that night—still the biggest crowd in team history. Bob Hope, the Braves' publicity man, had been working on the special night since the year before, not knowing that I would be tied with Ruth at the time. There were balloons and cannons and marching bands and a program that was like the old "This Is Your Life" television show. Important people from my past took their places on a map of the United States that covered the outfield—Ed Scott, my manager with the Mobile Black Bears; John Mullen, who signed me; Charlie Grimm, my first big-league manager; Donald Davidson, who had seen more of my home runs than anybody. Pearl Bailey sang the national anthem because she wanted to. Sammy Davis, Jr. was there and also Jimmy Carter, who at the time was still governor of Georgia. It seemed like the only people not there were the President of the United States and the commissioner of baseball. Nixon had a pretty good excuse—Congress was on his back to produce the Watergate tapes—but I couldn't say the same for Bowie Kuhn. He was in Cleveland speaking to the Wahoo Club. Kuhn sent Monte Irvin to stand in for him, and the Atlanta fans just about booed poor Monte out of the park. Kuhn knew that he would have been the one getting booed if he had come to Atlanta, because the whole town was mad at him for intervening in Cincinnati. He said later that his presence at the ballpark would have been a distraction and he stayed away so as not to blacken the occasion, but his absence was a much greater distraction. I was deeply offended that the commissioner of baseball would not see fit to watch me try to break a record that was supposed to be the most sacred in baseball. It was almost as if he didn't want to dignify the record or didn't want to be part of the surpassing of Babe Ruth. Whatever his reason for not being there, I think it was terribly inadequate. I took it personally, and, even though Kuhn and I have met and talked about it since then, I still do. . . .

My father threw out the first ball, and then we took the field against the Dodgers. Their pitcher was Al Downing, a veteran lefthander whom I respected. Downing always had an idea of what he was doing when he was on the mound, and he usually pitched me outside with sliders and screwballs. I crowded the plate against him to hit the outside pitch, but at the same time, I knew he would be trying to outthink me, which meant that I had to be patient and pick my spot. It didn't come in the second inning, when Downing walked me before I could take the bat off my shoulder. I scored when Dusty Baker doubled and Bill Buckner mishandled the ball in left field. Nobody seemed to care too much, but my run broke Willie Mays' National League record for runs scored—Willie had retired at the end of the 1973 season—and put me third all-time behind Ty Cobb and Ruth. I had always put great store in runs scored ever since Jackie Robinson pointed out that the purpose of coming up to the plate was to make it around the bases. The way I saw it, a run scored was just as important as one batted in. Apparently, though, Jackie and I were in the minority on that score.

I came up again in the fourth, with two outs and Darrell Evans on first base. The Dodgers were ahead 3–1, and I knew that Downing was not going to walk me and put the tying run on base. He was going to challenge me with everything he had—which was what it was going to take for me to hit my 715th home run. I knew all along that I wouldn't break the record against a rookie pitcher, because a rookie would be scared to come at me. It had to be a pitcher with some confidence and nerve—a solid veteran like Downing.

Downing's first pitch was a change of pace that went into the dirt. The umpire, Satch Davidson, threw it out, and the first-base umpire, Frank Pulli, tossed Downing another one of the specially marked infrared balls. Downing rubbed it up and then threw his slider low and down the middle, which was not where he wanted it but which was fine with me. I hit it squarely, although not well enough that I knew it was gone. The ball shot out on a line over the shortstop, Bill Russell, who bent his knees as if he were going to jump up and catch it. That was one of the differences between Ruth and me: he made outfielders look up at the sky, and I made shortstops bend their knees.

I used to say that I never saw one of my home runs land, but when I see photographs or films of myself hitting home runs, I'm always looking out toward left field. I never realized I was doing it, though, and I still don't think I was watching to see the ball go over the fence. I think it was just a matter of following the ball with my eyes. From the time the pitcher gripped it, I was focused on the ball, and I didn't look away until it was time to run the bases. Anyway, I saw this one go out. And before it did, I saw Buckner run to the fence like he was going to catch it. During the pregame warm-ups, Buckner had practiced leaping against the fence, as if he planned to take the home run away from me, and I believe he was thinking about doing that as he ran back to the wall and turned. But the ball kept going. It surprised him, and it surprised me. I'm still not sure I hit that ball hard enough for it to go out. I don't know—maybe I did but I was so keyed up that I couldn't feel it. Anyway, something carried the ball into the bullpen, and about the time I got to first base I realized that I was the all-time home run king of baseball. Steve Garvey, the Dodgers' first baseman, shook my hand as I passed first, and Davey Lopes, the second baseman, stuck out his hand at second. I'm not sure if I ever shook with Lopes, though, because about that time a couple of college kids appeared out of nowhere and started running alongside me and pounding me on the back. I guess I was aware of them, because the clips show that I sort of nudged them away with my elbow, but I honestly don't remember them being there. I was in my own little world at the time. It was like I was running in a bubble and I could see all these people jumping up and down and waving their arms in slow motion. I remember that every base seemed crowded, like there were all these people I had to get through to make it to home plate. I just couldn't wait to get there. I was told I had a big smile on my face as I came around third. I purposely never smiled as I ran the bases after a home run, but I suppose I couldn't help it that time. . . .

As I ran in toward home, Ralph Garr grabbed my leg and tried to plant it on the plate, screaming, "Touch it, Supe! Just touch it!" As soon as I did, Ralph and Darrell and Eddie and

Henry Aaron. April 8, 1974. The National Baseball Library, Cooperstown, New York. *Henry Aaron, baseball's all-time home-run king, takes his throne as number 715 sails over Atlanta-Fulton County Stadium's left-field wall, breaking Babe Ruth's record.*

everybody mobbed me. Somehow, my mother managed to make it through and put a bear hug on me. Good Lord, I didn't know Mama was that strong; I thought she was going to squeeze the life out of me. About that time, Tom House, a young relief pitcher, came sprinting in with the ball. He had caught it in the bullpen and he wasn't about to give it up to anybody but me. When he got to me, he stuck it in my hand and said, "Hammer, here it is!" Then they stopped the game for a little ceremony, and I stepped up to the microphone and said exactly what I felt: "Thank God it's over."

It started to rain while the ceremony was going on. Since it was only the fourth inning, the game would have been wiped out if it had kept raining. That would have meant that the whole moment never really happened and I still had 714 home runs. But the fates were with me that night. The rain stopped, and we went on to win the game, 7–4. By the look of the crowd, though, you'd have thought there had been a flash flood in the grandstand. By the next time I batted, there couldn't have been more than 20,000 people left in the park. It seemed more like a Braves game. I guess that's when it hit me that the whole thing was really over. As I walked out to the on-deck circle, Ralph Garr said, "Come on, Supe, break Hank Aaron's record." God, that sounded good. But I couldn't do it. . . .

There were already hundreds of telegrams piled up by the time the game was over. And President Nixon had called. I suppose with all that he was going through, he welcomed the chance to talk to a ballplayer for a few minutes. He phoned when I was in the outfield, and Donald Davidson disconnected him while they were trying to patch the call into the clubhouse. Donald tried to call him back, but the operator at the White House wouldn't let him through. Finally, Nixon called again and said some nice things and invited me to the White House. If I'd known he was such a baseball fan, I might have voted differently.

After the party in the clubhouse, there was one more press conference. It was a happier one this time, except that the reporters had to ask about Bowie Kuhn's absence and I had to tell them what I thought about it. And I had to have one more say about the Clay Kirby game. I wanted no misunderstanding about what had happened Sunday in Cincinnati. I had to get that off my chest before I could take my record home.

We had a little party at the house that night, mostly family and close friends. Billye and I were alone for a little while before everybody arrived, and while she was in the bedroom getting ready, I went off downstairs to be by myself for a few minutes. When I was alone and the door was shut, I got down on my knees and closed my eyes and thanked God for pulling me through. At that moment, I knew what the past twenty-five years of my life had been all about. I had done something that nobody else in the world had ever done, and with it came a feeling that nobody else has ever had—not exactly, anyway. I didn't feel a wild sense of joy. I didn't feel like celebrating. But I probably felt closer to God at that moment than at any other in my life. I felt a deep sense of gratitude and a wonderful surge of liberation all at the same time. I also felt a stream of tears running down my face.

Roger Angell

FROM FIVE SEASONS

"Agincourt and After"

Roger Angell, the game's poet laureate, recounts what might have been the greatest World Series ever played: the 1975 contest between the Cincinnati Reds (the victors) and the Boston Red Sox (forever the vanquished). Many say this series thrust baseball back to the forefront at a time when professional football had been gaining steadily in popularity and threatening for

COLORPLATE 51

MARJORIE PHILLIPS. *Night Baseball.* 1951.
Oil on canvas. 24¹/₄ x 36 in. © The Phillips Collection, Washington, D.C.

COLORPLATE 52

JOHN MARIN. *Baseball.* 1953. Colored pencil on paper. 8¹/₂ x 10¹/₂ in.
The Gladstone Collection of Baseball Art.

COLORPLATE 53

JACOB LAWRENCE. *Strike.* 1949. Tempera on board. 20 x 24 in.
The Howard University Gallery of Art, Washington, D.C. Permanent collection.

COLORPLATE 54

DICK PEREZ. *This is Next Year.* 1981. Watercolor. 30 x 20 in. The Gladstone Collection of Baseball Art.
In 1955, the Brooklyn Dodgers won their first—and only—World Championship when they defeated the
New York Yankees. Three years later, the Dodgers moved to Los Angeles.

COLORPLATE 55

HARVEY DINNERSTEIN. *The Wide Swing.* 1974. Oil on canvas. 24 x 32 in.
The Butler Institute of American Art, Youngstown, Ohio. Phil Desind Collection.

COLORPLATE 56

EARL MAYAN. *Yogi Berra. Saturday Evening Post* cover, March 20, 1957.

COLORPLATE 57

JOHN FALTER. *Stanley Musial.* *Saturday Evening Post* cover, May 1, 1954.
The National Baseball Library and Hall of Fame, Cooperstown, New York.

COLORPLATE 58

Norman Rockwell. *The Rookie (Red Sox Locker Room).*
Saturday Evening Post cover, March 2, 1957.
Oil on canvas. 41 x 39 in. Private collection.

the title of America's National Pastime. And it was in this series that Carlton Fisk waved and danced his way into New England's shared cultural consciousness, alongside Bunker Hill, Paul Revere's ride, and the Boston Tea Party.

———————————

Tarry, delight, so seldom met. . . . The games have ended, the heroes are dispersed, and another summer has died late in Boston, but still one yearns for them and wishes them back, so great was their pleasure. The adventures and discoveries and reversals of last month's World Series, which was ultimately won by the Cincinnati Reds in the final inning of the seventh and final game, were of such brilliance and unlikelihood that, even as they happened, those of us who were there in the stands and those who were there on the field were driven again and again not just to cries of excitement but to exclamations of wonder about what we were watching and sharing. Pete Rose, coming up to bat for the Reds in the tenth inning of the tied and retied sixth game, turned to Carlton Fisk, the Red Sox catcher, and said, "Say, this is some kind of game, isn't it?" And when that evening ended at last, after further abrupt and remarkable events, everyone—winners and losers and watchers—left the Fens in exaltation and disarray. "I went home," the Reds' manager, Sparky Anderson, said later, "and I was stunned."

The next day, during the last batting practice of the year, there was extended debate among the writers and players on the Fenway sidelines as to whether game six had been the greatest in Series history and whether we were not, in fact, in on the best Series of them all. Grizzled coaches and senior scribes recalled other famous Octobers—1929, when the Athletics, trailing the Cubs by eight runs in the fourth game, scored ten runs in the seventh inning and won; 1947, when Cookie Lavagetto's double with two out in the ninth ended Yankee pitcher Bill Bevens' bid for a no-hitter and won the fourth game for the Dodgers; 1960, when Bill Mazeroski's ninth-inning homer for the Pirates threw down the lordly Yankees. There is no answer to these barroom syllogisms, of course, but any recapitulation and reexamination of the 1975 Series suggests that at the very least we may conclude that there has never been a better one. Much is expected of the World Series, and in recent years much has been received. In the past decade, we have had the memorable and abrading seven-game struggles between the Red Sox and the Cardinals in 1967, the Cardinals and the Tigers in 1968, and the Orioles and the Pirates in 1971, and the astounding five-game upset of the Orioles by the Mets in 1969. Until this year, my own solid favorite—because of the Pirates' comeback and the effulgent play of Roberto Clemente—was the 1971 classic, but now I am no longer certain. Comebacks and late rallies are actually extremely scarce in baseball, and an excellent guaranteed cash-producing long-term investment is to wager that the winning team in any game will score more runs in a single inning than the losing team scores in nine. In this Series, however, the line scores alone reveal the rarity of what we saw:

In six of the seven games, the winning team came from behind.

In one of the games, the winning team came from behind twice.

In five games, the winning margin was one run.

There were two extra-inning games, and two games were settled in the ninth inning.

Overall, the games were retied or saw the lead reversed thirteen times.

No other Series—not even the celebrated Giants–Red Sox thriller of 1912—can match these figures.

It is best, however, not to press this search for the greatest Series any farther. There is something sterile and diminishing about our need for these superlatives, and the game of base-ball, of course, is so rich and various that it cannot begin to be encompassed in any set of seven games. This Series, for example, produced not one low-hit, low-score pitching duel—the classic and agonizing parade of double zeros that strains teams and managers and true fans to their limits as the inevitable crack in the porcelain is searched out and the game at last broken open. This year, too, the Reds batted poorly through most of the early play and offered indifferent front-line pitching, while the Red Sox made too many mistakes on the base paths, were unable to defend against Cincinnati's team speed, and committed some significant (and in the end fatal) errors in the infield. One of the games was seriously marred by a highly debatable umpire's decision, which may have altered its outcome. It was not a perfect Series. Let us conclude then—before we take a swift look at the season and the playoffs; before we return to Morgan leading away and stealing, to Yaz catching and whirling and throwing, to Eastwick blazing a fastball and Tiant turning his back and offering up a fluttering outside curve, to Evans' catch and Lynn's leap and fall, to Perez's bombs and Pete Rose's defiant, exuberant glare—and say only that this year the splendid autumn affair rose to our utmost expectations and then surpassed them, attaining at last such a level of excellence and emotional reward that it seems likely that the participants—the members of the deservedly winning, champion Reds and of the sorely disappointed, almost-champion Red Sox—will in time remember this Series not for its outcome but for the honor of having played in it, for having made it happen. . . .

Game Six, Game Six . . . what can we say of it without seeming to diminish it by recapitulation or dull it with detail? Those of us who were there will remember it, surely, as long as we have any baseball memory, and those who wanted to be there and were not will be sorry always. Crispin Crispian: for Red Sox fans, this was Agincourt. The game also went out to sixty-two million television viewers, a good many millions of whom missed their bedtime. Three days of heavy rains had postponed things; the outfield grass was a lush, Amazon green, but there was a clear sky at last and a welcoming moon—a giant autumn squash that rose above the right-field Fenway bleachers during batting practice.

In silhouette, the game suggests a well-packed but dangerously overloaded canoe—with the high bulge of the Red Sox' three first-inning runs in the bow, then the much bulkier hump of six Cincinnati runs amidships, then the counterbalancing three Boston runs astern, and then *way* aft, one more shape. But this picture needs colors: Fred Lynn clapping his hands once, quickly and happily, as his three-run opening shot flies over the Boston bullpen and into the bleachers . . . Luis Tiant fanning Perez with a curve and the Low-Flying Plane, then dispatching Foster with a Fall Off the Fence. Luis does not have his fastball, however. . . .

Pete Rose singles in the third. Perez singles in the fourth—his first real contact off Tiant in three games. Rose, up again in the fifth, with a man on base, fights off Tiant for seven pitches, then singles hard to center. Ken Griffey triples off the wall, exactly at the seam of the left-field and center-field angles; Fred Lynn, leaping up for the ball and missing it, falls backward into the wall and comes down heavily. He lies there, inert, in a terrible, awkwardly twisted position, and for an instant all of us think that he has been killed. He is up at last, though, and even stays in the lineup, but the noise and joy are gone out of the crowd, and the game is turned around. Tiant, tired and old and, in the end, bereft even of mannerisms, is rocked again and again—eight hits in three innings—and Johnson removes him, far too late, after Geronimo's first-pitch home run in the eighth has run the score to 6–3 for the visitors.

By now, I had begun to think sadly of distant friends of mine—faithful lifelong Red Sox fans all over New England, all over the East, whom I could almost see sitting silently at home and slowly shaking their heads as winter began to fall on them out of their sets. I scarcely noticed when Lynn led off the eighth with a single and Petrocelli walked. Sparky Anderson, flicking levers like a master back-hoe operator, now called in Eastwick, his sixth pitcher of the night, who fanned Evans and retired Burleson on a fly. Bernie Carbo, pinch-hitting, looked wholly overmatched against Eastwick, flailing at one inside fastball like someone fighting off a wasp with a croquet mallet. One more fastball arrived, high and over the middle of the plate, and Carbo smashed it in a gigantic, flattened parabola into the center-field bleachers, tying the game. Everyone out there—and everyone in the stands, too, I suppose—leaped to his feet and waved both arms exultantly, and the bleachers looked like the dark surface of a lake lashed with a sudden night squall.

The Sox, it will be recalled, nearly won it right away, when they loaded the bases in the ninth with none out, but an ill-advised dash home by Denny Doyle after a fly, and a cool, perfect peg to the plate by George Foster, snipped the chance. The balance of the game now swung back, as it so often does when opportunities are wasted. Drago pitched out of a jam in the tenth, but he flicked Pete Rose's uniform with a pitch to start the eleventh. Griffey bunted, and Fisk snatched up the ball and, risking all, fired to second for the force on Rose. Morgan was next, and I had very little hope left. He struck a drive on a quick, deadly rising line—you could still hear the loud *whock!* in the stands as the white blur went out over the infield—and for a moment I thought the ball would land ten or fifteen rows back in the right-field bleachers. But it wasn't hit quite that hard—it was traveling too fast, and there was no sail to it—and Dwight Evans, sprinting backward and watching the flight of it over his shoulder, made a last-second, half-staggering turn to his left, almost facing away from the plate at the end, and pulled the ball in over his head at the fence. The great catch made for two outs in the end, for Griffey had never stopped running and was easily doubled off first.

And so the swing of things was won back again. Carlton Fisk, leading off the bottom of the twelfth against Pat Darcy, the eighth Reds pitcher of the night—it was well into morning now, in fact—socked the second pitch up and out, farther and farther into the darkness above the lights, and when it came down at last, reilluminated, it struck the topmost, innermost edge of the screen inside the yellow left-field foul pole and glanced sharply down and bounced on the grass: a fair ball, fair all the way. I was watching the ball, of course, so I missed what everyone on television saw—Fisk waving wildly, weaving and writhing and gyrating along the first-base line, as he wished the ball fair, *forced* it fair with his entire body. He circled the bases in triumph, in sudden company with several hundred fans, and jumped on home plate with both feet, and John Kiley, the Fenway Park organist, played Handel's "Hallelujah Chorus," *fortissimo*, and then followed with other appropriately exuberant classical selections, and for the second time that evening, I suddenly remembered all my old absent and distant Sox-afflicted friends (and all the other Red Sox fans, all over New England), and I thought of them—in Brookline, Mass., and Brooklin, Maine; in Beverly Farms and Mashpee and Presque Isle and North Conway and Damariscotta; in Pomfret, Connecticut, and Pomfret, Vermont; in Wayland and Providence and Revere and Nashua, and in both the Concords and all five Manchesters;

Carlton Fisk's Home Run. October 21, 1975. UPI/The Bettmann Archive. *In one of baseball's most memorable moments, Fisk waves his home run fair against the Fenway Park foul pole, winning Game Six of the 1975 World Series and plunging much of New England into delirium.*

and in Raymond, New Hampshire (where Carlton Fisk lives), and Bellows Falls, Vermont (where Carlton Fisk was *born*), and I saw all of them dancing and shouting and kissing and leaping about like the fans at Fenway—jumping up and down in their bedrooms and kitchens and living rooms, and in bars and trailers, and even in some boats here and there, I suppose, and on back-country roads (a lone driver getting the news over the radio and blowing his horn over and over, and finally pulling up and getting out and leaping up and down on the cold macadam, yelling into the night), and all of them, for once at least, utterly joyful and believing in that joy—alight with it.

It should be added, of course, that very much the same sort of celebration probably took place the following night in the midlands towns and vicinities of the Reds' supporters—in Otterbein and Scioto; in Frankfort, Sardinia, and Summer Shade; in Zanesville and Louisville and Akron and French Lick and Loveland. I am not enough of a social geographer to know if the faith of the Red Sox fan is deeper or hardier than that of a Reds rooter (although I secretly believe that it may be, because of his longer and more bitter disappointments down the years). What I do know is that this belonging and caring is what our games are all about; this is what we come for. It is foolish and childish, on the face of it, to affiliate ourselves with anything so insignificant and patently contrived and commercially exploitative as a professional sports team, and the amused superiority and icy scorn that the non-fan directs at the sports nut (I know this look—I know it by heart) is understandable and almost unanswerable. Almost. What is left out of this calculation, it seems to me, is the business of caring—caring deeply and passionately, really *caring*—which is a capacity or an emotion that has almost gone out of our lives. And so it seems possible that we have come to a time when it no longer matters so much what the caring is about, how frail or foolish is the object of that concern, as long as the feeling itself can be saved. Naïveté—the infantile and ignoble joy that sends a grown man or woman to dancing and shouting with joy in the middle of the night over the haphazardous flight of a distant ball—seems a small price to pay for such a gift.

Red Smith

"Reggie Jackson's Three Home Runs"

Reggie Jackson, of whom someone once said, "There isn't enough mustard in the world to cover that hot dog," earned the nickname "Mr. October" when he swung his bat three consecutive times in Game Six of the 1977 World Series and turned a trio of Los Angeles Dodgers pitches into bleacher souvenirs. Always outspoken, always controversial, Jackson was one of the few "hot dogs" in baseball history whose bite lived up to his bark. His name and image defined the game for a whole generation of fans.

It had to happen this way. It had been predestined since November 29, 1976, when Reginald Martinez Jackson sat down on a gilded chair in New York's Americana Hotel and wrote his name on a Yankee contract. That day he became an instant millionaire, the big honcho on the best team money could buy, the richest, least inhibited, most glamorous exhibit in Billy Martin's pin-striped zoo. That day the plot was written for last night—the bizarre scenario Reggie Jackson played out by hitting three home runs, clubbing the Los Angeles Dodgers into submission and carrying his supporting players with him to the baseball championship of North America. His was the most lurid performance in 74 World Series, for although Babe

Ruth hit three home runs in a game in 1926 and again in 1928, not even that demigod smashed three in a row.

Reggie's first broke a tie and put the Yankees in front, 4–3. His second fattened the advantage to 7–3. His third completed arrangements for a final score of 8–4, wrapping up the championship in six games.

Yet that was merely the final act of an implausible one-man show: Jackson had made a home run last Saturday in Los Angeles and another on his last time at bat in that earthly paradise on Sunday. On his first appearance at the plate last night he walked, getting no official time at bat, so in his last four official turns he hit four home runs.

In his last nine times at bat, this Hamlet in double-knits scored seven runs, made six hits and five home runs and batted in six runs for a batting average of .667 compiled by day and by night on two seacoasts three thousand miles and three time zones apart. Shakespeare wouldn't attempt a curtain scene like that if he was plastered.

This was a drama that consumed seven months, for ever since the Yankees went to training camp last March, Jackson had lived in the eye of the hurricane. All summer long as the spike-shod capitalists bickered and quarreled, contending with their manager, defying their owner, Reggie was the most controversial, the most articulate, the most flamboyant.

Part philosopher, part preacher and part outfielder, he carried this rancorous company with his bat in the season's last fifty games, leading them to the East championship in the American League and into the World Series. He knocked in the winning run in the twelve-inning first game, drove in a run and scored two in the third, furnished the winning margin in the fourth and delivered the final run in the fifth.

Thus the stage was set when he went to the plate in last night's second inning with the Dodgers leading, 2–0. Sedately, he led off with a walk. Serenely, he circled the bases on a home run by Chris Chambliss. The score was tied.

Los Angeles had moved out front, 3–2, when the man reappeared in the fourth inning with Thurman Munson on base. He hit the first pitch on a line into the seats beyond right field. Circling the bases for the second time, he went into his home-run glide—head high, chest out. The Yankees led, 4–3. In the dugout, Yankees fell upon him. Billy Martin, the manager, who tried to slug him last June, patted his cheek lovingly. The dugout phone rang and Reggie accepted the call graciously.

His first home run knocked the Dodgers' starting pitcher, Burt Hooton, out of the game. His second disposed of Elias Sosa, Hooton's successor. Before Sosa's first pitch in the fifth inning, Reggie had strolled the length of the dugout to pluck a bat from the rack, even though three men would precede him to the plate. He was confident he would get his turn. When he did, there was a runner on base again, and again he hit the first pitch. Again it reached the seats in right.

When the last jubilant playmate had been peeled off his neck, Reggie took a seat near the first-base end of the bench. The crowd was still bawling for him and comrades urged him to take a curtain call but he replied with a gesture that said, "Aw, fellows, cut it out!" He did unbend enough to hold up two fingers for photographers in a V-for-victory sign.

Jackson was the leadoff batter in the eighth. By that time, Martin would have replaced him in an ordinary game, sending Paul Blair to right field to help protect the Yankees' lead. But did they ever bench Edwin Booth in the last act?

For the third time, Reggie hit the first pitch but this one didn't take the shortest distance between two points. Straight out from the plate the ball streaked, not toward the neighborly stands in right but on a soaring arc toward the unoccupied bleachers in dead center, where the seats are blacked out to give batters a background. Up the white speck climbed, dwindling, diminishing, until it settled at last halfway up those empty stands, probably 450 feet away.

This time he could not disappoint his public. He stepped out of the dugout and faced the multitude, two fists and one cap uplifted. Not only the customers applauded.

"I must admit," said Steve Garvey, the Dodgers' first baseman, "when Reggie Jackson hit his third home run and I was sure nobody was listening, I applauded into my glove."

Dan Shaughnessy

FROM ONE STRIKE AWAY

Bill Buckner was an outstanding ballplayer during his career with the Los Angeles Dodgers, the Chicago Cubs, the Boston Red Sox, the California Angels, and the Kansas City Royals. However, they might love him the most in New York, where his error at first base led to an implausible come-from-behind Mets win in Game Six of the 1986 World Series. That win forced a Game Seven, which the New Yorkers won, along with the championship. And in Boston, Red Sox fans continue to wait. And wait. And wait . . .

On January 3, 1920, owner Harry Frazee sold Ruth to the New York Yankees for $125,000. Frazee insisted that the Ruth deal was the only way he could retain the Red Sox, but then a year later he made $2 million financing a stage production of "No, No, Nanette."

Those who believe that the Red Sox will never win again usually mark this as the turning point. Since the sale of the Babe, Sox fans have supported bad teams, mediocre teams, and talented teams that somehow have failed to fulfill their potential. Since the sale of Ruth, New York has won twenty-nine championships; Boston, zero. The 1946 Red Sox were loaded with sluggers and able pitchers, but lost the seventh game of the World Series, 4–3. St. Louis scored the winning run when Enos Slaughter scrambled from first base on a hit to left-center by Harry Walker. The popular theory is that the Sox lost the Series because shortstop Johnny Pesky hesitated with a relay throw from the outfield while Slaughter didn't. But Sox slugger Ted Williams compiled no extra base hits with only one RBI in the Series, and was outhit by a talkative rookie, Cardinal catcher Joe Garagiola. Two years later another powerhouse Boston team finished in a first-place tie with the Cleveland Indians. A one-game playoff was held at Fenway Park. When Sox manager Joe McCarthy opted to start journeyman Denny Galehouse, the Tribe routed Galehouse en route to a 8–3 victory.

In 1949 the Red Sox finished the season in New York needing only one win in two games to clinch the American League flag. The Sox blew a 4–0 lead in the first game and lost 5–4 on Johnny Lindell's eighth-inning homer. New York won the finale by a 5–3 count. The 1967 Red Sox overcame 100 to 1 odds to win the American League pennant and took heavily favored St. Louis to the seventh game of the series in Fenway Park—but again the Sox were losers. Manager Dick Williams started Cy Young winner Jim Lonborg on two days' rest in Game Seven and Bob Gibson beat Lonborg and the Red Sox, 7–2. In 1972 Boston led the Tigers by half a game and needed to take two of three in Detroit in the final series of the season. The Sox lost the first game 3–1 as Luis Aparicio fell down rounding third base on a Carl Yastrzemski shot to center. And the next day they were eliminated.

In 1974 the Red Sox led the American League East by seven games on August 23 and led third-place Baltimore by eight games on August 29, but finally finished third themselves, seven games behind the Orioles. The Sox won the first game of the 1975 World Series and led, 3–0, in Game Seven before Bill Lee threw an ill-timed blooper pitch to Tony Perez. Cincinnati's proud first baseman deposited Lee's insult somewhere near the Citgo sign that rests atop Kenmore Square. In the ninth inning when Sox manager Darrell Johnson summoned rookie Jim Burton to stall the Red Machine, Burton gave up a two-out, two-on bloop single to Joe Morgan, and the Reds were 4–3 winners. The 1978 Sox season remains one by which all future folds will be measured. The mighty Red Sox led the Yankees by a whopping fourteen games on July 19 and eventually fell three and a half games behind New York before tying for the lead on the final day of the regular season. Yet another one-game playoff was hosted at Fenway and the Sox were 5–4 losers as Bucky Dent plopped a three-run homer into the left-field screen off Mike Torrez. It was left to Carl Yastrzemski to make the final out against Rich

Gossage. Starting in 1972, the Red Sox were in first place after the All Star break seven times in fourteen seasons, yet managed only one division flag over this span. Sox fans adopted "Won't Get Fooled Again" as their official song.

This was the legacy the 1986 Red Sox lugged into the bottom half of the tenth inning at Shea Stadium on the morning of October 26, 1986. Boston's precious 5–3 lead was entrusted to a twenty-four-year-old Texan with 94.2 innings of big league experience—Calvin Schiraldi—whose first name hinted that historical forces might be at work once again. No one is quite sure when the link was first observed between the sixteenth-century beliefs of theologian John Calvin and the fortunes of the Boston ballclub, but the two seem in perfect harmony. Calvin taught that some are chosen to be among the elect and some are not. Could it be that the Red Sox are victims of predestination or fate? Scholar A. Bartlett Giamatti, lifelong Sox fan, president of the National League and former head of Yale, observed, "There's an almost Calvinistic sense of guilt at success, that we must re-enact the Garden of Eden again and again. There's a sense that things will turn out poorly no matter how hard we work. Somehow the Sox fulfill the notion that we live in a fallen world. It's as though we assume they're here to provide us with more pain."

Calvinist clouds of self-doubt aside, it was the Mets' turn to bat and Mr. Schiraldi was set to slam the door. Wally Backman went out on a fly to left and Keith Hernandez lined to center. Two outs. No one on base. A 5–3 lead. Cake. Hernandez, the Met backbone, went into the clubhouse and later admitted that at that point he'd planned to "go out and get drunk and stay up all night." Aguilera was on the bench and said, "My heart was breaking." Hands in pockets, Met manager Davey Johnson sat down and smacked his head against the back of the dugout wall.

Mookie and the Mets. October 25, 1986. UPI/The Bettmann Archive. *Following Game Six of the 1986 World Series, New York Mets outfielder Mookie Wilson is mobbed by his teammates after his tenth-inning ground ball slipped past Red Sox first baseman Bill Buckner. Buckner's error allowed Met Ray Knight to score the game's winning run, forcing a seventh game which the Mets won for the championship.*

Across the field the Red Sox were standing on the top step of their dugout, waiting for the final out. Oil Can Boyd was slamdancing with anyone in his vicinity and Roger Clemens said, "I was sure we had it won." Mets assistant equipment manager John Rufino had already loaded twenty cases of Great Western champagne and had it carted over to the Red Sox clubhouse. Foil was peeled from the tops of the bottles. Bruce Hurst had won the MVP vote by a 4–1 count, and the championship trophy was making a rare appearance in the Red Sox locker room. An NBC crew was set up in the clubhouse and cellophane had been hung on the players' lockers to protect clothes from champagne spray. Commissioner Peter Ueberroth would present the trophy to Red Sox president Jean Yawkey and chief operating officer Haywood Sullivan and then read a congratulatory telegram from President Reagan. . . .

There was one happy pocket of fans in the Shea Stadium stands where Red Sox wives rose and cheered as Gary Carter came to bat. Yet one Boston wife remained seated. Most of the young women who marry ballplayers are high school sweethearts from southern California, Texas, Florida, and other sunny places that produce major league ballplayers. Sherry Gedman, like her husband Rich Gedman, the stoic Red Sox catcher, grew up forty miles from Boston. Unlike the other wives, Sherry did not marry into the Sox family—she was born into it and she knew that it was too early to celebrate.

As Carter came to the plate, Met scoreboard operator Mike Ryan pushed the wrong button and "Congratulations Boston Red Sox" flashed prematurely on the electronic message board. Ryan, a native of Pittsfield, Massachusetts, was red-faced and at least one person was prompted to recall the *Chicago Herald Tribune's* "Dewey Defeats Truman" headline in 1948. Meanwhile the revered baseball broadcaster Vin Scully was telling America that Marty Barrett had been named Player of the Game.

Carter singled to left on a 2–1 pitch. Pinch hitter Kevin Mitchell was next and he stroked an 0–1 pitch to center for another single. Sox pitching coach Bill Fischer visited Schiraldi at the mound, after which Schiraldi quickly got two strikes on Met third baseman Ray Knight. *One strike away.*

Knight singled to center, scoring Carter, moving Mitchell to third, "I did what I wanted to, but he hit it over the second baseman's head," Schiraldi said later.

Sox manager John McNamara summoned Bob Stanley, the human dartboard ornament of Fenway Park. Stanley was one of the most likeable and approachable personalities on the ballclub, but his hefty contract, hefty midsection, and chronic ineffectiveness turned Sox fans on him by 1985. Seven months earlier, after getting roughed up in the Sox home opener, Stanley said, "All I know is this. When I stand out there and save the final game of the season and we win the pennant and I'm waving in the air, I'll be waving to my wife and family. The rest of 'em can go to hell." The insertion of Stanley at this crucial juncture almost certainly was greeted with both anger and anguish back in Boston. . . .

Mookie Wilson, the fleet, switch-hitting Met outfielder, was the only batter Stanley faced. Stanley worked the count to 2–2. *One strike away.* . . .

Wilson fouled off a curveball. *One strike away.*

Wilson fouled off another curveball. Stanley lacked an out pitch and Wilson was able to spoil the Steamer's strikes. For the fourth and final time, a Sox hurler delivered a pitch with the championship *one strike away.*

This time the ball sailed in toward the batter. Wilson jackknifed away from the pitch and a weary Gedman lunged to his right. The ball grazed Gedman's glove and bounced to the backstop. Wild pitch. Mitchell danced across the plate and it was 5–5. Knight took second and the NBC crew set a record for moving equipment out of a locker room.

In Roslindale, Massachusetts, thirty-five-year-old Ed Duggan got up from his chair and walked out of his house, leaving his mother and brother to see the finish on television. A Sox fan his entire life, Duggan knew what was coming. He walked alone down dark Sycamore Street toward Cummins Highway, toward Roslindale Square, toward another date with disappointment.

Stanley said it was the first time his fastball had ever broken in toward a left-handed batter (some of the Mets thought it was a spitter). "Usually my ball goes backward toward a left-handed hitter," said the Charlie Brown reliever. "This one went the other way. I've never seen one of my pitches do that and, hey, I didn't try to throw it like that. It just happened. That's the story of my life, isn't it? I had the chance to be the hero; instead I'm the goat." . . .

After the wild pitch Stanley threw three more pitches to Wilson. Wilson hit two more fouls, then dribbled a slow grounder just inside the first base line. Boston's weary war horse Bill Buckner was playing behind the bag and failed to charge the ball. The ball bounced twice then bounced a third time and stayed down, skipping under Buckner's glove, between his legs, and into history. When Knight scored from second with ease, the Red Sox had provided a capsule summary of their last sixty-eight years in the span of one half inning.

In Stoughton, Masssachusetts, Tom Mulvoy, holding his week-old son, snapped off the TV. "Welcome to the club," he said to tiny Stephen Mulvoy. On the twenty-ninth floor of the plush apartment building in the heart of downtown Boston, Bob Rodophele slumped into a sofa, clutching the still unopened bottle of Korbel Extra Dry. On Nantucket Island Steve Sheppard said, "Knowing in my heart of hearts they couldn't do it, I could bet my marriage on it. We were willing to sacrifice our marriage for the good of the team. But even that didn't work. They get you every time They always find a way to blow it." In Roslindale, Ed Duggan was still walking alone toward the city square when the sounds of defeat broke the quiet autumn night. He knew what had happened. "People were pouring out of houses and bars and slamming car doors," he remembered. "I could tell they were agitated. The cars started coming down the street and there was rubber screeching all over the place. I knew the Red Sox had lost."

Nolan Ryan and Jerry Jenkins

FROM MIRACLE MAN: NOLAN RYAN, THE AUTOBIOGRAPHY

Nolan Ryan brings to Cooperstown an impressive pile of records, including more than three hundred wins, the all-time strikeout mark (more than fifty-five hundred and counting at the time of this writing), and seven no-hitters. In his 1992 autobiography, Ryan, who also pitched for the New York Mets, the California Angels, and the Houston Astros, describes no-no number seven, which came while he was on the mound for the Texas Rangers.

Things looked great for the Rangers for the 1991 season. We looked to have good hitting and a lot of pitching—at least until the first four games. I lost the opener to Milwaukee and then we lost three more straight. It was a good thing we won six of our next seven or we would have been in a real tailspin. By the time I started my fourth game, we were 6–6 and I was 2–1. I lost 5–2 to Cleveland on a Friday the thirteenth at Arlington, and I had thrown 133 pitches.

I was scheduled to pitch again the following Wednesday, May 1, with only four days' rest. I hadn't been that successful in '90 with less than five days' rest, but I was ready to give it a try. By game time we were 8–8 and needed to get on a winning track. We would be at home against the Toronto Blue Jays, one of the best hitting teams in the majors.

Ruth almost always comes to my home games, but if she can't she watches them on television. The only one she missed when I was with the Angels was when she was moving us back to Texas and I was making my last start in 1974. She still hasn't forgiven herself for missing that no-hitter.

So, when she found out, late in the afternoon, that the Toronto game wasn't going to be televised, she called one of my ranching partners, Jim Stinson, and asked if she could watch it at his place, because he has a satellite dish. "He's not pitchin' tonight," Jim told her. "He's pitchin' Friday in Detroit, right?"

"No," she said, "He's pitching tonight."

"Well, if I'd known that I'd have flown to the game. In fact, there's still time, Ruth. You wanna go?"

So Ruth flew into Arlington with Jim in his private plane. I was glad she was there. Harry Spilman, my old Astros teammate and now a neighbor who catches for me in January before spring training and whose wife Kim is my secretary, listened to the game on his car radio by driving all over the place. He thought it was going to be on television too. When I took a no-hitter into the seventh he called my kids, and they watched the end of it when ESPN cut away from the Detroit–Kansas City game to follow my progress.

I didn't expect to pitch well at all that night. I woke up with a sore back and took painkillers all day before leaving for the park. I went through extra stretching and exercises and even wore a heating pad during the scouting meeting where we go over the hitters. That wasn't the only thing wrong with me. While I was warming up I told Tom House, who was also forty-four years old at the time, "I don't know about you, but I feel old today. My back hurts, my finger hurts, my ankle hurts, everything hurts." Scar tissue tore open on the middle finger of my pitching hand in the bullpen, and I had one of my worst warmups ever. I didn't know it till later, but House told Bobby Valentine to keep an eye on me and not leave me in too long.

Before the game Bobby asked me how my back was. I told him that it was stiff. He said, "How will it be once you start pitching?" I said, "It'll be history." Adrenaline always takes over when I'm on the mound, and it did again, in the first inning.

With two out in the first, I lost Kelly Gruber on a full count and walked him. I was mad at myself, but settled down and got out of the inning by retiring Joe Carter. In the second I struck out the side on three curveballs. Steve Buechele, our third baseman, and shortstop Jeff Huson told each other as they came off the field that all we needed was one run that night if I had stuff like that. I had to admit my curve was really working, and I didn't have any trouble hitting my spots. The fastball was hopping too.

We scored our only three runs in the bottom of the third, two on a Ruben Sierra homer. After the Gruber walk in the first, I got eighteen straight hitters out before giving up another two-out, full-count walk in the seventh, this time to Joe Carter. Manny Lee had hit a blooper to center in the fifth, but Gary Pettis raced out from under his hat to catch it at his knees. He's one of the best. I'd thought that ball had a chance to drop in before Gary chased it down.

After the walk to Carter in the seventh, I retired the next seven hitters and the place went crazy. I had struck out sixteen, allowed only two base runners who never got past first, and had pitched my seventh no-hitter. Even I couldn't keep from grinning as the team raced out to the mound to congratulate me. I had been the oldest no-hit pitcher when my sixth came the year before. Who would have ever thought there'd be another one, especially in the condition I was in that day?

Ironically, my last out was a swinging strikeout of Blue Jay second baseman Robert Alomar. His father, Sandy, had been my second baseman for the Angels in my first two no-hitters eighteen years before. In fact I remember little Roberto asking me to help him become a pitcher someday.

They tell me I threw 122 pitches, 83 for strikes, 62 of those fastballs. Of the sixteen strike-outs, all but the three in the second inning were swinging. The radar gun showed my fastest pitch at ninety-six miles per hour against Carter in the fourth, with an average of ninety-three miles per hour for the game. My last pitch, the one that got Alomar, was also at ninety-three miles per hour.

There's a lot of debate about which of my seven no-hitters was the best and in which one I had my best stuff. I'm not sure myself, but I know that the seventh was especially gratifying because it was at home before that Arlington crowd. My stuff was surprisingly good, considering all that was wrong with me that day. Somebody said my teammates were like spectators because I was that dominant, but I know better than that.

Fifth Inning:

WHERE BASEBALL LIVES

No diamond is complete without a setting in which it can be displayed. These works profile some of the many places where the baseball faithful have gathered to worship.

The Chicago Baseball Grounds

Before Wrigley Field, before the two Comiskey Parks, fans in Chicago celebrated the opening of this grand edifice in 1884, which seated a whopping 10,000 fans, without, as the article reads, "invading the playing-field."

The grounds of the Chicago Ball Club, indisputably the finest in the world in respect of seating accommodations and conveniences, are located on what is known as the Lake Front property, the title to which is in the city of Chicago. The inclosure begins at Randolph Street on the

Wrigley Field, Chicago. Date unknown. The National Baseball Library, Cooperstown, New York.

The Opening of the New
Base-Ball Grounds at
Chicago, Illinois. 1884.
Newspaper illustration.
The National Baseball
Library, Cooperstown,
New York.

north, and extends along the east line of Michigan Avenue southward to a point about mid-way between Washington and Madison streets. On the east are the tracks and switch yards of the Illinois Central Railroad Company, which has for several years past made a standing offer of $800,000 (not one-half its value) for the property; but as the city has been enjoined either from selling the tract or from permitting its use for permanent buildings, the ball club has continued to enjoy the rare privilege of grounds situated within a two minutes' walk of State Street, the chief retail thoroughfare of Chicago. Partly on account of the convenient location of the grounds, but more by reason of the exceptional management of the Chicago ball team, and its success in winning the National League championship for three successive seasons, beginning with 1881, the game of base-ball is extremely popular in Chicago, and the average attendance at League championship games is considerably greater there than in any other city in the United States. During the season of 1882 the attendance at the forty-five League games played in Chicago was upward of 130,000, or an average of 3000 persons to a game. With this fine patronage, made up in good part of the better classes of the community, the Chicago Club is amply able to maintain its costly team of players, and to equip its grounds and fixtures in a manner that by comparison with the usual style of base-ball appurtenances might be termed palatial. At an outlay of $10,000 since the close of the playing season of 1882 the Chicago Club, under the direction of President Spalding, has completely remodelled its seating arrangements. Every exposed surface is painted, so as to admit of thorough cleansing from dust, the item of paint alone amounting to $1800. The grand stand seats 2000 people, and the uncovered seats will accommodate 6000 more, so that with the standing room the total capacity is fully 10,000, and this without invading the playing-field. A fence six feet high encircles the field in front of all the seats, which are elevated so as to command the best view of the play. Overlooking the main entrance is a handsomely ornamented pagoda, built for a band stand, and to be occupied by the First Cavalry Band throughout the season. Surmounting the grand stand is a row of eighteen private boxes, cozily draped with curtains to keep out wind and sun, and furnished with comfortable arm-chairs. By the use of the telephone and gong President Spalding can conduct all the preliminary details of the game without leaving his private box. Besides club officers and players, the services of forty-one persons are required at each game to attend the grounds and seating arrangements, viz., seven ushers, six policemen, four ticket-sellers, four gate-keepers, three field-men, three cushion-renters, six refreshment boys, and eight musicians. Aside from players' salaries, ground rent, and including advertising, the cost per game on the Chicago grounds is $200; add to this the salaries of players, rent of grounds, travelling and hotel expenses, and $10,000 expended this year on improvements, and the total outlay for the season is $60,000, so that the Chicago Club must average $525 for each of the ninety-six League championship games to be played during 1883. But the patronage attracted by the famous champion team both at home and in other cities may be depended upon to make good this large sum, and possibly leave something besides for stockholders. The fact that so large an outlay can be safely made tells its own story of the popularity of base-ball.

FROM *THE NEW YORK TIMES*, APRIL 6, 1913
"Ebbets Field Opening Victory for Superbas"

Ebbets Field remains a martyr to Golden Age baseball, even to fans who hadn't yet been born when the ballyard was demolished in 1960. Charles Ebbets, owner of the Dodgers (also known as the Superbas, Robins, and Bridegrooms during their time in Brooklyn), opened the ballpark in 1913 with an exhibition game against the rival New York Yankees.

All the dreams that President Charley Ebbets of the Brooklyns has had for the past twenty years came true yesterday. The new home of the Dodgers, Ebbets Field, was jammed with a crowd of 30,000 people, while outside the big new stadium 5,000 more howled in disappointment because they couldn't get in. The occasion for all this hullabaloo was to see the Dodgers and the New York Americans in the opening game at the new field. Mr. Ebbets felt sorry for all those folks outside the gates, but he didn't let that interfere with his joy when his fine young ball team trounced the Yankees by a score of 3 to 2.

Mr. Ebbets should worry.

Everyone in Brooklyn and half the same numbers of New Yorkers flocked to the Bedford section and startled the natives, who had never believed that there were so many people in the world. The New Yorkers' interest was not only to see Brooklyn's new ball yard, but also to see what kind of team Frank Leroy Chance is going to mold out of the old Yankees.

Chance, who, as leader of the great Cubs a few years back, fought both Brooklyn and New York tooth and nail, got a great reception in a New York uniform. When he first stepped up to the plate a mighty cheer went up from all over the large stands and lasted for several minutes, while the Peerless Leader stood there cool and collected, waiting for Nap Rucker to shoot the ball at him.

It was a well-played game for so early in the season, and it can easily be seen that Manager Bill Dahlen has a better ball club than he has had for the past few seasons.

The day was full of gladness for everybody in Brooklyn, for, in beating Chance's team, Charles Montgomery Stengel and Jacob Stogie Daubert both clouted forth glorious home runs which so electrified the multitude that it drove away the chill of the snappy Spring ozone. Then to make the day complete, the combat developed a real, vibrating baseball thrill in the nature of a blow up by pitcher Frank S. Allen in the ninth inning, when the Yanks pushed over two runs and tied the count.

Then came the climax of Col. Ebbets's joy when his Dodgers went into the last half of the ninth and snatched the game out of the fire.

And Mr. Ebbets could ask for nothing fairer than that.

There was an abundance of pomp and ceremony about the opening of the new park. Early in the afternoon, thousands of people were waiting at the gates and the police had their hands full getting the people into the marble rotunda. They admitted the fans in small droves, squirming and pushing and trampling on each other's feet, and then locked the gates until they were in their seats. Then they opened the gates again and admitted another howling squad. It was slow work, but finally the park was jammed before playing time.

The inside of the park was a picture. The great stand of steel and concrete loomed high in the air, holding its admiring thousands. The upper and lower tiers of boxes held the galaxy of Brooklyn's youth and beauty embellished and intensified by a glorious display of Spring finery and gaudy colors.

The girls of Brooklyn never turned out to a ball game like this before, and it's too bad they never did, because, from now on they will always be considered a big feature of a ball game at the new park.

The day was made to order. It was one of the nicest Spring days the oldest inhabitants of Flatbush could remember. And the sky—no baseball opening description could be complete without giving the sky a few lines. It was the same glorious canopy of pale blue, arched from horizon to horizon and flecked here and there with filmy clouds of white, which looked like little puffs of smoke.

Honest and true, it was just like that.

Passing on from the sky, look over the baseball field, with its diamond of green and as smooth as a billiard table. Isn't it great? Sure! And the band played and never stopped. The air was full of music and gladness, and when the crowd got restless and began to yell "Play Ball," the first act on the programme was staged.

President Ebbets, with First Vice President Edward J. McKeever and Mrs. McKeever, left their box and walked across the park to deep centre field, where stands the big flagpole.

Some day a pennant may wave from the pole, but what's the use of starting an argument at a pleasant time like this?

Mrs. McKeever wore an emerald green silk coat with hat to match, and wasn't a bit afraid of walking across the field in white shoes. The band played "The Star Spangled Banner" while the Stars and Stripes were unfurled to the breeze, and then the Brooklyn team paraded back to the bench. President Ebbets led the parade, and the band played "Here Comes Your Daddy Now," which made the old Colonel grin from ear to ear.

The snap-shot brigade followed the parade over to the lower row of boxes back of first base, where Miss Genevieve Ebbets, the youngest daughter of the President, tossed out a nice new white ball to Bob Emslie, the umpire. Miss Ebbets threw the ball straight, and wore a gown of cerise and one of those great big hats which you don't like to sit behind.

Washington Park, Brooklyn. 1887. The Brooklyn Historical Society. *This park was the home of Brooklyn baseball from 1883 to 1915.*

Aerial View of Ebbets Field. Date unknown. The National Baseball Library, Cooperstown, New York. *The famous scoreboard, which featured local tailor Abe Stark's HIT SIGN—WIN SUIT advertisement, stood in right field.*

Why say, it was just like the ceremony at the opening of a world's fair or something like that. There's no denying the fact that when Mr. Ebbets stages one of these dedication affairs he is right there with the dignity and the glitter and the history making.

And—do you know that this baseball park is built upon historic ground? Yes siree, on this very place where Jake Daubert spilled his home run, the battle of Long Island was fought, years and years ago, and it was back in those wild times that a well-known baseball expression was coined. A Revolutionary soldier at that time remarked that the British could cover lots of ground, but they couldn't hit.

Well, the Yankees play at Ebbets Field again on Monday, and perhaps they'll square matters.

At a late hour last night President Ebbets was still separating the $10 and $5 bills, and said it sure did look like a big season.

Gay Talese

FROM *THE NEW YORK TIMES,* FEBRUARY 24, 1960

"Ebbets Field Goes on the Scrap Pile"

When the Dodgers left Brooklyn for Los Angeles before the 1958 season, plans were made to build the Ebbets Field Apartments on the land occupied by the ballpark. Its demolition left a hole in the heart of Brooklyn that's still felt today.

At Ebbets Field yesterday men swung sledge hammers, the dugout crumbled and an iron ball crashed like Pete Reiser against the wall. After forty-four years as the home of the Dodgers and a monument to daffiness, the park began to vanish in favor of a proposed 1,317-family middle-income housing project.

About 200 spectators, a brass band and some former Brooklyn Dodger players gathered to watch a two-ton iron ball hammer against this arena where, between 1913 and 1957, baseball was played in a manner never before imagined or recommended.

It was here that fly balls bounced off Babe Herman's head, and here the Dodger Symphony band stayed out of tune for two decades. It was here that Leo Durocher snarled, Hilda Chester cheered and everybody said "Wait till next year."

Here was where they worshipped the Duke and dozens of zany characters; and here is where a little lady always bought one seat for herself and one for her cat—a gray tabby that sat behind first base and slept.

It was here that a fan once exclaimed, "We got three on base"—and his neighbor asked, "Which base?"

The haphazard tradition of the Dodgers continued yesterday when somebody had the flag flying upside down in centerfield. It was not intentional, although this is an international sign of distress.

Those present yesterday were not distressed, but they were a bit nostalgic. Roy Campanella, at homeplate in a wheelchair, remembered that he played his last game here on Sept. 24, 1957. Tommy Holmes, Carl Erskine and the old Dodger catcher, Otto Miller (who caught the first Ebbets Field game on April 9, 1913), remained quiet as the iron ball came down like a thumping foul atop the dugout—and fell through, knocking off the telephone to the bullpen.

The band played "Auld Lang Syne," and Tex Richards, who was the Dodgers' public address announcer for thirty-two years, said, for the final time, "Ladies and gentlemen, now coming in to pitch for the Dodgers, No. 14, Ralph Branca."

There was cheering from the spectators and the workmen—and Branca, an insurance sales-man in a camel's hair coat, came out of the crowd and smiled.

Campanella was awarded his locker, his No. 39 uniform, and a pot full of Ebbets Field dirt dug up from behind homeplate.

Then the big crane headed with the speed of Ernie Lombardi into centerfield. When it reached the 376-foot mark, the workman swung back on this iron ball painted white to resemble a baseball. It came spinning toward the wall and, after a few shots, there was a hole the size of Hugh Casey.

It will take ten weeks to destroy Ebbets Field.

Ebbets Field Demolition. 1960.
UPI/The Bettmann Archive.

COLORPLATE 59

Mission Bench with Baseball Motif. Undated. Wood.
38^1/$_2$ x 45 x 22^1/$_2$ in. The Gladstone Collection of Baseball Art.

COLORPLATE 60

SILAS KOPF. *Baseball Marquetry Cabinet.* 1988.
East Indian laurel and walnut. 85 x 29^3/$_4$ x 18^1/$_2$ in.
The Gladstone Collection of Baseball Art.

185

COLORPLATE 61

Japanese Silk Banner. 1941–42.
42 x 30 in. The Gladstone Collection
of Baseball Art. *This banner
was awarded semiannually to
winners of a baseball championship
in occupied China.*

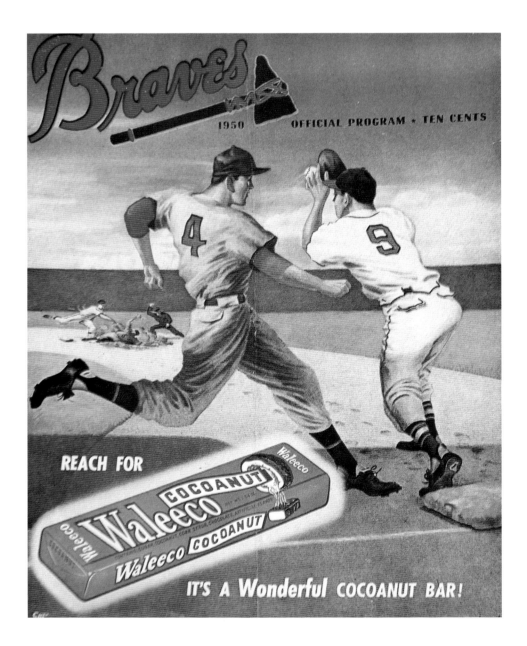

COLORPLATE 62

Boston Braves Program. 1950.
Transcendental Graphics.

COLORPLATE 63 *(opposite)*

History of Baseball Quilt. c. 1940.
Cotton. 96 x 62 in. The Gladstone
Collection of Baseball Art.

WAGNER, PITTSBURG

MAGIE, PHILA. NAT'L

PLANK, PHILA. AMER.

COLORPLATE 64 *(above, left)*

1909, T 206 Honus Wagner baseball card. $1\frac{1}{2}$ x $2\frac{5}{8}$ in.
Collection of Larry Fritsch, Stevens Point, Wisconsin.

COLORPLATE 65 *(above)*

1909, T 206 Sherry Magee baseball card. $1\frac{1}{2}$ x $2\frac{5}{8}$ in.
Collection of Larry Fritsch, Stevens Point, Wisconsin.

COLORPLATE 66 *(left)*

1909, T 206 Eddie Plank baseball card. $1\frac{1}{2}$ x $2\frac{5}{8}$ in.
Collection of Larry Fritsch, Stevens Point, Wisconsin.

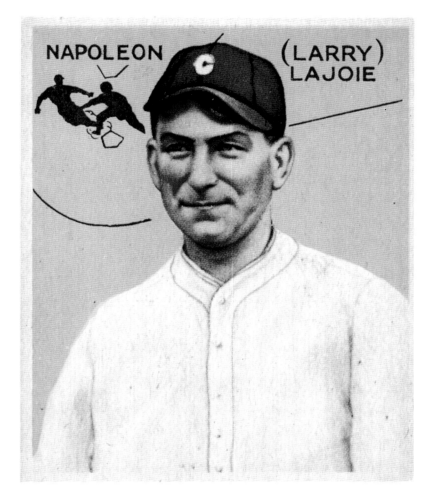

COLORPLATE 67

*1933, Goudey #106 Napoleon Lajoie
baseball card.* 2³/₈ x 2⁷/₈ in.
Collection of Larry Fritsch,
Stevens Point, Wisconsin.

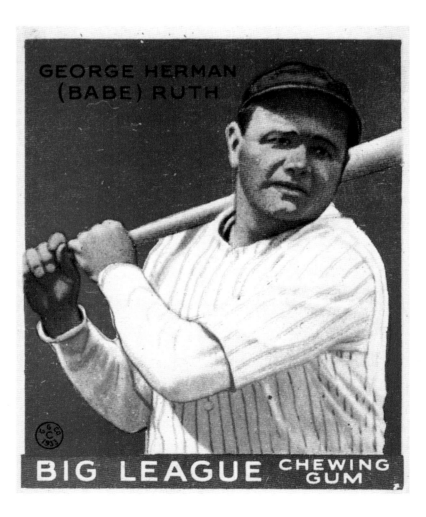

COLORPLATE 68

1933, Goudey Babe Ruth baseball card.
2³/₈ x 2⁷/₈ in. Collection of Larry Fritsch,
Stevens Point, Wisconsin.

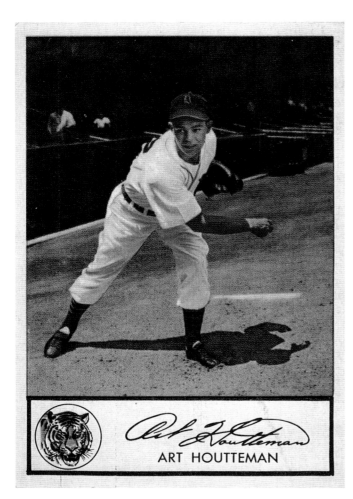

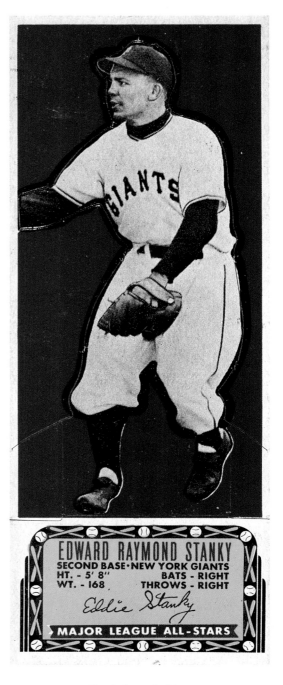

COLORPLATE 69 *(above left)*

1953, Glendale Meat Art Houtteman baseball card. 2⁵/8 x 3³/4 in. Collection of Larry Fritsch, Stevens Point, Wisconsin.

COLORPLATE 70 *(left)*

1952, Topps #311 Mickey Mantle baseball card. 2⁵/8 x 3³/4 in. Collection of Larry Fritsch, Stevens Point, Wisconsin.

COLORPLATE 71 *(above)*

1951, Topps Allstars Eddie Stanky baseball card. 2¹¹/16 x 5¹/4 in. Collection of Larry Fritsch, Stevens Point, Wisconsin.

COLORPLATE 72

MARILYNN GELFMAN. *PPF 61*. 1992.
Mixed media. 17 in. high; 10 in. diameter. Private collection.

COLORPLATE 73

Lance Richbourg. *Hobie Landrith.* 1983.
Oil on canvas. 37 x 68 in. Collection of Mrs. Monroe Meyerson.

Shibe Park, Philadelphia. Date unknown.
The National Baseball Library,
Cooperstown, New York.

Mike Bryan

FROM BASEBALL LIVES

"Joe Mooney"

If you know what it's like to maintain a house and a lawn, then you might imagine what it's like for a groundskeeper to keep a ballpark pristine and perfect despite the onslaught of rain, snow, blistering heat, and hundreds of thousands of house guests dropping garbage all over the place. If you can't imagine it, here's Joe Mooney's description.

IT'S A GORGEOUS DAY IN THE STANDS FORTY YARDS AWAY, BUT HE CHOOSES TO MEET IN A DINGY STORAGE ROOM AND SEATS HIMSELF ACROSS A FORMICA TABLE. A YOUNG KID COMES IN TO ASK HOW TO WORK A PAINT GUN. OTHER CREW MEMBERS ENTER AND HE ANSWERS ALL THIR QUESTIONS IN TEN WORDS OR LESS. HE IS BUILDING AND GROUNDS SUPERINTENDENT AT FENWAY PARK, AND EYES ME SUSPICIOUSLY.

It don't take an Einstein to put bolts into concrete and break out concrete with a jackhammer. That's the thing today: everybody wants to be an expert. They're all chiefs and nobody wants to be an Indian anymore. It's a way of life today. With the players it's the same way. The whole complex of living has changed.

   I'm here for eighteen years; before that, ten years at RFK Stadium in Washington, D.C. The crew size here depends on weather and other things. Sometimes it's thirty, sometimes it's forty, sometimes it's twelve. That's the grounds crew, maintenance, painting, everything. The guy who works here the longest is on the mound, Jim McCarthy. Forty-something years. He does the mound and home plate, and the watering when the team's on the road. I don't know if it's his *specialty*. He does it.

During the game I do everything. I walk the stadium, check and see if the restrooms are all right, check for broken water pipes. This and that. Anything. The easy days are a lot more common than the hard days. The crew don't tell you about when they just come in and sit around all day doing nothing.

The field is Marion bluegrass, which is a good grass for this part of the country all the way down to southern Pennsylvania, Maryland; below that you might move into Bermuda. Various spots get worn and we re-sod during the year. Bluegrass goes dormant in the winter; it's often under snow, ice, whatever. You're in New England, remember.

The infield and baselines are a sandy soil mixed with Turface, which we cut in two or three times a year. Otherwise, just good topsoil everywhere. Anytime the team goes on the road we re-level the dirt part of infield, especially at the edge of the infield and outfield grass, otherwise they get a lip. We cut the grass every day. It's an inch in the infield. And the clay around the plate and on the mound has to be good. They have a lot of trouble in Florida because the clay's not good enough, unless it's shipped in. It has to be *clay*.

Ninety percent of your people think, "Oh gee, you're off all the time, the whole winter. You've got a hell of a job." They think we have like government jobs where we don't work half the time and they have to support us. They don't know all the big maintenance jobs are off-season, a lot of concrete work. Right now we're replacing seats. In mid-August we make a list and set priorities, and they know how much money they want spent and we go by that when we decide in September. Nine million things to do in an old ballpark.

Right now the engineers are looking at "plan three": new screen behind home plate, new press box, dining room, other stuff. Plus they're going around to evaluate and see how much to spend to keep up Fenway Park. Is it worth it? How long will the concrete and everything last? But it's not falling down! It's not even close to that. This park's always been well maintained. The Red Sox have always spent money to keep it up and keep it clean. You can find modern equipment in this ballpark you can't find in new ones. The offices have the first-class computers. But just like anything else—cars or bodies—you can only get so many years out of something.

There's not a groundskeeper on earth that won any games for anybody. The field actually has nothing to do with the ball game. You see the kids on the sandlots, the minor leagues, city-owned fields—the field is nothing. Nobody does nothing out there but the players themselves between the lines. They throw the ball, they catch the ball, they hit the ball. That's the secret of the game. I hear these experts say they done this and that, I haven't seen it done.

It's the same thing with guys you see bless themselves before they bat. The guy on the mound, he could be a Catholic, too. What the hell? What if they *both* bless themselves?

I don't even go near the players. Never did, never will. I know them very little. Most people in my position are hero-worshippers. Not me. They're no better than you, me, or anyone else. They put their pants on the same way. But does it happen? With twenty-six big-league clubs, I'll guarantee it with twenty-four of them. People go gaga over the players. I pitched batting practice for years in Minneapolis; Washington, too. People ask me who's the greatest player I've ever seen. How can you say who's the greatest? Well, you might say Mickey Mantle except for his leg, but he had that leg. I personally have never seen a better hitter than Ted Williams. Wade Boggs here today: he's a tremendous hitter, and he's worked at it.

I never get involved with the other departments. I got enough of my own business without minding other people's business. They're paying people to run other things. I think they're qualified. John McNamara does a hell of a job and proved it in '86 with the American League pennant. Now a few things go bad and he's a bum [and was fired shortly afterward]. That's how the public is, so why get all shook up about it?

What do I want to go into another ballpark for? I wouldn't go across the street to watch a game. They don't play the game like I like it played. Back in Scranton, Pennsylvania, we had a team that won seventy-two straight games. Red Sox used to own the Scranton franchise. I was an infielder, but my favorite sport was college football.

Boston? I couldn't tell you how many games they're out now, five or fifteen. I watched games for years in Minneapolis in '58, '59, but I don't watch anymore.

Bob Wood

FROM DODGER DOGS TO FENWAY FRANKS

"Just Another Dome—Only Worse"

During the summer of 1985, junior high school teacher Bob Wood drove across America, visiting every major league ballpark. His evaluation of the Astrodome, home of the Houston Astros and hailed as "the Eighth Wonder of the World" during its unveiling, follows.

Aluminum bats are a curse to baseball. They belong on the end of a lightning rod or in a golf bag, not in an on-deck circle. Their rubber handles are too comfortable. Names on 'em are of a company not a ball player. They can't be flame treated, they never break. Worst of all, they sound sissyish. A "ping" instead of a "crack" has taken over Little League and high school practice fields. They've tainted baseball at its most important levels.

Bats aren't the only thing changing—all of baseball is. It's being invaded by technological efficiency. Aluminum bats, plastic grass, and domes are symbols of a new major league age. . . . Players are different, their values aren't the same. A good contract, lots of bucks, and free agency seem to be today's priority issues. Not "how on earth" to touch a Nolan Ryan fastball. Getting to the Series and beating the Yanks isn't enough incentive anymore. Now contracts are locked into how many folks are in the ballpark when you pitch or if you can get to the All-Star break without crashing on the 21-day DL. And the big payoff isn't that Series ring, it's more green. Baseball's just not as pure as it used to be.

I guess it's only natural, if ball players aren't the same that the ballparks aren't either. They're not ballparks anymore; the new ones are multipurpose stadiums. Roomy and comfortable, their biggest concern's no longer baseball, it's let's see how many sports we can fit inside. And let's do it as technologically efficiently as possible. Plastic chairs, plastic food, but most of all plastic grass has laid its roots. Durable and cheap, artificial turf has found a home. If a stadium is built today, odds are it'll have a plastic floor. That's just not right. Baseballs belong on grass, not skipping along some synthetic tablecloth. Half the spell of a ballpark is that first glimpse of the turf. Its fresh fragrance after a soft summer rain, the cut, the texture are locked into the very spirit of the place. To replace it with a sheet of plastic is criminal. It's like dining at Denny's on Thanksgiving or putting up a silver aluminum tree for Christmas. Tradition is ruined. Baseball becomes just another modern sport.

Seattle was my introduction to artificial baseball. My Midwest ballparks—Chicago's, Milwaukee's, and Detroit's—are as traditional as turkey on turkey day. But Seattle introduced me to the horrors of the ultramodern game. Not only did it provide an intro to synthetic grass, but it also showed me baseball's ultimate villain—THE DOME! For five summers now I've suffered through domed baseball. And unfortunately become somewhat of an indoor baseball expert. Domes destroy the notion that baseballs are meant to float high up into a blue sky and that sunshine is beautiful. In regions where Mother Nature won't allow the game to be played normally, domes have attempted to make it work. They've failed . . . miserably.

Baseball needs Mother Nature. It doesn't matter where—every climate offers something positive to the game. If a ball game is slow, sunshine and blue skies make the afternoon an enjoyable one. Sometimes in April or October cold biting rain pelts the stands. Not enough to call a game, it makes sitting there miserable. If I brave one of those, I feel significant. I tell myself only a real fan would've stayed all nine innings. Pride and hot coffee get me through. In a dome the excitement, the challenges vanish. No hot sunny days, no starry, starry nights. Like lukewarm bathwater, a dome is safe but boring. Instead of nature's surprises, year-round 72.8 degrees sterilizes baseball. . . .

Comiskey Park, Chicago. c. 1965. The National Baseball Library, Cooperstown, New York. *The home of the White Sox and baseball's first "exploding" scoreboard stood until 1990, the season before the Sox moved to a new Comisky Park built across the street.*

Going to Houston, I had sought to keep an open mind. I tried to forget that it was the Astrodome where that first polyseed for the first polyfloor was planted. That it was the first ballpark ever to kick out Mother Nature. I even tried to forget that the Texas dome was related to my retarded dome in Seattle. I promised myself I'd be objective. That I'd look at the bright side of Astro world. After baking in Arlington's oven, I figured I was ready for a dome. Not aluminum bats, not plastic grass, certainly not prima-donna clause-covered contracts, but maybe a dome.

Instead what I found was awful. Astro world convinced me of what I'd suspected all along. Baseball will never adapt to the computer age. Sophisticated equipment, faster playing surfaces, even fake cooler temperatures don't have a role. Baseball's almost oriental in its philosophy. Its beauty is found in a reflection of the past, not in a high-tech world of efficiency. And it must have Mother Nature. To feel right, it needs all the good and bad she has to offer. Sun, sky, even heat have to be around.

With outdoors removed from the dome, the game's left to the mercy of man and his man-made Astro things. For it to be anything better than dull, everything must perform perfectly. And even if it does, that's no assurance that indoor baseball will survive. It only means the place won't feel a total disaster. Disaster is a good dome description. In every traditional offering, the place is either too little or too much. It never lets baseball be itself.

At the top of the "too much" category is that obsession with its Astro color scheme. Everywhere inside those same colors flash their ugly faces. Uniforms, plastic seats, and, most revolting, on the scoreboard. Instead of baseball I was ready for Barnum and Bailey to bring in some circus acts.

Too little is almost as bad. Sleepwalking employees contrast with the loud colors. All night long in zombieville, they acted as though they didn't even know the temperature had fallen below 90 degrees. Fans followed their lead and spent most of the game in a trance. Rounds of applause were as wild and crazy as those at a funeral home. Lunacy and death! Together they create a strange, strange mood. An atmosphere for baseball it is not.

And still there is that plastic playing surface. Uglier even than the streets that lead into the stadium's potholed parking lot, it's the single biggest reason why the place has such a dull, dark, and dreary tone.

Not long ago Houston's Astrodome was considered a world wonder. People marveled at the brilliance of man. It was amazing how indoors could be made as good or better than the real thing. The Astrodome was the greatest discovery since the aluminum bat. Now that its personality has crystallized, its true character has emerged. And the result—a stadium designed and maintained with all the tactfulness of a *National Enquirer* headline story. To the baseball world Houston's tomb provides a new low in charisma, a bottom-of-the-ballpark barrel.

The Astrodome does, however, offer one single saving grace. Rejoice Seattle fans! There actually exists a place on earth that can make a night at the Kingdome seem natural.

Roger Angell

FROM SEASON TICKET

"Up at the Hall"

If Cooperstown, New York, isn't really the true birthplace of the game of baseball, then it should be. Go there in the dead of winter, visit the Hall of Fame, and the game is still aglow amidst the artifacts, the photographs, and the memories enshrined therein. Walk down Main Street, past the Short Stop Restaurant and Doubleday Field, and you'll forget that your team spent most of last season languishing in fifth place. As Roger Angell shows in his essay you'll remember why you love the game.

Summer 1987

Here we are, and here it all is for us: already too much to remember. Here's a meerschaum pipe presented to Cy Young by his Red Sox teammates after his perfect game in 1904. Here are Shoeless Joe Jackson's shoes. Here's a life-size statue of Ted Williams, beautifully done in basswood; Ted is just finishing his swing, and his eyes are following the flight of the ball, into the right-field stands again. Here is John McGraw's little black mitt, from the days when he played third base for the old Orioles; a blob of licorice, by the looks of it, or perhaps a small flattened animal, dead on the highway. Here's a ball signed by seventeen-year-old Willie McCovey and his teammates on the 1955 Class D Sandersville (Georgia) club—Stretch's first address in organized ball—and over *here* is a ball from a June 14, 1870, game between Cincinnati and the Brooklyn Atlantics; Brooklyn won, snapping the Red Stockings' astounding winning streak of two full years. Babe Ruth, in a floor-to-ceiling photomural, sits behind the wheel of an open touring car, with his manager, little Miller Huggins, almost hidden beside him. The Babe is wearing driving gauntlets, a cap, a fur-collared coat, and a sullen, assured look: Out of the way, world! Let's hum a song or two (from the sheet music for "Home Run Bill" or "The Marquard Glide" or "That Baseball Rag") while we think about some intrepid barnstormers of the game: the Chicago White Sox arrayed in front of the Egyptian Pyramids in 1889; King George V (in a derby) gravely inspecting a visiting American exhibition squad (in uniforms and spikes) in 1913; and shipboard high jinks by the members of a 1931 team headed for Japan (Mickey Cochrane is sporting white-and-tan wingtips). The 1935 Negro League Pittsburgh Crawfords were travellers, too; their blurry team photograph has them lined up, in smiles and baggy uniforms, in front of their dusty, streamlined team bus. Over here are some all-time minor-league records for us to think about: Ron Necciai pitched a no-hitter for the Appalachian League's Bristol Twins in 1952 and struck out all twenty-seven batters in the process; and Joe Wilhoit hit safely in sixty-nine consecutive games for the Wichita Wolves in

1919. Wilhoit was on his way down by then, after four undistinguished wartime seasons with four different big-league clubs, but Necciai's feat won him an immediate starting spot with the Pittsburgh Pirates—and a lifetime one-season 1–6 record in the majors, with a 7.08 earned-run average. Hard lines, but another kid made more of *his* chances after hitting safely in sixty-one consecutive games with the San Francisco Seals in 1933: Joe DiMaggio. . . .

What about bats? Pete Rose had a nearly knobless bat, with six separate strips of tape on the handle—or at least that's what he swung when he rapped out his four-thousandth hit (he was with the Expos then), against the Phillies, in 1984. Probably he wouldn't have done so well with Babe Ruth's thick-waisted model, or with Home Run Baker's mighty mace. Maybe weight isn't what matters: here's Jim Bottomley's modest-looking bat lying on its side in a case—the bat he used in a September 16, 1924 game, when he went six for six against the Dodgers (Sunny Jim played for the Cardinals, or course) and batted in twelve runs. I won't forget *that*, I'm sure, but here in the World Series section (there is a cutout silhouette of Joe Rudi making that beautiful catch up against the wall in 1974: I was there!) some text tells us that the Tigers batted .455 against the Padres' starting pitchers in the 1984 Series—and how in the world could I have forgotten that, now that I know forever that Cy Young's 1954 Ohio license plate was "C-511-Y" (Cy won five hundred and eleven games, lifetime) and that Mrs. Lou Gehrig's New York plate for 1942 (Lou had died the year before) was "1-LG"?

This clotted flow is an inadequate representation of the National Baseball Hall of Fame and Museum in Cooperstown, but it is perhaps a good tissue sample of one man's brain taken after a couple of hours in the marvelous place. What has been left out so far is the fans themselves—dozens and scores and hundreds of them, arrayed throughout the four floors of the modest Georgian edifice on any summer afternoon, with wives (or husbands) and kids and grandfathers and toddlers in tow, and all of them talking baseball a mile a minute: "Pop, look at *this!* Here's Roger Clemens' cap and his gloves and his shoes he wore on the day he struck out all those guys last year—you know, that twenty-strikeout game?" and "Ralph Kiner led the National League in home runs his first *seven* years running—how do you like that, honey!" and "Alison! Alison-n-n! Has anybody seen Alison?" I have done some museum time in my day—if I had to compare the Hall with any other museum in the world it would be the Victoria and Albert, in London—but I can't recollect a more willing and enthusiastic culture-crawl any-

The National Baseball Hall of Fame and Museum. The National Baseball Library, Cooperstown, New York.

Architect's Rendering of Oriole Park at Camden Yards, Baltimore. 1987. HOK Sports Facilities Group. *Oriole Park at Camden Yards, which opened for the 1992 season, began a trend of "retro-parks," which combined the charm of Golden Age ballyards with state-of-the-art amenities. Similar ballparks were soon planned in Texas and Cleveland.*

where. It took me a little while to dope this out, and the answer, it became clear, is geographical. The Hall of Fame draws a quarter of a million visitors every year—a total that cannot be fashioned out of drop-in locals from Cooperstown (pop. 2,300), plus a handful of idle music lovers, up for the nearby Glimmerglass Opera summer season, and a few busloads of kids from day camps scattered along adjoining Otsego Lake. (There are other tourist attractions in town as well: the Farmers' Museum and Fenimore House, the latter of which displays some furnishings of the eponymous and tireless non-Cleveland Indian publicist James Fenimore Cooper.) Cooperstown is an inviting little village, with flowering window baskets set out in front of its dignified old brick-front stores, but it isn't near anyplace else, unless you count Cobleskill or Cazenovia. From New York City, it's three hours up the New York Thruway and another hour out west of Albany before you hit the winding back-country road that takes you thirty miles to the lake and the town. Folks who come to the Hall are pilgrims, then; they want to be there, and most of the visitors I talked to during a couple of recent stays told me they had planned their trip more than a year before. The place is a shrine. . . .

Most of us fans fall in love with baseball when we are children, and those who come aboard as adults often do so in a rush of affection and attachment to a local team that has begun to win. These infatuations are ferociously battered and eroded by various forces—by the schlocky macho posturing and gossip and exaggerations of the media; by the failure of many players to live up to our expectations for them, both on the field and off the field; and, most of all, by the wearisome, heartbreaking difficulty of the sport, which inexorably throws down last year's champions, exposes rookie marvels as disappointing journeymen, and turns lithe young stars into straining old men, all in a very short space of time. Baseball is absorbing and sometimes thrilling, but it is also unrelenting; it is rarely pure fun for any of us, players or fans, for very long. Except at Cooperstown. The artifacts and exhibits in the Hall remind us, vividly and with feeling, of our hopes for bygone seasons and teams and players. Memories are jogged, even jolted; colors become brighter, and we laugh or sigh, remembering good times gone by. But the Hall of Famers themselves, with their plaques and pictures and citations, are the heart of something larger, for they tell us that there exists a handful of baseball players—it comes out to a bit over one percent of the thirteen thousand-odd men who have ever played major-league ball—who really did come close to our expectations. They played so well and so long, succeeding eventually at this almost impossible game, that we can think of them as something more useful than gods or heroes. We know they are there, tucked away up-country and in the back of our minds: old men, and younger ones on the way, who prove and sustain the elegance of our baseball dreams.

Sixth Inning:

THE VIEW FROM THE STANDS

There is no such thing as the common fan. Baseball has been more than just a game to a crowd of such great diversity that it includes a social philosopher, presidents of both Yale University and the United States of America, and one of Hollywood's most beloved actors. Here, they discuss the game's importance to both themselves and society as a whole.

Jacques Barzun

FROM GOD'S COUNTRY AND MINE

"Summer, or Sitting and Thinking"

Was a more keen observation of the American mind ever made than the oft-quoted opening line of this passage?

Whoever wants to know the heart and mind of America had better learn baseball, the rules and realities of the game—and do it by watching first some high school or small-town teams. The big league games are too fast for the beginner and the newspapers don't help. To read them with profit you have to know a language that comes easy only after philosophy has taught you to judge practice. Here is scholarship that takes effort on the part of the outsider, but it is so bred into the native that it never becomes a dreary round of technicalities. The wonderful purging of the passions that we all experienced in the fall of '51, the despair groaned out over the fate of the Dodgers, from whom the league pennant was snatched at the last minute, give us some idea of what Greek tragedy was like. Baseball *is* Greek in being national, heroic, and broken up in the rivalries of city-states. How sad that Europe knows nothing like it! Its Olympics generate anger, not unity, and its interstate politics follow no rules that a people can grasp. At least Americans understand baseball, the true realm of clear ideas.

That baseball fitly expresses the powers of the nation's mind and body is a merit separate from the glory of being the most active, agile, varied, articulate, and brainy of all group games. It is of and for our century. Tennis belongs to the individualistic past—a hero, or at most a pair of friends or lovers, against the world. The idea of baseball is a team, an outfit, a section, a gang, a union, a cell, a commando squad—in short, a twentieth-century setup of opposite numbers.

Baseball takes its mystic nine and scatters them wide. A kind of individualism thereby returns, but it is limited—eternal vigilance is the price of victory. Just because they're far apart, the outfield can't dream or play she-loves-me-not with daisies. The infield is like a steel net held in the hands of the catcher. He is the psychologist and historian for the staff—or else his signals will give the opposition hits. The value of his headpiece is shown by the ironmongery worn to protect it. The pitcher, on the other hand, is the wayward man of genius, whom others will direct. They will expect nothing from him but virtuosity. He is surrounded no doubt by mere talent, unless one excepts that transplanted acrobat, the shortstop. What a brilliant invention is his role despite its exposure to ludicrous lapses! One man to each base, and then the free lance, the trouble shooter, the movable feast for the eyes, whose motion animates the whole foreground.

The rules keep pace with this imaginative creation so rich in allusions to real life. How excellent, for instance, that a foul tip muffed by the catcher gives the batter another chance. It is the recognition of Chance that knows no argument. But on the other hand, how wise and just that the third strike must not be dropped. This points to the fact that near the end of any struggle life asks for more than is needful in order to clinch success. A victory has to be won, not snatched. We find also our American innocence in calling "World Series" the annual games between the winners in each big league. The world doesn't know or care and couldn't compete if it wanted to, but since it's us children having fun, why, the world is our stage. I said

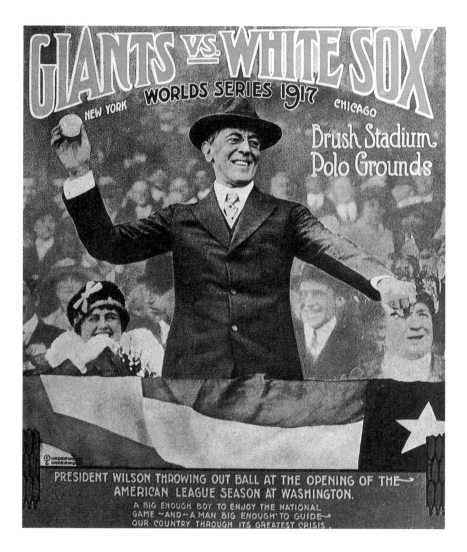

1917 World Series Program Cover. The National Baseball Library, Cooperstown, New York. *The caption on the lower cover calls President Woodrow Wilson "a big enough boy to enjoy the national game—and—a man big enough to guide our country through its greatest crisis."*

baseball was Greek. Is there not a poetic symbol in the new meaning—our meaning—of "Ruth hits Homer"?

Once the crack of the bat has sent the ball skimming left of second between the infielder's legs, six men converge or distend their defense to keep the runner from advancing along the prescribed path. The ball is not the center of interest as in those vulgar predatory games like football, basketball, and polo. Man running is the force to be contained. His getting to first or second base starts a capitalization dreadful to think of: every hit pushes him on. Bases full and a homer make four runs, while the defenders, helpless without the magic power of the ball lying over the fence, cry out their anguish and dig up the sod with their spikes.

But fate is controlled by the rules. Opportunity swings from one side to the other because innings alternate quickly, keep up spirit in the players, interest in the beholders. So does the profusion of different acts to be performed—pitching, throwing, catching, batting, running, stealing, sliding, signaling. Blows are similarly varied. Flies, Texas Leaguers, grounders, baseline fouls—praise God the human neck is a universal joint! And there is no set pace. Under the hot sun, the minutes creep as a deliberate pitcher tries his feints and curves for three strikes called, or conversely walks a threatening batter. But the batter is not invariably a tailor's dummy. In a hundredth of a second there may be a hissing rocket down right field, a cloud of dust over first base—the bleachers all a-yell—a double play, and the other side up to bat.

Accuracy and speed, the practiced eye and hefty arm, the mind to take in and readjust to the unexpected, the possession of more than one talent and the willingness to work in harness without special orders—these are the American virtues that shine in baseball. There has never been a good player who was dumb. Beef and bulk and mere endurance count for little, judgment and daring for much. Baseball is among group games played with a ball what fencing is to games of combat. But being spread out, baseball has something sociable and friendly about it that I especially love. It is graphic and choreographic. The ball is not shuttling in a confined space, as in tennis. Nor does baseball go to the other extreme of solitary whanging and counting stopped on the brink of pointlessness, like golf. Baseball is a kind of collective chess with arms and legs in full play under sunlight.

How adaptable, too! Three kids in a back yard are enough to create the same quality of drama. All of us in our tennis days have pounded balls with a racket against a wall, for practice. But that is nothing compared with batting in an empty lot, or catching at twilight, with a fella who'll let you use his mitt when your palms get too raw. Every part of baseball equipment is inherently attractive and of a most enchanting functionalism. A man cannot have too much leather about him; and a catcher's mitt is just the right amount for one hand. It's too bad the chest protector and shinpads are so hot and at a distance so like corrugated cardboard. Otherwise, the team is elegance itself in its striped knee breeches and loose shirts, colored stockings and peaked caps. Except for brief moments of sliding, you can see them all in one eyeful, unlike the muddy hecatombs of football. To watch a football game is to be in prolonged neurotic doubt as to what you're seeing. It's more like an emergency happening at a distance than a game. I don't wonder the spectators take to drink. Who has ever seen a baseball fan drinking within the meaning of the act? He wants all his senses sharp and clear, his eyesight above all. He gulps down soda pop, which is a harmless way of replenishing his energy by the ingestion of sugar diluted in water and colored pink.

Happy the man in the bleachers. He is enjoying the spectacle that the gods on Olympus contrived only with difficulty when they sent Helen to Troy and picked their teams. And the gods missed the fun of doing this by catching a bat near the narrow end and measuring hand over hand for first pick. In Troy, New York, the game scheduled for 2 P.M. will break no bones, yet it will be a real fight between Southpaw Dick and Red Larsen. For those whom civilized play doesn't fully satisfy, there will be provided a scapegoat in a blue suit—the umpire, yellproof and even-handed as justice, which he demonstrates with outstretched arms when calling "Safe!"

And the next day in the paper: learned comment, statistical summaries, and the verbal imagery of meta-euphoric experts. In the face of so much joy, one can only ask, Were you there when Dogface Joe parked the pellet beyond the pale?

Franklin D. Roosevelt

The "Green Light" Letter

One American, a president of the United States no less, shared his views on the importance of the game with Judge Kenesaw Mountain Landis after the commissioner offered to suspend play during World War II. Franklin Delano Roosevelt responded with the loudest "Play Ball!" ever heard.

THE WHITE HOUSE
WASHINGTON

January 15, 1942.

My dear Judge:—

Thank you for yours of January fourteenth. As you will, of course, realize the final decision about the baseball season must rest with you and the Baseball Club owners— so what I am going to say is solely a personal and not an official point of view.

I honestly feel that it would be best for the country to keep baseball going. There will be fewer people unemployed and everybody will work longer hours and harder than ever before.

And that means that they ought to have a chance for recreation and for taking their minds off their work even more than before.

Baseball provides a recreation which does not last over two hours or two hours and a half, and which can be got for very little cost. And, incidentally, I hope that night games can be extended because it gives an opportunity to the day shift to see a game occasionally.

President Franklin D. Roosevelt. c. 1940. UPI/The Bettmann Archive. *Roosevelt, who asked that baseball be played despite the outbreak of World War II, tosses out the ceremonial first pitch at Washington's Griffith Stadium.*

As to the players themselves, I know you agree with me that individual players who are of active military or naval age should go, without question, into the services. Even if the actual quality of the teams is lowered by the greater use of older players, this will not dampen the popularity of the sport. Of course, if any individual has some particular aptitude in a trade or profession, he ought to serve the Government. That, however, is a matter which I know you can handle with complete justice.

Here is another way of looking at it—if 300 teams use 5,000 or 6,000 players, these players are a definite recreational asset to at least 20,000,000 of their fellow citizens— and that in my judgment is thoroughly worthwhile.

With every best wish,

Very sincerely yours,

Franklin D. Roosevelt

Hon. Kenesaw M. Landis,
333 North Michigan Avenue,
Chicago,
Illinois.

Donald Hall

"Baseball and the Meaning of Life"

Some may not think that baseball has anything to do with the meaning of life; Donald Hall knows better.

———————————

I

Professor McCormick's suggestion is surely far-fetched. Although black-suited umpires may remind him of warlocks, although the pitcher's motion mimics dubious rituals, we must resist the suggestion that baseball retains elements of the Old Religion. We may admit the existence of "Seasonal Parallels" without lending credence to his speculations on the shape of home plate.

For baseball dies into the October ground as leaves fall, obscuring base path and pitcher's mound, littering empty dugouts and bullpens, flitting like spooked grounders over second base into the stiffening outfield grass. November rain expunges lime-powder foul lines from Centerville's Little League Park to Yankee Stadium, from Yakima to Bangor, from Key West to Iron Mountain. Soon in the north a colder powder, no less white, freezes diamond and foul territory together into an egalitarian alabaster plain below the cold green ranks of box, grandstand, and bleacher. The old game waits under the white; deeper than frozen grass, down at the frost line it waits . . .

. . . To return when the birds return. It starts to wake in the south where it had never quite stopped, where winter is a doze of hibernation interrupted by sleepy staggering momentary wakenings, like bears or skunks in a northern thaw. The game wakes gradually, gathering vigor to itself as the days lengthen late in February and grow warmer; old muscles grow limber, young arms throw strong and wild, legs pivot and leap, bodies hurtle into bright bases SAFE. . . . Clogged vein systems, in veteran oaks and left-fielders both, unstop themselves, putting forth leaves and line drives in Florida's March. Migrating North with the swallows, baseball and the grass's first green enter Cleveland, Kansas City, Boston. . . .

Ruth Visits the Bush League. April 1948. Yale Athletics Department. *During a ceremony at Yale University, Babe Ruth presents a manuscript of his autobiography to George Bush, the slick-fielding, light-hitting first baseman who would later serve as president of the United States. Ruth, fighting a losing battle against cancer, died four months after this photograph was taken.*

Silly he may be, but on the whole we sympathize with Professor McCormick's imaginative anthropology (*The Bat and the Wand*, Cooperstown: A. Doubleday, no date). At least we share the intuition that connects baseball with the meaning of life.

2

April baseball is tentative, exploratory, daring and timid together, poking a quivering finger into the risen year. May strengthens, sure-footed now, turning night into bright green day, springing with young manhood's energy and vanity toward the twilights of high summer. In June the animal-plant, full-leaved and muscled with maturity, invites us to settle secure for a season. We arrive at the ballpark early. The ballplayers have been here for hours, for batting practice and pepper and shagging outfield flies, as coaches with fungoes bang balls at the shins of shortstops, or raise cans of corn to the shallow outfield, or strike line drives off outfield walls and corners. We arrive and settle with score cards and Crackerjack and peanuts and Schlitz and hot dogs. There is a rasp in our voice, there is glory in our infant heart, there is mustard on our T-shirt.

While most of the players drink coffee in the locker room, smoke cigarettes, and sign baseballs, one or two wander on the grass in front of the dugouts. They want to be alone. Or, on the other hand, they want to sign autographs for kids or flirt with girls wearing jeans as tight as their own double-knits. Of the twenty-five players on the roster, these loners number themselves among the least active, though each of them knows that if he played every day . . . Most are young; a few show gray in the beard they will not shave until after the game—utility men, bullpen catchers, pinch hitters.

Then the tunnel disgorges three young men in bright suits carrying gloves, then two more, then six. "Play catch?" one says to another. They sort themselves by twos, throwing baseballs hard at each other without effort, drawing ruler-straight lines like chalk stripes between them. The soft pock of caught balls sounds in attentive ears.

The bullpen squad consists of a coach, a catcher, two long men, and two or three short men; they amble with fabulous unconcern, chewing as slowly as prize Holsteins, down the foul lines toward their condominium in right field. The ninth inning's fastballing superstar ace-relief man is not among them but is back in the trainer's room lying flat on his back, reading *Swann's Way* or *Looney Tunes*, waiting to trot his urgent trot from dugout to bullpen at the start of the eighth, the game 1–1, the one-man cavalry alerted to the threat of ambush at the mountain pass.

Anticipating cavalry, the organist assaults the score of the "Star-Spangled Banner," which we attempt to sing because of the fierce joy that fills us and threatens to choke our throats unless we loosen a joyful noise. Then we chew the song's ending and lean forward to watch the young men assume the field in their vain uniforms, to hear "Play ball," to allow the game's dance to receive our beings into its rhythms for two hours or three and then, in late afternoon, to release us again into the rubble of random streets.

Ah, the game! The game!

But what of the meaning of life . . .

3

Baseball connects American males with each other, not only through bleacher friendships and neighbor loyalties, not only through barroom fights but, most importantly, through generations. When you are small, you may not discuss politics or union dues or profit margins with your father's cigar-smoking friends when your father has gone out for a six-pack, but you may discuss baseball. It is all you have in common because your father's friend does not wish to discuss the assistant principal or Alice Bisbee Morgan. About the season's moment you know as much as he does; both of you may shake your heads over Lefty's wildness or the rookie who was called out last Saturday when he tried to steal home with two out in the ninth inning and his team down by one.

And you learn your first lessons of the rainbow arc all living makes but that baseball exaggerates. For when you are in sixth grade, the rook has fuzz on his face and throws to the wrong base; before you leave junior high school, he is a seasoned regular, his body filled out, his jowl rippled with tobacco; when you graduate from high school, he is a grizzled veteran—even if

The Brett Brothers. The National Baseball Library, Cooperstown, New York. *Ken last pitched for the Kansas City Royals in 1981, and retired with a career record of 83 wins and 85 losses. George, who reached the 3,000-hit milestone in September 1992, seems a sure bet for induction into the Hall of Fame.*

you are not certain what *grizzled* means. In a few years the green shoot becomes the withered stalk, and you learn the shape of the hill all beings travel down.

So Carl Yastrzemski enters his forty-second year. So Wilver Stargell's bones are stiff. While George Brett climbs the glorious mountain of his prime, all gut and muscle, his brother Ken watches with admiration and irony from the shadows of his quick sundown; Ken started the All Star game for the National League in 1974, his record thirteen and two, the lithe left arm bending sliders to catch the black—unbeatable, impervious, in his high stride hitting home runs from the ninth position. His brother George played AAA that year. That year somebody asked Ken Brett, "Why don't you play outfield when you're not pitching?" He smiled from his pleasant height, "Because they do not have that much money in Pittsburgh."

In 1980 Ken was released by the Dodgers and later signed on with George's Kansas City as a long man in the bullpen. This year or next he will begin to make "The Adjustment," as the players call it, when he leaves forever the game he doubtless began at the age of seven or eight. The light grows pale on the older players but never dwindles entirely away. . . . I remember Edd Roush, batting champion of 1917, ancient and glorious at an old-timer's game in 1975. Smokey Joe Wood, amazing fastballer of the 1912 Red Sox, signed autographs in Boston at a collector's convention in 1980.

Let it be. Players age, and baseball changes, as veterans slide off by way of jets to Japan instead of buses to Spokane. Baseball changes and we wish it never to change. Yet we know that inside the ball, be it horsehide or cowhide, the universe remains unaltered. Even if the moguls, twenty years from now, manage to move the game indoors and schedule twelve months a year, the seasons will remain implicit, like the lives of the players. Grow-lights do not legislate winter away; if the whole sport emigrates to Japan, baseball will remain a Zen garden.

For, surely, as Dr. McCormick fails to remind us, baseball sets off the meaning of life precisely because it is pure of meaning. As the ripples in the sand (in the Kyoto garden) organize and formalize the dust which is dust, so the diamonds and rituals of baseball create an elegant, trivial, enchanted grid on which our suffering, shapeless, sinful day leans for the momentary grace of order.

James Cagney
FROM CAGNEY BY CAGNEY

One of baseball's unique qualities is its ability to draw fans from all geographic locations and economic and social backgrounds. In his 1976 autobiography, legendary Hollywood actor James Cagney recalls not only his early love of baseball and his "reverence" for his childhood idols, but the way the game was intertwined with his rough, sometimes tragically violent upbringing on Manhattan's east side. And isn't it perfect that Cagney, the quintessential movie tough guy, was a catcher?

I returned to the Army and Columbia, but with war's end and the birth of Jeannie, the need to keep the family exchequer in good shape came back as strongly as ever. As respite from my various jobs, I played a lot of baseball on Sundays with the Nut Club, and this was an endeavor right in harmony with the times. In those days our idols weren't movie stars or ham politicians. We revered the great men of baseball, and how wonderful those names sound even now all these years after: John McGraw, Christy Mathewson, Hooks Wiltse, Larry Doyle, Fred Merkel, Roger Bresnahan, and Art Fletcher! Not long ago my wife was going through some

Christy Mathewson. c. 1910. The National Baseball Library, Cooperstown, New York. *Mathewson was a Hall of Fame pitcher and an idol to young New Yorkers like James Cagney: "We revered the great men of baseball, and how wonderful those names sound even now all these years after. . . ."*

old trunks and found the baseball uniform I wore with the Nut Club. I also managed to save my old catcher's mask; it's hanging on a nail in my dressing room today.

My favorite baseball memory is of the time when the prisoners' association at Sing Sing, the Mutual Welfare League, invited our ball team up to play. Numbered on their teams were a few ex–minor leaguers, so a game between us was not going to be Amateur Night by any means. When we arrived on the field, as catcher, I naturally began to warm up our pitcher. Then, right next to me, a voice said, "Hello, Red." We had been warned not to speak to the convicts so I pretended not to hear, but the voice continued, "What's the matter, you getting stuck up?" I looked and there was a kid who had sat next to me in school. "Bootah, how are you?" I said, and shook hands, another violation of the rules. I asked him what the rap was, and he said, "Five to ten. Shot a cop. Russell's up here on the same rap." There beside Bootah was a kid I knew named Russell, a fine-looking boy. They had nicked a cop during a stick-up and were sent up for assault.

The first inning began, and who should step up to the plate but another old neighborhood boy, "Dirty Neck" Jack Lafferty. He had been a particular chum of my dad's, and he told me how sorry he was to hear of his death. I remember my dad telling me that Lafferty at a very young age felt sure sometime somewhere he was going to kill someone. My dad told him not to be silly. Lafferty was the first saloon brawler my dad ever saw break a beer mug on the bar and carve another man's face with it. Later, Lafferty tried to steal an automobile belonging to a guy named Bull Mahoney, who came along in time to prevent the theft. Lafferty stuck a gun in Mahoney's belly and blew him wide open. So Lafferty's instinct as a youngster that he was bound to kill came sadly true, and for the Mahoney murder he was sentenced to twenty years-to-life. My old man, using some Tammany Hall connections, went to bat for Lafferty, and the sentence was reduced to fourteen years. And now here he was with my other neighborhood pals, playing baseball in Ossining.

Later in the game I went down to coach first base, and a man there said, "Hey, Red! You go down to the East Side House anymore?" Another old chum, and before the game was over, I had met two more. Everybody on our team knew *somebody* there. That is proof, if proof be wanted, that our neighborhood produced something more than ex-vaudevillians. I will always remember July 21, 1927, a night some years after that Sing Sing ball game, because that was the night Jack Dempsey fought Jack Sharkey, it was the night I was playing in a Broadway show, and it was the night that Bootah died in the electric chair.

COLORPLATE 74

DAVID LEVINE. *Crowd at Ebbets Field.* c. 1960.
Oil on canvas. 36 x 28 3/4 in. Forum Gallery, New York.

COLORPLATE 75

ROBERT GWATHMEY. *World Series.* 1958.
Oil on canvas. 32¹/₂ x 45¹/₂ in. Private collection.
© Estate of Robert Gwathmey/VAGA, New York 1993.

COLORPLATE 76

MARJORIE PHILLIPS. *Giants vs. Mets.* 1964. Oil on canvas. 36¼ x 42 in. © The Phillips Collection,
Washington, D.C. *The New York Mets versus the San Francisco Giants at the Polo Grounds.*
The Giants made the Polo Grounds their home from 1891 until their move west in 1958. The Mets
re-opened the oddly-shaped ballpark in 1962, but moved to the newly-built Shea Stadium two years later.

COLORPLATE 77

RAOUL DUFY. *Ball Park—Boston.* c. 1950. Watercolor on paper. 19½ x 25½ in.
Rose Art Museum, Brandeis University, Waltham, Massachusetts.

COLORPLATE 78 *(opposite, above)*

RALPH FASANELLA. *Sandlot Game #2.* 1967.
Oil on canvas. 36 x 40 in. Private collection.

COLORPLATE 79 *(opposite, below)*

HELEN FABRI SMOGORINSKY. *The Red Wings at Silver Stadium.*
(Game between the Rochester Red Wings and the Toledo Mud Hens.) 1983.
Oil on canvas. 20 x 25 in. The Gladstone Collection of Baseball Art.

COLORPLATE 80

MIKE SCHACHT. *Willie Mays.* 1989.
Acrylic on paper. 12 x 15 in. Collection of Robert Rose.

COLORPLATE 81

TINA HOGGATT. *Ernie Banks Hits 500th Home Run, May 12th, 1970, Wrigley Field.* 1987. Watercolor. 25 x 15 in. Collection of the artist.

COLORPLATE 82

MICHAEL LANGENSTEIN. *Play Ball.* 1982.
Postcard collage. 4 x 6 in. Collection of Mr. and Mrs. Samuel A. Ramirez.

Pete Hamill

FROM *THE NEW YORK POST*, OCTOBER 3, 1988
"Never Forgive, Never Forget"

In 1988, the New York Mets faced the Los Angeles Dodgers in the National League Championship Series. For New York Post *columnist Pete Hamill, the series meant one thing—revenge. The Dodgers, however, broke New York's heart once more by winning the series, four games to three.*

LOS ANGELES—Across all the years, I kept the solemn vow. In 1957, led by the man my father afterward always referred to as That Son of a Bitch O'Malley, the Dodgers left Brooklyn forever. And with millions of others, I made the vow: Never Forgive, Never Forget.

That vow was made in a state of holy fury. It was a blood oath shouted from Bay Ridge to Brownsville, from Red Hook to Canarsie, becoming the rallying cry of the Brooklyn jihad. The Dodgers, you see, had committed an unforgivable crime: They had destroyed our innocence. In one filthy act, they told us that we fans were just a pack of gullible marks—romantic fools who believed all the myths about America.

They told us that baseball wasn't the most beautiful game ever devised by man nor were the Dodgers its most elegant artists. Baseball was a racket, said That Son of a Bitch O'Malley, a businessman's hustle, like any other. The innocent fable was a lie. Money was everything, greed the ruling principle.

So the Dodgers went off to whore after gold in California, and back home, giant cranes rumbled up Empire Boulevard to Ebbets Field and huge steel balls smashed against the outfield

WILLARD MULLIN. *Goodbye Now.* 1940. Ink and graphite on paper. 17 1/4 x 14 5/8 in. The National Art Museum of Sport. *Mullin's cartoon celebrated the Bums of Brooklyn as they entered the ranks of the National League's upper division.*

The Brooklyn Dodger Sym-phony Drum. c. 1950. The Gladstone Collection of Baseball Art. *Like the Dodgers themselves, this famous drum was beaten during crucial games at Ebbets Field.*

walls, creating rubble where Pete Reiser broke his head for us, where Furillo played the caroms, where Snider roamed with his special grace. The bulldozers scraped away the grass and churned up the infield where Reese and Robinson, Hodges and Cox had owned the earth. Business was business, they said.

Yeah.

So we vowed never to forget this atrocity and never, ever to forgive it; most of us didn't. Across the years, I came often to California to practice my trade, even lived here for a while. But I never took the trip up to Dodger Stadium. For an entire decade, I wouldn't even watch the dirty lamsters on television. We who had once prayed at the command of the Brooklyn archbishop for God to deliver Gil Hodges from a slump now wished these people only the Calvinist punishments of eternal damnation.

We weren't wrong. When the Yankees played them in the 1978 World Series, the Dodgers looked like everything I hated. Most of my bile was centered on the figure of Steve Garvey, whose clean-cut, blow-dried, all-American, West Coast, white-bread, good-guy act made me physically sick. This cardboard creature couldn't have survived for an hour on Bedford Avenue. That year, the Yankees of Reggie, Nettles, Gossage and Munson seemed more like Dodgers than these surfheads from the West. I did something undreamed of in my youth: I actually rooted for the Yankees.

But during the same period, I was shifting treacherously inside the confines of the vow. This softening was caused by the arrival of one Dodger player: Fernando Valenzuela. He was a great pitcher. But he also looked right. That lumpy body had not been assembled on a Nautilus machine in Malibu; he resembled a Mexican Hugh Casey. Fernando was smart, too. He played hard; he never whined. You were not likely to hear that he was now channeling, delving into past life experiences or carrying crystals in his palm. He was a pitcher. Oh, man, was he a pitcher.

The Dodger manager, Tommy Lasorda, pitched him too often, let him tear his arm apart with the screwball, and his career might be over too soon. But I must confess: When Fernando pitched against the Mets, I always secretly wanted him to win. And the reason was simple: Fernando is the only man on the Los Angeles team who would have looked right playing for Brooklyn.

The hell with the rest of them. As the Mets go up against the Dodgers in the playoffs, I will at last walk into the stadium in Chavez Ravine, like some old Spanish Republican entering Spain after the death of Franco. Thirty years have passed and I have grown soft in many ways. That Son of a Bitch O'Malley is dead and so is my father. But some wounds never heal. I go to the enemy camp as a hostile witness. And the vow still holds. Never forgive. Never, ever forget.

FROM *THE NEW YORK TIMES*, SEPTEMBER 16, 1952

"Russians Say U.S. Stole 'Beizbol,' Made It a Game of Bloody Murder"

Build an Iron Curtain across Europe—fine. Stockpile nuclear warheads in Cuba—no problem. But start trying to steal America's National Pastime, and them's fightin' words. This article appeared on the front page of The New York Times, *and featured photos of ballplayers "Babis Rut" and "Tai Kopb" under the heading, "Beizbol Slaves."*

Moscow Sept. 15—The magazine Smena, under the title "Beizbol," explained to its readers today that baseball, the American national sport, was a "beastly battle, a bloody fight with mayhem and murder" and furthermore nothing but a Yankee perversion of an ancient Russian village sport called lapta.

Smena presented a vivid description of the American national sport for its readers, declaring that, far from being "amusing," "noble" or "safe," beizbol actually was a dangerous game in which both players and spectators frequently suffered terrible wounds or even death.

[The carnage in the National League was unabated yesterday. The Giants slaughtered the St. Louis Cardinals, 12 to 1, only one day after the Cardinals had slaughtered the Giants. The Dodgers maintained their three-game lead by ruthlessly putting down Cincinnati's non-political Reds, 11 to 5.]

"Let us leave to one side the national American origin of this game," said Smena. "It is well known that in Russian villages they played lapta, of which beizbol is an imitation. It was played in Russian villages when the United States was not even marked on the maps."

The Soviet Encyclopedia describes lapta in the following terms:

"At opposite ends of a broad square there are marked 'cities.' The players are divided into two teams. The players in turn with a blow of a round stick knock a ball up and ahead, and during its flight run around to the 'city' of the opposing team and back. The latter tries to catch the ball and strike the runner with it."

To illustrate the bloody nature of beizbol, Smena published a photograph described as revealing "an episode in the play of 'Sen Louis' and the 'Rodjers.' Del Rois having received a blow on the head is carried unconscious from the field."

The article quoted the memoirs of the famous American player, Tai Kopb, published last March in the magazine Laif, which reported that after years of play his body was covered from head to foot with scars.

The article said American businessmen "intensively implanted" this bloody sport among 14-year-old and 15-year-old adolescents who "supplement their lack of technique by a surplus of rough play."

The article explained that the "New York club Rodjers" had a special training camp to train youths in this "beastly battle."

The article said that baseball betting annually in the United States ran to $5,000,000,000 and baseball admissions to 14,000,000 or 15,000,000 and that advertising was also a source of big income.

Indication of the bloody character of the game, said Smena, is provided by the names of some of the teams, such as "Tigrov" and "Piratov."

Despite the huge profits, said Smena, the players "are in a situation of slaves: as in football, baseball and other sports, they are bought and sold and thrown out the door when they become unnecessary."

It revealed that the "most famous American baseball player, Babis Rut," was sold against his wishes to another club for $150,000.

The life of a big league player, it said, was only six or seven years, "after which, with ruined health and often also crippled, he increases the army of American unemployed."

Typical of the fate of discarded veterans of this cruel and bloody sport, said Smena, is what happened to the famous player, Garri Kellman. "For several years he played on the best teams," said Smena, "and having gone into retirement, he died of starvation."

There has been only one fatality in the history of major league baseball. A ball thrown by Carl Mays, a Yankee pitcher, struck Ray Chapman, Cleveland shortstop, on the head and resulted in his death. That happened at the Polo Grounds in 1920.

All baseball clubs have special training camps. Under Branch Rickey, however, the "Rodjers" set up a vast camp at Vero Beach, Fla., which has been described by tongue-in-cheek writers as "a baseball assembly line."

No one can begin to estimate how much money is bet on baseball. Big league attendance a year ago continued its slow decline from the post-war peak of almost 20,000,000 spectators to a total of 18,025,035.

Members of the St. Louis Cardinals expressed surprise yesterday to learn that Del Rois, or

Del Rice. c. 1956. The National Baseball Library, Cooperstown, New York. *Former St. Louis Cardinal and Milwaukee Brave Del Rice was known as "Del Rois" in the Soviet Union, where it was claimed that he and thousands of other athletes played a "cruel and bloody" American sport that left players "with ruined health and often also crippled."*

Del Rice, had once been carried unconscious from the field. Traveling Secretary Leo Ward, who has seen every game Rice played, declared:

"I can't remember Rice ever being carried from the field unconscious. He's too tough. I once saw him hit on the head with a bat. But he merely shook it off and caught the rest of the game."

Babe Ruth was sold by the Red Sox to the Yankees for $100,000. However, it certainly was not against his wishes. He went from a poverty-stricken owner to a rich one and eventually earned $80,000 a year. When his playing days were almost over, he was given his unconditional release so that he could make a deal for himself.

The career of a big league player now averages close to ten years, night baseball having trimmed it from its normal expectancy by three or four years. The longevity record is twenty-five years, held by Eddie Collins. Most great stars of the past lasted more than twenty years.

If "Garri Kellman" is the late Harry Heilmann of the Detroit Tigers, he prospered mightily after leaving baseball. When he died of a heart attack last July, he was earning more as a baseball broadcaster than he ever had as a baseball player.

The Russian alphabet does not have the symbol "h." To transliterate "h" from English to Russian, the Soviet press sometimes uses the letter "g" and sometimes the Russian letter "x" which is then retransliterated into English as "kh" with the sound of the hard "ch" in German.

As a result, Harry Hopkins' name was usually given in Russian as Garry Gopkins, while the last name of William Randolph Hearst was usually given as Khearst. These difficulties of transliteration apparently account for the unusual spellings of the names of American baseball players in the Moscow dispatch.

Robert Whiting

FROM YOU GOTTA HAVE WA

"Oendan"

". . . take me out with the crowd. Buy me some sushi and miso soup . . ." No, it doesn't have quite the same ring to it, but Japanese baseball has become as much a reflection of that country's culture as American baseball has for the U.S. In this passage from his study of the Japanese game, Robert Whiting takes us to the home of the Hanshin Tigers to watch a game among the sarariman.

The wind blows from Mount Rokko   Ohh . . . ohh . . . ohh . . .
The sun beats high in the sky;   Hanshin Tigers,
The passion of youth is beautiful,   Fure . . . fure . . . fure . . .
Oh, glorious Hanshin Tigers.   Hooray . . . hooray . . . hooray.

from "The Hanshin Tigers Song,"
lyrics by Sonosuke Sato

On the outskirts of the sprawling industrial zone that is Osaka, at the base of Mount Rokko, stands a musty, ivy-covered edifice known as Koshien Stadium. It has housed the Hanshin Tigers for half a century.

At three o'clock on the day of a Tiger home night game, the gates to the outfield seats open up and a familiar ritual unfolds. Within minutes, the bleachers in the right and center field area are a sea of people, over ten thousand in all, which comprises the Tiger cheering section. Each person is equipped with the contents of a Tiger Kit, sold outside the stadium for the nominal fee of one thousand yen; a *happi* coat, a cap, and a megaphone in the Tiger colors of yellow and black.

Many young women in the crowd sport artificial Tiger tails and Tiger whiskers. Others have their hair dyed yellow and black. Several fans have their heads shaved in the shape of the Chinese character *tora*, meaning tiger. One or two carry an American flag.

In the crowd are several splinter booster groups and ad hoc organizations identified by distinctive headbands and badges. They bear names like the "I love Koshien Club," the "Tiger Fanatics Club," the "Kyoto Tiger Association," the "Right Field Stands Club," and the "Tora, Tora, Tora Group."

Two hours before game time, with the bleacher crowd already overflowing into the aisles, the cheerleaders arrive, their places in the front row respectfully reserved by other fans. They have just come from the Tiger shrine, located in a nearby supermarket owned by rabid Tiger fans, where they prayed for the success of the team.

One of them, a leathery-faced man with twinkling eyes and thick callouses on his hands from waving a ponderous Tiger banner, cracks open a can of Tiger Beer, an Asahi product bearing the Hanshin Tiger logo. "It's good to be a little drunk out here," he says to no one in particular.

At 5:00 P.M., exactly one hour before the first pitch, the cheering section rises en masse to sing the Tiger song, "The Wind Blows Down from Mount Rokko." Then the chanting begins:

Japan's all-time home-run leader, Sadaharu Oh.
The National Baseball Library, Cooperstown, New York.

"*Katobase Tai-ga-zu*" (Knock 'em out Tigers), "*Katobase Tai-ga-zu*." It is a resounding, deafening cry that will go on in varying forms until the end of the game approximately four-and-a-half hours away.

The fans interrupt their cheering only to celebrate the seventh-inning stretch, when they unleash a huge cloud of colored balloons.

All in all, it is an awesome display of energy. And even when the game is over, the crowd seems reluctant to leave. Many remain standing in place, still chanting as if under some magic spell.

"Baseball is a lot clearer than our daily lives," says one *sarariman*, dressed in a dark-blue suit with his tie still in place. "The strong and the best win. That's all there is to it."

For others, the attraction is even more basic. Says one young man in a voice hoarse from screaming, "I really didn't come here to see pro ball. I just like the atmosphere." "It's like a rock concert," declares his girlfriend. "We just have a lot of fun yelling."

"To tell the truth," one of the cheerleaders, a man in his fifties, confesses, "I come here because it gives me a chance to get away from my wife." He adds with a wink, "That's also why I go on the road with the team."

There are a lot of extraordinary things about Japan's national sport of baseball: Bands that play Mahler and Beethoven in opening day ceremonies. Umpires that practice their strike and ball calling form in pregame warmups. And commentators who use sophisticated computer studies to evaluate a player's ability, then blithely cite his blood type in the popular belief that it somehow affects performance. (Types A and O purportedly make good batters, Type B makes good pitchers, and so forth.) But perhaps most unusual of all is the Japanese fan himself, who is a fascinating study in contrasts.

Generally speaking, Japanese people are reserved and tend to concentrate all their energy inside. They are shy, low-key, and only occasionally are they given to eruption, like the volcanic mountains that dot their island country. It takes several drinks after work, for example, before the Japanese *sarariman* loses his inhibitions and reveals his other, boisterous self.

Nowhere is this dichotomy more apparent than at the ballpark. Observing fan conduct there is akin to taking a crash course in Japanese psychology. The typical fan, left alone and to his own devices, will sit quietly through a nine-inning game, behaving with proverbial Japanese decorum, eschewing the sort of loud and vulgar conduct common in many U.S. major league ballparks. He will even politely return foul balls to the stadium ushers, as prescribed by long-held custom in Japanese baseball.

Yet, put him in one of the highly organized cheering groups, or *oendan*, that can be found at all baseball stadiums in Japan, and he quickly sheds his traditional restraint. Spurred on by energetic cheerleaders, and the pounding rhythm of *taiko* drums, horns, whistles, and other noisemakers, he becomes a veritable wildman, yelling and screaming nonstop for nine solid innings.

Said one New York television producer after spending an entire game in the midst of the several-thousand-member Yomiuri Giants *oendan*, "These people are lunatics! There is more noise here than the World Series and the Army-Navy game combined. How do they keep it up?"

Oendan exist at every level of Japanese sport, from amateur to professional, and date back to the nineteenth century, when they were a major presence at college baseball games—highly organized, extremely loud, and more than a little militant. Participating in the *oendan* was considered a way of demonstrating school loyalty, and postgame confrontations between rival cheering groups were a vivid adjunct to the athletic activity on the field.

In 1904, after a game in which Keio had defeated its crosstown Tokyo rival Waseda, the Keio *oendan* performed a rousing *banzai* cheer in front of the on-campus residence of the Waseda University president. Stung by this grievous insult, the Waseda *oendan* repaid in kind after the next contest, which Waseda won, with a noisy demonstration of its own in front of the Keio president's house.

By the time the third game was scheduled to be played, there was homicide in the air. Both cheering groups had swollen in size to several hundred students, fortified with members of their respective school judo clubs, who were ready to do battle. University authorities were so alarmed that they canceled the contest and any further play between the two schools was subsequently banned for the next two years.

Today, college *oendan* bear little resemblance to their fun-loving counterparts in the West. They are strictly ordered by rank and seniority, and otherwise marked by militaristic tendencies. All members wear the same black cadet uniforms and often white headbands emblazoned with a red rising sun and stirring inscriptions like *hissho* (desperate victory).

The *oendan* are also known for their association with right-wing organizations and their devotion to traditional Japanese values of loyalty and discipline. Said the leader of one *oendan*, "Japan is losing its sense of order. It's our job to help restore it."

One of the more successful college baseball managers was Kichiro Shimaoka, a rotund Wallace Beery look-alike who guided the fortunes of the Meiji University team for some thirty years. He led them to several Big Six League titles and also managed a Japanese college all-star team to a victory over the Americans in College World Series competition.

Yet, Shimaoka never played organized baseball and had only a cursory knowledge of the game. As a student at Meiji in the 1930s, he had been head of the cheering section and he was regarded as a good leader and motivator of youth. In 1939, after several years as manager of the Meiji Middle School baseball team, he was asked to step up to the college level.

Shimaoka had spirit and that was enough. He would sit on the bench and exhort his team to greater efforts. "*Yare! Yare!*" (Do it! Do it!) he would yell, and his players would play their hearts out for him.

A. Bartlett Giamatti

FROM *YALE ALUMNI MAGAZINE,* NOVEMBER 1977

"The Green Fields of the Mind"

A. Bartlett Giamatti, the late commissioner of baseball who left us far too soon, demonstrated in this essay what were his strongest qualifications for the office: a deep love and understanding of the game, combined with wisdom and articulation.

It breaks your heart. It is designed to break your heart. The game begins in the spring, when everything else begins again, and it blossoms in the summer, filling the afternoons and evenings, and then as soon as the chill rains come, it stops and leaves you to face the fall alone. You count on it, rely on it to buffer the passage of time, to keep the memory of sunshine and high skies alive, and then just when the days are all twilight, when you need it most, it stops. Today, October 2, a Sunday of rain and broken branches and leaf-clogged drains and slick streets, it stopped, and summer was gone.

Somehow, the summer seemed to slip by faster this time. Maybe it wasn't this summer, but all the summers that, in this my fortieth summer, slipped by so fast. There comes a time when every summer will have something of autumn about it. Whatever the reason, it seemed to me that I was investing more and more in baseball, making the game do more of the work that keeps time fat and slow and lazy. I was counting on the game's deep patterns, three strikes, three outs, three times three innings, and its deepest impulse, to go out and back, to leave and to return home, to set the order of the day and to organize the daylight. I wrote a few things this last summer, this summer that did not last, nothing grand but some things, and yet that work was just camouflage. The real activity was done with the radio—not the all-seeing, all-falsifying television—and was the playing of the game in the only place it will last, the enclosed green field of the mind. There, in that warm, bright place, what the old poet called Mutability does not so quickly come.

But out here on Sunday, October 2, where it rains all day, Dame Mutability never loses. She was in the crowd at Fenway yesterday, a gray day full of bluster and contradiction, when the Red Sox came up in the last of the ninth trailing Baltimore 8–5, while the Yankees, rain-delayed against Detroit, only needing to win one or have Boston lose one to win it all, sat in New York washing down cold cuts with beer and watching the Boston game. Boston had won two, the Yankees had lost two, and suddenly it seemed as if the whole season might go to the last day, or beyond, except here was Boston losing 8–5, while New York sat in its family room and put its feet up. Lynn, both ankles hurting now as they had in July, hits a single down the right-field line. The crowd stirs. It is on its feet. Hobson, third baseman, former Bear Bryant quarterback, strong, quiet, over 100 RBIs, goes for three breaking balls and is out. The goddess smiles and encourages her agent, a canny journeyman named Nelson Briles.

Now comes a pinch hitter, Bernie Carbo, one-time Rookie of the Year, erratic, quick, a shade too handsome, so laid back he is always, in his soul, stretched out in the tall grass, one arm under his head, watching the clouds and laughing; now he looks over some low stuff unworthy of him and then, uncoiling, sends one out, straight on a rising line, over the center-field wall, no cheap Fenway shot, but all of it, the physics as elegant as the arc the ball describes.

New England is on its feet, roaring. The summer will not pass. Roaring, they recall the evening, late and cold, in 1975, the sixth game of the World Series, perhaps the greatest base-ball game played in the last fifty years, when Carbo, loose and easy, had uncoiled to tie the game that Fisk would win. It is 8–7, one out, and school will never start, rain will never come, sun will warm the back of your neck forever. Now Bailey, picked up from the National League recently, big arms, heavy gut, experienced, new to the league and the club; he fouls off two and then, checking, tentative, a big man off balance, he pops a soft liner to the first base-man. It is suddenly darker and later, and the announcer doing the game coast to coast, a New Yorker who works for a New York television station, sounds relieved. His little world, well-lit, hot-combed, split-second-timed, had no capacity to absorb this much gritty, grainy, contrary reality.

Cox swings a bat, stretches his long arms, bends his back, the rookie from Pawtucket, who broke in two weeks earlier with a record six straight hits, the kid drafted ahead of Fred Lynn, rangy, smooth, cool. The count runs two and two, Briles is cagey, nothing too good, and Cox swings, the ball beginning toward the mound and then, in a jaunty, wayward dance, skipping past Briles, feinting to the right, skimming the last of the grass, finding the dirt, moving now like some small, purposeful marine creature negotiating the green deep, easily avoiding the jagged rock of second base, traveling steady and straight now out into the dark, silent recesses of center field.

The aisles are jammed, the place is on its feet, the wrappers, the programs, the Coke cups and peanut shells, the detritus of an afternoon; the anxieties, the things that have to be done tomorrow, the regrets about yesterday, the accumulation of a summer: all forgotten, while hope, the anchor, bites and takes hold where a moment before it seemed we would be swept out with the tide. Rice is up, Rice whom Aaron had said was the only one he'd seen with the ability to break his records, Rice the best clutch hitter on the club, with the best slugging per-centage in the league, Rice, so quick and strong he once checked his swing halfway through and snapped the bat in two, Rice the Hammer of God sent to scourge the Yankees, the sound was overwhelming, fathers pounded their sons on the back, cars pulled off the road, house-holds froze, New England exulted in its blessedness, and roared its thanks for all good things, for Rice and for a summer stretching halfway through October. Briles threw, Rice swung, and it was over. One pitch, a fly to center, and it stopped. Summer died in New England, and like rain sliding off a roof, the crowd slipped out of Fenway, quickly, with only a steady murmur of concern for the drive ahead remaining of the roar. Mutability had turned the seasons and translated hope to memory once again. And once again, she had used baseball, our best invention to stay change, to bring change on. That is why it breaks my heart, that game—not because in New York they could win because Boston lost; in that, there is a rough justice, and a reminder to the Yankees of how slight and fragile are the circumstances that exalt one group of human beings over another. It breaks my heart because it was meant to, because it was meant to foster in me again the illusion that there was something abiding, some pattern and some impulse that could come together to make a reality that would resist the corrosion; and because after it had fostered again that most hungered-for illusion, the game was meant to stop, and betray precisely what it promised.

Of course, there are those who learn after the first few times. They grow out of sports. And there are others who were born with the wisdom to know that nothing lasts. These are the truly tough among us, the ones who can live without illusion, or without even the hope of illusion. I am not that grown-up or up-to-date. I am a simpler creature, tied to more primitive patterns and cycles. I need to think something lasts forever, and it might as well be the state of being that is a game; it might as well be that, in a green field, in the sun.

Fenway Park, Boston. c. 1975. The National Baseball Library, Cooperstown, New York.

Seventh Inning:
BASEBALL LIT. 101

The humorist, the novelist, the poet, and the musician have all used the game as a medium through which they convey their artistry. In this chapter, baseball is celebrated in story and song.

Robert L. Harrison

FROM *SPITBALL MAGAZINE*

"The Hellenic League"

Baseball, with its penchant for mythology, seems to be perfectly suited to the ancient Greeks. Could the Acropolis really have been a giant concession stand? Was the rivalry between Greece and Troy as heated as the one between the Cubs and Cardinals?

They uncovered the site
of that old ballpark,
where Homer once
recorded the scores.

The burn marks from
Mercury's slides still
scorched the earth,
and "Pop" Zeus'
footprints were
found in the
home team's dugout.

The section where the Sirens
sang their songs
(after the visitors got on first)
was found near the
gyro stands by the wall
that Hercules once called
"the marble monster."

What shots must have flown
from Apollo's bat.

What glory after
the Trojan nine was creamed.

The nectar poured
from Bacchus's concession stands
after Hades threw
his famous heater
and Vulcan etched in stone
the final out.

The most marvelous find
was a Grecian urn
that turned out to be
a season's pass.

William Shakespeare

Shakespeare on Baseball

So who was the first person to write about baseball? An argument could be made for William Shakespeare, the immortal Babe—that is, Bard—*of Stratford-upon-Avon, who penned some of these lines 250 years before the first pitch was thrown.*

———————

"Just kind death, umpire of men's miseries"

    —*Henry VI*, Part I, Act II, Scene v

"Of all base passions, fear is the most accursed."

    —V, ii

"Small things make base men proud."

    —IV, i

"I will make it felony to drink small beer."

    —IV, ii

"To seek their fortunes further than at home,
Where small experience grows."

    —*The Taming of the Shrew*, I, ii

"Such an injury would vex a saint."

    —III, ii

"O! How this spring of love resembleth
The uncertain glory of an April day!"

    —*The Two Gentlemen of Verona*, I, iii

"This is very midsummer madness."

    —*Twelfth Night*, III, iv

"The play, I remember, pleased not the million; 'twas caviare to the general."

    —*Hamlet*, II, ii

"A hit, a very palpable hit!"

    —V, ii

"He capers, he dances, he has eyes of youth, he writes verses, he speaks holidays, he smells
April and May."

    —*The Merry Wives of Windsor*, III, ii

"Like a strutting player, whose conceit
Lies in his hamstring, and doth think it rich
To hear the wooden dialogue and sound
'Twixt his stretched footing and the scaffoldage."

    —*Troilus and Cressida*, I, iii

   "O! it is excellent
To have a Giant's strength; but is tyrannous
To use it like a Giant."

    —*Measure for Measure*, II, ii

"They laugh that win."

    —*Othello*, IV, i

"Upon such sacrifices, my Cordelia,
The Gods themselves throw incense."

    —*King Lear*, V, iii

"Fair is foul and foul is fair."

    —*Macbeth*, I, i

"My arm is sore."

    —*Antony and Cleopatra*, II, v

DOUGLAS TILDEN.
The Baseball Player.
1888–1889. Bronze,
medium brown patina.
34 1/4 in. high. The
National Baseball Library,
Cooperstown, New York.

David E. Brand

FROM BASEBALL MAGAZINE

"A Batter's Soliloquy"

David E. Brand offered this revised version of Hamlet's famous speech in the September 1911 issue of Baseball Magazine. *You can almost hear the announcer: "And now, ladies and gentlemen, stepping up to the plate, the Melancholy Dane."*

———————————

To bunt, or not to bunt: that is the question:
Whether 'tis nobler in the mind to suffer
The slings and arrows of the outraged bleachers,
Or gain their approbation by a swing
Well placed and well advised? To strike: to hit,
Perhaps; and by a hit to say we end
The heartache and the thousand natural shocks
Batters are heir to, 'tis a consummation
Devoutly to be wished. To strike, to hit;
To hit; perchance to short: ay, there's the rub;
For in that double play what outs may come
When we have thus connected with the pill,

Wee Willie Keeler. c. 1904. The National Baseball Library, Cooperstown, New York. *"To bunt, or not to bunt: that is the question." Wee Willie Keeler was among the best bunters of all time, and by consistently "hitting 'em where they ain't," achieved a .343 lifetime average and induction into the Hall of Fame.*

Must give us instant pause: There's the respect
That makes calamity of so rash a blow.
For who would bear the whips and scorns of fans
The umpire's wrong, the team-mates' contumely,
The insolence of rooters and the spurns
The embryonic Honus then receives,
When he might of himself a hero make
By a home run? Who then would weakly bunt,
But that the dread of grounding out to third,
That speedy little baseman from whose whip
No runner ere escapes, puzzles the will
And makes us rather try to play it safe
Than fly to fielders that we know not of?
And thus the native wish to lose the ball
Is sicklied over with a sacrifice,
And mighty swats of long remembered fame
That might have been home runs of record lengths
With this regard, are stifled ere they're born.

Mark Twain

FROM A CONNECTICUT YANKEE IN KING ARTHUR'S COURT

In Mark Twain's dark classic, a nineteenth-century Hartford blacksmith was struck on the head during a "misunderstanding conducted with crowbars" and transported back in time to Camelot. In this portion of the novel, published in 1888, we see that he brought the best of the modern world back with him.

At the end of a month I sent the vessel home for fresh supplies, and for news. We expected her back in three or four days. She would bring me, along with other news, the result of a certain experiment which I had been starting. It was a project of mine to replace the tournament with something which might furnish an escape for the extra steam of the chivalry, keep those bucks entertained and out of mischief, and at the same time preserve the best thing in them, which was their hardy spirit of emulation. I had had a choice band of them in private training for some time, and the date was now arriving for their first public effort.

This experiment was baseball. In order to give the thing vogue from the start, and place it out of the reach of criticism, I chose my nines by rank, not capacity. There wasn't a knight in either team who wasn't a sceptered sovereign. As for material of this sort, there was a glut of it, always, around Arthur. You couldn't throw a brick in any direction and not cripple a king. Of course I couldn't get these people to leave off their armor; they wouldn't do that when they bathed. They consented to differentiate the armor so that a body could tell one team from the other, but that was the most they would do. So, one of the teams wore chain-mail ulsters, and the other wore plate armor made of my new Bessemer steel. Their practice in the field was the most fantastic thing I ever saw. Being ballproof, they never skipped out of the way, but stood still and took the result; when a Bessemer was at the bat and a ball hit him, it would bound a hundred and fifty yards, sometimes. And when a man was running, and threw himself on his stomach to slide to his base, it was like an ironclad coming into port. At first I appointed men of no rank to act as umpires, but I had to discontinue that. These people were no easier to please than other nines. The umpire's first decision was usually his last; they broke him in two with a bat, and his friends toted him home on a shutter. When it was noticed that no umpire ever survived a game, umpiring got to be unpopular. So I was obliged to appoint somebody whose rank and lofty position under the government would protect him.

Here are the names of the nines:

BESSEMERS.	ULSTERS.
KING ARTHUR.	EMPEROR LUCIUS.
KING LOT OF LOTHIAN.	KING LOGRIS.
KING OF NORTHALIS.	KING MARHALT OF IRELAND.
KING MARSIL.	KING MORGANORE.
KING OF LITTLE BRITAIN.	KING MARK OF CORNWALL.
KING LABOR.	KING NENTRES OF GARLOT.
KING PELLAM OF LISTENGESE.	KING MELIODAS OF LIONES.
KING BAGDEMAGUS.	KING OF THE LAKE.
KING TOLLEME LA FEINTES.	THE SOWDAN OF SYRIA.

Umpire—CLARENCE.

The first public game would certainly draw fifty thousand people; and for solid fun would be worth going around the world to see. Everything would be favorable; it was balmy and beautiful spring weather, now, and Nature was all tailored out in her new clothes.

Walter R. Hirsch

FROM *BASEBALL MAGAZINE*

"A Coming Fanette: The Mournful Ballad of a Girl and a Baseball Game"

While there are some today who would brand this piece as sexist, readers will be forced to admit that it poses some worthwhile and difficult questions.

———————

Why is a baseball a baseball? And why did they make it round?
And why did they coat it with leather? And why does it bounce and bound?
What did it do to the batter that he swings with all his might,
And tries to put that baseball far away and out of sight?
Why is a pitcher a twirler? And why does he stand on a mound?
What makes him want to go up in the air? Why doesn't he stay on the ground?
Why is a fielder a fielder? And why does he go out so far?
Why doesn't he play in closer? He should use a motor car.
Why is a shortstop a shortstop? Is a "long-stop" just as good?
Why is the plate made of rubber? And why is a bat made of wood?
And I wonder why is a first baseman? Oh, he's first to bat I suppose!

COLORPLATE 83

LeRoy Neiman. *Reggie Jackson.* 1982.
Oil on panel. 10³/₄ x 8 in. Private collection.

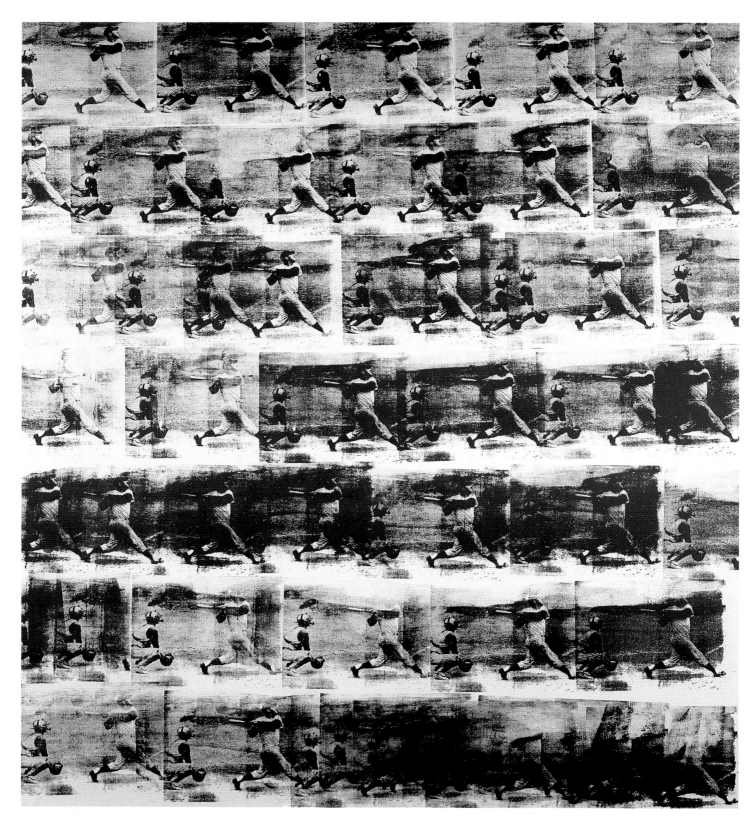

COLORPLATE 84

ANDY WARHOL. *Baseball*. 1962. Silkscreen ink and oil on canvas. 91^1/$_2$ x 82 in.
The Nelson-Atkins Museum of Art, Kansas City, Missouri.

COLORPLATE 85 *(opposite)*

CLAES OLDENBERG. *Bat Spinning at the Speed of Light*. 1975. Lithograph on paper. 37 x 25^1/$_8$ in.
Collection of the Butler Institute of American Art, Youngstown, Ohio.

COLORPLATE 86

GERALD GARSTON. *Spring Training*. 1981. Oil on canvas. 40 x 49 in.
Collection of the Law Firm of Wiggin & Dana, New Haven, Connecticut.

COLORPLATE 87

TINA CHADEN. *The Baseball Fan.* 1985.
Paper, clay, and egg tempera. 15 x 30 x 40 in. Private collection.

COLORPLATE 88

JANET BRAUN-REINITZ.
*Report from the Fire Zone,
Scroll XV.* 1985.
Acrylic on paper. 96 x 48 in.
Collection of the artist.

COLORPLATE 89

DERYL DANIEL MACKIE. *Smokey Joe Williams.* 1985.
Acrylic on canvas. 64 x 54 in. Collection of the artist.

COLORPLATE 90

WAYNE THIEBAUD. *Hats*. 1988.
Oil on paper. 19 x 18 in. Private collection.

MARK RUCKER. *Angel Hermosa's Double Play.* 1974. Graphite on paper. 27 ¹/₂ x 22 in. Collection, University Art Museum, University at Albany.

And why did they throw that bottle and break the umpire's nose?
Now why does that ugly catcher act so terribly tough and mad?
Oh, look! the ball's gone over the fence. Why isn't the pitcher glad?
And why did that man yell "Rotten!" and then say "Get the hook?"
Now why do they start to argue? They called the umpire a crook!
What is a "sub"?—a subject, or a submarine diving boat?
Why is a fan a rooter? Where does he keep his goat?
Why is the ground called a diamond? Why not a ruby or pearl?
What is the score now, Tommy? Is that the shortstop's girl?
Why don't they have him arrested? He stole a base, you say.
Why are they yelling "Slam 'er out"? Why are the ball suits gray?
Where has the foul ball gone, dear? Why don't they use that, too?
Why does the batter spit on his hands? Why doesn't he use some glue?
Why is a bunt a bunt, Tom? Who made the sacrifice?
He's certainly a gentleman, and I think he's very nice.
Why don't they bleach the bleachers and bring the outfield in?
Why aren't the visitors sociable and let the home team win?
Oh, Tom, the game is over! Who won, and what's the score?
Oh, I know the game so perfectly that I'm going to come some more.
I'm going home to father and tell him that we won,
It was a close game, Tommy: the score was ten to one!

Ring Lardner

"Alibi Ike"

Legendary sportswriter Ring Lardner possessed a nimble, cutting wit and little tolerance for the kind of player so savagely lampooned in his most famous short story.

His right name was Frank X. Farrell, and I guess the X stood for "Excuse me." Because he never pulled a play, good or bad, on or off the field, without apologizin' for it.

"Alibi Ike" was the name Carey wished on him the first day he reported down South. O' course we all cut out the "Alibi" part of it right away for the fear he would overhear it and bust somebody. But we called him "Ike" right to his face and the rest of it was understood by everybody on the club except Ike himself.

He ast me one time, he says:

"What do you all call me Ike for? I ain't no Yid."

"Carey give you the name," I says. "It's his nickname for everybody he takes a likin' to."

"He mustn't have only a few friends then," says Ike. "I never heard him say `Ike' to nobody else."

But I was goin' to tell you about Carey namin' him. We'd been workin' out two weeks and the pitchers was showin' somethin' when this bird joined us. His first day out he stood up there so good and took such a reef at the old pill that he had everyone lookin'. Then him and Carey was together in left field, catchin' fungoes, and it was after we was through for the day that Carey told me about him.

"What do you think of Alibi Ike?" ast Carey.

"Who's that?" I says.

"This here Farrell in the outfield," says Carey.

"He looks like he could hit," I says.

"Yes," says Carey, "but he can't hit near as good as he can apologize."

Then Carey went on to tell me what Ike had been pullin' out there. He'd dropped the first fly ball that was hit to him and told Carey his glove wasn't broke in good yet, and Carey says the glove could easy of been Kid Gleason's gran'father. He made a whale of a catch out o' the next one and Carey says "Nice work!" or somethin' like that, but Ike says he could of caught the ball with his back turned only he slipped when he started after it and, besides that, the air currents fooled him.

"I thought you done well to get to the ball," says Carey.

"I ought to been settin' under it," says Ike.

"What did you hit last year?" Carey ast him.

"I had malaria most o' the season," says Ike. "I wound up with .356."

"Where would I have to go to get malaria?" says Carey, but Ike didn't wise up.

I and Carey and him set at the same table together for supper. It took him half an hour longer'n us to eat because he had to excuse himself every time he lifted his fork.

"Doctor told me I needed starch," he'd say, and then toss a shovelful o' potatoes into him. Or, "They ain't much meat on one o' these chops," he'd tell us, and grab another one. Or he'd say: "Nothin' like onions for a cold," and then he'd dip into the perfumery.

"Better try that apple sauce," says Carey. "It'll help your malaria."

"Whose malaria?" says Ike. He'd forgot already why he didn't only hit .356 last year.

I and Carey begin to lead him on.

"Whereabouts did you say your home was?" I ast him.

"I live with my folks," he says. "We live in Kansas City—not right down in the business part—outside a ways."

How's that come?" says Carey. "I should think you'd get rooms in the post office."

But Ike was too busy curin' his cold to get that one.

"Are you married?" I ast him.

"No," he says. "I never run around much with girls, except to shows onct in a wile and parties and dances and roller skatin'."

"Never take 'em to the prize fights, eh?" says Carey.

"We don't have no real good bouts," says Ike. "Just bush stuff. And I never figured a boxin' match was a place for the ladies."

Well, after supper he pulled a cigar out and lit it. I was just goin' to ask him what he done it for, but he beat me to it.

"Kind o' rests a man to smoke after a good work-out," he says. "Kind o' settles a man's supper, too."

"Looks like a pretty good cigar," says Carey.

"Yes," says Ike. "A friend o' mine give it to me—a fella in Kansas City that runs a billiard room."

"Do you play billiards?" I ast him.

"I used to play a fair game," he says. "I'm all out o' practice now—can't hardly make a shot."

We coaxed him into a four-handed battle, him and Carey against Jack, Mack and I. Say, he couldn't play billiards as good as Willie Hoppe; not quite. But to hear him tell it, he didn't make a good shot all evenin'. I'd leave him an awful-lookin' layout and he'd gather 'em up in one try and then run a couple o' hundred, and between every carom he'd say he'd put too much stuff on the ball, or the English didn't take, or the table wasn't true, or his stick was crooked, or somethin'. And all the time he had the balls actin' like they was Dutch soldiers and him Kaiser William. We started out to play fifty points, but we had to make it a thousand so as I and Jack and Carey could try the table.

The four of us set round the lobby a wile after we was through playin', and when it got along toward bedtime Carey whispered to me and says:

"Ike'd like to go to bed, but he can't think up no excuse."

Carey hadn't hardly finished whisperin' when Ike got up and pulled it:

"Well, good night, boys," he says. "I ain't sleepy, but I got some gravel in my shoes and it's killin' my feet."

We knowed he hadn't never left the hotel since we'd came in from the grounds and changed our clo'es. So Carey says:

"I should think they'd take them gravel pits out o' the billiard room."

But Ike was already on his way to the elevator, limpin'.

"He's got the world beat," says Carey to Jack and I. "I've knew lots o' guys that had an alibi for every mistake they made; I've heard pitchers say that the ball slipped when somebody cracked one off'n 'em; I've heard infielders complain of a sore arm after heavin' one into the stand, and I've saw outfielders tooken sick with a dizzy spell when they've misjudged a fly ball. But this baby can't even go to bed without apologizin', and I bet he excuses himself to the razor when he gets ready to shave."

"And at that," says Jack, "he's goin' to make us a good man."

"Yes," says Carey, "unless rheumatism keeps his battin' average down to .400."

Well, sir, Ike kept whalin' away at the ball all through the trip till everybody knowed he'd won a job. Cap had him in there regular the last few exhibition games and told the newspaper boys a week before the season opened that he was goin' to start him in Kane's place.

"You're there, kid," says Carey to Ike, the night Cap made the 'nnouncement. "They ain't many boys that wins a big league berth their third year out."

"I'd of been up here a year ago," says Ike, "only I was bent over all season with lumbago." . . .

And you ought to heard him out there on that field! They wasn't a day when he didn't pull six or seven, and it didn't make no difference whether he was goin' good or bad. If he popped up in the pinch he should of made a base hit and the reason he didn't was so-and-so. And if he cracked one for three bases he ought to had a home run, only the ball wasn't lively, or the wind brought it back, or he tripped on a lump o' dirt, roundin' first base.

They was one afternoon in New York when he beat all records. Big Marquard was workin' against us and he was good.

In the first innin' Ike hit one clear over that right field stand, but it was a few feet foul. Then he got another foul and then the count came to two and two. Then Rube slipped one acrost on him and he was called out.

"What do you know about that!" he says afterward on the bench. "I lost count. I thought it was three and one, and I took a strike."

"You took a strike all right," says Carey. "Even the umps knowed it was a strike."

"Yes," says Ike, "but you can bet I wouldn't of took it if I'd knew it was the third one. The score board had it wrong."

"That score board ain't for you to look at," says Cap. "It's for you to hit that old pill against."

"Well," says Ike, "I could of hit that one over the score board if I'd knew it was the third."

"Was it a good ball?" I says.

"Well, no, it wasn't," says Ike. "It was inside."

"How far inside?" says Carey.

"Oh, two or three inches or half a foot," says Ike.

"I guess you wouldn't of threatened the score board with it then," says Cap.

"I'd of pulled it down the right foul line if I hadn't thought he'd call it a ball," says Ike. . . .

Along in the fifth we was one run to the bad and Ike got on with one out. On the first ball throwed to Smitty, Ike went down. The ball was outside and Meyers throwed Ike out by ten feet.

You could see Ike's lips movin' all the way to the bench and when he got there he had his piece learned.

"Why didn't he swing?" he says.

"Why didn't you wait for his sign?" says Cap.

"He give me his sign," says Ike.

"What is his sign with you?" says Cap.

"Pickin' up some dirt with his right hand," says Ike.

"Well, I didn't see him do it," Cap says.

"He done it all right," says Ike.

Well, Smitty went out and they wasn't no more argument till they come in for the next innin'. Then Cap opened it up.

"You fellas better get your signs straight," he says.

"Do you mean me?" says Smitty.

"Yes," Cap says. "What's your sign with Ike?"

"Slidin' my left hand up to the end o' the bat and back," says Smitty.

"Do you hear that, Ike?" ast Cap.

"What of it?" says Ike.

"You says his sign was pickin' up dirt and he says it's slidin his hand. Which is right?"

"I'm right," says Smitty. "But if you're arguin' about him goin' last innin', I didn't give him no sign."

"You pulled your cap down with your right hand, didn't you?" ast Ike.

"Well, s'pose I did," says Smitty. "That don't mean nothin'. I never told you to take that for a sign, did I?"

"I thought maybe you meant to tell me and forgot," says Ike.

They couldn't none of us answer that and they wouldn't of been no more said if Ike had of shut up. But wile we was settin' there Carey got on with two out and stole second clean.

"There!" says Ike. "That's what I was tryin' to do and I'd of got away with it if Smitty'd swang and bothered the Indian."

"Oh!" says Smitty. "You was tryin' to steal then, was you? I thought you claimed I give you the hit and run."

"I didn't claim no such a thing," says Ike. "I thought maybe you might of gave me a sign, but I was goin' anyway because I thought I had a good start."

Cap prob'ly would of hit him with a bat, only just about that time Doyle booted one on Hayes and Carey come acrost with the run that tied.

Well, we go into the ninth finally, one and one, and Marquard walks McDonald with nobody out.

"Lay it down," says Cap to Ike.

And Ike goes up there with orders to bunt and cracks the first ball into that right-field stand! It was fair this time, and we're two ahead, but I didn't think about that at the time. I was too busy watchin' Cap's face. First he turned pale and then he got red as fire and then he got blue and purple, and finally he just laid back and busted out laughin'. So we wasn't afraid to laugh ourselfs when we seen him doin' it, and when Ike come in everybody on the bench was in hysterics.

But instead o' takin' advantage, Ike had to try and excuse himself. His play was to shut up and he didn't know how to make it.

"Well," he says, "if I hadn't hit quite so quick at that one I bet it'd of cleared the center-field fence."

Cap stopped laughin'.

"It'll cost you plain fifty," he says.

"What for?" says Ike.

"When I say 'bunt' I mean 'bunt,'" says Cap.

"You didn't say 'bunt,'" says Ike.

"I says 'Lay it down,'" says Cap. "If that don't mean 'bunt,' what does it mean?"

"'Lay it down' means 'bunt' all right," says Ike, "but I understood you to say 'Lay on it.'"

"All right," says Cap, "and the little misunderstandin' will cost you fifty."

Ike didn't say nothin' for a few minutes. Then he had another bright idear.

"I was just kiddin' about misunderstandin' you," he says. "I knowed you wanted me to bunt."

"Well, then, why didn't you bunt?" ast Cap.

"I was goin' to on the next ball," says Ike. "But I thought if I took a good wallop I'd have 'em all fooled. So I walloped at the first one to fool 'em, and I didn't have no intention o' hittin' it."

"You tried to miss it, did you?" says Cap.

"Yes," says Ike.

"How'd you happen to hit it?" ast Cap.

"Well," Ike says, "I was lookin' for him to throw me a fast one and I was goin' to swing under it. But he come with a hook and I met it right square where I was swingin' to go under the fast one."

"Great!" says Cap. "Boys," he says, "Ike's learned how to hit Marquard's curve. Pretend a fast one's comin' and then try to miss it. It's a good thing to know and Ike'd ought to be willin' to pay for the lesson. So I'm goin' to make it a hundred instead o' fifty."

The game wound up 3 to 1. The fine didn't go, because Ike hit like a wild man all through that trip and we made pretty near a clean-up. The night we went to Philly I got him cornered in the car and I says to him:

"Forget them alibis for a wile and tell me somethin'. What'd you do that for, swing that time against Marquard when you was told to bunt?"

"I'll tell you," he says. "That ball he throwed me looked just like the one I struck out on in the first innin' and I wanted to show Cap what I could of done to that other one if I'd knew it was the third strike."

"But," I says, "the one you struck out on in the first innin' was a fast ball."

"So was the one I cracked in the ninth," says Ike. . . .

Frank Sullivan

FROM *THE NEW YORKER*

"The Cliché Expert Testifies on Baseball"

Ace writer Frank Sullivan really chalked one up with this timeless gem, which was published in 1949.

———————————

Q—Mr. Arbuthnot, you state that your grandmother has passed away and you would like to have the afternoon off to go to her funeral.

A—That is correct.

Q—You are an expert in the clichés of baseball—right?

A—I pride myself on being well versed in the stereotypes of our national pastime.

Q—Well, we'll test you. Who plays baseball?

A—Big-league baseball is customarily played by brilliant outfielders, veteran hurlers, powerful sluggers, knuckle-ball artists, towering first basemen, key moundsmen, fleet base runners, ace southpaws, scrappy little shortstops, sensational war vets, ex-college stars, relief artists, rifle-armed twirlers, dependable mainstays, doughty right-handers, streamlined back-stops, power-hitting batsmen, redoubtable infielders, erstwhile Dodgers, veteran sparkplugs, sterling moundsmen, aging twirlers, and rookie sensations.

Q—What other names are rookie sensations known by?

A—They are also known as aspiring rookies, sensational newcomers, promising freshmen, ex-sandlotters, highly touted striplings, and youngsters who will bear watching.

Q—What's the manager of a baseball team called?

A—A veteran pilot. Or youthful pilot. But he doesn't manage the team.

Q—No? What does he do?

A—He guides its destinies.

Q—How?

A—By the use of managerial strategy.

Q—Mr. Arbuthnot, please describe the average major-league-baseball athlete.

A—Well, he comes in three sizes, or types. The first type is tall, slim, lean, towering, rangy, huge, husky, big, strapping, sturdy, handsome, powerful, lanky, rawboned, and rugged.

Q—Quite a hunk of athlete.

A—Well, those are the adjectives usage requires for the description of the Type One, or Ted Williams, ballplayer.

Q—What is Type Two like?

A—He is chunky or stocky—that is to say, Yogi Berra.

Q—And the Third?

A—The third type is elongated and does not walk. He is Ol' Satchmo, or Satchel Paige.

Q—What do you mean Satchmo doesn't walk?

A—Not in the sports pages, he doesn't. He ambles.

Q—You mentioned a hurler, Mr. Arbuthnot. What is a hurler?

A—A hurler is a twirler.

Q—Well, what is a twirler?

A—A twirler is a flinger, a tosser. He's a moundsman.

Q—Moundsman?

A—Yes. He officiates on the mound. When the veteran pilot tells a hurler he is to twirl on a given day, that is a mound assignment, and the hurler who has been told to twirl is the mound nominee for that game.

ARMAND LA MONTAGNE. *Ted Williams.*
1985. Wood. Approx. 8 ft. high.
The National Baseball Library,
Cooperstown, New York.

Q—You mean he pitches?

A—That is right. You have cut the Gordian knot.

Q—What's the pitcher for the other team called?

A—He is the mound adversary, or mound opponent, of the mound nominee. That makes them rival hurlers, or twirlers. They face each other and have a mound duel, or pitchers' battle.

Q—Who wins?

A—The mound victor wins, and as a result he is a mound ace, or ace moundsman. He excels on the mound, or stars on it. He and the other moundsmen on his team are the mound corps.

Q—What happens to the mound nominee who loses the mound duel?

A—He is driven off the mound.

Q—What do you mean by that?

A—He's yanked. He's knocked out of the box.

Q—What's the box?

A—The box is the mound.

Q—I see. Why does the losing moundsman lose?

A—Because he issues, grants, yields, allows, or permits too many hits or walks, or both.

Q—A bit on the freehanded side, eh? Where does the mound victor go if he pitches the entire game?

A—He goes all the way.

Q—And how does the mound adversary who has been knocked out of the box explain his being driven off the mound?

A—He says, "I had trouble with my control," or "my curve wasn't working," or "I just didn't have anything today."

Q—What happens if a mound ace issues, grants, yields, allows, or permits too many hits and walks?

A—In that case, sooner or later, rumors are rife. Either that or they are rampant.

Q—Rife where?

A—In the front office.

Q—What's that?

A—That's the place where baseball's biggies—also known as baseball moguls—do their asking.

Q—What do they ask for?

A—Waivers on erratic southpaw.

Q—What are these baseball biggies further known as?

A—They are known as the Shrewd Mahatma or as Horace Stoneham, but if they wear their shirt open at the neck, they are known as Bill Veeck.

Q—What do baseball biggies do when they are not asking for waivers?

A—They count the gate receipts, buy promising rookies, sell aging twirlers, and stay loyally by Manager Durocher.

Q—And what does Manager Durocher do?

A—He guides the destinies of the Giants and precipitates arguments with the men in blue.

Q—What men in blue?

A—The umpires, or arbiters.

Q—What kind of arguments does Durocher precipitate?

A—Heated arguments.

Q—And the men in blue do what to him and other players who precipitate heated arguments?

A—They send, relegate, banish, or thumb them to the showers.

Q—Mr. Arbuthnot, how do you, as a cliché expert, refer to first base?

A—First base is the initial sack.

Q—And second base?

A—The keystone sack.

Q—What's third base called?

A—The hot corner. The first inning is the initial frame, and an inning without runs is a scoreless stanza.

Q—What is one run known as?

A—A lone run, but four runs are known as a quartet of tallies.

Q—What is a baseball?

A—The pill, the horsehide, the old apple, or the sphere.

Q—And what's a bat?

A—The bat is the willow, or the wagon tongue, or the piece of lumber. In the hands of a mighty batsman, it is the mighty bludgeon.

Q—What does a mighty batsman do?

A—He amasses runs. He connects with the old apple. He raps 'em out. He belts 'em and he clouts 'em.

Q—Clouts what?

A—Circuit clouts.

Q—What are they?

A—Home runs. Know what the mighty batsman does to the mighty bludgeon?

Q—No. What?

A—He wields it. Know what kind of orgies he fancies?

Q—What kind?

A—Batting orgies. Slugfests. That's why his team pins.

Q—Pins what?

A—All its hopes on him.

Q—Mr. Arbuthnot, what is a runner guilty of when he steals home?

A—A plate theft.

Q—And how many kinds of baseball games are there?

A—Five main classifications: scheduled tussles, crucial contests, pivotal games, drab frays, and arc-light tussles.

MURRAY TINKELMAN. *Joe DiMaggio.*
Pen and ink on bristol. 11 x 14 in.
In the collection of the Baseball Hall
of Fame, Cooperstown, New York.

Q—And what does the team that wins—

A—Sir, a baseball team never wins. It scores a victory, or gains one, or chalks one up, or it snatches.

Q—Snatches what?

A—Victory from the jaws of defeat.

Q—How?

A—By a ninth-inning rally.

Q—I see. Well, what do the teams that chalk up victories do to the teams that lose?

A—They nip, top, wallop, trounce, rout, down, subdue, smash, drub, paste, trip, crush, curb, whitewash, erase, bop, slam, batter, check, hammer, pop, wham, clout, and blank the visitors. Or they zero them.

Q—Gracious sakes! Now I know why ballplayers are old at thirty-five.

A—Oh, that isn't the half of it. They do other things to the visitors.

Q—Is it possible?

A—Certainly. They jolt them, or deal them a jolt. They also halt, sock, thump, larrup, vanquish, flatten, scalp, shellac, blast, slaughter, K.O., mow down, topple, whack, pound, rap, sink, baffle, thwart, foil, maul, and nick.

Q—Do the losers do anything at all to the victors?

A—Yes. They bow to the victors. And they taste.

Q—Taste what?

A—Defeat. They trail. They take a drubbing, pasting, or shellacking. They are in the cellar.

Q—What about the victors?

A—They loom as flag contenders. They're in the first division . . .

Q—Mr. Arbuthnot, what is the first sign of spring?

A—Well, a robin, of course.

Q—Yes, but I'm thinking of our subject here. How about when the ballplayers go south for spring training?

A—Ballplayers don't go south for spring training.

Q—Why, they do!

A—They do *not*. They wend their way southward.

Q—Oh, I see. Well, do all ballplayers wend their way southward?

A—No. One remains at home.

Q—Who is he?

A—The lone holdout.

Q—Why does the lone holdout remain at home?

A—He refuses to ink pact.

Q—What do you mean by that?

A—He won't affix his Hancock to his contract.

Q—Why not?

A—He demands a pay hike, or salary boost.

Q—From whom?

MURRAY TINKELMAN. *Wade Boggs*. Pen and ink on bristol. 16 x 20 in. In the collection of Don Gage—The Upper Deck.

A—From baseball's biggies.

Q—And what do baseball's biggies do to the lone holdout?

A—They attempt to lure him back into the fold.

Q—How?

A—By offering him a new contract.

Q—What does lone holdout do then?

A—He weighs offer. If he doesn't like it, he balks at terms. If he does like it, he inks pact and gets pay hike.

Q—How much pay hike?

A—An undisclosed amount in excess of.

Q—That makes him what?

A—One of the highest-paid baseball stars in the annals of the game, barring Ruth.

Q—What if baseball's biggies won't give lone holdout pay hike?

A—In that case, lone holdout takes pay cut, old salary, or job in filling station in home town.

Q—Now, when baseball players reach the spring training camp and put on their uniforms—

A—May I correct you again, sir? Baseball players do not put on uniforms. They don them.

Q—I see. What for?

A—For practice session or strenuous workout.

Q—And why must they have a strenuous workout?

A—Because they must shed the winter's accumulation of excess avoirdupois.

Q—You mean they must lose weight?

A—You put it in a nutshell. They must be streamlined, so they plunge.

Q—Plunge into what?

A—Into serious training.

Q—Can't get into serious training except by plunging, eh?

A—No. Protocol requires that they plunge. Training season gets under way in Grapefruit and Citrus Leagues. Casey Stengel bars night life.

Q—Mr. Arbuthnot, what is the opening game of the season called?

A—Let me see-e-e. It's on the tip of my tongue. Isn't that aggravating? Ah, I have it—the opener! At the opener, fifty-two thousand two hundred and ninety-three fans watch Giants bow to Dodgers.

Q—What do those fifty-two thousand two hundred and ninety-three fans constitute?

A—They constitute fandom.

Q—And how do they get into the ballpark?

A—They click through the turnstiles.

Q—Now, then, Mr. Arbuthnot, the climax of the baseball season is the World Series, is it not?

A—That's right.

Q—And what is the World Series called?

A—It's the fall classic, or crucial contest, also known as the fray, the epic struggle, and the Homeric struggle. It is part of the American scene, like ham and eggs or pumpkin pie. It's a colorful event.

Q—What is it packed with?

A—Thrills. Drama.

Q—What kind of drama?

A—Sheer or tense.

Q—Why does it have to be packed with thrills and drama?

A—Because if it isn't, it becomes drab fray.

Q—Where does the fall classic take place?

A—In a vast municipal stadium or huge ballpark.

Q—And the city in which the fall classic is held is what?

A—The city is baseball mad.

Q—And the hotels?

A—The hotels are jammed. Rooms are at a premium.

Q—Tickets also, I presume.

A—Ticket? If you mean the cards of admission to the fall classic, they are referred to as elusive series ducats, and they *are* at a premium, though I would prefer to say that they are scarcer than the proverbial hen's teeth.

Q—Who attends the series?

A—A milling throng, or great outpouring of fans.

Q—What does the great outpouring of fans do?

A—It storms the portals and, of course, clicks through the turnstiles.

Q—Causing what?

A—Causing attendance records to go by the board. Stands fill early.

Q—What else does the crowd do?

A—It yells itself hoarse. Pent-up emotions are released. It rides the men in blue. . . .

Q—Now, the team that wins the series—

A—Again, I'm sorry to correct you, sir. A team does not win a series. It wraps it up. It clinches it.

Q—Well, then what?

A—Then the newly crowned champions repair to their locker room.

Q—What reigns in that locker room?

A—Pandemonium, bedlam, and joy.

Q—Expressed how?

A—By lifting youthful pilot, or his equivalent, to the shoulders of his teammates.

Q—In the locker room of the losers, what is as thick as a day in—I mean so thick you could cut it with a knife?

A—Gloom. The losers are devoid.

Q—Devoid of what?

A—Animation.

Q—Why?

A—Because they came apart at the seams in the pivotal tussle.

Q—What happens to the newly crowned champions later?

A—They are hailed, acclaimed, and fêted. They receive mighty ovations, boisterous demonstrations, and thunderous welcomes.

Q—And when those are over?

A—They split the series purse and go hunting.

Q—Mr. Arbuthnot, if a powerful slugger or mighty batsman wields a mighty bludgeon to such effect that he piles up a record number of circuit clouts, what does that make him?

A—That is very apt to make him most valuable player of the year.

Q—And that?

A—That makes the kids of America look up to him as their hero.

Q—If most valuable player of the year continues the batting orgies that make the kids of America worship him, what then?

A—Then he becomes one of Baseball's Immortals. He is enshrined in Baseball's Hall of Fame.

Q—And after that?

A—Someday he retires and becomes veteran scout, or veteran pilot. Or sports broadcaster.

Q—And then?

A—Well, eventually a memorial plaque is unveiled to him at the opener.

Q—Thank you, Mr. Arbuthnot. You have been most helpful. I won't detain you any longer, and I hope your grandmother's funeral this afternoon is a tense drama packed with thrills.

A—Thanks a lot. Good-by now.

Q—Hold on a moment, Mr. Arbuthnot. Just for my own curiosity—couldn't you have said "thanks" and "good-by" and let it go at that, without adding the "lot" and "now" malarkey?

A—I could have, but it would have cost me my title as a cliché expert.

Bernard Malamud

FROM THE NATURAL

In this excerpt from what might be the best-known baseball novel of all, a young Roy Hobbs, on his way to a major league tryout, faces the Whammer, a Babe Ruth clone, on a field somewhere in America. This passage epitomizes baseball's ability to highlight a one-on-one confrontation within a team game. It also lets us enjoy, for a few moments, a perfect summer evening.

Toward late afternoon the Whammer, droning on about his deeds on the playing field, got very chummy with Harriet Bird and before long had slipped his fat fingers around the back of her chair so Roy left the club car and sat in the sleeper, looking out of the window, across the aisle from where Eddie slept sitting up. Gosh, the size of the forest. He thought they had left it for good yesterday and here it still was. As he watched, the trees flowed together and so did the hills and clouds. He felt a kind of sadness, because he had lost the feeling of a particular place. Yesterday he had come from somewhere, a place he knew was there, but today it had thinned away in space—how vast he could not have guessed—and he felt like he would never see it again.

The forest stayed with them, climbing hills like an army, shooting down like waterfalls. As the train skirted close in, the trees leveled out and he could see within the woodland the only place he had been truly intimate with in his wanderings, a green world shot through with weird light and strange bird cries, muffled in silence that made the privacy so complete his inmost self had no shame of anything he thought there, and it eased the body-shaking beat of his ambitions. Then he thought of here and now and for the thousandth time wondered why they had come so far and for what. Did Sam really know what he was doing? Sometimes Roy had his doubts. Sometimes he wanted to turn around and go back home, where he could at least predict what tomorrow would be like. Remembering the white rose in his pants pocket, he decided to get rid of it. But then the pine trees flowed away from the train and slowly swerved behind blue hills; all at once there was this beaten gold, snow-capped mountain in the distance, and on the plain several miles from its base lay a small city gleaming in the rays of the declining sun. Approaching it, the long train slowly pulled to a stop.

Eddie woke with a jump and stared out the window.

"Oh, oh, trouble, we never stop here."

He looked again and called Roy.

"What do you make out of that?"

About a hundred yards ahead, where two dirt roads crossed, a moth-eaten model-T Ford was parked on the farther side of the road from town, and a fat old man wearing a broad-brimmed black hat and cowboy boots, who they could see was carrying a squat doctor's satchel, climbed down from it. To the conductor, who had impatiently swung off the train with a lit red lamp, he flourished a yellow telegram. They argued a minute, then the conductor, snapping open his watch, beckoned him along and they boarded the train. When they passed through Eddie's car the conductor's face was sizzling with irritation but the doctor was unruffled. Before disappearing through the door, the conductor called to Eddie, "Half hour."

"Half hour," Eddie yodeled and he got out the stool and set it outside the car so that anyone who wanted to stretch, could.

Only about a dozen passengers got off the train, including Harriet Bird, still hanging on to her precious hat box, the Whammer, and Max Mercy, all as thick as thieves. Roy hunted up the bassoon case just if the train should decide to take off without him, and when he had located Sam they both got off.

"Well, I'll be jiggered." Sam pointed down about a block beyond where the locomotive had halted. There, sprawled out at the outskirts of the city, a carnival was on. It was made up of try-your-skill booths, kiddie rides, a freak show and a gigantic Ferris wheel that looked like a stopped clock. Though there was still plenty of daylight, the carnival was lit up by twisted ropes of blinking bulbs, and many banners streamed in the breeze as the calliope played.

"Come on," said Roy, and they went along with the people from the train who were going toward the tents.

Once they had got there and fooled around a while, Sam stopped to have a crushed cocoanut drink which he privately spiked with a shot from a new bottle, while Roy wandered over to a place where you could throw three baseballs for a dime at three wooden pins, shaped like pint-size milk bottles and set in pyramids of one on top of two, on small raised platforms about twenty feet back from the counter. He changed the fifty-cent piece Sam had slipped him on leaving the train, and this pretty girl in yellow, a little hefty but with a sweet face and nice ways, who with her peanut of a father was waiting on trade, handed him three balls. Lobbing one of them, Roy easily knocked off the pyramid and won himself a naked kewpie doll. Enjoying the game, he laid down another dime, again clattering the pins to the floor in a single shot and now collecting an alarm clock. With the other three dimes he won a brand-new boxed baseball, a washboard, and baby potty, which he traded in for a six-inch harmonica. A few kids came over to watch and Sam, wandering by, indulgently changed another half into dimes for Roy. And Roy won a fine leather cigar case for Sam, a "God Bless America" banner, a flashlight, can of coffee, and a two-pound box of sweets. To the kids' delight, Sam, after a slight hesitation, flipped Roy another half dollar, but this time the little man behind the counter nudged his daughter and she asked Roy if he would now take a kiss for every three pins he tumbled.

Roy glanced at her breasts and she blushed. He got embarrassed too. "What do you say, Sam, it's your four bits?"

Sam bowed low to the girl. "Ma'am," he said, "now you see how dang foolish it is to be a young feller."

The girl laughed and Roy began to throw for kisses, flushing each pyramid in a shot or two while the girl counted aloud the kisses she owed him.

Some of the people from the train passed by and stayed to watch when they learned from the mocking kids what Roy was throwing for.

The girl, pretending to be unconcerned, tolled off the third and fourth kisses.

As Roy fingered the ball for the last throw the Whammer came by holding over his shoulder a Louisville Slugger that he had won for himself in the batting cage down a way. Harriet, her pretty face flushed, had a kewpie doll, and Max Mercy carried a box of cigars. The Whammer had discarded his sun glasses and all but strutted over his performance and the prizes he had won.

Roy raised his arm to throw for the fifth kiss and a clean sweep when the Whammer called out to him in a loud voice, "Pitch it here, busher, and I will knock it into the moon."

Roy shot for the last kiss and missed. He missed with the second and third balls. The crowd oohed its disappointment.

"Only four," said the girl in yellow as if she mourned the fifth.

Angered at what had happened, Sam hoarsely piped, "I got ten dollars that says he can strike you out with three pitched balls, Wambold."

The Whammer looked at Sam with contempt.

"What d'ye say, Max?" he said.

Mercy shrugged.

"Oh, I love contests of skill," Harriet said excitedly. Roy's face went pale.

"What's the matter, hayfoot, you scared?" the Whammer taunted.

"Not of you," Roy said.

"Let's go across the tracks where nobody'll get hurt," Mercy suggested.

"Nobody but the busher and his bazooka. What's in it, busher?"

"None of your business." Roy picked up the bassoon case.

The crowd moved in a body across the tracks, the kids circling around to get a good view, and the engineer and fireman watched from their cab window.

Sam cornered one of the kids who lived nearby and sent him home for a fielder's glove and his friend's catcher's mitt. While they were waiting, for protection he buttoned underneath his coat the washboard Roy had won. Max drew a batter's box alongside a piece of slate. He said he would call the throws and they would count as one of the three pitches only if they were over or if the Whammer swung and missed.

When the boy returned with the gloves, the sun was going down, and though the sky was aflame with light all the way to the snowy mountain peak, it was chilly on the ground.

Breaking the seal, Sam squeezed the baseball box and the pill shot up like a greased egg. He tossed it to Mercy, who inspected the hide and stitches, then rubbed the shine off and flipped it to Roy.

"Better throw a couple of warm-ups."

"My arm is loose," said Roy.

"It's your funeral."

Placing his bassoon case out of the way in the grass, Roy shed his coat. One of the boys came forth to hold it.

"Be careful you don't spill the pockets," Roy told him.

Sam came forward with the catcher's glove on. It was too small for his big hand but he said it would do all right.

"Sam, I wish you hadn't bet that money on me," Roy said.

"I won't take it if we win, kiddo, but just let it stand if we lose," Sam said, embarrassed.

"We came by it too hard."

"Just let it stand so."

He cautioned Roy to keep his pitches inside, for the Whammer was known to gobble them on the outside corner.

Sam returned to the plate and crouched behind the batter, his knees spread wide because of the washboard. Roy drew on his glove and palmed the ball behind it. Mercy, rubbing his hands to warm them, edged back about six feet behind Sam.

The onlookers retreated to the other side of the tracks, except Harriet, who stood without fear of fouls up close. Her eyes shone at the sight of the two men facing one another.

Mercy called, "Batter up."

The Whammer crowded the left side of the plate, gripping the heavy bat low on the neck, his hands jammed together and legs plunked evenly apart. He hadn't bothered to take off his coat. His eye on Roy said it spied a left-handed monkey.

"Throw it, Rube, it won't get no lighter."

Though he stood about sixty feet away, he loomed up gigantic to Roy, with the wood held like a caveman's ax on his shoulder. His rocklike frame was motionless, his face impassive, unsmiling, dark.

Roy's heart skipped a beat. He turned to gaze at the mountain.

Sam whacked the leather with his fist. "Come on, kiddo, wham it down his whammy."

The Whammer out of the corner of his mouth told the drunk to keep his mouth shut.

"Burn it across his button."

"Close your trap," Mercy said.

"Cut his throat with it."

"If he tries to dust me, so help me I will smash his skull," the Whammer threatened.

Roy stretched loosely, rocked back on his left leg, twirling the right a little like a dancer, then strode forward and threw with such force his knuckles all but scraped the ground on the follow-through.

At thirty-three the Whammer still enjoyed exceptional eyesight. He saw the ball spin off Roy's fingertips and it reminded him of a white pigeon he had kept as a boy, that he would send into flight by flipping it into the air. The ball flew at him and he was conscious of its bird-form and white flapping wings, until it suddenly disappeared from view. He heard a noise like the bang of a firecracker at his feet and Sam had the ball in his mitt. Unable to believe his ears he heard Mercy intone a reluctant strike.

Sam flung off the glove and was wringing his hand.

"Hurt you, Sam?" Roy called.

"No, it's this dang glove."

Though he did not show it, the pitch had bothered the Whammer no end. Not just the speed of it but the sensation of surprise and strangeness that went with it—him batting here on the railroad tracks, the crazy carnival, the drunk catching and a clown pitching, and that queer dame Harriet, who had five minutes ago been patting him on the back for his skill in the batting cage, now eyeing him coldly for letting one pitch go by.

He noticed Max had moved farther back.

"How the hell you expect to call them out there?"

"He looks wild to me." Max moved in.

"Your knees are knockin'," Sam tittered.

"Mind your business, rednose," Max said.

"You better watch your talk, mister," Roy called to Mercy.

"Pitch it, greenhorn," warned the Whammer.

Sam crouched with his glove on. "Do it again, Roy. Give him something simular."

"Do it again," mimicked the Whammer. To the crowd, maybe to Harriet, he held up a vaunting finger showing there were other pitches to come.

Roy pumped, reared and flung.

The ball appeared to the batter to be a slow spinning planet looming toward the earth. For a long light-year he waited for this globe to whirl into the orbit of his swing so he could bust it to smithereens that would settle with dust and dead leaves into some distant cosmos. At last the unseeing eye, maybe a fortuneteller's lit crystal ball—anyway, a curious combination of circles—drifted within range of his weapon, or so he thought, because he lunged at it ferociously, twisting round like a top. He landed on both knees as the world floated by over his head and hit with a *whup* into the cave of Sam's glove.

"Hey, Max," Sam said, as he chased the ball after it had bounced out of the glove, "how do they pernounce Whammer if you leave out the W?"

"Strike," Mercy called long after a cheer (was it a jeer?) had burst from the crowd.

"What's he throwing," the Whammer howled, "spitters?"

"In the pig's poop." Sam thrust the ball at him. "It's drier than your granddaddy's scalp."

"I'm warning him not to try any dirty business."

Yet the Whammer felt oddly relieved. He liked to have his back crowding the wall, when there was a single pitch to worry about and a single pitch to hit. Then the sweat began to leak out of his pores as he stared at the hard, lanky figure of the pitiless pitcher, moving, despite his years and a few waste motions, like a veteran undertaker of the diamond, and he experienced a moment of depression.

Sam must have sensed it, because he discovered an unexpected pity in his heart and even for a split second hoped the idol would not be tumbled. But only for a second, for the Whammer had regained confidence in his known talent and experience and was taunting the greenhorn to throw.

Someone in the crowd hooted and the Whammer raised aloft two fat fingers and pointed where he would murder the ball, where the gleaming rails converged on the horizon and beyond was invisible.

Roy raised his leg. He smelled the Whammer's blood and wanted it, and through him the worm's he had with him, for the way he had insulted Sam.

The third ball slithered at the batter like a meteor, the flame swallowing itself. He lifted his club to crush it into a universe of sparks but the heavy wood dragged, and though he willed to destroy the sound he heard a gong bong and realized with sadness that the ball he had expected to hit had long since been part of the past; and though Max could not cough the fatal word out of his throat, the Whammer understood he was, in the truest sense of it, out.

The crowd was silent as the violet evening fell on their shoulders.

For a night game, the Whammer harshly shouted, it was customary to turn on lights. Dropping the bat, he trotted off to the train, an old man.

COLORPLATE 91

ANDREW RADCLIFFE. *The Baseball Game.* 1986. Oil on canvas. 18 x 22 in.
Nancy Hoffman Gallery, New York.

COLORPLATE 92

PETER DE SÈVE. *The Bums of Summer.* 1989.
Watercolor and ink. 10 x 13 in. Collection of C.F. Payne.

COLORPLATE 93

PETER DE SÈVE. *Spring Training*. 1986.
Watercolor and ink. 11 x 15 in. Collection of Roger de Sève.

COLORPLATE 94

MICHAEL HURSON. *Baseball Player (At Bat).* 1982. Pencil, pastel, ink and conte crayon
on paper. 21 x 16½ in. Collection of Elizabeth Murray, New York.

COLORPLATE 95

JANET BRAUN-REINITZ. *The Bad Trade (Mookie Wilson)*. 1989.
Acrylic on paper. 48 x 84 in. Gallery 53 Artworks, Cooperstown, New York.

COLORPLATE 98

TIM SWARTZ. *Klondike.* 1990.
Watercolor. 18 x 22 in. Gallery 53 Artworks, Cooperstown, New York.

COLORPLATE 96 *(opposite, above)*

VINCENT SCILLA. *Hebrew National.* 1989. Oil on canvas. 24 x 30 in.
Gallery 53 Artworks, Cooperstown, New York.

COLORPLATE 97 *(opposite, below)*

VINCENT SCILLA. *Hit the Hat and Win Five Bucks.* 1988. Acrylic on canvas. 24 x 32 in.
S. Ralbovsky and Gallery 53 Artworks, Cooperstown, New York.

COLORPLATE 99

JAMES RIZZI. *Take Me Out to the Ballgame.* 1990.
Silkscreen with 3-D construction. 25³/4 x 35³/4 in. John Szoke Graphics, Inc.

Douglass Wallop

FROM THE YEAR THE YANKEES LOST THE PENNANT

By the time this novel was published in 1954, the New York Yankees had won sixteen of their twenty-two World Championships. The novel, later adapted for the stage and screen in the form of the musical Damn Yankees, *tells the story of Joe Boyd, a fan of the hapless Washington Senators who sells his soul to the devil for a chance to lead the Nats to a pennant over the hated Bronx Bombers. In this excerpt, Joe, walking off another Senators loss, has his first encounter with the King of the Underworld (who is, not surprisingly, an ardent Yankee fan).*

———————————

Joe stopped short, but after a second of silent self-encouragement forced his legs forward again, wondering if he was about to be robbed and then remembering with relief that he had left his wallet on the bureau.

"Good evening, Mr. Boyd," the man said.

"Good evening," Joe said, mystified that his name was known. He hurried on, but the man fell into step beside him, and as they neared a street lamp, Joe took a sidelong glance. Although even at this hour the temperature was still over ninety and the humidity unworldly, the stranger wore a black topcoat, the lapels turned up and crossed to hide his chin and mouth. A black hat was pulled low over his brow.

"How did the team make out tonight?" the stranger asked.

They had reached the corner now and Joe halted. "You mean the baseball team?" he said.

"Naturally."

"They lost. Eleven to three."

The stranger made a clucking noise of sympathy. "That's a shame," he said. "It must be hard for you."

Joe found the man's voice singular. Although its owner seemed trying very hard for an effect of mellifluous cordiality he was gravely handicapped for it was a deeply rasping voice, at times hoarse.

"I'm used to it by now," Joe said. He paused, scraping his shoe against the curb. "Or partly used to it, anyway."

"And incidentally, how was your trip to Quebec this year?" the stranger asked, disregarding Joe's question.

"It wasn't bad," Joe said. "Say, do you live around here? I don't remember seeing you before. Where do you get all your information, anyway?" . . .

"I was reading through your file," the stranger said.

"My file!"

"Sure. Your file. We have a file on quite a few of you older fellows."

"Who is we, if you don't mind my asking?"

The stranger chuckled. "My name is Applegate, but that's of no importance," he said. "What's important right at the moment is that punk baseball team you've been rooting for all these years."

"I wouldn't call them punk exactly," Joe said, and a coolness came into his voice.

"And conversely, it is the New York Yankees who are also important," the stranger said. "You say you wouldn't call that team of yours punk? Let me ask you how long it's been since they won the pennant.

"Well, let's see . . ."

"It's fast approaching three decades," the stranger said. "Am I right? Now if the file is accurate, and—"

Washington Senator Harmon Killebrew On Deck.
c. 1960. The National Baseball Library, Cooperstown,
New York. *The Washington team, "first in war, first in
peace, and last in the American League," won its last
pennant in 1933—not counting the fictitious pennant
won in Douglass Wallop's 1954 novel* The Year the
Yankees Lost the Pennant. *The Senators would later
move to Minnesota and become the Twins, while a
second Senators team would be established; but it too
would move, to Texas to become the Rangers.*

"I don't get this file stuff," Joe broke in.

". . . and there's no reason to believe it's anything less, you were just short of twenty-five at the time they last won, and now you're fifty. Did it ever occur to you that you may even die before you see them win the pennant again? For that matter you may die before any team other than the Yankees wins it. There's something rather tragic about that, something very sad."

Joe admitted that it was so, although he did not reply.

"On your death bed," the stranger went on, "it would be very sad to think back and realize—well, I mean this period of barrenness spans the best years of your life . . . all those years in the second division, you know what I mean."

"They just picked up a couple of pretty good pitchers on waivers," Joe said. "I think they'll probably pull themselves together in a few days."

The stranger chuckled scornfully. "Just like every spring you read they're bringing up some hot rookies from the minors and this year it's going to be different, eh, Mr. Boyd? Only it never is."

"Maybe so and maybe not," Joe said, "but you still haven't explained what you mean by my file. What kind of file? I'm no communist."

"Communist?" The stranger began laughing without control, finally saying weakly, "Communist! What memories that stirs! No, of course you're not a communist."

"Well, then what are you talking about?"

For a few seconds longer the stranger laughed. Then straightening to his full height, he folded the lapels of his coat more carefully over his chin and touched his nose lightly. "Mr. Boyd," he said, "I've got a proposition for you. How would you like to be a baseball player?"

"A baseball player? Where? In the old men's softball league?"

"In the American League, Mr. Boyd. Playing for that team of yours. You can be Moses and lead them out of the wilderness, to use a metaphor I've never particularly cared for."

"Was it a good party?" Joe asked.

"What do you mean, was it a good party?"

"That party you went on tonight. It must have been good."

"Don't make light, Mr. Boyd," the stranger said sternly. "My time isn't so plentiful that I can spend it in levity."

"You mean when you say I can be a baseball player I should take you seriously?" Joe asked.

"Very seriously."

"How's all this going to happen?"

"It's easy," the stranger said. "Just say the word and you can be the finest baseball player in the world."

"But how? I'm fifty years old. Besides I was never much good at baseball anyway. This is ridiculous."

"Age is a very flexible thing," the stranger said. "You don't have to be fifty years old, you know. What's most important is the will to be a good baseball player. And Mr. Boyd, in all this country we've never found anybody with as great a will as yours."

"Listen, who are you, for heaven's sake?" Joe demanded.

"Not exactly," the stranger said. "But as I told you before, my name is Applegate."

"Well, Mr. Applegate," Joe said, starting off, "I suggest you see a doctor. Or at least go sleep it off."

Joe heard the low chuckle following him up the block. Then it seemed to overtake him and a moment later his heart pounded violently. Just ahead, a dark figure stepped from the shadows.

"Now as I was saying, Mr. Boyd," the stranger began, and then chuckled again. "I'm sorry I startled you, my friend," he went on. "But there's certainly no reason to be startled. I have nothing but friendly intentions. My only wish is to help you lead a more fruitful life. Now if you'll just stand still a second or two so I can make myself clear. . . . Cigarette?"

Joe declined and a second later felt his body again grow weak. The stranger had lit his own cigarette but not by match or lighter. He had merely snapped his fingers.

"Now then," he said, "suppose we find a place to sit down and talk this over. Here's a bench up at the corner. Let's have a seat."

Joe looked and there was a bench next to the bus-stop sign, although to his certain knowledge there had never been a bench there before.

"By the way," the stranger said, settling himself and stretching his legs, "do you mind if I call you Joe? And you can call me App, if you like. That's what my friends call me. . . . Come on, Joe, have a seat."

Joe stood a moment longer and then gingerly sat down, as far away from Applegate as the width of the bench permitted. A few blocks away he could see the lights of a bus approaching, and it was a welcome sight. His strength was returning. His jaw tightened. He would now restore the whole interview to normalcy. With a calm phrase or two . . . He could, instead, get up and go home, but that seemed cowardly on the face of it. There was no reason to go home. It was nothing but normal. The man was drunk. The fire had started—well, he could have been lighting a kitchen match with his thumbnail. And he had simply run along through the shrubbery. That's how he had gotten ahead again so quickly.

On the strength of these self-assurances, Joe squared his shoulders and asked, "What kind of liquor were they feeding you tonight?" But his voice quavered and lacked conviction. The bus sped past without stopping.

"Oh, come now, Joe," Applegate said. "Let's not be sophomoric about this. Let's get down to business. Now first of all I'd like to ask you a question. How long has it been since you ran?"

"Ran?"

"Sure, ran."

"I don't know. I can't remember exactly."

"Will you do me a favor, Joe? Stand up, if you will. Now walk a few steps away. That's right. Now head back down the block the way we came from. Good! Now—run!"

"I don't feel like running," Joe said.

"Well, just jog a little. Just get yourself started."

Joe began to jog, and then, suddenly, as though beyond his own will, he was running at great speed. His body felt light; indeed it felt thin. Thin and hard and wiry. In midflight he thumped his stomach. It was flat as a board, and as hard. It was not his own stomach, he thought headily, but all the better. Breathing easily, his head reared back, he tasted something from the distant past: The way the air had felt, warm spring air as he remembered it, rushing past his head; the sense of headlong flight, a feeling he had not experienced since—since the last time he had run, and that was not since his youth.

At the end of the block he stopped, and when he touched his stomach it was again his own. Flabby.

"Now run back," Applegate called.

Joe began running, but slowly, sluggishly, with heavy legs. After only a few steps he was breathing hard. His temples pounded. His stomach quivered out ahead of him. He clenched his fists and dug harder, but he could not recapture the swiftness of the trip down and already he missed it.

"Out of condition, Joe?" Applegate asked sympathetically, as Joe finally arrived. "How did it feel on the way down, though?"

Gasping, Joe sank to the bench, fearful of the strain on his heart. He shouldn't have done it. And yet, going down, it had seemed no strain at all. "It felt good," he managed to say.

"You could run like that all the time," Applegate said. "The question is, would you like it?"

"You mean be able to run like that?" Joe asked, still panting.

"Yes, and more besides. To have your youth, to have almost unheard of skill in baseball— to be able to carry that team of yours on your back—all the way to the pennant."

Joe stood, trying to suck in deep breaths, looking off toward the corner store—in his earliest memory a meat market, later a dry goods and notions store, once a cleaning and pressing place, and now, about to become something else. He saw a man and woman moving about, placing things on shelves.

"You mean you're trying to tell me they could still win the pennant this season?" he asked.

"Sure, it's not too late. A couple of good winning streaks for you boys and a little tough luck for the Yankees—that's all it would take."

"That's ridiculous," Joe said between pantings.

"It's not ridiculous, boy. It can be done. Just trust in me."

"And who are you?" Joe asked again, although by now he thought perhaps he knew.

"Applegate is the name. A-P-P—" he broke off and chuckled. "I told you that was of no importance, my boy. The question is—do you accept?"

Another bus was approaching. This one stopped and a woman got off.

"Oh, good evening, Mr. Boyd," she said.

"Good evening, Mrs. Stewart."

"What are you doing standing here on the corner all by yourself?" she asked.

It was not until then that Joe saw Applegate was gone.

"Oh, just getting a little air," he said.

The woman started off. "Do you think it will ever rain?" she called back. Joe didn't answer and her heels clicked off up the hill, out of hearing.

"Hey," Joe called. Then, "Where are you Applegate? Hey, *Apple*gate."

There was no answer, no sign. Joe looked about in each direction, peering into the shadows, and when he turned back, the bench too had disappeared.

Philip Roth

FROM THE GREAT AMERICAN NOVEL
"Home Sweet Home"

In his 1973 account of the fictitious Patriot League, Philip Roth documents the fateful on-the-field confrontation between maverick rookie phenom Gil Gamesh of the Tri-City Greenbacks and umpiring legend Mike "The Mouth" Masterson.

The Greenbacks went into the final day of the year only half a game out in front of the Tycoons; whichever Tri-City team should win the game, would win the flag. And Gamesh, by winning his forty-second, would have won more games in a season than any other pitcher in history. And of course there was the chance that the nineteen-year-old kid would pitch his third consecutive no-hitter . . .

Well, what happened was more incredible even than that. The first twenty-six Tycoons he faced went down on strikes: seventy-eight strikes in a row. There had not even been a foul tip—either the strike was called, or in desperation they swung at the ozone. Then, two out in the ninth and two strikes on the batter (thus was it ever, with Gilbert Gamesh) the left-hander fired into the catcher's mitt what seemed not only to the sixty-two thousand three hundred and forty-two ecstatic fans packed into Greenback Stadium, but to the helpless batter himself—who turned from the plate without a whimper and started back to his home in Wilkes-Barre, Pa.—the last pitch of the '33 Patriot League season. Strike-out number twenty-seven. Victory number forty-two. Consecutive no-hitter number three. The most perfect game ever pitched in the major leagues, or conceived of by the mind of man. The Greenbacks had won the pennant, and how! Bring on the Senators and the Giants!

Or so it had seemed, until Mike the Mouth Masterson got word through to the two managers that the final out did not count, because at the moment of the pitch, *his back had been turned to the plate.*

In order for the game to be resumed, tens of thousands of spectators who had poured out onto the field when little Joe Iviri, the Tycoon hitter, had turned away in defeat, had now to be forced back up through the gates into the stands; wisely, General Oakhart had arranged beforehand for the Tri-City mounted constabulary to be at the ready, under the stands, in the event of just such an uprising as this, and so it was that a hundred whinnying horses, drawn up like a cavalry company and charging into the manswarm for a full fifteen minutes, drove the enraged fans from the field. But not even policemen with drawn pistols could force them to take their seats. With arms upraised they roared at Mike the Mouth as though he were their Fuehrer, only it was not devotion they were promising him.

General Oakhart himself took the microphone and attempted to address the raging mob. "This is General Douglas D. Oakhart, President of the Patriot League. Due to circumstances beyond his control, umpire-in-chief Mike Masterson was unable to make a call on the last pitch because his back was turned to the plate at that moment."

"KILL THE MOUTH! MURDER THE BUM!"

"According to rule 9.4, section e, of the Official—"

"BANISH THE BLIND BASTARD! CUT OFF HIS WHATSIS!"

"—game shall be resumed prior to that pitch. Thank you."

"BOOOOOOOOOOOOOOOOOOOOOOOOOOOOOOO!"

In the end it was necessary for the General to step out onto the field of play (as once he had stepped onto the field of battle), followed behind by the Tri-City Symphony Orchestra; by his order, the musicians (more terrified than any army he had ever seen, French, British,

Americans, or Hun) assembled for the second time that day in center field, and with two down in the ninth, and two strikes on the batter, proceeded to play the National Anthem again.

"'O say can you see,'" sang the General.

Through his teeth, he addressed Mike Masterson, who stood beside him at home plate, with his cap over his chest protector. "What happened?"

Mike said, "I—I saw him."

Agitated as he was, he nonetheless remained at rigid attention, smartly saluting the broad stripes and bright stars. "Who? When?"

"The one," said Mike.

"The one *what?*"

"Who I've been looking for. There! Headed for the exit back of the Tycoon dugout. I recognized him by his ears and the set of his chin," and a sob rose in his throat. "Him. The kidnapper. The masked man who killed my little girl."

"Mike!" snapped the General. "Mike, you were seeing things! You were imagining it!"

"It was *him!*"

"Mike, that was thirty-five years ago. You could not recognize a man after all that time, not by his ears, for God's sake!"

"Why not?" Mike wept. "I've seen him every night, in my sleep, since 12 September 1898."

"'O say does that Star-Spangled Banner yet wave/O'er the land of the free, and the home—'"

"Play ball!" the fans were shouting, "Play the God damn game!"

It had worked. The General had turned sixty-two thousand savages back into baseball fans with the playing of the National Anthem! Now—if only he could step in behind the plate and call the last pitch! Or bring the field umpire in to take Mike's place on balls and strikes! But the first was beyond what he was empowered to do under the Rules and the Regulations; and the second would forever cast doubt upon the twenty-six strike-outs already recorded in the history books by Gamesh, and on the forty-one victories before that. Indeed, the field umpire had wisely pretended that he had not seen the last Gamesh pitch either, so as not to compromise the greatest umpire in the game by rendering the call himself. What could the General do then but depart the field?

On the pitcher's mound, Gil Gamesh had pulled his cap so low on his brow that he was in shadows to his chin. He had not even removed it for "The Star-Spangled Banner"—as thousands began to realize with a deepening sense of uneasiness and alarm. He had been there on the field since the last pitch thrown to Iviri—except for the ten minutes when he had been above it, bobbing on a sea of uplifted arms, rolling in the embrace of ten thousand fans. And when the last pack of celebrants had fled before the flying hooves, they had deposited him back on the mound, from whence they had plucked him—and run for their lives. And so there he stood, immobile, his eyes and mouth invisible to one and all. What was he thinking! What was going through Gil's mind?

Scrappy little Joe Iviri, a little pecking hitter, and the best lead-off man in the country at that time, came up out of the Tycoon dugout, sporting a little grin as though he had just been raised from the dead, and from the stands came an angry Vesuvian roar. . . .

"Play!"

Iviri stepped in, twitching his little behind.

Gamesh pitched.

It was a curve that would have shamed a ten-year-old boy—or girl, for that matter. While it hung in the clear September light, deciding whether to break a little or not, there was time enough for the catcher to gasp, "Holy aloha!"

And then the baseball was ricocheting around in the tricky right-field corner, to which it had been dispatched at the same height at which it had been struck. A stand-up triple for Iviri.

From the silence in Greenback Stadium, you would have thought that winter had come and the field lay under three feet of snow. You would have thought that the ballplayers were all down home watching haircuts at the barber shop, or boasting over a beer to the boys in the local saloon. And all sixty-two thousand fans might have been in hibernation with the bears.

LAWRENCE KARASEK. *Mike's Mask.* 1991.
Lithograph of charcoal on paper drawing.
30 x 23 in. Gallery 53 Artworks,
Cooperstown, New York.

Pineapple Tawhaki moved in a daze out to the mound to hand a new ball to Gamesh. Immediately after the game, at the investigation conducted in General Oakhart's office, Tawhaki—weeping profusely—maintained that when he had come out to the mound after the triple was hit, Gamesh had hissed at him, "Stay down! Stay low! On your knees, Pineapple, if you know what's good for you!" "So," said Pineapple in his own defense, "I do what he say, sir. That all. I figger Gil want to throw drop-drop. Okay to me. Gil pitch, Pineapple catch. I stay down. Wait for drop-drop. That all, sir, that all in the world!" . . .

It was clear from the moment the ball left Gil's hand that it wasn't any drop-drop he'd had in mind to throw. Tawhaki stayed low—even as the pitch took off like something the Wright Brothers had invented. The batter testified at the hearing that it was still picking up speed when it passed him, and scientists interviewed by reporters later that day estimated that at the moment it struck Mike Masterson in the throat, Gamesh's rising fastball was probably traveling between one hundred and twenty and one hundred and thirty miles per hour. In his vain attempt to turn from the ball, Mike had caught it just between the face mask and the chest protector, a perfect pitch, if you believed, as the General did, that Masterson's blue bow tie was the bull's-eye for which Gamesh had been aiming.

The calamity-sized black headline MOUTH DEAD; GIL BANISHED proved to be premature. To be sure, even before the sun went down, the Patriot League President, with the Commissioner's approval, had expelled the record-breaking rookie sensation from the game of baseball forever. But the indestructible ump rallied from his coma in the early hours of the morning, and though he did not live to tell the tale—he was a mute thereafter—at least he lived.

The fans never forgave the General for banishing their hero. To hear them tell it, a boy destined to be the greatest pitcher of all time had been expelled from the game just for throwing a wild pitch. Rattled by a senile old umpire who had been catching a few Zs back of home plate, the great rookie throws *one bad one*, and that's it, for life! Oh no, it ain't Oakhart's favorite ump who's to blame for standin' in the way of the damn thing—it's Gil!

Nor did the General's favorite ump forgive him either. The very day they had unswathed the bandages and released him from the hospital, Mike Masterson was down at the league office, demanding what he called "justice." Despite the rule forbidding it, he was wearing his blue uniform off the field—in the big pockets once heavy with P. League baseballs, he carried an old rag and a box of chalk; and when he entered the office, there was a blackboard and an easel strapped to his back. Poor Mike had lost not only his voice. He wanted Gamesh to be indicted and tried by the Tri-City D.A.'s office for attempted murder.

"Mike, I must say that it comes as a profound shock to me that a man of your great wisdom should wish to take vengeance in that way."

STUFF MY WISDOM (wrote Mike the Mouth on the blackboard he had set before the General's desk) I WANT THAT BOY BEHIND BARS!

"But this is not like you at all. Besides, the boy has been punished plenty."

SAYS WHO?

"Now use your head, man. He is a brilliant young pitcher—and he will never pitch again."

AND I CAN'T TALK AGAIN! OR EVEN WHISPER! I CAN'T CALL A STRIKE! I CAN'T CALL A BALL! I HAVE BEEN SILENCED FOREVER AT SEVENTY-ONE!

"And will seeing him in jail give you your voice back, at seventy-one?"

NO! NOTHING WILL! IT WON'T BRING MY MARY JANE BACK EITHER! IT WON'T MAKE UP FOR THE SCAR ON MY FOREHEAD OR THE GLASS STILL FLOATING IN MY BACK! IT WON'T MAKE UP (here he had to stop to wipe the board clean with his rag, so that he would have room to proceed) FOR THE ABUSE I HAVE TAKEN DAY IN AND DAY OUT FOR FIFTY YEARS!

"Then what on earth is the use of it?"

JUSTICE!

"Mike, listen to reason—what kind of justice is it that will destroy the reputation of our league?"

STUFF OUR LEAGUE!

"Mike, it would blacken forever the name of baseball."

STUFF BASEBALL!

Here General Oakhart rose in anger—"It is a man who has lost his sense of values entirely, who could write those two words on a blackboard! Put that boy in jail, and, I promise you, you will have another Sacco and Vanzetti on your hands. You will make a martyr of Gamesh, and in the process ruin the very thing we all love."

HATE! wrote Mike, HATE! And on and on, filling the board with the four-letter word, then rubbing it clean with his rag, then filling it to the edges, again and again.

On and on and on.

Fortunately the crazed Masterson got nowhere with the D.A.—General Oakhart saw to that, as did the owners of the Greenbacks and the Tycoons. All they needed was Gil Gamesh tried for attempted murder in Tri-City, for baseball to be killed for good in that town. Sooner or later, Gamesh would be forgotten, and the Patriot League would return to normal . . .

Wishful thinking. Gamesh, behind the wheel of his Packard, and still in his baseball togs, disappeared from sight only minutes after leaving the postgame investigation in the General's office. To the reporters who clung to the running board, begging him to make a statement about his banishment, about Oakhart, about baseball, about anything, he had but five words to say, one of which could not even be printed in the papers: "I'll be back, you————!" and the Packard roared away. But the next morning, on a back road near Binghamton, New York, the car was found overturned and burned out—and no rookie sensation to be seen anywhere. Either the charred body had been snatched by ghoulish fans, or he had walked away from the wreck intact.

GIL KILLED? the headlines asked, even as the stories came in from people claiming to have seen Gamesh riding the rails in Indiana, selling apples in Oklahoma City, or waiting in a soup line in L.A. A sign appeared in a saloon in Orlando, Florida, that read GIL TENDING BAR HERE, and hanging beside it in the window was a white uniform with a green numeral, 19—purportedly Gil's very own baseball suit. For a day and a night the place did a bang-up business, and then the sallow, sullen, skinny boy who called himself Gil Gamesh took off with the contents of the register. Within the month, every bar in the South had one of those signs printed up and one of those uniforms, with 19 sewn on it, hanging up beside it in the window for a gag. Outside opera houses, kids scrawled, GIL SINGING GRAND OPERA HERE TONIGHT. On trolley cars it was GIL TAKING TICKETS INSIDE. On barn doors, on school buildings, in rest rooms around the nation, the broken-hearted and the raffish wrote, I'LL BE BACK, G.G. His name, his initials, his number were everywhere. . . .

And Mike the Mouth? He went from bad to worse and eventually took to traveling the league with a blackboard on his back, setting himself up at the entrance to the bleachers to plead his hopeless cause with the fans. Kids either teased him, or looked on in awe at that ghostly ump, powdered white from the dozen sticks of chalk that he would grind to dust in a single day. Most adults ignored him, either fearing or pitying the madman, but those who remembered Gil Gamesh—and they were legion, particularly in the bleachers—told the once-great umpire to go jump in a lake, and worse.

BUT I COULD NOT CALL WHAT I DID NOT SEE!

"You couldn't a-seed it anyway, you blind bat!"

NONSENSE! I WAS TWENTY-TWENTY IN BOTH EYES ALL MY LIFE! I HAD THE BEST VISION IN BASEBALL! . . .

"You wuz a lousy ump, Mike. You wuz a busher all your life."

WHERE IS YOUR EVIDENCE FOR THAT SLANDEROUS REMARK?

"Common knowledge is my evidence. The whole world knows. Even my little boy, who don't know nothin', knows that. Hey, Johnny, come here—who is the worst ump who ever lived? Tell this creep."

"Mike the Mouth! Mike the Mouth!"

NONSENSE! SLANDER! LIES! I DEMAND JUSTICE, ONCE AND FOR ALL!

"Well, you're gettin' it, slow but sure. See ya, Mouth."

Paul Simon

"Night Game"

Simple and melancholy, this song always sounds like the end of the season. It was released in 1975 on Paul Simon's album Still Crazy After All These Years.

There were two men down
And the score was tied
In the bottom of the eighth
When the pitcher died

And they laid his spikes
On the pitcher's mound
And his uniform was torn
And his number was left on the ground

Then the night turned cold
Colder than the moon
The stars were white as bones
The stadium was old
Older than the screams
Older than the teams

There were three men down
And the season lost
And the tarpaulin was rolled
Upon the winter frost

John E. Maxfield
FROM BASEBALL DIAMONDS
"Hard Core Support"

In any given season, twenty-seven teams will not win the World Series, leaving their fans frustrated and longing for the renewal of spring, when all the records are wiped clean. But like the rest of us, John E. Maxfield's mother-in-law couldn't help spending her lost summers checking her team's pulse even long after she knew the shroud had been drawn.

———————

My mother-in-law is a Senators' fan.
Even now—the team long moved,
The first to Minnesota
The second, Texas.
She'd root for anyone in Washington.

I watched her, years ago
During a particularly long drought.
Once again an early lead blown
The pitcher wild,
Seemed planted in the mound.

She stomped across and stretched
   to reach the mantel
Switched off her small transistor:
"I can't stand listening to another
Mismanaged baseball game!"

But every little while she'd stop—
Click it on, confirm and click it off
Then stalk away, red hair flying—
A bristling banty hen whose chicks
Persisted in their foolish straying.

Linda Mizejewski
FROM BASEBALL DIAMONDS
"Season Wish"

How many daughters of fathers who had no sons have lived through the experience of this poem? Linda Mizejewski (how wonderful that last name would look on the back of a uniform jersey!) brings the reader to the rocky, deserted diamonds of her youth.

———————

In turns of season
come exchanges,
transformations—daughters, even,
traded to gods for wheat or rain.
Rapunzel, before she was even born,
was traded away for cabbage leaves
on a risk her father took one night
for love. A man might think of dowry
on a night that pivots warmth and cold

during Indian summers, false
springs, sudden August cool.
A miller might say his daughter
can spin horses' straw to gold.
A man might offer in sudden hope
a crop, a dove, his youngest girl.

In spring, my father
took me out at dusk

to lots the boys had left,
seeing each year if I could spin
the winning curve ball back to him
and learn the catch, the grip and swing
of a missing son; hoping there was magic
in the glove or sneakers or wooden bat
like the power children found
in the legend in pauper's clothes
that created a man from balls of snow.
The cap, perhaps, might keep my hair
forever clipped; holding the glove
against my chest might stop
my breasts; and if I learned
the grip and stance, perhaps my wrists
would thicken, hard, around the bat.

My father made the diamond
out of stones he piled like altars
into three small mounds.
Pitching to him underhand,
sometimes I threw him winning runs
and watched him round our bases,
touch the stones and then
take home. He hoped

the season would never come
when something more important
would keep me on an April night
from trespassing with him into lots
till boys came back
to claim their ground
and kick our home and bases
into rocks again.

Year by year he built for me
the things he thought
a man one day would want me for:
investments, a name
the family business—stock
to insure a fair exchange
for a man who might try
to be a son. My father's
spring trades always failed:
I always came back being
still a girl who couldn't play
the way he'd hoped while he
built for me stone bases
on his knees there in the dirt.

William Kennedy

FROM IRONWEED

This Pulitzer Prize-winning novel by William Kennedy tells the story of former ballplayer Francis Phelan, now an alcoholic vagabond, who, in this excerpt, returns to his home and family in Albany, New York.

———————————

Annie was setting the dining-room table with a white linen tablecloth, with the silver Iron Joe gave them for their wedding, and with china Francis did not recognize, when Daniel Quinn arrived home. The boy tossed his schoolbag in a corner of the dining room, then stopped in midmotion where he saw Francis standing in the doorway to the kitchen.

"Hulooo," Francis said to him.

"Danny, this is your grandfather," Annie said. "He just came to see us and he's staying for dinner." Daniel stared at Francis's face and slowly extended his right hand. Francis shook it.

"Pleased to meet you." Daniel said.

"The feeling's mutual, boy. You're a big lad for ten."

"I'll be eleven in January."

"You comin' from school, are ye?"

"From instructions, religion."

"Oh, religion. I guess I just seen you crossin' the street and didn't even know it. Learn anything, did you?"

"Learned about today. All Saints' Day."

"What about it?"

"It's a holy day. You have to go to church. It's the day we remember the martyrs who died for the faith and nobody knows their names."

"Oh, yeah," Francis said. "I remember them fellas."

"What happened to your teeth?"

"Daniel."

"My teeth," Francis said. "Me and them parted company, most of 'em. I got a few left."

"Are you Grampa Phelan or Grampa Quinn?"

"Phelan," Annie said. "His name is Francis Aloysius Phelan."

"Francis Aloysius, right," said Francis with a chuckle. "Long time since I heard that."

"You're the ball player," Danny said. "The big-leaguer. You played with the Washington Senators."

"Used to. Don't play anymore."

"Billy says you taught him how to throw an inshoot."

"He remembers that, does he?"

"Will you teach me?"

"You a pitcher, are ye?"

"Sometimes. I can throw a knuckle ball."

"Change of pace. Hard to hit. You get a baseball, I'll show you how to hold it for an inshoot." And Daniel ran into the kitchen, then the pantry, and emerged with a ball and glove, which he handed to Francis. The glove was much too small for Francis's hand but he put a few fingers inside it and held the ball in his right hand, studied its seams. Then he gripped it with his thumb and one and a half fingers.

"What happened to your finger?" Daniel asked.

"Me and it parted company too. Sort of an accident."

"Does that make any difference throwing an inshoot?"

"Sure does, but not to me. I don't throw no more at all. Never was a pitcher, you know, but talked with plenty of 'em. Walter Johnson was my buddy. You know him? The Big Train?"

The boy shook his head.

"Don't matter. But he taught me how it was done and I ain't forgot. Put your first two fingers right on the seams, like this, and then you snap your wrist out, like this, and if you're a righty—are you a righty?"—and the boy nodded—"then the ball's gonna dance a little turn-around jig and head right inside at the batter's belly button, assumin', acourse, that he's a righty too. You followin' me?" And the boy nodded again. "Now the trick is, you got to throw the opposite of the outcurve, which is like this." And he snapped his wrist clockwise. "You got to do it like this." And he snapped his wrist counterclockwise again. Then he had the boy try it both ways and patted him on the back.

"That's how it's done," he said. "You get so's you can do it, the batter's gonna think you got a little animal inside that ball, flyin' it like an airplane."

"Let's go outside and try it," Daniel said. "I'll get another glove."

"Glove," said Francis, and he turned to Annie. "By some fluke you still got my old glove stuck away somewheres in the house? That possible, Annie?"

"There's a whole trunk of your things in the attic," she said. "It might be there."

"It is," Daniel said. "I know it is. I saw it. I'll get it."

"You will not," Annie said. "That trunk is none of your affair."

"But I've already seen it. There's a pair of spikes too, and clothes and newspapers and old pictures."

"All that," Francis said to Annie. "You saved it."

"You had no business in that trunk," Annie said.

WILLIAM MERRITT CHASE. *The Baseball Player.*
c. 1872. Pencil on paper. 5 3/4 x 3 1/2 in.
The Gladstone Collection of Baseball Art.

"Billy and I looked at the pictures and the clippings one day," Daniel said. "Billy looked just as much as I did. He's in lots of 'em." And he pointed at his grandfather.

"Maybe you'd want to have a look at what's there," Annie said to Francis.

"Could be. Might find me a new shoelace."

Annie led him up the stairs, Daniel already far ahead of them. . . .

When Francis opened the trunk lid the odor of lost time filled the attic air, a cloying reek of imprisoned flowers that unsettled the dust and fluttered the window shades. Francis felt drugged by the scent of the reconstituted past, and then stunned by his first look inside the trunk, for there, staring out from a photo, was his own face at age nineteen. The picture lay among rolled socks and a small American flag, a Washington Senators cap, a pile of newspaper clippings and other photos, all in a scatter on the trunk's tray. Francis stared up at himself from the bleachers in Chadwick Park on a day in 1899, his face unlined, his teeth all there, his collar open, his hair unruly in the afternoon's breeze. He lifted the picture for a closer look and saw himself among a group of men, tossing a baseball from bare right hand to gloved left hand. The flight of the ball had always made this photo mysterious to Francis, for the camera had caught the ball clutched in one hand and also in flight, arcing in a blur toward the glove. What the camera had caught was two instants in one: time separated and unified, the ball in two places at once, an eventuation as inexplicable as the Trinity itself. Francis now took the picture to be a Trinitarian talisman (a hand, a glove, a ball) for achieving the impossible: for he had always believed it impossible for him, ravaged man, failed human, to reenter history under this roof. Yet here he was in this aerie of reconstitutable time, touching untouchable artifacts of a self that did not yet know it was ruined, just as the ball, in its inanimate ignorance, did not know yet that it was going nowhere, was caught.

But the ball is really not yet caught, except by the camera, which has frozen only its situation in space.

And Francis is not yet ruined, except as an apparency in process.

The ball still flies.

Francis still lives to play another day.

Doesn't he?

The boy noticed the teeth. A man can get new teeth, store teeth. Annie got 'em.

W. P. Kinsella

FROM SHOELESS JOE

Later adapted for the screen under the title Field of Dreams, *this novel tells the story of an Iowa farmer who cuts a baseball diamond into his cornfield and watches in awe as Shoeless Joe Jackson and the rest of the Chicago Black Sox make their return to the playing field.*

———————

A ground mist, like wisps of gauze, snakes in slow circular motions just above the grass.

"The grass is soft as a child's breath," I say to the moonlight. On the porch wall I find the switch, and the single battery of floodlights I have erected behind the left-field fence sputters to life. "I've tended it like I would my own baby. It has been powdered and lotioned and loved. It is ready."

Moonlight butters the whole Iowa night. Clover and corn smells are thick as syrup. I experience a tingling like the tiniest of electric wires touching the back of my neck, sending warm sensations through me. Then, as the lights flare, a scar against the blue-black sky, I see

Shoeless Joe Jackson standing out in left field. His feet spread wide, body bent forward from the waist, hands on hips, he waits. I hear the sharp crack of the bat, and Shoeless Joe drifts effortlessly a few steps to his left, raises his right hand to signal for the ball, camps under it for a second or two, catches it, at the same time transferring it to his throwing hand, and fires it to the infield.

I make my way to left field, walking in the darkness far outside the third-base line, behind where the third-base stands would be. I climb up on the wobbly bleacher behind the fence. I can look right down on Shoeless Joe. He fields a single on one hop and pegs the ball to third.

"How does it play?" I holler down.

"The ball bounces true," he replies.

"I know." I am smiling with pride, and my heart thumps mightily against my ribs. "I've hit a thousand line drives and as many grounders. It's true as a felt-top table."

"It is," says Shoeless Joe. "It is true."

I lean back and watch the game. From where I sit the scene is as complete as in any of the major-league baseball parks I have ever visited: the two teams, the stands, the fans, the lights, the vendors, the scoreboard. The only difference is that I sit alone in the left-field bleacher and the only player who seems to have substance is Shoeless Joe Jackson. When Joe's team is at bat, the left fielder below me is transparent, as if he were made of vapor. He performs mechanically but seems not to have facial features. We do not converse.

A great amphitheater of grandstand looms dark against the sky, the park is surrounded by decks of floodlights making it brighter than day, the crowd buzzes, the vendors hawk their wares, and I cannot keep the promise I made myself not to ask Shoeless Joe Jackson about his suspension and what it means to him.

While the pitcher warms up for the third inning we talk.

"It must have been . . . It must have been like . . ." But I can't find the words.

"Like having a part of me amputated, slick and smooth and painless." Joe looks up at me and his dark eyes seem about to burst with the pain of it. "A friend of mine used to tell about the war, how him and a buddy was running across a field when a piece of shrapnel took his friend's head off, and how the friend ran, headless, for several strides before he fell. I'm told that old men wake in the night and scratch itchy legs that have been dust for fifty years. That was me. Years and years later, I'd wake in the night with the smell of the ballpark in my nose and the cool of the grass on my feet. The thrill of the grass . . ."

How I wish my father could be here with me. If he'd lasted just a few months longer, he could have watched our grainy black-and-white TV as Bill Mazeroski homered in the bottom of the ninth to beat the Yankees 10-9. We would have joined hands and danced around the kitchen like madmen. "The Yankees lose so seldom you have to celebrate every single time," he used to say. We were always going to go to a major-league baseball game, he and I. But the time was never right, the money always needed for something else. One of the last days of his life, late in the night while I sat with him because the pain wouldn't let him sleep, the radio picked up a static-y station broadcasting a White Sox game. We hunched over the radio and cheered them on, but they lost. Dad told the story of the Black Sox Scandal for the last time. Told of seeing two of those World Series games, told of the way Shoeless Joe Jackson hit, told the dimensions of Comiskey Park, and how, during the series, the mobsters in striped suits sat in the box seats with their colorful women, watching the game and perhaps making plans to go out later and kill a rival.

"You must go," Dad said. "I've been in all sixteen major-league parks. I want you to do it too. The summers belong to somebody else now, have for a long time." I nodded agreement.

"Hell, you know what I mean," he said, shaking his head.

I did indeed.

"I loved the game," Shoeless Joe went on. "I'd have played for food money. I'd have played free and worked for food. It was the game, the parks, the smells, the sounds. Have you ever held a bat or a baseball to your face? The varnish, the leather. And it was the crowd, the excitement of them rising as one when the ball was hit deep. The sound was like a chorus. Then there was the chub-a-lug of the tin lizzies in the parking lots, and the hotels with their

Shoeless Joe Jackson. c. 1919. The National Baseball Library, Cooperstown, New York. *"Dad told the story of the Black Sox Scandal for the last time. Told of seeing two of those World Series games, told of the way Shoeless Joe Jackson hit . . . and how, during the series, the mobsters in striped suits sat in the box seats with their colorful women, watching the game and perhaps making plans to go out later and kill a rival."* (W. P. Kinsella)

brass spittoons in the lobbies and brass beds in the rooms. It makes me tingle all over like a kid on his way to his first double-header, just to talk about it."

The year after Annie and I were married, the year we first rented this farm, I dug Annie's garden for her; dug it by hand, stepping a spade into the soft black soil, ruining my salesman's hands. After I finished, it rained, an Iowa spring rain as soft as spray from a warm hose. The clods of earth I had dug seemed to melt until the garden leveled out, looking like a patch of black ocean. It was near noon on a gentle Sunday when I walked out to that garden. The soil was soft and my shoes disappeared as I plodded until I was near the center. There I knelt, the soil cool on my knees. I looked up at the low gray sky; the rain had stopped and the only sound was the surrounding trees dripping fragrantly. Suddenly I thrust my hands wrist-deep into the snuffy-black earth. The air was pure. All around me the clean smell of earth and water. Keeping my hands buried I stirred the earth with my fingers and knew I loved Iowa as much as a man could love a piece of earth.

When I came back to the house Annie stopped me at the door, made me wait on the veran-dah and then hosed me down as if I were a door with too many handprints on it, while I tried to explain my epiphany. It is very difficult to describe an experience of religious significance while you are being sprayed with a garden hose by a laughing, loving woman.

"What happened to the sun?" Shoeless Joe says to me, waving his hand toward the banks of floodlights that surround the park.

"Only stadium in the big leagues that doesn't have them is Wrigley Field," I say. "the owners found that more people could attend night games. They even play the World Series at night now."

Joe purses his lips, considering.

"It's harder to see the ball, especially at the plate."

"When there are breaks, they usually go against the ballplayers, right? But I notice you're three-for-three so far," I add, looking down at his uniform the only identifying marks a large *S*

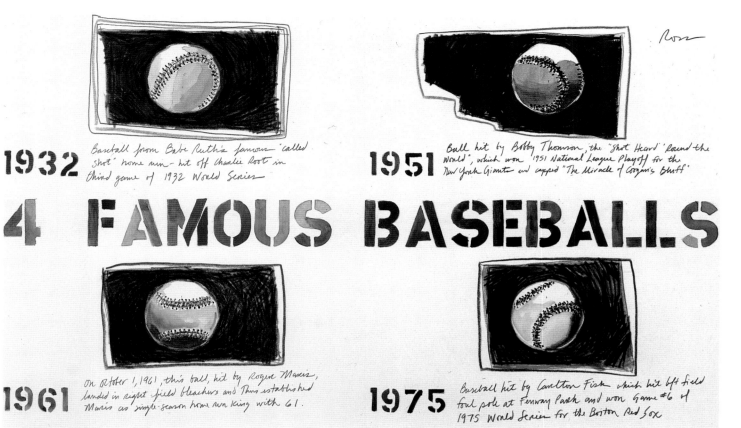

1932 — Baseball from Babe Ruth's famous "called shot" home run - hit off Charlie Root in third game of 1932 World Series

1951 — Ball hit by Bobby Thomson, the "Shot Heard 'Round the World", which won 1951 National League Playoff for the New York Giants and capped "The Miracle of Coogan's Bluff"

4 FAMOUS BASEBALLS

1961 — On October 1, 1961, this ball, hit by Roger Maris, landed in right field bleachers and thus established Maris as single-season home run king with 61.

1975 — Baseball hit by Carlton Fisk which hit left field foul pole at Fenway Park and won Game #6 of 1975 World Series for the Boston Red Sox

COLORPLATE 100

THOM ROSS. *Four Famous Baseballs*. 1991.
Mixed media on paper. 26 x 38 in. Squash Blossom Gallery.

COLORPLATE 101

CHARLES MUNRO. *Fourth of July Townball at the Farmers Museum.* 1989.
Mixed media on paper. 24 x 32 in. Gallery 53 Artworks, Cooperstown, New York.

COLORPLATE 102

JANET MUNRO. *Night Game—Cooperstown, New York.* 1991.
Mixed media on masonite. 24 x 32 in. Gallery 53 Artworks, Cooperstown, New York.

COLORPLATE 103

LEROY NEIMAN. *Los Angeles Dodgers*. 1990.
Oil on board. 48 x 72 in.
Collection of the Los Angeles Dodgers.

COLORPLATE 105

JOHN HULL. *Bullpen: Pawtucket.* 1990.
Acrylic on canvas. 36 x 60 in. Private collection.

COLORPLATE 104 *(opposite)*

JOHN HULL. *Top Step: Shepherd.* 1990.
Acrylic on canvas. 48 x 36 in. Collection of Richard C. Anderson.

COLORPLATE 106

GEORGE WRIGHT. *A Tradition of Excellence.* 1991.
Oil on canvas. 38 x 45 in. Baltimore Oriole Hall of Fame Museum at Camden Yards.

288

with an *O* in the top crook, an *X* in the bottom, and an American flag with forty-eight stars on his left sleeve near the elbow.

Joe grins. "I'd play for the Devil's own team just for the touch of a baseball. Hell, I'd play in the dark if I had to."

I want to ask about that day in December 1951. If he'd lived another few years things might have been different. There was a move afoot to have his record cleared, but it died with him. I wanted to ask, but my instinct told me not to. There are things it is better not to know.

It is one of those nights when the sky is close enough to touch, so close that looking up is like seeing my own eyes reflected in a rain barrel. I sit in the bleacher just outside the left-field fence. I clutch in my hand a hot dog with mustard, onion, and green relish. The voice of the crowd roars in my ears. Chords of "The Star-Spangled Banner" and "Take Me Out to the Ballgame" float across the field. A Coke bottle is propped against my thigh, squat, greenish, the ice-cream-haired elf grinning conspiratorially from the cap.

Below me in left field, Shoeless Joe Jackson glides over the plush velvet grass, silent as a jungle cat. He prowls and paces, crouches ready to spring as, nearly 300 feet away, the ball is pitched. At the sound of the bat he wafts in whatever direction is required, as if he were on ball bearings.

Then the intrusive sound of a slamming screen door reaches me, and I blink and start. I recognize it as the sound of the door to my house, and, looking into the distance, I can see a shape that I know is my daughter, toddling down the back steps. Perhaps the lights or the crowd have awakened her and she has somehow eluded Annie. I judge the distance to the steps. I am just to the inside of the foul pole, which is exactly 330 feet from home plate. I tense. Karin will surely be drawn to the lights and the emerald dazzle of the infield. If she touches anything, I fear it will all disappear, perhaps forever. Then, as if she senses my discomfort, she stumbles away from the lights, walking in the ragged fringe of darkness well outside the third-base line. She trails a blanket behind her, one tiny fist rubbing a sleepy eye. She is barefoot and wears a white flannelette nightgown covered in an explosion of daisies.

She climbs up the bleacher, alternating a knee and a foot on each step, and crawls into my lap silently, like a kitten. I hold her close and wrap the blanket around her feet. The play goes on; her innocence has not disturbed the balance. "What is it?" she says shyly, her eyes indicating she means all that she sees.

"Just watch the left fielder," I say. "He'll tell you all you ever need to know about a baseball game. Watch his feet as the pitcher accepts the sign and gets ready to pitch. A good left fielder knows what pitch is coming, and he can tell from the angle of the bat where the ball is going to be hit, and, if he's good, how hard."

I look down at Karin. She cocks one green eye at me, wrinkling her nose, then snuggles into my chest, the index finger of her right hand tracing tiny circles around her nose.

The crack of the bat is sharp as the yelp of a kicked cur. Shoeless Joe whirls, takes five loping strides directly toward us, turns again, reaches up, and the ball smacks into his glove. The final batter dawdles in the on-deck circle.

"Can I come back again?" Joe asks.

"I built this left field for you. It's yours anytime you want to use it. They play one hundred sixty-two games a season now."

"There are others," he says. "If you were to finish the infield, why, old Chick Gandil could play first base, and we'd have the Swede at shortstop and Buck Weaver at third." I can feel his excitement rising. "We could stick McMullin in at second, and Eddie Cicotte and Lefty Williams would like to pitch again. Do you think you could finish center field? It would mean a lot to Happy Felsch."

"Consider it done," I say, hardly thinking of the time, the money, the backbreaking labor it would entail. "Consider it done," I say again, then stop suddenly as an idea creeps into my brain like a runner inching off first base.

"I know a catcher," I say. "He never made the majors, but in his prime he was good. Really good. Played Class B ball in Florida and California . . ."

"We could give him a try," says Shoeless Joe. "You give us a place to play and we'll look at your catcher."

I swear the stars have moved in close enough to eavesdrop as I sit in this single rickety bleacher that I built with my unskilled hands, looking down at Shoeless Joe Jackson. A breath of clover travels on the summer wind. Behind me, just yards away, brook water plashes softly in the darkness, a frog shrills, fireflies dazzle the night like red pepper. A petal falls.

"God what an outfield," he says. "What a left field." He looks up at me and I look down at him. "This must be heaven," he says.

"No. It's Iowa," I reply automatically. But then I feel the night rubbing softly against my face like cherry blossoms; look at the sleeping girl-child in my arms, her small hand curled around one of my fingers; think of the fierce warmth of the woman waiting for me in the house; inhale the fresh-cut grass smell that seems locked in the air like permanent incense; and listen to the drone of the crowd, as below me Shoeless Joe Jackson tenses, watching the angle of the distant bat for a clue as to where the ball will be hit.

"I think you're right, Joe," I say, but softly enough not to disturb his concentration.

George Herman "Babe" Ruth. c. 1930. The National Baseball Library, Cooperstown, New York. *Ruth considered Shoeless Joe Jackson one of the greatest hitters he'd ever seen, and the Babe patterned his swing after that of the White Sox outfielder.*

Eighth Inning:

ON AND OFF THE FIELD

The trappings of the game of baseball are as unique as the game itself. Here's a look at the equipment, the rules, the strategy, the business of the big leagues, the unique relationship between the manager and the umpire, and the passion of the collector for his baseball cards.

Robert K. Adair

FROM THE PHYSICS OF BASEBALL

"The Pitcher's Task"

We know what makes a fastball fast, but what puts the yellow in the ol' yellowhammer, the yak in the yakker, and the uncle in Uncle Charlie? Remember when you thought you'd have no use for high school physics? Robert K. Adair explains the physical aspects of one of baseball's greatest mysteries, the curveball.

The most important person on the team, in any one game is the pitcher.[1] The pitcher's job is simply defined—if not simply executed. From the pitcher's mound, 60'6" from the rear point of home plate, he must throw the ball over the plate for strikes. But within that constraint he must project the ball in patterns of trajectories, velocities, and placements so that the batter cannot hit the ball squarely. But what is a strike?

A STRIKE is a legal pitch when so called by the umpire, which (b) is not struck at, if any part of the ball pass through any part of the strike zone.

The STRIKE ZONE is that space over home plate which is between the batter's armpits

---

[1] Though over the whole season, the best hitter in baseball—Babe Ruth—was judged to be more valuable than one of the best pitchers in baseball—Babe Ruth. In 1919, Ruth was moved from the Boston Red Sox pitcher's box, where he worked every fourth day, to an everyday job in right field.

and the top of his knees when he assumes his natural stance [*Official Baseball Rules*, 1987, page 22].

1.05 Home base . . . [is] 17 inches long . . . with the 17-inch edge facing the pitcher's plate [*Official Baseball Rules*, page 5].

A typical six-foot-tall batter stands naturally at the plate with his armpits about 46" above the plate. The tops of his knees will be about 22" above the plate. With these definitions, a ball he does not swing at will be called a strike if it passes over the plate so that it knicks a five-sided box, with a cross section the shape of the plate, 17" wide, 24" high, and 17" deep, which might be suspended with the bottom edge 22" above the plate. As a matter of practice, umpires define the high boundary of the strike zone about 4" lower than the armpits so the effective zone is about 17" by 20". Hence, the center of the ball must strike a three-dimensional target about 20" wide by 23" high and 17" deep. Control pitchers hit corners with an uncertainty of about 3". One must be a fairly good shot to shoot a pistol with that accuracy. A mistake, usually an error of a foot that puts the ball in the center of the strike zone, on one pitch of a hundred, may lose the ball in the bleachers—and the game.

The pitcher must not only throw the ball so that it passes through the strike zone, he must throw so that the batter does not hit the ball squarely. He does this by throwing the ball so that it passes through specific places at or near the strike zone that the batter finds difficult to reach, by throwing the ball at different velocities to upset the batter's timing, and by applying spin to the ball in such a manner that the ball passes the batter with different trajectories, confusing and confuting him. Thus, the pitcher varies the placement, the velocity, and the movement of the ball. The pitcher's action up to the release of the ball is part of the art of pitching; the action of the ball after release, determined by the laws of nature, is addressed by physics and is subject to our analyses.

THE CURVE BALL

Interest in the left-right curvature of balls sailing through the air is probably as old as ball games themselves. Isaac Newton, at the age of 23, discussed the curvature of tennis balls in terms that make good sense today. In the nineteenth-century genesis of mathematical physics, Lord Rayleigh analyzed the curvature of the path of spinning balls, and P. G. Tait, the eminent Scottish physicist, wrote extensively on the curves of golf balls—perhaps in an attempt to understand and cure a slice. The Baseball Hall of Fame in Cooperstown, New York, gives precedence to Candy Cummings as the first baseball pitcher to throw a curve ball, though the rules of the 1860s required Cummings to throw underhand rather as a softball pitcher today. Freddy Goldsmith and others confounded batters with curve balls at about the same time.

Balls curve as a consequence of asymmetries in the resistance of the air through which they pass. If the air resistance is greater on the third-base side than on the first-base side of a ball thrown from the pitcher to the batter, the ball will be forced—curve—toward first. Aside from generating curved paths, this resistance affects the flight of the pitched ball by reducing the velocity of a ball thrown from the pitcher's mound at a speed of 100 mph to a velocity of 90 mph as it crosses the plate about 0.40 seconds after it leaves the pitcher's hand. If the ball is not spinning very fast, during the time of flight it will fall almost three feet below the original flight line. If the ball is rotating quickly, differences in the force of the air on the ball transverse to the spin axis are induced that cause the trajectory of the ball to deviate from the original horizontal direction of motion and deviate vertically from the trajectory determined solely by gravity. Such asymmetric forces follow from the rotation of the ball when a curve or hopping (rising) fast ball is thrown or from differential forces on the seams for a slowly rotating knuckle ball. The action of a curve ball and knuckle ball are quite different.

First we consider the curve ball.

As we have noted, the force on a baseball is greater on the side of the ball that passes more quickly through the air due to the Magnus effect. The diagram at the top of Figure 1 shows the trajectory (reconstructed from Briggs's wind tunnel measurements) of a rather wide-breaking curve ball thrown so as to rotate counterclockwise—as seen from above in the figure—by a right-handed pitcher. This ball is thrown with an initial velocity of 70 mph, spinning at a rate of 1600 rpm, to cross the plate about 0.6 seconds later at a speed of about 61 mph. Although the radius of curvature is nearly constant throughout the ball's flight, the deflection from the original direction increases approximately quadratically with distance, i.e., four times the deflection at twice the distance. Halfway from pitcher to the plate, the ball has moved about 3.4 inches from the original line of flight, which is directed toward the inside corner and is moving toward the center of the plate. At the plate, the deflection is 14.4 inches and the ball passes over the outside corner. From the perspective of the batter—or pitcher—the ball that started toward the inside corner has "curved" 14.4 inches to pass over the outside corner. Moreover, one half of the deflection occurred during the last 15 feet of the path to the plate. (We realize that the most useful curve from a tactical view curves down much more than side-ways, but we discuss the transverse motion for expositional simplicity.) Does a curve ball then travel in a smooth arc like the arc of a circle? Yes. Does the ball "break" as it nears the plate? Yes. Neither the smooth arc nor the break is an illusion but a different description of the same reality.

Though the deflection as seen, correctly, by batter and pitcher is 14.4", the sagitta—the largest deviation from the straight line drawn from the beginning to the end of the ball's flight as shown in the figure—is but 3.4". Hence, it is difficult to throw a ball with a diameter of 2.9" through three aligned rods so that the ball will pass to the left of one rod, to the right of the second, and to the left of the third. In the course of arguments in 1870 as to whether a curve ball really curves, Freddy Goldsmith performed that feat in New Haven.

But Goldsmith probably threw a slower curve. For slow curves thrown with a definite spin rate, the deflection is approximately proportional to the time the ball is in the air. Hence, a ball thrown with an initial velocity of 65 mph with a 1600 rpm spin, which takes about 8 percent longer to reach the plate than the 70 mph pitch, will curve about 8 percent more.

Conversely, it is almost impossible to throw a fast ball that curves strongly. The transverse Magnus force that induces the curved trajectory is smaller for velocities greater than 70 mph. Also, since the faster ball reaches the plate sooner, the force has a shorter time in which to act; for the same transverse force, the ball that travels 10 percent faster will curve 20 percent less.

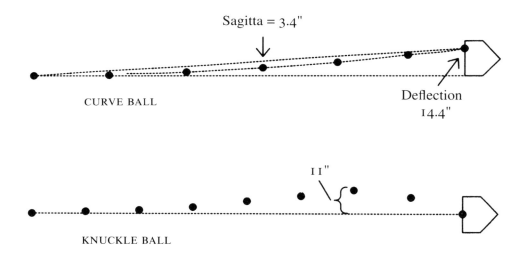

The trajectories of a curve ball and a knuckle ball on their way from a right-handed pitcher to a batter. The curve ball is rotating counterclockwise as viewed from above the ball's line of flight.

There are other pitches of interest. The slider—sometimes called a "nickel curve" 70 years ago—is a kind of fast curve. Thrown at a higher velocity than the standard curve ball, the break of the slider is smaller than the deflection of the curve ball and the spin axis is such that the deflection is more nearly left-right than the curve—which, at best, is more of a pure drop.

The screwball thrown by Carl Hubbell and others, and called the fadeaway by Christy Mathewson, is a kind of reverse curve thrown by a right-handed pitcher to break away from a left-handed batter a little like a left-handed curve ball.

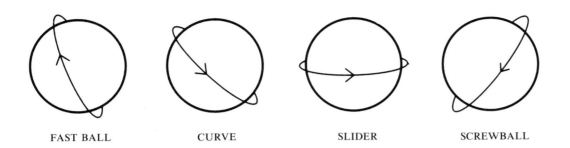

FAST BALL   CURVE   SLIDER   SCREWBALL

Ball rotation directions, as seen by the batter, for pitches thrown almost straight overhand by a right-handed pitcher. The arrow shows the direction of rotation, which is also the direction of the Magnus force.

Mike Bryan

FROM BASEBALL LIVES

"Ronald Bryant"

Players sand them, bone them, wrap them in tape, and cover them with pine tar. They carry them on planes and buses, kiss them for good luck, and make bonfires out of them during hitting slumps. Nowhere in sports is there a relationship as close, as deadly serious, and as unusual as there is between the ballplayer and his "business partner"—the bat.

———————

HE'S A SLIGHT MAN WITH THINNING HAIR, SAFETY GOGGLES, A DIRECT GAZE, AND A CIGA-RETTE. HIS DOMAIN IS THE LOUISVILLE SLUGGER BAT FACTORY IN JEFFERSONVILLE, INDIANA, RIGHT ACROSS THE OHIO RIVER FROM LOUISVILLE. ON THE OTHER SIDE OF THE PLANT THEY MAKE POWER-BILT GOLF CLUBS. THE FACILITY IS AS LARGE AS A FOOTBALL FIELD, WITH STACKS OF TIMBER AND BATS IN VARIOUS STAGES OF PRODUCTION JAMMED EVERYWHERE. HIS JOB IS TO KNOW THE STATUS OF EACH ONE OF THEM.

If we got the timber the way we want it we could produce a lot faster. But when you're fooling with Mother Nature, it's not like an iron golf club. Man-made stuff you can push, this stuff you just have to wait until it grows. We cull about 40 percent, maybe 50 percent, because it's not good enough for a ballplayer. It's a good bat but it doesn't have the cosmetics, the straight grain; it just doesn't *look hard*. The ballplayer's not going to take it. He'll say this is just trash. But that doesn't mean we throw it away. That goes into your store bats. . . .

    If they're not good bats I'm the one who hears about it. We just got a bad bat back from Dave Concepcion. Chuck [Schupp, the sales representative] brought it back in here the other day, said Concepcion was griping about his model. I look at the bat and says, "He's right. It's not even close." We can't figure out what happened. We checked the master model and it was a little off but not that much off. We allow one-tenth of an inch for sanding. After they're turned on the lathe they get rough sanded, then fine sanded. But if they happen to put new sandpaper in there, it cuts a little more. What somebody done maybe, they pulled that machine in until it fitted the exact model, and they didn't allow for sanding. Plus they had just put new sandpaper in there. It changed that whole bat. Thirty-second of an inch. Enough that you could see it. Concepcion could tell by *feeling* it. These guys can start with the handle and work their hands up and tell you whether the barrel is big or small. They can pick 'em up and I guarantee come within half an ounce of what it weighs. I can do it and they can do it, too. Concepcion's been using our bats for nineteen years, and that type of person we don't like to give a wrong bat.

Kal Daniels sent some bats back; the handles were a little small. They was a little small, but not that small. He said they just weren't right, but if he'd been hitting, he wouldn't have paid any attention to it. I'd be the same way. These guys make a living with that bat.

They can specify from one end to the other, from the end of the knob to the end of the barrel, how big, how they want it tapered. And they know it, too. Handles, say, come with cone knob, semi-cone, then you've got your extra-large knob, your regular knob, and your small knob.

In every case but one the letter of the model stands for the player's name. The C-243, that's Rod Carew. If Rickey Henderson wanted to use that model his name would be on the bat, but it would be Carew's model, and that model number will never change. If Carl Yastrzemski had a model made it would be Y so-and-so. There's one exception: the C-271. That *C* actually stands for "cup bat." Lou Brock brought one of them back from Japan, a cupped bat, because the Japanese had trouble getting wood and that's the way they took weight off. Brock liked it and it really caught on. What it is, they can get a heavier, harder piece of wood and still get it lighter, because a cup takes an ounce off. That is a very popular model. We can't keep it in stock.

The T-141: you've got players all the way down to the lower and all the way up to the higher use that bat. The most popular are probably your C-271, M-110, and P-72.

With a lot of 'em, I know what they want. Some change so much it's hard. Don Mattingly is using the T-141. The *T* is Cesar Tovar. Mattingly's also got one out now that's his, M-1728, the birthdays of his kids.

They know you can't always find exactly what they want, but you've got to give them the best. Particular ballplayers like knots in the barrels, some like wide grain, some like narrow. Most of 'em like the wide grain. They think it's harder. It's in their head. There's no science to it. I've always been told, actually, your narrow grain is your stronger bat because the narrow grain has took its time by nature and grown, and the wide grain has been shot with juice, growing fast.

Ted Williams, as great a player as he was, wanted narrow grain. He didn't want the wide grain. He said that tree grew too fast.

Harmon Killebrew kept calling me saying, "I want narrow grain, narrow grain." He got this from Ted Williams. I kept sending him narrow grain, so narrow you couldn't hardly see it.

"Too wide, too wide."

He raised cattle, and right before he retired he came down here to the big cattle show at the fairgrounds, and he came over and I just asked him personally, "Harmon, show me what you're talking about, 'narrow grain.'" And he went over and picked out a bat that in my opinion was a cull; something we probably wouldn't give a minor leaguer. He wanted *no grain at all*, what we call brashie, no texture at all, going all over the place. I said, "For two years I dug craters trying to get narrow as I could and I could have walked up and picked any of them out of the rack for you."

And he said, "Well that's what I want. That's natural-grown wood. That hasn't had the juice shot to it."

But most of your players today want the wide grain. Mattingly has to be real wide grain—half inch or better—or he'll send it back.

With the knots, I think there is science. You ever sawed a piece of wood and got a knot? It's hard. I think the knots help in the barrel. They do not want them in the *handle*; it makes the handle weak. The older ballplayers almost all asked for knots in the barrel; they don't do it as much today. A lot of the new ones coming up don't even know about it. Babe Ruth was

BILL WILLIAMS. *They Blossom Every Spring.* 1990. Oil on canvas. 20 x 24 in. Collection of the artist.

one of the first who started asking for knots in the barrel. We've got a record of it. Carl Yastrzemski, he'd ask for knots. Ted Williams would. Willie Stargell would. It's on the order. "Knots in barrel if possible."

Hickory went out about when I came in. It has no grain at all, just fiber; that's why they put the dark finish on hickory, to cover it up. It's all ash now, mainly because it's more workable, I think, and it's got a grain to it and you can get a bigger bat with lighter weight—and nowadays these ballplayers they want lighter bats. They do not use heavy bats. I'd say your average weight now is between thirty and thirty-one ounces. Used to be thirty-three, thirty-four, thirty-five. We had some guys using forty-one-ounce bats. Back then the pitcher comes up after being in the minor leagues for years; he's in his thirties when he makes the big-league club, so he wasn't throwing that hundred-mile-an-hour fastball. Now you get these kids coming up, they're eighteen years old throwin' that dude a hundred, a hundred and ten miles an hour. You're not going to get no forty-one-ounce bat around on *that*. You've got to get that bat *through* there, the way they pitch today.

You get your order, get the model he wants, the specifications, the finish, then you go over and pick out the timber by weight to make the certain length and model of bat. That piece of wood is called the billet. You have to really dig through the racks, the trucks, the bins, keep looking till you find what they want, to the best of your ability. Coming out of the hothouse they can be 8 to 10 percent moisture. That's what we want. You don't want them completely bone dry, but you want 'em dry enough to where they won't lose weight.

My favorite job is picking out the billets. That's the whole job, to me. If it's not right at the front it's not going to be right at the back. These clubs'll order 450 to 500 bats for spring training, then they'll turn around three weeks later and order another 500 for their Opening Day. That hurts our timber situation, really takes it down. Right now [May] we're behind. Right now I've got 12,000 bats on order to get off that [computer] screen. Imagine. It'd probably take me a half a day to get out a special order. If I walked right over and found the timber ready, I could probably get them out of here in three hours. I've done it.

The billets used to be square or round. Now they're all round because they're easier for us to turn. After I pick the billet I mark the barrel end, turn it so the knots will be in the barrel. Then we semi-rough it down to what's called a rough-out. Then it goes to either the tracer lathe or the lathe, and it's turned into a bat. The only difference in the lathes is that the tracer is automatically fed, instead of manually. And it's computerized; that machine is exact and twice as fast. The hand turners can turn pretty close to the model, but that tracer spits 'em out exact. But if the tracer's not set up just right it will turn the bat wrong. Or a lot of times on your automatic lathe over here, where you slide the bat in, if there's a lot of wood chips behind it and you don't notice it, it'll make a difference in that bat. The slide won't go all the way in. . . .

After the bat is turned it's checked for size, for weight. If it's okay it goes on to the brander, then on to the finisher.

They can specify eight different finishes: flame-burned; hickory; filler; Hornsby (a lighter brown than the hickory); Walker (hickory halfway down with a light-brown handle—that's the two-toned bat I like, that's a pretty bat); black; unfinished; and waxed. A lot of 'em like the black bats; they think that gives them a hard look. Don Mattingly uses the plain bat.

You have the sawing man, the man roughing out and weighing, the tracer lathe is two more people, the rough sander is a person, the fine sander is a person, your brander is a person, your sealer is a person, your dipper is a person. You're talking roughly fourteen, sixteen hands handle that bat. Right now our seniority here is fifteen years, on the average. It seems like once people come here they stay. I'd say for every six people they hire, five of 'em retire from here. It's hard work. You'd classify it as manual work. You have the machinery but still the man has to pick the bat up, feed the machine most of the time.

For as many bats as we put out I think we do a super job. We don't get many back. Not satisfying the ballplayer—not getting it to him on time, not getting it right—that disturbs me more than anything. To me, that bat there *is* Dale Murphy. The bat is his personality. It's him. I think he's a super guy, and I try to give him what he wants, give him the best. Of course I do that with all 'em. I don't do any favors. My favorite team's Boston, but they don't get any better bats than the Reds, the Yankees—which I hate, of course.

When guys at the plant hear we got some bats out late they'll come up to me and say, "How come we got his bats out so late?" Or, "Why'd those bats come back? What was wrong with them?" I'll have people from the factory come up, people who don't even have anything to do with the ballplayer bats, and ask what was wrong with those bats? They want to know.

Richard H. Durbin

FROM *THE CONGRESSIONAL RECORD*

On July 26, 1989, Representative Richard H. Durbin of Illinois made national headlines when he spoke out against the rising proliferation of aluminum baseball bats. Hopefully, his speech will help keep us from hearing the following scenario over the radio: "Ripken steps up to the plate. Here's the pitch. (Clank!) And there's a long fly ball to left . . ."

"Mr. Speaker, I rise to condemn the desecration of a great American symbol. No, I am not referring to flag burning; I am referring to the baseball bat.

"Several experts tell us that the wooden baseball bat is doomed to extinction, that major league baseball players will soon be standing at home plate with aluminum bats in their hands.

"Baseball fans have been forced to endure countless indignities by those who just cannot leave well enough alone.

"Designated hitters, plastic grass, uniforms that look like pajamas, chicken clowns dancing on the baselines, and of course the most heinous sacrilege, lights in Wrigley Field.

"Are we willing to hear the crack of a bat replaced by the dinky ping? Are we ready to see the Louisville slugger replaced by the aluminum ping dinger? Is nothing sacred?

"Please, do not tell me that wooden bats are too expensive, when players who cannot hit their weight are being paid more money than the president of the United Sates.

"Please, do not try to sell me on the notion that these metal clubs will make better hitters.

"What is next? Teflon baseballs? Radar-enhanced gloves? I ask you.

"I do not want to hear about saving trees. Any tree in America would gladly give its life for the glory of a day at home plate.

"I do not know if it will take a constitutional amendment to keep the baseball traditions alive, but if we forsake the great Americana of broken-bat singles and pine tar, we will have certainly lost our way as a nation."

Chester L. Smith

FROM *THE PITTSBURGH PRESS*
"Uniforms Shouldn't Be—Uniform"

If he could have seen the technicolor aberrations later inflicted upon the fans by the Houston Astros, or the short pants and knee socks eventually perpetrated by the Chicago White Sox, Chester L. Smith might not have argued quite so strongly for more variety in uniforms when this article was published in 1948.

Sartorially, the Chicago Cubs' catchers have set a new and intriguing style. After the outfielders and infielders are in position, and the pitcher is ready on the mound, out strolls Clyde McCullough, or whoever is to do the receiving for the day, wearing a beautiful blue chest protector.

The mitt, the mask and the shin-guards are the old, familiar colors, but the protector—ah, you must see it.

Just peachy, that's all. A marine blue, I believe, and there's no denying it sets off Mr. McCullough and his fellow backstops no end.

Now this is not a fashion merely for the sake of adding something new—like the new look for the ladies, for instance. The blue protector is in answer to a long-standing complaint of the infielders. Not only the Cubs, but others.

They have maintained that the orthodox light tan color of protectors makes for a bad background. The ball blends into it and there is a split second after the batter connects before they can adjust their eyes to the course the sphere is taking.

But the contrast of white against blue is another matter.

How many smashes that would have been base hits with the lesser visibility and will now be turned into putouts no one will ever reckon. Maybe none. Perhaps it's only in the minds of the infielders. But everybody is happy, especially Cholly Grimm's catchers who are now by far the sportiest dressers on the field.

It also is too much to hope that this will prove to be the opening wedge in the successful termination of our long and fruitless campaign to dress ball players like individuals and

ANDY JURINKO.
Wrigley Field. 1983.
Charcoal and pastel on
paper. 30 x 44 in.

with some degree of originality. That would be asking too much of a game that has so much tradition.

My idea is that each of the sixteen major league clubs should adopt a distinctive uniform and stick by it, at home and on the road.

College football teams do it. Notre Dame's green or blue is unmistakable anywhere. Pitt has always been identified by its blue or gold.

Yale is the Blue, Princeton, the Black and Harvard the Crimson, Penn State the Blue and White.

But not baseball. Except for certain differences in the lettering, trimmings and stockings, the home team is in white and the visitors wear gray. In Cleveland, the Yanks look like the White Sox and in New York the Indians can't be told from the Browns.

A baseball team expresses about as much personality in its uniforms as a crate of oranges.

There were days when the old New York Highlanders and also the White Sox were natty in blue with white piping. There could be no mistaking them when you saw them on the ball field.

There is scarcely a club that couldn't turn instantly to an exclusive suiting. Pittsburgh's city colors of black and gold could, with the aid of a qualified designer, be made into a uniform with distinction. The Cincinnati Reds and Boston Red Sox might clash, but not if they laid their problem before an expert—and anyhow, they're not in the same league.

One day I mentioned the idea to Ford Frick, the president of the National League, and got in return a startled stare, as though I had suggested making the diamond a circle.

Always the same answer: "We must have uniformity. The home team must wear white and the road team gray." Why?

I am fully aware that nothing will be done, just as the football fathers may take centuries getting around to throwing out the senseless and game-corrupting point-after touchdown. But a good, wholesome crusade is as much a tonic as sulphur and molasses in the spring, so I'm going to keep on beating my head against the wall.

Ron Rapoport

FROM *THE CHICAGO SUN-TIMES*

"The Pirates Rank No. 1 in the Fashion Parade!"

Although it took almost thirty years, someone finally listened to Chester L. Smith. This article about Smith's hometown Pittsburgh Pirates appeared was originally published in The Chicago Sun-Times, *and in the September 1977 issue of* Baseball Digest.

It has not been Dave Parker, Willie Stargell, John Candelaria or Rich Gossage that has made the strongest impression as the Pirates travel around the National League this season. It's their uniforms.

Not just the fact that they have three different kinds: gold, black and striped. Charlie Finley brought colors other than white and gray to the big leagues years ago and the other teams rapidly followed suit.

But the Pirates have carried this concept one step further. They play mix and match with their uniforms. Gold shirts with black pants today. Striped shirts with gold pants tomorrow. All stripes the day after. They're like the guy who bought a suit with contrasting sports coat and slacks—a complete wardrobe for $149.50.

In all, the Pirates can get nine different combinations out of their shirts and pants. But things are actually more complicated than that. After all, man does not play ball by shirts and pants alone.

There are long stockings to be worn. And T-shirts. And hats.

The Pirates have two sets of each of those items as well—one black and one gold.

The truth is, nobody knows how many combinations there are. The Pirates' front office toyed with the idea of putting the equation through a computer, but never got around to it.

It goes without saying that the uniform situation has to be kept under tight control or the Pirates could end up on the field one day in an unruly galaxy of uniforms. This would be not only an aesthetic affront, but also a breach of baseball rules that state all players on a team must be similarly dressed down to their shoetops.

This awesome responsibility at Three Rivers Stadium falls upon June Schant, secretary to Pirates' vice president Joe O'Toole. She heads up Uniform Control and her word is law.

Ms. Schant works up her rotation far in advance and distributes it to various checkpoints. The Pirates' bulletin board announces which color each of the items will be for the next week or so. Lists for road trips are handed out with meal money and itineraries.

Thus did the Pirates learn that for a recent weekend series against the Cubs their Friday attire would be striped shirt, gold pants and cap, black socks and T-shirt. Saturday, it was gold top and socks with black pants, cap and T-shirt. Sunday, it was striped top and pants with gold cap, socks and T-shirt.

Ms. Schant's sergeant-major in charge of carrying out the orders is equipment man John Hallahan. He makes it easy on everybody by simply laying out the uniform of the day in each locker.

"If they didn't lay it out in the lockers," admits infielder Phil Garner, "I wouldn't know what to wear."

Even manager Chuck Tanner says he peeks around to check out what everybody else is wearing and make sure he's properly dressed. Tanner once got as far as the field before realizing he was wearing the wrong hat.

In Pittsburgh, some fans have gotten up a pool trying to guess which player will make the first mistake. It is not known if anybody has his money on the Pirates' ballgirls, who have their own multi-uniforms right down to tight-fitting shorts.

Other non-players have gotten into the spirit as well. While discussing the uniforms the other day, O'Toole was wearing a pair of white slacks with the Pirates' black-and-gold stripe down the side.

Even though the Pirates have a history of uniform innovation—in 1971, they were the first to introduce the now universally worn double-knits—they were concerned about the reaction of the National League to their new plans. But its OK was quickly given once some sketches were submitted.

The uniforms have created some controversy among the fans, and the least-liked combination seems to be striped shirt or pants mixed with a solid color. But television viewers and magazine photographers seem to be intrigued and the Pirates are getting the national exposure they were hoping for.

None of the players has voiced any displeasure either. To date, there have been no reported instances of a player going 4-for-4 and then refusing to change the next day for fear it will change his luck.

Which is probably just as well. The list of volunteers to tell Willie Stargell what he can and can't wear is not likely to be a long one.

John Bowman and Joel Zoss

FROM DIAMONDS IN THE ROUGH

"Enter the Villain"

Think about how hard an umpire works. While each player has at least every half-inning off to sit on the bench and enjoy a cold drink, the umpire stands out there for the whole game, praying that nothing will happen for which he'll be noticed or remembered. Why, then, does the fan hate him so much?

———————————

How umpires came to be treated as paid professionals, how they came to be separated from their home-team ties, how their uniforms and gear developed, and how their mastery of the increasingly more detailed rules came to be crucial to the game is part of the standard histories of the game. Less known is the way the umpire developed into a kind of "villain"—like a stage character in a melodrama, a character whom the paying public felt they had a right, almost an obligation, to hiss and boo, the difference being that the umpire had to operate in a real world where public attacks went far beyond hissing and booing. David Q. Voigt, one of the premier historians of the game, has traced this development in his article "America's Manufactured Villain—The Baseball Umpire," but few of today's fans or even sportswriters realize what a long tradition of umpire-baiting lies behind contemporary "rhubarbs" involving umpires and managers such as Earl Weaver, Billy Martin, or Pete Rose. (The career record for ejections from games seems to be held by Earl Weaver—ninety-eight.) The distinguishing characteristic of these modern confrontations, in fact, is their tameness in comparison to the late-nineteenth-century treatment of umpires. Nothing that managers or players or owners or fans do or say these days comes anywhere close to the despicable treatment umpires were subjected to in the last decades of the nineteenth century.

The vilification began in the early 1870s and was directly related to the growing complexity and seriousness of the game, which in turn grew out of baseball's growing professionalism.

When the Cincinnati Red Stockings openly declared themselves a paid professional team in 1869, other teams soon followed, and right on their heels came gamblers. A new kind of spectator began to dominate the big-city ballparks where professional teams were playing, spectators who came to bet on their favorites, to drink with their cronies, and generally to raise a bit of hell. They were not apt to have given much thought to the nature of the game, and the obvious focus for their ignorance and frustration was the umpire. Players were only too willing to exploit this blatant partisanship among the fans, especially at their home field, and some owners even encouraged it.

So it was that, starting in the 1870s, there began a constant series of incidents involving umpires, confrontations that often led to violence and ultimately led to umpires being cast as villains. Umpires were frequently assaulted both during and after games, by players as well as fans, and there are at least two references to killings of umpires in the minor leagues: Samuel White at Lowndesborough, Alabama, in 1889, and Ora Jennings at Farmersburg, Indiana, in 1891—both struck with bats by irate players. Sometimes games were tainted by gambling money riding on their outcome, enabling players to accuse umpires of being "bought"; conversely, umpires might accuse players of having "sold out." One notoriously feisty umpire, Bob Ferguson, accused a New York Mutuals player of holding back for the gamblers, and when the player called him a liar, Ferguson hit him with a bat. Ferguson had to be escorted off the field by the local police.

But Ferguson's assault was an exception to the usual situation. Accounts by umpires during this era are full of tales of flights from the field, fights with players and fans, police escorts out of town, and hiding in hotel rooms or under stands to escape the locals' wrath. Crowds turned into brute mobs and hurled dangerous missiles of all kinds, chasing umpires off the field both during and after games. Once an umpire named Johnstone was denied entrance to the Polo Grounds by the Giants management, which said the crowd was so unhappy with his calls of the previous day's game that there'd be a riot. Johnstone retaliated by declaring the game forfeited by the Giants. Understandably, umpires in this era were known to have carried and produced guns, although there is no case of their having shot anyone. (A Chicago judge in 1909 ruled that an umpire had no right to draw a gun even when confronted by an angry mob.)

Between 1870 and 1900, owners actually encouraged attacks against umpires, either through some naive notion that it was all "part of the game" or through a more calculated desire to attract spectators with a bit of violence. One of the ways owners contributed to this pervasive umpire-baiting was to refuse either to fine their players or to pay the fines levied against them for their attacks on umpires. Some of the most prominent and presumably respectable figures in baseball during these years participated in this guerrilla warfare against umpires. Even the great Albert Spalding, upholder of baseball as the American Ideal Incarnate, would claim that in attacking umpires the fans were simply demonstrating their democratic right to oppose tyrants. In 1887, National League President Nicholas Young told an umpire to give "the closest and most doubtful decisions to the home club" in order to avoid arousing the mob.

Baseball historian David Q. Voigt has documented the many headlines, poems, songs, and newspaper articles that openly whipped on the fans to dislike and assault umpires. The Chicago *Tribune* in 1886 printed a "humorous" poem typical of the era:

Mother, may I slug the umpire　　　　Let me clasp his throat, dear mother,
　May I slug him right away　　　　　　In a dear, delightful grip
So he cannot be here, Mother,　　　　With one hand, and with the other
　When the clubs begin to play?　　　　Bat him several in the lip.

The effect of such propaganda on the umpires themselves was understandably devastating. The rules for baseball were evolving, and no one had much experience with the subtleties that underlie close situations in a ballgame. Umpires were thus in an almost impossible situation as they tried their best to apply the new rules under the hateful glare of ballpark crowds.

One of the most touching expressions of the plight of umpires came in an article written for *Lippincott's Monthly Magazine* of October 1886 by one Joe J. Ellick, a former baseball

player and manager who had retired to go into business but had accepted an invitation in July 1885 from the National League to serve as an umpire. His account of his brief career gives a sad glimpse into the state of baseball in that era: Within weeks he quit and went back to his business career, unable to stomach the conduct of players and fans and journalists. His parting advice says it all: "Some defensive armor for protecting the umpire against bad language and beer-glasses is imperatively called for."

Is all this a thing of the past? Not entirely. It is customary to say that the end of such atrocious treatment of umpires came with the establishment of the American League in 1901, for its founder and president, Ban Johnson, was a staunch defender of the inviolability of umpires. Indeed, when Johnson suspended a Baltimore pitcher for spitting in the face of an umpire that first year, team manager John McGraw was reportedly so furious that the incident contributed to his quitting the team and going over to the National League. (To even the score, though, it should be admitted that umpire Tim Hurst in 1909 spit in the face of Eddie Collins—and Johnson fired Hurst.) In 1907, umpire Bill Evans had his skull fractured by a bottle tossed from the stands. In 1917, John McGraw hit umpire Bill Byron in the jaw (and was fined five hundred dollars and suspended sixteen days).

Most fans today have no idea of how many umpires continue to leave the profession simply because they cannot take the abuse. (Dave Pallone's quitting in 1988 after his fracas with Rose seems to have been based on more complex matters.) Even the courts tend to sanction umpires' status as punching bags. As recently as August 1987, a New York State appeals court upheld George Steinbrenner's right to proclaim publicly that a particular American League umpire was "not a capable umpire. He doesn't measure up." The court's decision went on to say that "this action of defamation brings into play one of the most colorful American traditions—the razzing of the umpire. . . . General Douglas MacArthur is reported to have said he was proud to protect American freedoms like the freedom to boo umpires."

Billy Martin in Action. UPI/The Bettmann Archive. *Billy Martin was as well known for his stormy relationship with umpires (as well as Yankee boss George Steinbrenner) as he was for the managerial acumen that brought a world championship to the Bronx in 1977. Here, Martin administers a layer of top-soil to an unfortunate umpire.*

Ron Luciano and David Fisher

FROM THE UMPIRE STRIKES BACK

"Managers"

The snake and the mongoose. The dolphin and the shark. Add to that list of natural enemies former umpire Ron Luciano and former Baltimore Orioles manager Earl Weaver. We hear first from Luciano in this excerpt from his 1982 book The Umpire Strikes Back.

———————

The strangest protest in which I've ever been involved was lodged by Earl Weaver, although I don't think anything concerning me and Earl could really be considered strange. . . . Once, for example, before a game, we were having a very calm discussion about managing. He tried to convince me that the most a manager can do is try to arrange things so that certain hitters will face certain pitchers. I told him he didn't know what he was talking about, because I had been watching him outmanage people in four leagues over fifteen years. He told me I was crazy. I told him he was twice as crazy as I was. Finally one of his coaches stepped in and told us to stop shouting at each other. We were in the middle of an argument and didn't even realize it.

Our serious problems started in 1976. I was out in Oakland and a local reporter asked me who my favorite manager was. Naturally I told him it was former Oakland manager Alvin Dark. Couldn't hurt, right? . . .

Then, unfortunately, the reporter asked me which manager I liked least. Naturally I tried to avoid a direct answer. "WEAVER," I shouted. "EARL WEAVER." I would have spelled it for him, I would have written it down, I would even have hired skywriters if necessary.

The only problem I've ever had with newspapermen is that they write for newspapers. If they would just have kept my opinions to themselves I never would have had any trouble. Weaver read my comments and did not appreciate my sense of humor. He requested that the league bar me from Baltimore's Municipal Stadium, the State of Maryland and the entire East Coast. Lee MacPhail suggested I keep my mouth locked.

I knew MacPhail was right and did my best to avoid any more problems with Weaver. My best lasted until spring training the following year. I was in Arizona and a reporter asked me a trick question: which teams did I think would win the division races in the American League.

"It doesn't matter to me," I said. "Lee MacPhail signs my paychecks no matter who wins." When pressed further, I said I thought Oakland would win the West and I didn't care who won the East, "As long as it isn't Baltimore."

When I said it I didn't think it was a terrible thing to say. That was the way I felt as a fan, but I knew that my feelings would never and had never affected my judgment on the field. Anytime I missed a play it was simply because I missed it, not because I was partial to one team or one player.

In retrospect it was an incredibly stupid thing to say. The league fined me four hundred dollars and ordered me to apologize publicly to Weaver and the Orioles. I agreed to apologize, but not pay the fine.

Three months later my crew was in Anaheim and had Baltimore for the first time that season. I was prepared to be on my best behavior, but I could afford to be—Bill Haller was angry. Weaver had questioned his honesty by saying he should not be allowed to work Detroit Tiger games because his brother was catching for the Tigers—and the league actually removed Bill from our crew every time we had Detroit.

Haller and Weaver had had difficulties for a long time. One Saturday afternoon Haller was working the plate and looked over at the Oriole dugout and spotted Weaver on his knees on the steps. Bill wandered over there and quietly asked him to leave the premises without hesitation.

COLORPLATE 107

MARK BRAUGHT. *Three and Two.* 1991.
Pastel and oil. 25 x 35 in. Collection of the artist.

 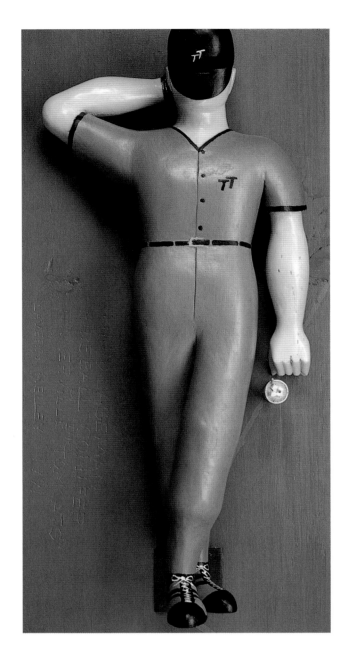

COLORPLATE 108

JACK DOWD. *Bases Loaded.* 1991.
Basswood. 72 in. tall. Collection of Bill Griffin.

COLORPLATE 109 *(above, right)*

LAVERN KELLEY. *Third Baseman Fireball Confier of the Tinkerville Tomcats.*
1991. Pine, acrylic. 10 x 20 x 6 in. Gallery 53 Artworks, Cooperstown, New York.

COLORPLATE 110 *(opposite, above)*

TIM SWARTZ. *Pre-Game Visit.* 1991. Watercolor. 10 x 15 in.
Gallery 53 Artworks, Cooperstown, New York.

COLORPLATE 111 *(opposite, below)*

TIM SWARTZ. *Stretching II.* 1990. Watercolor. 26 x 34 in.
Gallery 53 Artworks, Cooperstown, New York.

COLORPLATE 112

ANDY JURINKO. *Tiger Stadium Panorama*. 1991. Oil on canvas. 64 x 144 in.
Collection of the artist.

COLORPLATE 113

PAMELA PATRICK. *The Rookie*. 1991. Pastel. 30 x 40 in.
Collection of MBNA.

COLORPLATE 114

MICHAEL HESLOP. *Contact.* 1991.
Oil on canvas. 18 x 26 in. Collection of the artist.

COLORPLATE 115

WREN PANZELLA. *Two-One Count.* 1991. Hand-colored lithograph.
18¹/₂ x 14¹/₂ in. Gallery 53 Artworks, Cooperstown, New York.

Weaver couldn't believe it. "What're you throwing me out for?" he demanded. "I'm just praying. You can't throw me out for praying."

"You Jewish?"

"No," Weaver admitted.

Haller smiled. "Well, it's Saturday, and you don't pray on Saturday if you're not Jewish. So get outta here."

For the first game of this Oriole–Angel series I was at second and Haller was at third. I had a close play at second that went against Baltimore, and before I took my thumb down I knew Weaver would want to discuss it. Sure enough, I looked up and saw him coming toward me. Even before he reached me he had grabbed his hat and thrown it on the ground, and I knew he was going to go. But as I flexed my thumb I spotted Haller racing toward me from third. "I got him," he was screaming gleefully. "Lemme, lemme." I stepped aside and let Haller tell Weaver how much he had appreciated his remarks about the Tiger games.

While Haller was giving him explicit directions to the clubhouse, I looked wistfully at Weaver's cap lying on the ground and nostalgically remembered the night 6'2" Don Denkinger had eased over to Weaver's cap while I was arguing with him and first stepped on it with the very sharp golf cleats on his right foot, and then the very sharp golf cleats on his left foot, and then started twisting back and forth, back and forth.

Upon arriving in Anaheim I had announced a press conference at which I would make a formal apology for my ill-considered remarks in spring training. Before the second game a group of writers, Weaver and American League Supervisor of Umpires Dick Butler squeezed into the umpires' dressing room.

My press conference began well. "To start with, I've got a big mouth and I said a lot of dumb things. Everyone makes mistakes and I guess I'm at the top of the ladder when it comes to saying dumb things.

"It was just a dumb, stupid statement that should never have been printed . . . Earl and his players are professionals—they know I'm not going to do anything intentionally to hurt them. I like Baltimore, and I like the Orioles team. They're a good defensive team, and that always makes it easier on an umpire."

Suddenly I heard a familiar voice from the back of the small crowd. "But you did say it," Weaver said.

"Well, sure, yeah, I did say it," I admitted, "but hey, Earl, you've said a lot of things you're sorry for, too."

"No," he said, "I'm not sorry about anything I ever said about you or to you. I've meant every word of it."

"Well, then," I replied, getting warmed up, "I haven't been too far wrong when I said those things about you, you know."

Dick Butler tried to interrupt. "Thanks, Ron . . ."

"So you meant it, huh?" Weaver snapped, "I knew it."

"No," I told him, "I didn't mean what I said about Baltimore."

"But you meant it about me!"

By this time we were shouting at each other. "Well, you're the only guy I have trouble with all the time, and you have trouble with every umpire in the league, so don't you think you're the problem?"

"I yell at you because you're biased."

"Oh, yeah? Well you're more biased than anyone!"

My attempt to apologize turned out to be a disaster. The American League had no choice but to take me off Baltimore games. I objected, but there really wasn't anything I could do about it.

I didn't work an Oriole game for an entire year. I didn't miss Weaver, but I did miss his team. The Orioles were always such a pleasure to watch—and they played quick games. To my surprise, when I received my monthly schedule for June 1979, I had been assigned to a Baltimore–White Sox series in Chicago. Haller was taking his vacation during this period and I assumed the league had gotten confused and thought I was going to be on vacation. I didn't say a word. I was looking forward to seeing my pal Earl again.

We arrived in Chicago on a Friday morning. There had been a rock concert held in Comiskey Park the previous weekend and the field had been badly torn up. New sod had been lain down, but it had rained hard during the week. When I walked across the field I sank in over my shoes. I decided that if I couldn't walk on water, certainly nobody playing major league baseball could. I declared the field unplayable and called the game.

White Sox manager Tony LaRussa objected, but I told him I wasn't going to be responsible for players getting hurt on a muddy field. Weaver agreed with me, so our first confrontation in a year went smoothly.

The sun was shining on Saturday, but the field was still in terrible shape. I still didn't think we should play, but I wasn't sure. Players on both teams signed a petition claiming the field was not playable, so I called it again. This was the only time I've known of a game called because of rain on a gorgeous June afternoon.

We played a doubleheader on Sunday. The field was not good, but life rafts were no longer necessary, either. I had the plate and Weaver started on me in the very first inning. "Looked like a strike from here." "Bend over and look at it." It took him three pitches to make me feel right at home. In the third inning I called a strike on Doug DeCinces and Weaver really let me have it. "Wherewasitlookedhighfromherebenddownbeardown . . ." Maybe he was right, maybe it wasn't a strike. I had only called about 150,000 pitches from behind the plate and he had called many more than that from the dugout, but it looked like a good pitch to me. I probably would not have thrown out any other manager in baseball for complaining, but this wasn't any other manager. This was Weaver. I turned and looked directly at him. I carefully loaded my finger. I pointed it right at him and shot him out of the game. Then I calmly blew the smoke away.

He sprinted out of the dugout to confront me. "Are you throwing me out of the game?"

I'd been waiting a long time for this moment. I smiled broadly. "Earl," I said, "I haven't seen you in a year. *Of course* I'm throwing you out of the game."

He then proceeded to criticize my work and concluded by protesting the game.

"Earl? What? What are you going to protest? You lasted until the third inning. You should be flattered."

It was then he invented the strangest protest I'd ever heard. "I'm protesting the game on account of the umpire's integrity."

"What?"

"Umpire's integrity. And I want it announced over the loudspeaker."

"Earl," I said sympathetically, "you know you don't want me to do that."

"I'm not leaving the field until it's announced over the loudspeaker." This was a man who had faked a heart attack on the field. This was a man who had stolen second base and wouldn't give it back. I knew he wasn't bluffing: he wasn't going to leave the field until that announcement was made.

I was thrilled. I knew I had him. There was no way he was not going to get suspended for publicly attacking an umpire's integrity. "Okay, buddy," I told him, "you got it." I called the public address announcer and told him exactly what Weaver wanted.

"You don't want me to announce that," he said.

"Oh, yes, I do," I chimed happily. "Oh, yes, I do."

The p.a. announcer still did not believe I was serious. He announced that the Orioles were playing the game under protest, but did not give the reason.

That brought Weaver back onto the field. "What're you doing here?" I asked him. "You're not here anymore. You're gone."

"That's not what I said I wanted," he reminded me.

I tried to be sensible. "Earl, leave it at this. It isn't going to hurt me, but it is going to hurt you."

Announce it, he insisted.

I had it announced, and play resumed.

Assistant Supervisor of Umpires Johnny Stevens was waiting for me in the umpires' dressing room at the conclusion of the first game. Fuming. He had been in contact with Lee MacPhail, he told me.

"How is Lee?" I asked.

First, Stevens told me I was not to discuss the incident with any reporters. I was not to talk to Weaver during the second game of the doubleheader under any circumstances. I wasn't to smile at him. I wasn't to tell him that I couldn't hear him to draw him out of the dugout and then when he came out give him the boot. I wasn't to allow him to back me into a corner. If the ballpark caught on fire, I wasn't even to warn him.

I began to realize this was getting serious.

At the beginning of the second game we met at home plate during the exchange of lineups. He looked at me and asked, "What's going on?"

I opened my mouth to tell him that it had taken me an entire year, but I'd finally gotten him for his performance at that press conference. But before I could utter a single syllable, umpire Russell Goetz stepped between us. "Ron says everything is fine, Earl. Now, listen, both of you, it's a new game and we're not going to talk about the first game. It's over. That's it."

I worked third base that game and only had two calls. One was a line drive hit by an Oriole that landed just foul and I called it foul at least fifteen times. The other was a sliding tag play in which a White Sox player was out. That might have been the toughest out I ever called in baseball.

Weaver was suspended for three games.

Although I didn't realize it at the time, that was the last time Weaver and I would meet between the foul lines. The following year I was up in the broadcast booth, looking down upon him. I'd like to be able to report that the three-day suspension taught him an important lesson, that from that day on Earl Weaver had acted differently toward umpires, paying them the respect that he knows they have earned by their tireless efforts.

I would really like to be able to report that. Unfortunately I can't. Weaver will be winning games and screeching at umpires on every pitch until they drag him into the Hall of Fame.

During my career on the field I got to know, and like, numerous men who managed big league ballclubs. It's an elite, exclusive fraternity, limited to a membership of twenty-six men at any one time. But as I learned, old managers never die; they just end up working for George Steinbrenner.

Earl Weaver with Berry Stainback

FROM IT'S WHAT YOU LEARN AFTER YOU KNOW IT ALL THAT COUNTS

Here, Mr. Weaver, the former Baltimore Orioles manager, takes a few moments for rebuttal of Mr. Luciano in the form of this passage from his 1982 autobiography.

———————————

Ron Luciano . . . was an umpire I preferred not to associate with right up until he retired a few years ago to work for NBC-TV. I say that not merely because Luciano ejected me more times (seven) in fewer games than any other umpire.

I've known Luciano from my days in the minors when he was definitely one of the better umpires in the league. I remember offering him counsel, though, based on my fifteen years in professional baseball. We had a big argument in York, Pennsylvania, and I'll never forget standing there looking up at Ron's chin and hollering about all the dedication it takes for a ballplayer to go to the big leagues. And I suggested that anyone who wants to advance has to bear down all the time. I don't know whether Ron heeded that advice, but he did move up to the majors rather quickly.

Earl Weaver. c. 1970. The National Baseball Library, Cooperstown, New York. *Here, Weaver, the former manager of the Baltimore Orioles and scourge of American League umpires, stalks his prey. "You've got to go and tell a guy when he's wrong, just as you've got to tell a guy when you feel he may be harboring some kind of grudge."*

And he introduced a new style of umpiring, one that had more entertainment value in it than anyone I'd seen since Emmet Ashford. Luciano wouldn't just call a man "safe." He'd make the call a dozen times, dramatically slicing his arms through the air like a non-swimmer trying to stay afloat. And his "out" signals looked like a spastic trying to hitch a ride on an L.A. freeway. But it was fun and gave fans something else to cheer about.

Luciano, who is a massive man, about six-foot-six and 300 pounds, was indeed a show-man. I think his antics were definitely good for the game . . . until he began putting more effort into them than he did into his work. It suffered along with those of us who were engaged in our profession that particular day. Luciano just got caught with his thumb up his butt too many times. I remember a game in which he was working the bases. During the fifth-inning break when they drag the infield, Ron grabbed a Coke and began talking to fans in the stands. He was still standing there chatting when the first pitch of the next inning was thrown. He looked like a fool and so did his crew chief, Bill Haller, who is supposed to be sure all the umpires are in position before an inning begins.

And I don't know how many times Luciano gave one of his multiple "out" signals, then suddenly realized he had yelled "Safe" and had to switch signs. *That* was entertaining, too, but more than a little confusing. We'd be jumping around in the dugout saying, "What the fungo did that big boob call? Can't he make up his goddamn mind?" Then someone would say, "He ain't got one."

Still, I didn't have any more problems with Luciano than I did with other umpires until he started saying publicly that he hated Earl Weaver. The quote appeared in a California newspaper in 1975 and was picked up all over. Now I did not feel that a man who admits that he hates you should be umpiring your games. After I questioned Luciano's attitude and protested his performance in a game against us, he proceeded to eject me from both games of a subsequent doubleheader, and I wasn't even fined. That suggested that MacPhail saw some merit in my charges.

It didn't do me much good, though, because in the first Oriole game Luciano worked behind the plate in 1976 he got me for nothing. He'd missed some calls on Jim Palmer in the first two innings, and when the initial pitch of the third was "Ball one" I called to catcher Dave Duncan:

"Was that a strike, Dave?" He motioned that it had been.

"Where did Luciano say the pitch was?" Duncan motioned high.

Then Luciano, who had been staring at me, gave a little jerk with his thumb. I went out to him incredulously. "Are you throwing me out?"

"You're out, Earl. You know you can't question balls and strikes."

"I wasn't! I was asking my catcher about the pitch! I have every right to question my catcher!"

Luciano turned his back on me. I charged him, cupped my hands by my mouth, and hollered as loud as I could into Luciano's face that he was a disgrace to his profession and several other unprintable things. Then I kicked dirt all over home plate and went into the runway. I saw Palmer start to pitch with the plate still covered. Luciano didn't clean it off until Jim walked in as if to clean it himself.

After the game, which we lost 3–1, I was still enraged and I told the writers, "I wish Luciano hadn't uncovered the plate. If he'd let Palmer do it, Lee MacPhail would have had to fire Luciano, which he should have done long ago."

Just a few weeks later Ron Luciano gave MacPhail incontestable reasons for relieving him of his duties. In an interview with a Chicago *Sun-Times* writer that was syndicated nationally, Luciano said, "I don't care who wins the pennant as long as it isn't Baltimore." He also said he didn't like Earl Weaver and "I hope he doesn't win another game."

Now, how can a man who openly admits that he roots against a ball club and its manager, how can that man possibly be objective in umpiring any of that ball club's games? The Orioles front office called for Luciano's immediate termination.

In July, before we played the Angels in Anaheim, Luciano called a press conference and apologized to me for his anti-Weaver, anti-Oriole comments. "To start with," Luciano began, "I've got a big mouth and I've said a lot of dumb things. Everybody makes mistakes, and I'm at the top of the ladder when it comes to saying dumb things."

I certainly agreed with that, but I was still unconvinced that I could rely on Luciano to be impartial. I said, "I'll try to forgive and forget. But the first time a close play goes against us, I'm gonna feel it was a chance to get the knife in deeper."

In all truth, by making that statement after Luciano's public apology to me I thought he would not dare give us any quick thumbs. And in the game against the Angels that night Luciano was exemplary. But his crew chief, Bill Haller, ejected me in the fifth inning. The next night he got me two innings earlier.

Both were blatant instances of Haller standing up for the Umpire's Association in what amounted to a slap in the face of the president of the American League and the supervisor of umpires . . . with me paying the price. In other words, *no* authority was going to chastise an umpire without the umpires retaliating. As I said after the second successive ejection, "We got no chance with this crew. Evidently Luciano will stand back and let the other members of the crew get me."

Luciano didn't work any of our other games that season and very few in subsequent seasons. The next time we saw the Haller crew in 1976, Dale Ford had replaced Luciano, and again we received no bargain. During a Sunday afternoon game in Baltimore, Lee May contested a called third strike, and once again it was a case of an umpire ejecting a player before I even had a chance to try and protect him. I don't think anything infuriates me more than the gratuitous loss of a player. By the time I reached the plate umpire, May was already gone and I really tore into Dale Ford. Unfortunately, in waving my hands in Ford's face my fingers accidentally cut his lips. When MacPhail asked me if there had been contact with Ford, I said yes.

But I also told him that the entire incident could have been avoided if the league had used a little foresight and not assigned the Haller crew to Baltimore. Taking Luciano off of the crew just alienated the others, in my opinion. That crew had already thrown me out of five games, fined me once, and I now received a three-game suspension—and the season was only half over!

But we had very few inordinate problems with the Haller crew thereafter, and I don't know as we even saw Luciano again until the 1979 season. Of course, I heard from him occasionally, or rather I heard from what he has characterized as his "big, dumb mouth," particularly after he had appeared at off-season banquets.

Luciano made a speech in Rochester in the spring of '79 and said, "I hate Earl Weaver with a passion. I met Weaver in my second year in baseball. I threw him out that first night and three nights after that. Our relationship has gone downhill ever since. He's about three-foot-one and I have to tell him to get his nose off my kneecap."

When the writers sprang these quotes on me I got annoyed and said, "I'm sorry Luciano's mentally ill and won't umpire any of our games again this season. He's a sick man."

The only time Luciano worked one of our '79 games, on August 26 in Chicago, he grabbed the first opportunity that presented itself to eject me—and I ended up with another three-day suspension. There were no problems whatsoever through the first four innings. But Doug DeCinces led off the fifth and worked the count to 3–2. The next pitch was so far off the plate that Doug flipped his bat and was 25 feet down the base path when Luciano called strike three . . . another of Ron's cute mannerisms. Doug turned and charged Luciano, and I jumped out of the dugout to get between them—when Doug suddenly stopped and headed for the dugout. So I was left standing there, bare and exposed five feet from the dugout. I threw my hands in the air helplessly. Someone thought I was raising my arms to the heavens imploring a higher power to grant us patience . . . if He couldn't provide us with another home-plate umpire.

It seemed to me Luciano had just been waiting to get me out of the dugout to throw me out. He made only the slightest pointing motion at me, then quickly brought three fingers to his lips and gave me the kiss-off.

"Are you throwing me out?" I asked.

"Yes."

I went right to crew chief Russ Goetz. "I am protesting this game," I told him, "on the grounds of the umpire's integrity." Then I went to the White Sox p.a. man, Bob Finnigan, and had him make the announcement to the 25,000 people in the stands. Lee MacPhail happened to be one of them, and I felt it was about time he took Luciano off our case permanently.

MacPhail was of a different mind. "I exploded when I heard that announcement," he said. "I sure as hell can't let him publicly question the integrity of an umpire. What does that mean? He's dishonest? We had Luciano apologize when he said what he said." Thanks, Lee, I thought, that did me a world of good. "We've tried to keep Luciano away [from Oriole games]," MacPhail went on, "but you can't carry these things on forever. Earl Weaver is suspended for three games. That strike call was the first decision even debated today."

The fact that the call led to my ejection raised legitimate questions in my mind about the umpire's integrity—particularly since my part in the "debate" consisted of stretching my arms to the skies. Is that just cause for ejection? I could have been airing my pits, for all anyone knew.

Oriole GM Hank Peters was angry, too. "I don't like the grounds of the suspension," Hank said. "They don't suspend an umpire when he calls Earl 'baseball's Son of Sam.' Luciano has said all those things about how he doesn't want the Orioles to win. We asked Lee to fire him and he refused. I haven't seen why Luciano hasn't been suspended."

I didn't waste my time protesting the suspension. But then suspending managers is really a waste of time, because every manager has a means of communicating with his ball club following an ejection or suspension from games. It certainly would not be difficult to communicate if I so desired. I have closed-circuit TV and a phone to the dugout in my office, as well as messengers available if needed. I can sit back in comfort and see when the count goes 3–0 with a man on second and put on the hit sign just as I would if I were in the dugout. But I cannot confirm the reports that I have continued to manage after being thrown out of a game. There is no way I would want to give Lee MacPhail any groundless grounds to suspend me.

George F. Will
FROM MEN AT WORK
"The Manager"

Essayist George F. Will's 1990 study of baseball included a profile of Oakland A's manager Tony LaRussa. In this passage, we see that explicitly illegal acts within the game are nonetheless an integral part of the game's strategy.

At precisely 8:00 A.M. on Wednesday, August 31, 1988, Tony LaRussa strides into the coffee shop of a motel hard by the Oakland–Alameda County Coliseum. That is where the Athletics play and where LaRussa spent the night. Nine hours earlier his team had beaten the Boston Red Sox and they will do so again in four hours. LaRussa is wearing running shoes, blue sweat pants and a T-shirt the distinctive orange of a Wheaties cereal box. The front of the shirt is emblazoned with the Wheaties logo. When a fan who recognizes him compliments him on the shirt, LaRussa replies, tersely, "Read the back." The back says: "Commitment to Excellence."

Last night the mighty Athletics, who play "bashball" and after hitting home runs bump forearms rather than merely swap high fives, beat the Red Sox, 1–0. The Red Sox pitcher was Roger Clemens, who struck out 9 in 6$\frac{1}{3}$ innings. When you are facing Clemens, you come to the park knowing you are going to scratch for runs. The Athletics scratched. The runner who scored, Carney Lansford, reached first on a single to left, stole second and went to third on a wild pitch. He scored on a ball that traveled 30 feet. It was a suicide squeeze bunt laid down by Glenn Hubbard, who stands 5 feet 7. Funny business, baseball. Why is LaRussa not laughing?

Laughing? He is not even eating. All he has ordered is a wedge of melon, and he is barely picking at it. His stomach is, he says, not exactly upset, but he is still too tense, too drained to eat. The squeeze was only the third attempted by the Athletics that season. It was the first that had worked. Going into the ninth, Dave Stewart had thrown 120 pitches. He struck out Ellis Burks on three pitches. He did the same to Todd Benzinger. He got an 0–2 count on Jim Rice, then missed with a borderline ball. Rice fouled off two, then struck out. It was, LaRussa says, one of the most draining games of his career.

Today's game starts at noon. No one will have had enough sleep. It is the last day in August. Tomorrow begins the month when, for the best baseball teams, life is real, life is earnest. Emotions are high, as are the stakes. Nerves are often raw and tempers are short. Last night one player on each team was hit by a pitch. It is time to think about the ethical and prudential problems of batters being thrown at, and of retaliating when it happens to your batters. LaRussa's policy is the result of much reflection. He has thought often and hard about his reputation as a man with a hard side.

"If a guy is hitting well against our club, I have never, *ever* told a pitcher, 'Let's go ahead and hit him.' Some guys do that." In 1987, when McGwire was setting a record for rookies with 49 home runs, he hit 2 home runs on a Saturday against the Red Sox and got hit on Sunday. Hit on the head. LaRussa's normally muted tone changes as disgust fills his voice when he speaks about the practice some teams have of saying, "This guy's wearing us out—knock him on his ass." Gary Gaetti, the Twins' third baseman, embodies everything LaRussa likes in a player—intelligence, intensity, hustle. Once when an Athletics pitcher deliberately hit Gaetti, at a time when Gaetti was blistering Athletics pitching, LaRussa called the pitcher on the carpet and told him, "You'll never pitch for me again if you do that again." LaRussa explains, "We can make him [a hot hitter] uncomfortable pitching in on his hands. But that is it."

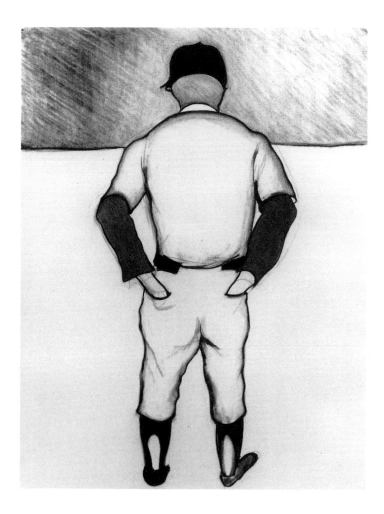

BASIL KING. *The Manager*. 1983.
Charcoal on paper. 30 x 22 ¹/₄ in.
Gallery 53 Artworks, Cooperstown, New York.

Regarding retaliation, LaRussa has a doctrine of measured response. "It's a 2–1 game and your big guy gets bopped in the bottom of the eighth inning. Now you've got to go out in the top of the ninth with a one-run lead and you need three outs. Who should make the decision whether you retaliate? It's got to be the manager. Sometimes you walk up to your player who got hit and say, 'I really believe this guy took a shot at you. We'll get somebody in the first inning tomorrow.'" LaRussa is a stickler for proportionality in punishment. "You try to match, as best you can. If they take a shot at your big producer, then you take a shot at their big producer. If they've just cold-cocked McGwire and their first batter in the inning is their light-hitting second baseman, that's not the guy. If someone takes a shot at Walter Weiss, then you look for their promising rookie or their second-year player who is a big star."

In game three of the 1983 American League Championship Series between LaRussa's White Sox and the Orioles, the Orioles' pitcher, Mike Flanagan, hit Ron Kittle with a slider. A slider is a good pitch to hit someone with because it is two to three miles per hour slower than a fastball and it is more apt to look like an accident. LaRussa knew that Kittle was Flanagan's biggest problem. So in the next inning someone comparable to Kittle—a young power hitter named Cal Ripken—got hit. "We will never, ever retaliate above the shoulder. So the guy will get stung but he will play again," LaRussa stresses.

"Once you establish that you'll protect your players, that is a part of the game you shouldn't have to worry about. Then the only things left are those natural, unavoidable confrontations between two competitive teams trying to beat each other. If someone throws a fastball outside and Jose hits a home run to right field, they may try to throw a fastball inside to get him out. If they miss they might hit him. You'll never avoid those. We are a very aggressive, pitching inside-off-the-plate club."

Two changes, one in equipment and one in teaching, have complicated the problem of deciding what is and what is not fair in the war between pitchers and batters for control of the inside and outside edges of the strike zone. Batting helmets, which were not made mandatory until 1971, increased batters' aggressiveness by decreasing fear. And the batting style taught by the late Charlie Lau has made many hitters seem (to pitchers) excessively, provocatively aggressive. Lau, whose most famous work of art is George Brett, was the White Sox batting instructor when LaRussa was the White Sox manager.

The gospel according to Lau is: Shift your weight to your back foot as the pitcher winds up, then stride in toward the plate, shifting your weight to provide the power at the moment of contact. Striding in is dangerous to the hitter—and to the pitcher's career if he lets it occur without any resistance. It gives the batter too much control of the outside corner.

"You want to hit?" LaRussa asks. "First you have to see the ball, and you have to stay on it. Second, you need a positive move toward the pitcher. You can't wait to see whether the ball is coming at you. You can't be on your heels. If you are, you flinch when a guy throws a breaking ball, you take too many pitches because you're a little leery. If you have a whole club like that, you can't hit. They won't step into the ball and take their chances. If you don't protect yourself, it's just one of those edges that people will take away. It's a little bit scary to go up there and face that ball being thrown hard. If you know your club isn't going to protect you, you're going to lose a big edge at the plate. Everyone is going to go up there a little timid, a little farther from the plate.

"Some umpires get a little ticked off when somebody takes a cheap shot, messes with their game. They'll hold off on a warning until you retaliate. But sometimes the minute your guy gets hit, they'll put the warning in and tie your hands. Then you tell the umpires between innings—I've never lied to them about this—'I understand the warning. We've got six innings to play and we're not going to take a shot at anybody. But our basic pitching philosophy against this club is that they crowd the plate. I don't want to lose this game because our pitchers stayed out over the plate. So I'm telling you we're going to be pitching inside to get guys out. If at any time in this game or this series I want to take a shot, I'll come and tell you it's coming.' Otherwise an umpire puts in a warning, and your pitcher is afraid to throw inside. He might get thrown out of the game. So he moves out over the plate and starts getting creamed."

All this theorizing at the breakfast table will become intensely practical on the field in a few hours. The Red Sox pitcher, Mike Smithson, will get hit hard right from the start. He will get exasperated and will throw at the Athletics' third baseman, Carney Lansford, who has done some of this early damage to Smithson. Lansford will duck the pitch, but the fact that Smithson deliberately threw at him was obvious to everyone, including the person who mattered most, the home plate umpire, Richie Garcia. His response illustrated one of the nuances of governance inside the game.

Garcia came to umpiring from the Marine Corps, which is good training for a vocation that an umpire once summed up in seven words: "Call 'em fast and walk away tough." Toughness is not enough, but it is necessary. Once when Babe Pinelli called Babe Ruth out on strikes, Ruth made a populist argument. Ruth reasoned fallaciously (as populists do) from raw numbers to moral weight: "There's 40,000 people here who know the last one was a ball, tomato head." Pinelli replied with the measured stateliness of John Marshall: "Maybe so, but mine is the only opinion that counts." Or, as Garcia tells young umpires (and every parent should tell every child): "Just because they are yelling at you doesn't mean you are wrong." Long ago the ethic of umpiring was expressed with great dignity by Bill Guthrie: "Der ain't no close plays, me lad. Dey is either dis or dat." That is true, *de jure*. De fact is, however, that, *de facto*, things are different.

When Smithson threw at Lansford, Garcia took off his mask, looked out to the mound and for a moment seemed about to issue a warning. That would have required both teams to behave. Anyone henceforth convicted (by the home plate umpire's instant and of course unappealable judgment) of throwing at anyone would be ejected. Garcia's brief pregnant pause ended not with a warning but with a brisk brushing off of home plate with his whisk broom. His message was muted but clear: The Athletics would get to retaliate. They did, in strict accordance with LaRussa's principle of proportionality. In the next inning Lansford's counterpart, Wade Boggs, the Red Sox third baseman, got thrown at. He was not hit but he had to bail out of the batter's box. The game continued. The Athletics won.

They had played 134 games and were in first place by nine. Their manager was, in his fashion, almost content as he looked ahead to a trip to Texas.

Joe Gergen

FROM THE SPORTING NEWS 1992 BASEBALL YEARBOOK

"Expansion"

At the time of this writing, in the summer of 1992, the Colorado Rockies and the Florida Marlins have yet to play a single game on the field. Off the field, though, the two teams have been gearing up for their inaugural seasons. Joe Gergen takes a behind-the-stands look at the construction of two modern baseball franchises.

In time, the Rockies may crumble. First, though, the franchise must be built, and that process is under way in Denver.

There may be plenty of fish in the adjacent ocean, but only the Marlins are marketed by baseball now that the National League has embraced Miami.

Twenty-four years after its last expansion, which came in 1969, the senior circuit will welcome two more members, the Colorado Rockies and the Florida Marlins. The 1993 coming-out party invites a plaintive question: Where have you gone, Coco Laboy?

The Rockies, having exhumed the name of a late, unlamented hockey team, and the Marlins, borrowing from the region's minor league heritage, already have taken the initial steps toward competing in '93, filling out front-office positions, scouting staffs and expense accounts. Before 1992 is over, they will have received the first tangible returns on their $95 million entry fee, bodies to place in those new big-league uniforms.

With a nucleus of 36 players culled from the operative franchises in both major leagues and one crop of amateur free agents in tow, the Rockies and Marlins will be ready to face the inevitable fate of expansion teams: losing. Optimists might note that the New York Mets, whose first collection of athletes established a modern major league standard for losses (120, in 1962), won a World Series in their eighth season. Pessimists can point to the Seattle Mariners, who didn't clear the .500 barrier until last season, their 15th year in the American League.

Indeed, of the 10 previous expansion teams, starting with the Los Angeles/California Angels and Washington Senators II/Texas Rangers, who began play in 1961, only the Kansas City Royals (born in 1969) have won more games than they've lost. Their percentage of .521 ranks favorably with the most successful franchises in baseball history, topped by the New York Yankees (.566). The Angels actually managed a winning season in their second year, but they have lost 137 more games than they've won (2,410–2,547) overall. And the Mets, whose two World Series championships are an expansion record, have a dismal career mark of 2,241–2,547.

Since only one of the majors' 10 expansion clubs in the last three decades has won as many as 70 games in its first season and the average amount of time required for a first-year team to achieve .500 is 8.5 years, it's apparent that the success of any expansion outfit rests on the youngsters developed in its farm system. Yet, the greatest attention will be focused on the "name" players acquired from a major league talent pool in November.

As a result of Fay Vincent's decision to involve both leagues in the selection process (in the past, drafts were held only within the expanding league), there will be more players from which to choose. While that may result in a better harvest than enjoyed by previous expansion clubs, it adds to the workload of the new teams.

For that reason, Dave Dombrowski, the general manager of the Marlins, suggested that one of the most important acquisitions of the Florida franchise was a satellite dish. He plans to watch more games than ever this season, supplementing the reports filed by the five people hired to scout at the major league level. "This is going to be our future," he said.

There are innumerable details that require attention in a new operation. Dombrowski is responsible for the construction of offices, clubhouses and a baseball press box at Joe Robbie Stadium, the hiring of clubhouse men, trainers and physical-fitness people, even the design of the uniforms. Rockies General Manager Bob Gebhard, who has scheduled his team to play in Mile High Stadium for two years while he oversees the project to be known as Coors Field, said "trying to find a location for one or two rookie clubs" was among the foremost items on his agenda. The Little Rockies (Foothills?) will be formed in June after the amateur draft. (Some of the junior Rockies will surely wind up in Bend, Ore., site of the franchise's first farm club. Bend is a member of the short-season Class A Northwest League.)

Still, there was little doubt that the top priority for both men was assessing talent. Gebhard, who served as vice president, player personnel, for the Minnesota Twins before casting his lot with Colorado, talked of assembling a staff of "quality scouts." In that respect, the Marlins held a clear advantage. Dombrowski, former Expos general manager, was given permission to bring his scouting director as well as other key assistants with him from Montreal.

Among them was Angel Vazquez, who had the task of implementing a scouting network in Latin America. The Expos have been one of the most successful franchises at mining the region, and there is reason to expect the Marlins will be no less aggressive in pursuing the abundant talent in that area.

Even the National Football League Dolphins, the original tenants of Joe Robbie Stadium, were conscious of the benefits to be derived from the presence of an extensive Latino community. One year, they decided to take a chance on a free-agent lineman named Manny Fernandez, in part because they thought he would make a fine spokesman for football among Hispanics. As it developed, the only language with which Fernandez, a native of California, was familiar was English. On a positive note, Fernandez became one of the best defensive tackles in the league, a solid and occasionally spectacular contributor to the No-Name Defense that helped the 1972 Dolphins to a 17–0 record.

Unlike football, of course, baseball already is wildly popular in Latin countries. "I think because of where we are located," Dombrowski said, "we're envisioned as Latin America's team. Latin players will be comfortable with the language, the weather and the proximity to home." Not to mention the ethnic composition of the fans.

It's said that one of the prime reasons for the appointment of Cookie Rojas as a Marlins scout was his connections to his homeland. If and when Cuban stars are allowed to pursue U.S. dollars, Rojas will be there to deliver them. Marlins sí, Yankees no!

Along with its multicultural diversity, of course, Miami also offers a tropical climate, virtually guaranteeing late-afternoon thundershowers during the summer months. Since one of the prime attractions of each new franchise was an open-air stadium with a grass field, this will leave the Marlins and their opponents exposed to the elements. "You can't beat the weather," Dombrowski said. "We plan for rain from 4 to 6 P.M."

Because that may play havoc with the pregame schedule, Dombrowski said many batting cages and mounds would be set up under the stands. The Rockies may have more trouble working around the snow that sometimes blankets the area in April and has been known to stage a surprise raid in August. Last summer, while attending a reunion of the 1951 New York Giants, former catcher Sal Yvars recalled a spring-training encounter between his team and the Cleveland Indians in Denver.

"They had a terrific snowstorm," Yvars said, "but the game was completely sold out. So they played with big banks of snow rimming the outfield fence. Bobby Thomson was playing center field and George Wilson—he couldn't play but he volunteered for everything—was in right."

According to Yvars, Luke Easter hit a long drive into the gap in right-center. Thomson was in position to spear the ball but Wilson cut in front and attempted a backhanded catch. The outfielder and the ball both fell to the ground, with the ball rolling into a nearby mound of snow. Undeterred, Wilson quickly fashioned a snowball and fired it to the infield. It was relayed to the plate in time for Yvars to tag out the runner.

The catcher rolled the sphere back toward the mound, where it became part of the frozen landscape. "Al Lopez and Tony Cuccinello [manager and coach, respectively, for the Indians] screamed at the umpire that it was a snowball," Yvars said. "He told them, 'Go find it.' They couldn't."

So perhaps the ball will have to be checked after each putout in mile-high Denver and the standard ground rules amended. A National League study already has confirmed that batted balls travel farther and that breaking balls tend to be straighter at such altitude. Pittsburgh Manager Jim Leyland has predicted that a manager might be tempted to use up an entire pitching staff in the course of a series in Denver. He must be patient in the face of high-scoring games.

"We'll play under the existing conditions," Gebhard said. But the thin air will be taken into account in the design of the new ballpark. In the meantime, with a relatively short distance to the stands in straightaway left field (345 feet) at Mile High Stadium, it's reasonable to suggest that the Rockies would benefit from the presence of right-handed batters prone to hitting fly balls. Gary Redus of the Pirates is one who springs to mind.

The Florida team, which is expected to be placed in the N.L. East, is more likely to opt for speed. Although the Marlins will play home games on grass, Dombrowski took note of the prevailing artificial turf in four East Division parks—Montreal, Philadelphia, Pittsburgh and St. Louis. "We have to be cognizant of that," he said, especially if the league adopts—as expected—an unbalanced schedule.

It goes without saying that both organizations, as well as the managers they choose, will have to exhibit patience on a major league scale. And that many of the so-called major leaguers that the Rockies and Marlins pick in November will not be with the team on opening day of 1993. Perhaps one will get lucky at the other's expense.

During spring training in 1969, the first-year Royals decided they were short a righthanded-hitting outfielder and placed a call to their fledgling counterparts, the Seattle Pilots, who were in need of a lefthanded-hitting outfielder. So the teams swapped players they had acquired from the expansion pool, with the Royals giving up Steve Whitaker (plus pitcher John Gelnar) for Lou Piniella.

Piniella went on to win the American League's Rookie of the Year award in '69 and played 15 additional seasons in the majors before becoming a successful batting coach and executive and manager of a World Series champion. Whitaker appeared in 69 games for the Pilots and 16 more for the Giants the following year before his big-league career ended. He was not the sole reason that the Pilots departed Seattle for Milwaukee after one season, but he didn't help the franchise sink any pilings into the Washington soil.

Perhaps the slickest move perpetrated by any expansion franchise was engineered by the 1969 Montreal Expos when they sent two players acquired in the allocation draft—first baseman Donn Clendenon and outfielder Jesus Alou—to Houston for young outfielder Rusty Staub. Clendenon declined to report to the Astros, but Montreal got to keep Staub by sending Houston two more expansion-draft picks (pitchers Jack Billingham and Skip Guinn) and cash. Staub, of course, became the Expos' most productive hitter and most popular player.

So the moral is, don't judge the new teams by their November rosters.

To be sure, there will be some big names on the lists made available to the Rockies and Marlins. But they are likely to be older players bearing lucrative, long-term contracts.

"We have to decide whether those players are in the best interest of our team," said Gebhard, a former pitcher who served as farm director of the Expos before joining the Twins in 1986. "We're not going for the quick fix. In three or four years, we want to have our young players coming through the system, ready to contribute."

In the meantime, the franchises representing Colorado and Florida should hope for the best but brace for the worst. "You realize you're going to take a beating for a while," Dombrowski said.

Even with guys like Coco Laboy. Surely you remember Coco.

A veteran of 10 minor league seasons, Laboy was chosen by the Expos off the St. Louis Cardinals' roster in the expansion draft that stocked the Montreal and San Diego teams for the '69 season. And this obscure infielder proceeded to sock 18 home runs for the Expos, including a decisive blast in their opening-day game.

Alas, even with Coco around, the Expos finished their first season with 110 losses.

Leonard Koppett

FROM THE NEW THINKING FAN'S GUIDE TO BASEBALL

"Spring Training"

In this piece, Leonard Koppett discusses baseball's annual rite of renewal, and why, in the author's words, "no civilization that has produced baseball spring training can be all bad."

PALO ALTO—This is a hymn of praise, a paean, a celebration, a jubilation for baseball spring training, a glory of the Western World not found in any other time and place but America of the last 80 years.

It has been written (by me, years ago, and I'm sure by many others) that Florida is a state of mind, not a geographical location. Arizona and Palm Springs are, of course, equivalent in this sense. The very special combination of attitude and surroundings, of work and play, of hope, enthusiasm and occasional discomfort that make up spring training just doesn't exist in any other context.

Let us ruminate on the three words: baseball, and spring, and training.

Of all the major team games, baseball is the most leisurely by nature. It is often attacked for this by people who, I am convinced, must be incredibly obtuse or selling some other product. The comparatively slow and relaxed pace of baseball is one of its greatest assets, not a drawback; it is what makes possible those elements that make baseball enjoyable. You don't have to like baseball, of course; many people don't. But if you do, it is the leisurely element that underlies your enjoyment—and no other game offers that particular complex of enjoyments.

But put that aside. If we have to talk about what makes baseball enjoyable at this stage of the game, our minds won't meet anyhow. Let's go on to "spring."

The depth of mankind's feeling about the spring season goes back to pre-history. Re-birth, the warming of the seasons, the revival of nature after a cold winter—such concepts are built into earth's creatures, including us. The imagery of a new beginning around the time of the vernal equinox permeates religion, art, psychology and even science.

What better time, then, to start a new season, a hopeful new year? Baseball is the only sport (among the large promotions) that has its competitive schedule coincide with the subliminal feelings of a new year.

Both geography and history have played a major role in forming this pattern. Baseball began, grew and developed in the northeastern quadrant of the continental United States, where winter weather is too severe to contemplate playing an outdoor game requiring fine control of a ball in flight.

People who live in Boston, New York, Philadelphia, Cleveland, Detroit, Pittsburgh, Cincinnati, Washington, Chicago and St. Louis know how deep the yearning can become, by mid-February, for sunshine and warmth and beaches and gentle breezes. And for more than 50 years, that's where all major league baseball teams were located.

So the annual ritual of baseball clubs going south in the spring struck deep resonances in the hearts of all the fans back home. It might be sheer envy, it might be the most fully experienced vicarious thrill, but it was a response, and a response that reached far into the subconscious. Spring is here, and another baseball season is starting.

This is something that Californians don't really understand, since they live in a much more even climate all year round, in the populated areas. Spring, in California, means less rain, but

Lou Gehrig in Spring Training with the Yankees. c. 1930. The National Baseball Library, Cooperstown, New York.

not a long-awaited respite from a long, dark, confining mini–ice age. I've felt this change myself. To go from Palo Alto to Arizona for a few weeks is certainly pleasant, but it is in no sense an escape, as it used to be to go from New York to Florida. The destination is nice—but the contrast is not as compelling.

Which brings us to "training," and that's probably the most striking difference of all with respect to other sports.

Anyone who has been through basic training in the Army has a good idea of what a football training camp is like, and if you went through a Marine boot camp, you have a better idea than others. Basketball and hockey camps may not be quite as confining, but they are, like football, at isolated locations under fairly strict supervision.

But baseball teams train at resorts. That's right, resorts. Think about that a minute.

Miami, Fort Lauderdale, St. Petersburg, Tampa, West Palm Beach, Orlando, Palm Springs and Phoenix, with its satellites of Scottsdale, Tempe and Mesa—these and the other spring training locations are communities that have made recreation a primary business. They are good at what they do. Their goal is to make visitors happy and comfortable, because that's how a resort makes its living.

And the baseball crowd gets all the benefits of such surroundings.

Each person, of course, makes use of it his own way. Club owners don't go to the same restaurants, or golf courses, that clubhouse attendants do—but on whatever level, from rookie through super star, there is something in a resort setting for everyone: entertainment, good food, recreational facilities and, above all, an atmosphere of people trying to have a good time according to their tastes.

The effect on everyone of such an atmosphere should not be underestimated. It is a pleasure that football, basketball and hockey players don't get during their training season.

Baseball practice also is far more pleasant—batting and throwing—than scrimmaging in those other games. The type of physical conditioning sought is less painful. A large proportion of practice time is devoted to actual games (30 or so exhibitions). And with relatively few exceptions, jobs are not really on the line during spring training.

Besides, baseball mystique calls for brandishing confidences. Everyone starts out expecting great things. (In football, by contrast, the prevailing approach to every game is carefully stimulated apprehension. A football coach always talks of how tough the other team will be; a baseball manager shamelessly overpraises his own team.)

So, we have optimism, untarnished by any result that will count in the standings; spring-time, with all its overtones; and resort setting, with all their opportunities and time to enjoy them. One word sums up the whole baseball spring training scene: Beautiful.

Frank Dolson

FROM BEATING THE BUSHES
"The Axeman Cometh"

In this chapter from his 1982 study of the minor leagues, Frank Dolson describes the slow tor-ture of Cutdown Day, where we see that it's far less painful to be a player on a losing team that it is to be a player without a team.

_____

Cutdown day is the cruelest day of all. Spring training is just about over. Bags are packed. Plans are made. In many cases wives and children have headed for the city in which they think—or at least hope—they'll be spending the summer. There's one problem, though. The big league roster contains 26 names. By opening day, under the rules, it cannot contain more than 25. Somebody's got to go.

There might be three fringe guys, or four fringe guys, or only two fringe guys who aren't sure where they stand. When that plane leaves late in the afternoon for the trip north, will they be on it? Will they be going to New York or Columbus, Ohio? To Baltimore or Rochester, N.Y.? To Chicago or Edmonton, Canada? To St. Louis or Louisville? To the big leagues or the minors?

In the next few hours one of those three or four fringe guys will get the terrible news. A coach will walk over to him in the clubhouse, or on the field, and say, "The Skip wants to see you," or something to that effect. Those words have the ring of death about them. There isn't a man in camp on that day who doesn't know what they mean.

There aren't many things worse in sports than finding out, on the last day of spring train-ing, that you're the 26th man on a 25-man team. Finishing fourth in the Olympic Trials is worse because only three go to the Olympic Games and an athlete has to wait four years for the next chance. But at least in the Olympic Trials it normally comes down to a person's perfor-mance on a given day; in that sense, the athlete controls his or her own fate. In baseball, the decision will be made behind closed doors in a meeting room. It doesn't always matter if you hit .300 in spring training or had an earned run average under 2.00. Anything is liable to hap-pen behind those closed doors. Maybe the manager doesn't like you. Or the general manager doesn't like you. Or the top scout doesn't think you can hack it in the big leagues. Maybe you have an option left, and the guy fighting you for that 25th spot doesn't and so, rather than risk losing him, the club decides to send you out. On cutdown day, the world is filled with maybes.

So you show up at the ball park, the way you've been showing up all spring, and you try to act unconcerned. You make small talk in the clubhouse. You put on your uniform. You do your work. And you sweat bullets. A coach approaches and you die a thousand deaths. Is he coming over to say hello, or is he coming over to say goodbye? Is he coming over to say, "You're playing the first three innings at third base today," or is he coming over to say, "The Skip wants to see you?"

Occasionally, of course, a man headed for the minors doesn't get the news in the customary manner. Mike Fremuth, a righthanded pitcher, nearly made the Phillies' pitching staff in the early '70s. Came the final day of spring training and 11 pitchers remained in the big league camp. One had to go. Fremuth turned out to be the one, but at least he got the word in a rather novel way. Before a coach had the opportunity to track him down and tell him the manager wanted to see him, a sportswriter walked up, extended a hand and said, "Good luck, Mike. I'm sorry to see you go." It was only when he asked Fremuth when he had found out about it and the pitcher replied, "Just now, from you," that the writer, Bus Saidt of *The Trenton Times*, realized that his well-intentioned words had let the cat out of the bag. Happily, Fremuth had that rare ability to laugh at the bizarre happenings that he recognized as being part of life in a baseball uniform. If anything, the news was probably less painful coming from a friendly writer than it would have been coming from a considerably less friendly manager. Anyhow, Fremuth survived the jolt quite well, thank you. After getting released later that season, he went to Stanford Law School. He is now an attorney in Washington, D.C.

For most, though, getting sent down at the very end of spring training is an exceptionally difficult experience, one that can produce a lingering feeling of anger and frustration.

Take the case of Don McCormack. A highly-regarded catcher, he came up through the Phillies' organization. Called up by the big club in September of '80, he was behind the plate in the final innings of the dramatic, division-title-clinching game in Montreal on the next-to-last day of the regular season. He had worked hard for that opportunity, spending seven years in the minor leagues, and he handled himself well that day at Olympic Stadium. McCormack felt like a million dollars when he went home at the end of the '80 season. He couldn't wait for spring training to start. Finally, he was on the verge of earning a big league job. . . .

But as so often happens, there were a number of problems. And McCormack had an option left, which meant the Phillies could send him out without risk of losing him. As spring training wound down, the uncertainties mounted. Sure, McCormack had done well. Sure, he had earned a place on the team as a backup catcher. But still, that was no guarantee.

"The last three days were really tough," he said. "There were 26 people and that even made it tougher. I heard both sides. I heard people saying, 'Yeah, you're going to make it,' and I heard others saying, 'Ah, they don't want to carry three catchers.'"

The Phillies had Bob Boone and Keith Moreland. They could get along without McCormack. The waiting grew progressively harder.

A camera crew from a cable TV outfit had been following Don McCormack since early in spring training, preparing a piece on a rookie's struggle to make it to the big leagues. It had been fun for a while, but by the final day of spring training—with the camp count still at 26—nothing was fun any more.

"That last day—phwew!" Don McCormack said. "My wife drove me to the park and the film crew was waiting for me outside. They were going to interview me after the decision was made."

McCormack said hello and walked inside the clubhouse. "Everybody was sitting there," he said. "I took my time getting dressed. No use me getting dressed if they're going to cut me. Here I am in a cold sweat and these guys with a camera are standing right there in front of my locker, and that didn't help, either. And then Dallas [Dallas Green, who was managing the Phillies then] comes out, points a finger at me, and I knew it was all over. I just kind of—my whole mental outlook completely dropped. Boy, there were so many things went through my mind in those 10, 15 steps into his little room back there. In fact, my whole life just flashed right in front of me."

Devastated by the news, Don McCormack walked out of Green's office and found the camera crew waiting for him. Under the circumstances, he might have told them to get lost, to come back another time, anything to save himself from having to answer questions at a time like this. But he didn't, which tells you a lot about Don McCormack. "That was really tough," he said about that TV interview. "We went out there in the bullpen. I didn't know what to do, what to say. All I knew was, I had to go out and talk to them."

The following spring, McCormack went through it again. No TV crew this time, but what happened was even worse. Since he was now out of options, the Phillies gave him his uncon-

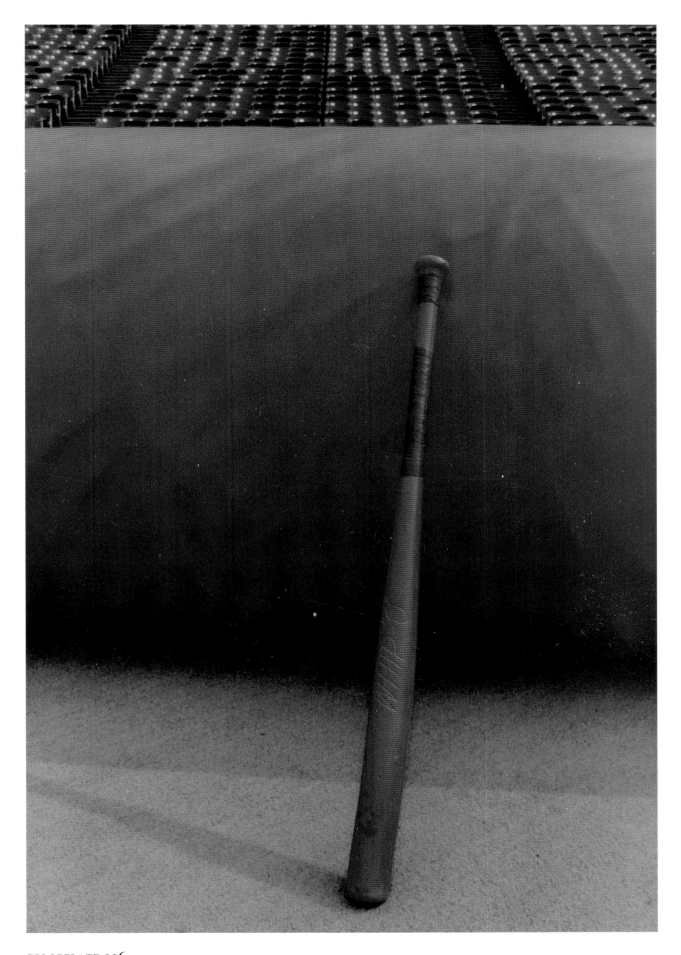

COLORPLATE 116

JOHN WEISS. *"Whip-O" Fungo Bat.* 1984.
Photograph.

COLORPLATE 117
JOHN WEISS. *Phillies Trainer Jeff Cooper with Jeff Stone*. 1984.
Photograph.

COLORPLATE 118 *(opposite)*

JOHN WEISS. *Paul Molitor (center)*. 1988.
Photograph.

COLORPLATE 119

JOHN WEISS. *Tommy Kelly, son of Twins Manager, Tom Kelly.* 1985.
Photograph.

COLORPLATE 120

JOHN WEISS. *The Phillie Phanatic Kisses Orel Hershiser.* 1986.
Photograph.

COLORPLATE 121

JEFF GOLDBERG. *Oriole Park at Camden Yards.* 1992. Esto Photographics.
*Oriole Park at Camden Yards opened April 8, 1992. The B & O Warehouse building
looms over right field, where a bar owned by Babe Ruth's father once stood.*

COLORPLATE 122

JIM DOW. *Rear of Grandstand, Dudley Field, El Paso, Texas.* El Paso Diablos, Texas League, AA. (Stadium now demolished.) 1989. Colorprint from 8 x 10 in. negative. Gallery 53 Artworks, Cooperstown, New York.

COLORPLATE 123

JOHN WEISS. *Dennis "Oil Can" Boyd Interview*. 1986.
Photograph.

ditional release. Eight years in the organization and suddenly he was gone. But baseball gets in a man's blood. As hard a blow as it was, as seriously as he thought about getting out of the game and embarking on a new career, McCormack eventually chose to return to the minor leagues with another organization.

If you want to talk to an expert on late-spring axings, try Yankee pitcher George Frazier. Starting in '78, it happened to him three times in four years when he belonged to the St. Louis Cardinals.

"The craziest thing," said George, "you're getting sent out the last day and your wife's headed for the town you think you're playing in because they haven't told you anything. The truck's gone with all your belongings on it. The only thing you've got is a suitcase with two pairs of jeans in it."

Frazier's worst experience came in the spring of '81. The day before the Cardinals were scheduled to leave St. Petersburg, Fla., and head north George told manager Whitey Herzog that he wanted to take his car over to the garage to have some work done on it before his wife drove home. "He said, 'Okay, go ahead. You can miss batting practice,'" Frazier said. "So I rushed out. I got the car fixed. After the game Whitey asked me, 'You get the car fixed? Everything set for your wife?' I said, 'Yeah, fine.' Next morning I get dropped off at the ball park at 7:30 in the morning and as soon as I walked in the door Whitey calls me in and tells me I've been sent down."

Frazier was stunned. He had just flown his mother in so she could be with his wife and kids on the long drive back to St. Louis. And to compound matters, they were already on their way. "I mean," said George, "they're five minutes up the highway. I could call the police and get them to find them for me and stop them. But what sense is there for me to flag them down? There's no room for me to ride in the car, anyway. That kind of stuff can drive you up a wall."

A lot of baseball players have made a trip up that wall. "I've seen so many guys," said Frazier. "They've rented houses because they've been told, 'You're on the ball club,' and then, boom, they're gone. . . .

You don't have to tell Joe Kerrigan about it. He knows. He's been through it, too.

A righthanded relief pitcher, Kerrigan has appeared in 131 big league games. Five years ago, he saved 11 and won three for a Montreal team that finished in fifth place in the National League East. But that winter he was traded to the Baltimore Orioles—"the worst thing that probably happened to me in my life," he said.

At the time, though, it looked like a great thing. He was going from an also-ran to a contender. Then Joe Kerrigan found out that in baseball the way things look isn't necessarily the way things are.

He made it through the '78 season in Baltimore, winning three and saving three in 26 appearances. He had no reason to think his place on the team was in jeopardy in the spring of '79. "I was doing promos for the team—for bat day and ball night, that kind of thing," he said.

They don't ask guys who aren't going to be on the team to make TV and radio commercials. Besides, Joe had a good spring on the mound, pitching 12 scoreless innings.

"It came out of the clear blue sky," Kerrigan said. "The last day, as we were getting ready to go on the plane, I get called into his [manager Earl Weaver's] office. Tippy Martinez says to me, 'You lucky dog. You've been traded.' I said, 'All right, maybe I'll go to a place where I can pitch more.'

"I'll never forget walking into the room, sitting down on that chair. I had my suit on, ready to get on that plane. He [Weaver] said, 'I got some bad news, Joe. We've got to send you down because [Tim] Stoddard and [Sammy] Stewart, we found out, are out of options.' I mean, that was something. Phwew! That was the hardest moment of my life.". . .

The first time around, the minor leagues don't look that bad. It's the second time around—after a man's been in the big leagues—that the negative side of the minor leagues experience stands out in bold, bitter relief.

"You go down a second time," said Kerrigan, "and all of a sudden the lights are darker than they used to be and the fields aren't as good. The first time you didn't know the difference. You didn't know if the lights were good or bad. You didn't mind the bus trips. But going down the ladder, it's not quite as sweet."

And when the financial pinch hits home, it can get downright sour.

A pro baseball career for a man who goes through what a Joe Kerrigan or a Don McCormack goes through is a constant struggle. Common sense says, "Get out." But there's something inside you that won't let you break away, even if the price you're paying in dollars and cents and heartache is absurdly high.

"It's like a total war between your heart and your mind," Joe Kerrigan said on the spring day in 1982 when the Phillies sent him to their Oklahoma City farm club.

More often than not, it seems, the heart wins. Surely, it did in Kerrigan's case. A few years ago, when he thought his big league status was secure, Joe and his wife bought a house in Bucks County, Pa. "You think you're going to stay in the big leagues for a while," he said. "Then the bottom drops out."

It's a long, hard fall.

"We're down to our last $500 in the bank," Joe Kerrigan said last spring. "We've got a $700-a-month mortgage, and we've got the house up for sale. You've got to have a good family to stick in this game. There were times my wife said to me, 'Why don't you get out? You're crazy for staying in this business.' That's the realistic side of it. But you're always chasing that dream."

That dream again. Always, it's that dream of making it some day, making it big. A few of them do. Most of them don't.

The Kerrigans had to sell some of their furniture just to keep their house going. Joe's wife had to get a job. Joe's mother had to baby-sit for them. Joe had to get a second job. "If you want to stay in the game, that's the price you've got to pay," he said. "Eddie Farmer will tell you that." . . .

Farmer, like so many others, has felt the sharp edge of the ax on cutdown day. And he knows the feeling of being out of the game, if only temporarily. He worked in a warehouse the year he was hurt, and he has never forgotten it.

"I never lost sight of picking up a box of nuts and bolts and putting it on a shelf for $3.25 an hour," he said. "I never have and I never will . . . I'll tell you what, this [pitching] beats the shit out of working in a warehouse."

Most of the time, it does. But sometimes—say, when you're the 26th man on a 25-man team on the last day of spring training and a coach walks over and says, "Uh, the Skip wants to see you"—it doesn't really beat it by all that much.

The A. G. Spalding Trophy.
The National Baseball Library,
Cooperstown, New York.

Denton True "Cy" Young. c. 1955. The National Baseball Library, Cooperstown, New York. *Baseball's annual award for the best pitcher in each league bears his name. Born in 1867 in Gilmore, Ohio, Young won a record 507 games in his major league career. He died in 1955 at the age of 88.*

Dan Rea

FROM NEWSWEEK

"Sociology 101 in a Shoe Box"

Somewhere in America, there's a landfill containing hundreds of billions of old baseball cards thrown out years ago by all of our mothers. Today, with the ever-increasing value of these cards, it might be cheaper to throw out Dad's stock portfolio than the kid's card collection. In this essay, Dan Rea discusses a baseball card's real value. Rea has worked as a television reporter in Boston since 1976, and he has been a baseball fan since 1954.

Hardly a month passes these days without some newspaper article or television report on the "bull market" in old baseball cards. There are some who suggest that no single investment from the 1950s has resulted in a better financial return than a baseball-card collection. Those Topps and Bowmans are now more valuable than some stocks and bonds. Such stories prompt every young collector from the 1950s to review his player portfolio in high hopes of finding a Mantle in mint condition. Yet the quick cash to be made in today's boom market does not necessarily measure the real worth of that cache of old baseball cards.

Way back in the days of Sputnik and Dwight Eisenhower, baseball cards taught me how to read. They were infinitely more interesting than any silly stories about Dick, Jane and Spot. Better yet, flip those cards over and those columns of statistics of at-bats, hits and runs batted in gave arithmetic purpose. What better way to teach an 8-year-old to multiply and divide than to introduce him or her to the magical calculation of an earned-run average?

For just five pennies, throw in a tour of America—pre–New Frontier. No geography book ever held my interest longer than those old cards; they introduced me to the far regions of all

48 states, the hometowns of my heroes. Decades later, my work as a television reporter has taken me to more than 30 states to cover news stores. When the Vatican appointed a new archbishop of Boston, I found myself in Springfield, Mo., the bishop's previous diocese. There, with complete confidence, I was able to surprise my cameraman with an extemporaneous explanation of the Sherm Lollar (a great White Sox catcher from the '50s) Bowling Alley.

This fall, the end of a long day following the Bush campaign found me on the road from South Bend, Ind., to Kalamazoo, Mich. In the middle of that stretch of road, at 65 miles an hour, a small oasis: a sign pointed to Paw Paw, Mich. My crew soon learned the name of the town's most famous resident, Charlie (Paw Paw) Maxwell, a left-handed, power-hitting Detroit Tiger of summers long past.

No collector of baseball cards in the 1950s could long ignore that players with strong ethnic names like Kluszewski, Malzone and Skowron probably came from a Northern city, while any player with initials for a first name was almost assuredly from below the Mason-Dixon line. Sociology 101 with a stick of bubble gum tossed in.

From the lengthening perspective of a quarter century, there are even more valuable lessons to be gleaned from those old cards. For virtually all the players, the game between the lines is now over. But as the box scores of life came in, not all those fortunate young men were treated alike. Fate cruelly deserted the young Chicago Cubs infielder, Ken Hubbs, who died in an off-season plane crash. His death introduced mortality to any serious young baseball-card collector at a time of genuine innocence—long before Vietnam. Later, much later, few deaths of world figures rivaled the loss of Roberto Clemente as far as I was concerned. A New Year's Eve airplane disaster in the early '70s deprived the world of the Pittsburgh Pirates Hall of Famer. Clemente surrendered his life and his career at the height of his talent, helping to transport much-needed supplies to earthquake victims in Managua, Nicaragua.

As the years passed, so did the immortals. Roger Maris, for me the Babe Ruth of my generation, stroked more home runs in one single season than any other player in history. Yet Maris was never able to remotely rival his epic season of 1961. He won world championships in both leagues, retired early and passed away much too soon. Every year now the sports pages carry the obituaries of great players like Elston Howard, Ken Boyer, Jerry Adair, Dick Farrell and Norm Cash—young men of the '50s and '60s who will never lose their youth. Meanwhile, others lost their innocence. More than a few of my heroes ended up on the wrong side of the law. Perhaps best known is Denny McLain, the Cy Young Award winner of 1968 who last year pleaded guilty to racketeering and cocaine possession, thus proving that the blessings of youth do not necessarily last a lifetime.

For the athlete, life is often a cruel irony. The greatest triumphs come too easily and too early, leaving him in later life with a frustrating inability to repeat past achievements. Still, some of my baseball-card heroes took their lives far beyond the days of summer. Congressman Jim Bunning of Kentucky threw no-hitters in both the American and National leagues, and former congressman Wilmer (Vinegar Bend) Mizell of North Carolina wears a Pittsburgh Pirates ring from their world championship of 1960. Former Washington Senators outfielder Chuck Hinton now practices his craft as a baseball coach at Howard University. And a few like Vern Law, Marty Keough, Dick Ellsworth and Gus Bell have the unimaginable thrill of watching their own sons 30 years later follow their footsteps down big-league base paths.

I have held onto my baseball-card collection for a quarter of a century, even though that collection was complete by my early teens. Those cards accompanied me through my boyhood while taking me to a world far beyond my imagination. Baseball games on the back-porch radio at night assumed an additional dimension with a stack of baseball cards nearby for easy reference. A leisurely perusal of those old cards would lead me through the lives of players, time and again showing me that nothing—in life or in baseball—is accomplished without hard work and, sometimes, great disappointment.

Those lessons from so long ago now sitting in a shoe box are still relevant today. And those lessons convince me that any catalog price these old baseball cards might attract will never fully measure their genuine value.

Seller beware: childhood memories and lifelong lessons have no price tag.

Ninth Inning:

YOU CAN LOOK IT UP

Some interesting facts about the game are followed by baseball's greatest players and the feats that made them legendary. The plaques pictured in this chapter hang in the National Baseball Hall of Fame in Cooperstown, New York, and honor the hall's 215 inductees.

Nicknames of the Major League Clubs

Readers are cautioned to look on any such list with a wary eye, as much of the history of the game of the late nineteenth and early twentieth centuries has been lost to antiquity. That having been noted, this is a list of the nicknames used by all the clubs from the various major leagues.

———————————

UNION ASSOCIATION (1884)

Altoona Mountain Citys
Baltimore Monumentals
Boston Reds
Chicago Browns
Cincinnati Outlaw Reds
Kansas City Unions
Milwaukee Cream Citys
Philadelphia Keystones
Pittsburgh Stogies
St. Louis Maroons
St. Paul Saints
Washington Nationals
Wilmington Quicksteps

FEDERAL LEAGUE (1914–15)

Baltimore Terrapins
Brooklyn Tip-Tops
Buffalo Buffeds (1914)
Buffalo Blues (1915)
Chicago Chi-Feds (1914)
Chicago Whales (1915)
Indianapolis Hoosiers
Kansas City Packers
Newark Peppers
Pittsburgh Rebels
St. Louis Terriers

PLAYERS' LEAGUE (1890)

Boston Reds
Brooklyn Wonders
Buffalo Bisons
Chicago Pirates
Cleveland Infants
New York Giants
Philadelphia Quakers
Pittsburgh Burghers

AMERICAN ASSOCIATION (1882–91)

Baltimore Orioles (1882–91)
Boston Reds (1891)
Brooklyn Trolley-Dodgers (1884–88)
Brooklyn Bridegrooms (1889)
Brooklyn Gladiators (1890)
Cincinnati Red Stockings (1882–89)
Cincinnati Kellys (1891)
Cleveland Blues (1887–88)
Columbus Buckeyes (1883–84)
Columbus Buckeyes (1889–91)
Indianapolis Hoosiers (1884)
Kansas City Cowboys (1888–89)
Louisville Eclipse (1882–84)
Louisville Colonels (1885–91)
Milwaukee Brewers (1891)
New York Metropolitans (1883–87)
Philadelphia Athletics (1882–91)
Pittsburgh Alleghenys (1882–86)
Richmond Virginians (1884)
Rochester Hop-Bitters (1890)
St. Louis Brown Stockings (1882)
St. Louis Browns (1883–91)
Syracuse Stars (1890)
Toledo Blue Stockings (1884)
Toledo Maumees (1890)
Washington Nationals (1884)
Washington Statesmen (1891)

NATIONAL ASSOCIATION (1871–75)

Baltimore Lord Baltimores (1872–74)
Baltimore Marylands (1873)
Boston Red Stockings (1871–75)
Brooklyn Atlantics (1872–75)
Brooklyn Eckfords (1872)
Chicago White Stockings (1871, 1874–75)
Cleveland Forest Citys (1871–72)
Elizabeth Resolutes (1873)
Ft. Wayne Kekiongas (1871)
Hartford Dark Blues (1874–75)
Keokuk Westerns (1875)
Middletown Mansfields (1872)
New Haven Elm Citys (1875)

New York Mutuals (1871–75)
Philadelphia Athletics (1871–75)
Philadelphia Centennials (1875)
Philadelphia Whites (1873–75)
Rockford Forest Citys (1871)
St. Louis Brown Stockings (1875)
St. Louis Red Stockings (1875)
Troy Haymakers (1871–72)
Washington Olympics (1871–72)
Washington Nationals (1872)
Washington Nationals (1875)

AMERICAN LEAGUE (1901–)

Baltimore Orioles (1901–02)
Baltimore Orioles (1954—)
Boston Somersets (1901–02)
Boston Pilgrims (1903–06)
Boston Red Sox (1907—)
California Angels (1965—)
Chicago White Stockings (1901–03)
Chicago White Sox (1904—)
Cleveland Blues (1901–04)
Cleveland Naps (1905–14)
Cleveland Indians (1915—)
Detroit Tigers (1901—)
Kansas City Athletics (1955–67)
Kansas City Royals (1969—)
Los Angeles Angels (1961–64)
Milwaukee Brewers (1901)
Milwaukee Brewers (1970—)
Minnesota Twins (1961—)
New York Highlanders (1903–12)
New York Yankees (1913—)
Oakland Athletics (1968—)
Philadelphia Athletics (1901–54)
St. Louis Browns (1902–53)
Seattle Pilots (1969)
Seattle Mariners (1977—)
Texas Rangers (1972—)
Toronto Blue Jays (1977—)
Washington Nationals (1901–56)
Washington Senators (1957–71)

NATIONAL LEAGUE (1876–)

Atlanta Braves (1966—)
Baltimore Orioles (1892–99)
Boston Red Caps (1876–82)
Boston Beaneaters (1883–1906)
Boston Doves (1907–10)
Boston Rustlers (1911)
Boston Braves (1912–35, 1941–52)
Boston Bees (1936–40)
Brooklyn Bridegrooms (1890–98)
Brooklyn Superbas (1899–1910)

Brooklyn Dodgers (1911–13, 1932–57)
Brooklyn Robins (1914–31)
Buffalo Bisons (1879–85)
Chicago White Stockings (1876–89)
Chicago Colts (1890–97)
Chicago Orphans (1898–1901)
Chicago Cubs (1902—)
Cincinnati Red Stockings (1876–77)
Cincinnati Reds (1878–80)
Cincinnati Reds (1890–1952, 1959—)
Cincinnati Redlegs (1953–58)
Cleveland Blues (1879–84)
Cleveland Spiders (1889–99)
Colorado Rockies (1993—)
Detroit Wolverines (1881–88)
Florida Marlins (1993—)
Hartford Dark Blues (1876–77)
Houston Colt .45's (1962–64)
Houston Astros (1965—)
Indianapolis Hoosiers (1878)
Indianapolis Hoosiers (1887–89)
Kansas City Cowboys (1886)
Los Angeles Dodgers (1958—)
Louisville Grays (1876–77)
Louisville Colonels (1892–99)
Milwaukee Cream Citys (1878)

Milwaukee Braves (1953–65)
Montreal Expos (1969—)
New York Mutuals (1876)
New York Gothams (1883–84)
New York Giants (1885–1957)
New York Mets (1962—)
Philadelphia Athletics (1876)
Philadelphia Quakers (1883–89)
Philadelphia Phillies (1890–1943, 1946—)
Philadelphia Blue Jays (1944–45)
Pittsburgh Alleghenys (1887–90)
Pittsburgh Pirates (1891—)
Providence Grays (1878–85)
St. Louis Brown Stockings (1876–77)
St. Louis Maroons (1885–86)
St. Louis Browns (1892–98)
St. Louis Perfectos (1899)
St. Louis Cardinals (1900—)
San Diego Padres (1969—)
San Francisco Giants (1958—)
Syracuse Stars (1879)
Troy Trojans (1879–82)
Washington Statesmen (1886–89)
Washington Senators (1892–99)
Worcester Ruby Legs (1880–82)

J. N. Hook

FROM ALL THOSE WONDERFUL NAMES

"How the 26 Major League Baseball Teams Got Their Names"

Once again, the reader is warned that there are varying accounts as to how some teams received their monikers. Also, this list was originally published before the birth of the Colorado Rockies and the Florida Marlins, both of whom were named after one time minor league teams from those two states.

---

1. ATLANTA BRAVES: The Braves inherited their name from Boston and Milwaukee. The Boston National League baseball team had been called, officially or unofficially, Red Caps, Beanies, Beaneaters, Doves, Rustlers, Pilgrims. Baseball club president Jim Gaffney, member of a political organization called Tammany, recommended Braves, honoring the Tammany "Wigwam." The name was accepted in 1912, and retained except for 1936 to 1941, when Bees was substituted. The name Braves followed the team to Milwaukee in 1953, and to Atlanta in 1966.

2. BALTIMORE ORIOLES: The name was adopted in the 1890s. The oriole (formerly called the Baltimore oriole but now the Northern oriole) is Maryland's state bird. Nicknames: Birds, O's.

3. BOSTON RED SOX: Originally they were called Somersets (1901) for the owner, Charles W. Somers. Nicknames at the time included Speed Boys, Puritans, Plymouth Rocks. After the National League Braves, the other Boston team of the time, changed from red stockings to white, the American League team adopted red stockings and took the name Red Sox. Nicknames: Bosox, Sox.

4. CALIFORNIA ANGELS: In 1961 they were the Los Angeles Angels, the name of the city's earlier Pacific Coast League club. On moving to Anaheim in 1965, they became the California Angels.

5. CHICAGO CUBS: The team was originally called the White Stockings. From 1880 through 1886, the Chicago National League club won five pennants, but on the departure of their beloved manager, "Pop" or "Cap" (really Adrian) Anson, the team was called Orphans. Later, at a time when they had numerous rookies, they were nicknamed Babes, Colts, and Cubs. The last name stuck. Unofficially: Bruins.

6. CHICAGO WHITE SOX: In 1901, this team tried to take over the old name of the Cubs, which was White Stockings. On objections from the National League, they changed to White Sox. For short: Sox or Chisox.

7. CINCINNATI REDS: In 1866 they were Red Stockings, quickly shortened to Reds. In 1953, because of Joseph McCarthy's Communist-scare tactics, club officers changed to Redlegs, but fans thought the decision silly, so the team soon became Reds again.

8. CLEVELAND INDIANS: The Cleveland team's pre-big-league name was Spiders because so many players were thin and gangling. When they entered the American League, they became the Blues or Bluebirds because of the color of their uniforms. In 1902 the players voted for Broncos, but fans liked Naps better, to honor their favorite player, second baseman Napoleon ("Nap") Lajoie. After he left to play for Philadelphia in 1914, the fans chose Indians.

9. DETROIT TIGERS: The Detroit team was originally called Wolverines because Michigan is the Wolverine State, but their black and yellow stockings suggested the name Tigers. They were nicknamed Tygers during Ty Cobb's great career with them (1904–26). Nickname: Bengals.

10. HOUSTON ASTROS: In 1962 they were the Colt .45's or Colts, but the gun company objected, especially when they couldn't hit. In 1964 they became the Astronauts, which wouldn't fit headlines. Hence they are the Astros, who play in the Astrodome.

11. KANSAS CITY ROYALS: Vociferous protests and threatened legal action followed the 1968 move of the Kansas City A's to Oakland, but peace returned when baseball authorities permitted a new team to be formed two years later. The club asked for name suggestions and received over 17,000. The name should be "of significance to the area, and one that would be suitable for emblematic purposes, as well as appropriate in length for newspapers, radio and TV." The winner, a Kansan named Sanford Porte, referred to Kansas City's "nationally known American Royal parade and pageant" and added, "The team colors of royal blue and white would be in harmony with the State Bird, the Bluebird, the State Flag, the old Kansas City Blues baseball team, and our current hockey team."

12. LOS ANGELES DODGERS: The name dates back to Brooklyn. Originally they were the Brooklyn Bridegrooms because that's what several of the first players were. New York Giants fans ridiculed them as "trolley dodgers" (a street kids' game of playing "chicken" with trolleys), and Dodgers stuck. Sportswriters also liked Robins (for a one-time manager), Kings, and Superbas, and fans lived and died with their beloved but often erratic Bums. The name Dodgers accompanied the team to the West Coast.

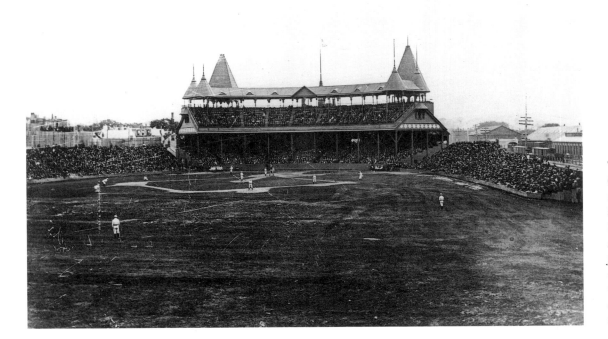

The Walpole Street
Grounds, Boston. c. 1880
(pre-1894). Albumin print.
8 x 10 in. The Bostonian
Society. *Also known as the
South End grounds, this
facility was the original
home of the Braves, and
was Boston's only double-
decked stadium. It housed
teams from 1871 to 1915.*

13. MILWAUKEE BREWERS: From 1878 to 1953 Milwaukee had Brewers alternately as a major and a minor league club, named for the city's most famous industry. In 1953 Milwaukee secured the Braves and kept that name. After the Braves moved to Atlanta, Milwaukee took over the Seattle Pilots and changed back to the name Brewers.

14. MINNESOTA TWINS: In 1960 a team secured from Washington, DC, was renamed the Twin City Twins, for Minneapolis and St. Paul. (In Washington the team had first been called the Statesmen, but was demoted to Senators. After that came the Nationals [the team from the capital city was supposedly the national team], the Nats, and then the Senators again.) The Twin City Twins' name was soon changed to Minnesota Twins to suggest that the team represented the whole state.

15. MONTREAL EXPOS: In 1968, a year after the Montreal world's fair called Expo 67, the team was named Expos.

16. NEW YORK METS: The team is officially called the Metropolitans. In 1883 an American Association team had that name. The new version arrived in 1962, when New York had been without National League baseball for four years. Fans revived Metropolitans, which headline writers and conversationalists had to shorten.

17. NEW YORK YANKEES: The New York team was originally called the Highlanders or the Hilltoppers because of the highlands of the Hudson. New York sportswriters preferred the shorter Yankees. Nicknames include Yanks and, starting with the years of Ruth and Gehrig, Bronx Bombers. Once-numerous Yankee haters were known to call them Damyankees.

18. OAKLAND A'S: The Philadelphia Athletics, often called A's for short, have existed as amateurs or professionals since 1860. They were sometimes nicknamed the White Elephants, but not often while Cornelius McGillicuddy (better known as Connie Mack) was their manager (1901–1950). The name Athletics or A's followed the team to Kansas City, then to Oakland in 1968.

19. PHILADELPHIA PHILLIES: The name has been used most of the time since 1883, although Bob Carpenter, an owner from 1943 to 1950, unsuccessfully tried to foist the name Blue Jays on fans who preferred the short name of their favorite city. Nicknames: Phils, Quakers.

20. PITTSBURGH PIRATES: Originally they were the Alleghenies (for the river and the mountains), then Innocents (for unknown reasons). Since 1891 they have been the Pirates, so called

because of their intensive efforts to lure star players from other clubs (now considered a legitimate part of the business).

21. ST. LOUIS CARDINALS: The earliest St. Louis team was called the Browns, but the Browns of 1899 changed their colors to red, causing a female fan to refer to "that lovely shade of cardinal." So Cardinals they became, although another team in the American League took over the old name and existed (barely) as the St. Louis Browns into the 1940s, when they lost in their only World Series appearance—to the Cardinals. Nicknames: Redbirds, Cards.

22. SAN DIEGO PADRES: An earlier Pacific Coast team had been the Padres, a popular name in an area with many priests and many speakers of Spanish, so the big-league team took it over during a time of expansion.

23. SAN FRANCISCO GIANTS: The team was originally the New York Giants, which had at first been called the Gothams. The name is sometimes attributed to President Benjamin Harrison, who thought the players looked like giants. It remained with the team when in 1958 it moved from the East to the West Coast.

24. SEATTLE MARINERS: They were preceded in Seattle by the Pilots, who moved to Milwaukee. In a contest open to fans, Mariners was one of the names suggested and was chosen by the six owners. The older players are of course Ancient Mariners. Nickname: M's.

25. TEXAS RANGERS: Formerly the Washington Senators of 1961 to 1971. They moved to Arlington, TX (from Dallas), in 1972, and were named for the famous Texas lawmen.

26. TORONTO BLUE JAYS: In a contest to name the expansion team, 154 persons (out of 30,000) suggested Blue Jays, pointing out that Ontario has many of those birds and—this may have been decisive—that a beer called Blue was made by one of the owners, the LaBatt Breweries.

David Nemec

FROM GREAT BASEBALL FACTS AND FEATS
"The 20 Most Lopsided Trades Since 1901"

Perhaps we can add to this list the trade that sent Steve Carlton (who went on to win four Cy Young Awards) from the St. Louis Cardinals to the Philadelphia Phillies in exchange for Rick Wise. Or the 1983 trade that brought first baseman Keith Hernandez to the New York Mets in exchange for relief pitcher Neil Allen. There are many more examples to cite, but those listed here are indisputably some of the most ill-advised trades of all time.

At the conclusion of the 1965 season the Reds felt they needed more quality pitchers to become a contender and sent Frank Robinson to Baltimore for starting pitcher Milt Pappas, reliever Jack Baldschun and a promising young outfielder named Dick Simpson. Simpson never panned out, Baldschun proved to be almost through, and the trade began to seem just about the worst one ever made when Robinson won the American League Triple Crown in 1966 and led Baltimore to its first World Championship while the Reds faded from fourth place to seventh. No question the swap worked out badly for the Reds, but it was far from being the all-time worst deal. While Robinson went on to hit 586 career home runs and make the Hall of Fame, Pappas didn't do all that shabbily either. He won 99 games in the National League before retiring and 207 altogether, not exactly the figures of a washout. Here are 20 swaps that, I think, make the Robinson–Pappas transaction look rather good. Excluded are all deals in which a sizable chunk of cash—more than $25,000—sweetened the package and made it too tempting for impoverished club owners to resist. Also excluded is the infamous trade in which the Giants got Christy Mathewson from the Reds for a washed-up Amos Rusie. Not only did it occur near the end of 1900, but the prime mover in the deal, John Brush, knew that he'd soon be leaving the Reds to join the Giants and hence was acting clandestinely in his own best interest.

1905: The Red Sox send rookie George Stone to the Browns for aging Jesse Burkett. Stone leads the American League in total bases in 1905; Burkett hits .257. The following year Stone wins the AL batting title, Burkett is playing out the string in the minors, and the Red Sox plummet to the cellar two years after winning the pennant.

1907: Cleveland deals rebellious holdout pitcher Earl Moore to the Yankees for Walter Clarkson, brother of 328-game winner John Clarkson. Moore doesn't get along in New York either and drops to the minors but resurfaces with the Phillies late in the 1908 season and becomes the ace of their staff. Walter Clarkson wins four games for Cleveland and is cut in 1908 as the Indians, short of pitching, lose the pennant by half a game.

1910: The Cardinals swindle the Reds out of Miller Huggins, Rebel Oakes and Frank Corridon for the price of Fred Beebe and Al Storke. Storke dies before spring training begins, and Beebe plays only one year for the Reds.

1919: Cleveland gets Larry Gardner, Charlie Jamieson and Elmer Myers from the A's for Braggo Roth. Gardner and Jamieson become vital cogs in the Indians' 1920 World Championship team; the A's ship Roth to the Red Sox in midseason. For the Indians, the deal makes up, partially, for the 1915 transaction with the White Sox in which they got Roth for Shoeless Joe Jackson.

1934: Convinced that Wes Ferrell's lame arm won't recover, the Indians send him to the Red Sox along with Twitchy Dick Porter in return for Bob Weiland and Bob Seeds. Ferrell wins 59 games for the Red Sox over the next three seasons. Weiland wins one game for Cleveland, and Seeds is cut after being unable to crack the Indians lineup.

1938: The Phillies send Dolf Camilli to Brooklyn for Eddie Morgan. Morgan never plays a single game for the Phils; Camilli has four 100-plus RBI seasons for the Dodgers and in 1941 leads the NL in both homers and RBIs. (In the Phillies' defense, some sources claim that owner Gerry Nugent got a fair-sized wad of cash too.)

1947: The Phils get Al Lakeman from the Reds for Ken Raffensberger and Hugh Poland. Lakeman hits .159 as the Phils' backup catcher; for the next six years Raffensberger is one of the NL's top pitchers. With Raffensberger, the Phils conceivably could have won two more pennants in that period; without him they are lucky to win one.

1950: The A's send Nellie Fox to the White Sox for catcher Joe Tipton. Tipton never becomes more than a sub; Fox should one day become a Hall of Famer.

1954: The Orioles give up on Roy Sievers and send him to Washington for Gil Coan. Coan turns out to be about finished; in 1957 Sievers becomes the Senators' first home run king.

1959: The Pirates package Frank Thomas, Jim Pendleton, Whammy Douglas and Johnny Powers and ship them to the Reds for Harvey Haddix, Smokey Burgess and Don Hoak. Thomas is a bust in 1959 for the Reds; the others are even bigger disappointments. In 1960 Haddix, Burgess and Hoak lead the Pirates to their first flag since 1927.

1960: The Indians get Norm Cash in a deal with the White Sox and swiftly present him to the Tigers in return for Steve Demeter, whom they expect will fill their third base hole. Which Demeter does—for all of three games. Cash leads the AL in batting in 1961 and goes on to a long and productive career.

1969: The Seattle Pilots snare Lou Piniella from Cleveland in the expansion draft, grow disenchanted with him in spring training and swap him to their sister expansion club, the Kansas City Royals, for John Gelnar and Steve Whitaker. Piniella wins the Rookie of the Year award in 1969; Seattle wins a move to Milwaukee.

1969: Not content with aging third baseman Ed Charles, the Mets deal Amos Otis and Bob Johnson to the Royals for Joe Foy. Foy hits .236 in 1970 and is out of the majors the following year; Otis plays until 1985 and posts higher career totals in every major batting department than any of the Mets' career leaders.

1971: The greatest year ever for trades if you're not a fan of the Mets, Giants or Astros. The Giants start off the season by passing future home-run king George Foster along to the Reds for Frank Duffy and Vern Geishert.

1971: Still in quest of a third baseman, the Mets grab Jim Fregosi from the Angels for Leroy Stanton, Don Rose and Francisco Estrada . . . and throw in pitcher Nolan Ryan.

1971: At the end of the season the Astros deliver John Mayberry to the Royals for Jim York and Lance Clemons. In a three-year period the Royals have now acquired Mayberry, Lou Piniella and Amos Otis just about for free.

1971: Duffy's not what they're looking for, so when the season's over the Giants send him to Cleveland for sore-armed Sam McDowell and manage in the same deal to unload aging Gaylord Perry, who has only 179 wins left in his right arm.

1972: To get Danny Cater the Red Sox divest themselves of Sparky Lyle. Lyle posts 35 saves for the Yankees in 1972 and later wins the Cy Young award; Cater never again plays regularly.

1975: In December, the Yankees obtain Willie Randolph, Dock Ellis and Ken Brett from the Pirates for Doc Medich. Medich wins eight games for Pittsburgh in 1975; Ellis wins 17 for the Yankees, and Randolph becomes one of the top second basemen in the American League for the next decade.

1978: The Indians test switch-hitting shortstop Alfredo Griffin in a few games, find him wanting and ship him to Toronto for reliever Victor Cruz. Cruz wins three games for Cleveland in 1979; Griffin wins the Rookie of the Year award and becomes one of the AL's best glove men at shortstop for the next decade.

MEMBERS OF THE NATIONAL BASEBALL HALL OF FAME

This is baseball's Roll of Honor, making up, as pointed out by Roger Angell, roughly 1 percent of all the players ever to take the field.

1936 TYRUS R. COBB
WALTER P. JOHNSON
CHRISTOPHER MATHEWSON
GEORGE H. "BABE" RUTH
JOHN P. "HONUS" WAGNER

1937 MORGAN G. BULKELEY
BYRON B. "BAN" JOHNSON

NAPOLEON "LARRY" LAJOIE
CONNIE MACK
JOHN J. McGRAW
TRISTRAM E. SPEAKER
GEORGE WRIGHT
DENTON T. "CY" YOUNG

1938 GROVER C. ALEXANDER

ALEXANDER J. CARTWRIGHT, JR.
HENRY CHADWICK

1939 ADRIAN C. "CAP" ANSON
EDWARD T. COLLINS
CHARLES A. COMISKEY
WILLIAM A. "CANDY" CUMMINGS
WILLIAM B. "BUCK" EWING
H. LOUIS GEHRIG
WILLIAM H. "WILLIE" KEELER
CHARLES G. RADBOURNE
GEORGE H. SISLER
ALBERT G. SPALDING

1942 ROGERS HORNSBY

1944 KENESAW M. LANDIS

1945 ROGER P. BRESNAHAN
DENNIS "DAN" BROUTHERS
FREDERICK C. CLARKE
JAMES J. COLLINS
EDWARD J. DELAHANTY
HUGH DUFFY
HUGH A. JENNINGS
MICHAEL J. "KING" KELLY
JAMES H. O'ROURKE
WILBERT ROBINSON

1946 JESSE C. BURKETT
FRANK L. CHANCE
JOHN D. CHESBRO
JOHN J. EVERS
CLARK C. GRIFFITH
THOMAS F. McCARTHY
JOSEPH J. McGINNITY
EDWARD S. PLANK
JOSEPH B. TINKER
GEORGE E. "RUBE" WADDELL
EDWARD A. WALSH

1947 GORDON S. "MICKEY" COCHRANE
FRANK F. FRISCH
ROBERT M. "LEFTY" GROVE
CARL O. HUBBELL

1948 HERBERT J. PENNOCK
HAROLD J. "PIE" TRAYNOR

1949 MORDECAI P. BROWN
CHARLES L. GEHRINGER
CHARLES A. "KID" NICHOLS

1951 JAMES E. FOXX
MELVIN T. OTT

1952 HARRY E. HEILMANN
PAUL G. WANER

1953 EDWARD G. BARROW
CHARLES A. "CHIEF" BENDER
THOMAS H. CONNOLLY
JAY H. "DIZZY" DEAN
WILLIAM L. KLEM
ALOYSIUS H. SIMMONS
RODERICK J. "BOBBY" WALLACE
WILLIAM H. "HARRY" WRIGHT

1954 WILLIAM M. DICKEY
WALTER J. "RABBIT" MARANVILLE
WILLIAM H. TERRY

1955 J. FRANKLIN BAKER
JOSEPH P. DIMAGGIO
CHARLES L. "GABBY" HARTNETT
THEODORE A. LYONS
RAYMOND W. SCHALK
ARTHUR C. "DAZZY" VANCE

1956 JOSEPH H. CRONIN
HENRY B. GREENBERG

1957 SAMUEL E. CRAWFORD
JOSEPH V. McCARTHY

1959 ZACHARIAH D. WHEAT

1961 MAX G. CAREY
WILLIAM R. HAMILTON

1962 ROBERT W. A. FELLER
WILLIAM B. McKECHNIE
JACK R. ROBINSON
EDD J. ROUSH

1963 JOHN G. CLARKSON
ELMER H. FLICK
EDGAR C. "SAM" RICE
EPPA RIXEY

1964 LUCIUS B. "LUKE" APPLING
URBAN C. "RED" FABER
BURLEIGH A. GRIMES
MILLER J. HUGGINS
TIMOTHY J. KEEFE
HENRY E. "HEINIE" MANUSH
JOHN M. WARD

1965 JAMES F. "PUD" GALVIN

1966 CHARLES D. "CASEY" STENGEL

THEODORE S. WILLIAMS

1967 W. BRANCH RICKEY
      CHARLES H. "RED" RUFFING
      LLOYD J. WANER

1968 HAZEN S. "KIKI" CUYLER
      LEON A. "GOOSE" GOSLIN
      JOSEPH M. MEDWICK

1969 ROY CAMPANELLA
      STANLEY A. COVELESKI
      WAITE C. HOYT
      STANLEY F. MUSIAL

1970 LOUIS BOUDREAU
      EARLE B. COMBS
      FORD C. FRICK
      JESSE J. "POP" HAINES

1971 DAVID J. BANCROFT
      JACOB P. BECKLEY
      CHARLES J. "CHICK" HAFEY
      HARRY B. HOOPER
      JOSEPH J. KELLEY
      RICHARD W. "RUBE" MARQUARD
      LEROY R. "SATCHEL" PAIGE
      GEORGE M. WEISS

1972 LAWRENCE P. "YOGI" BERRA
      JOSHUA GIBSON
      VERNON L. "LEFTY" GOMEZ
      WILLIAM HARRIDGE
      SANFORD KOUFAX
      WALTER F. "BUCK" LEONARD
      EARLY WYNN
      ROSS M. YOUNGS

1973 ROBERTO W. CLEMENTE
      WILLIAM G. EVANS
      MONFORD "MONTE" IRVIN
      GEORGE L. KELLY
      WARREN E. SPAHN
      MICHAEL F. WELCH

1974 JAMES T. "COOL PAPA" BELL
      JAMES L. BOTTOMLEY
      JOHN B. "JOCKO" CONLAN
      EDWARD C. "WHITEY" FORD
      MICKEY C. MANTLE
      SAMUEL L. THOMPSON

1975 H. EARL AVERILL
      STANLEY R. "BUCKY" HARRIS
      WILLIAM J. HERMAN

WILLIAM J. "JUDY" JOHNSON
RALPH M. KINER

1976 OSCAR M. CHARLESTON
      ROGER CONNOR
      R. CAL HUBBARD
      ROBERT G. LEMON
      FREDERICK C. LINDSTROM
      ROBIN E. ROBERTS

1977 ERNEST BANKS
      MARTIN DIHIGO
      JOHN H. LLOYD
      ALFONSO R. LOPEZ
      AMOS W. RUSIE
      JOSEPH W. SEWELL

1978 ADRIAN JOSS
      LELAND S. "LARRY" MacPHAIL
      EDWIN L. MATHEWS

1979 WARREN C. GILES
      WILLIE H. MAYS
      LEWIS R. "HACK" WILSON

1980 ALBERT W. KALINE
      CHARLES H. KLEIN
      EDWIN D. "DUKE" SNIDER
      THOMAS A. YAWKEY

1981 ANDREW "RUBE" FOSTER
      ROBERT GIBSON
      JOHN R. MIZE

1982 HENRY L. AARON
      ALBERT B. "HAPPY" CHANDLER
      TRAVIS C. "STONEWALL" JACKSON
      FRANK ROBINSON

1983 WALTER E. ALSTON
      GEORGE C. KELL
      JUAN A. MARICHAL
      BROOKS C. ROBINSON, JR.

1984 LUIS E. APARICIO
      DONALD S. DRYSDALE
      RICHARD B. FERRELL
      HARMON C. KILLEBREW
      HAROLD H. "PEE WEE" REESE

1985 LOUIS C. BROCK
      ENOS B. "COUNTRY" SLAUGHTER
      JOSEPH F. "ARKY" VAUGHAN
      JAMES HOYT WILHELM

1986	ROBERT N. P. DOERR	1991	RODNEY C. CAREW
	ERNEST LOMBARDI		FERGUSON A. JENKINS
	WILLIE L. "STRETCH" McCOVEY		ANTHONY M. LAZZERI
			GAYLORD J. PERRY
1987	RAYMOND E. DANDRIDGE		BILL VEECK
	JAMES A. "CATFISH" HUNTER		
	BILLY L. WILLIAMS	1992	ROLAND G. FINGERS
			WILLIAM A. McGOWAN
1988	WILVER D. "WILLIE" STARGELL		HAROLD NEWHOUSER
			GEORGE THOMAS SEAVER
1989	ALBERT J. BARLICK		
	JOHNNY L. BENCH	1993	REGINALD MARTINEZ JACKSON
	ALBERT F. "RED" SCHOENDIENST		
	CARL M. "YAZ" YASTRZEMSKI	1994	STEPHEN N. CARLTON
			LEO E. DUROCHER
1990	JOE L. MORGAN		PHILLIP F. RIZZUTO
	JAMES A. PALMER		

THE HALL OF FAME GALLERY

The collection of plaques honoring inductees to the Hall of Fame makes up the heart of base-ball's ultimate shrine. Here, the plaques are presented in order of induction.

CONNIE MACK
A STAR CATCHER BUT FAMED MORE
AS MANAGER OF THE PHILADELPHIA
ATHLETICS SINCE 1901.
WINNER OF 9 PENNANTS AND 5
WORLD CHAMPIONSHIPS.
RECEIVED THE BOK AWARD
IN PHILADELPHIA FOR 1929.

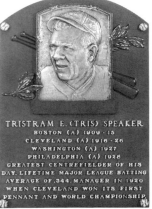

JOHN J. McGRAW
STAR THIRD-BASEMAN OF THE
GREAT BALTIMORE ORIOLES, NATIONAL
LEAGUE CHAMPIONS IN THE '90'S. FOR
30 YEARS MANAGER OF THE NEW YORK
GIANTS STARTING IN 1902.
UNDER HIS LEADERSHIP THE
GIANTS WON 10 PENNANTS AND 3
WORLD CHAMPIONSHIPS.

TRISTRAM E. (TRIS) SPEAKER
BOSTON (A) 1909-15
CLEVELAND (A) 1916-26
WASHINGTON (A) 1927
PHILADELPHIA (A) 1928
GREATEST CENTREFIELDER OF HIS
DAY. LIFETIME MAJOR LEAGUE BATTING
AVERAGE OF .344. MANAGER IN 1920
WHEN CLEVELAND WON ITS FIRST
PENNANT AND WORLD CHAMPIONSHIP

GEORGE WRIGHT
STAR OF BASEBALL'S FIRST
PROFESSIONAL TEAM, THE
CINCINNATI RED STOCKINGS OF 1869.
GREAT SHORTSTOP AND CAPTAIN OF
CHAMPION BOSTONS IN NATIONAL
LEAGUE'S PIONEER YEARS.

DENTON T. (CY) YOUNG
CLEVELAND (N) 1890-98
ST. LOUIS (N) 1899-1900
BOSTON (A) 1901-08
CLEVELAND (A) 1909-11
BOSTON (N) 1911
ONLY PITCHER IN FIRST HUNDRED
YEARS OF BASEBALL TO WIN 500 GAMES.
AMONG HIS 511 VICTORIES WERE 3
NO-HIT SHUTOUTS. PITCHED PERFECT
GAME MAY 5, 1904, NO OPPOSING
BATSMAN REACHING FIRST BASE.

GROVER CLEVELAND ALEXANDER
GREAT NATIONAL LEAGUE PITCHER
FOR TWO DECADES WITH PHILLIES,
CUBS AND CARDINALS STARTING
IN 1911. WON 1926 WORLD CHAMPIONSHIP
FOR CARDINALS BY STRIKING OUT
LAZZERI WITH BASES FULL IN
FINAL CRISIS AT YANKEE STADIUM.

ALEXANDER JOY CARTWRIGHT, Jr.
"FATHER OF MODERN BASE BALL."
SET BASES 90 FEET APART.
ESTABLISHED 9 INNINGS AS GAME
AND 9 PLAYERS AS TEAM. ORGANIZED
THE KNICKERBOCKER BASEBALL CLUB
OF N.Y. IN 1845. CARRIED BASEBALL
TO PACIFIC COAST AND HAWAII
IN PIONEER DAYS.

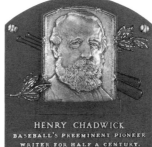

HENRY CHADWICK
BASEBALL'S PREEMINENT PIONEER
WRITER FOR HALF A CENTURY.
INVENTOR OF THE BOX SCORE.
AUTHOR OF THE FIRST RULE-BOOK
IN 1858. CHAIRMAN OF RULES
COMMITTEE IN FIRST NATION-WIDE
BASEBALL ORGANIZATION.

ADRIAN CONSTANTINE ANSON
"CAP"
GREATEST HITTER AND GREATEST
NATIONAL LEAGUE PLAYER-MANAGER
OF 19TH CENTURY. STARTED WITH
CHICAGOS IN NATIONAL LEAGUE'S
FIRST YEAR 1876. CHICAGO MANAGER
FROM 1879 TO 1897, WINNING 5 PENNANTS.
WAS .300 CLASS HITTER 20 YEARS,
BATTING CHAMPION 4 TIMES.

EDWARD TROWBRIDGE COLLINS
PHILADELPHIA - CHICAGO
PHILADELPHIA, A.L. - 1906-1930
FAMED AS BATSMAN, BASE RUNNER
AND SECOND BASEMAN AND ALSO AS
FIELD CAPTAIN. BATTED .333 DURING
MAJOR LEAGUE CAREER, SECOND ONLY
TO TY COBB IN MODERN BASE STEALING.
MADE 3313 HITS IN 2826 GAMES.

CHARLES A. COMISKEY
"THE OLD ROMAN"
STARTED 50 YEARS OF BASEBALL AS
ST. LOUIS BROWNS FIRST-BASEMAN IN 1882
AND WAS FIRST MAN AT THIS POSITION TO
PLAY AWAY FROM THE BAG FOR BATTERS. AS
BROWNS' MANAGER-CAPTAIN-PLAYER WON
4 STRAIGHT AMERICAN ASSOCIATION
PENNANTS STARTING 1885. WORLD CHAMPIONS
FIRST 2 YEARS. OWNER AND PRESIDENT
CHICAGO WHITE SOX 1900 TO 1931.

W. A. "CANDY" CUMMINGS
PITCHED FIRST CURVE BALL IN BASEBALL
HISTORY. INVENTED CURVE AS AMATEUR
ACE OF BROOKLYN STARS IN 1867. ENDED
LONG CAREER AS HARTFORD PITCHER IN
NATIONAL LEAGUE'S FIRST YEAR 1876.

WM. B. "BUCK" EWING
GREATEST 19TH CENTURY CATCHER. GIANT
IN STATURE AND GIANT CAPTAIN OF
NEW YORK'S FIRST NATIONAL LEAGUE
CHAMPIONS 1888 AND 1889. WAS GENIUS
AS FIELD LEADER, UNSURPASSED IN
THROWING TO BASES. GREAT LONG-RANGE
HITTER. NATIONAL LEAGUE CAREER
1881 TO 1899 TROY, N.Y. GIANTS AND
CLEVELAND; CINCINNATI MANAGER.

HENRY LOUIS GEHRIG
NEW YORK YANKEES 1923-1939
HOLDER OF MORE THAN A SCORE OF
MAJOR AND AMERICAN LEAGUE RECORDS,
INCLUDING THAT OF PLAYING 2130
CONSECUTIVE GAMES, WHEN HE RETIRED
IN 1939, HE HAD A LIFE TIME BATTING
AVERAGE OF .340.

WILLIE KEELER
"HIT 'EM WHERE THEY AINT!"
BASEBALL'S GREATEST PLACE-HITTER;
BEST BUNTER. BIG LEAGUE CAREER
1892 TO 1910 WITH N.Y. GIANTS,
BALTIMORE ORIOLES, BROOKLYN SUPERBAS,
N.Y. HIGHLANDERS. NATIONAL LEAGUE
BATTING CHAMPION '97-'98.

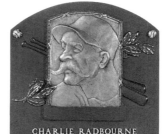

CHARLIE RADBOURNE
"OLD HOSS"
PROVIDENCE, BOSTON AND CINCINNATI
NATIONAL LEAGUE 1881 TO 1891, GREATEST
OF ALL 19TH CENTURY PITCHERS, WINNING
1884 PENNANT FOR PROVIDENCE. RADBOURNE
PITCHED LAST 27 GAMES OF SEASON, WON
26. WON 3 STRAIGHT IN WORLD SERIES.

COLORPLATE 124

WREN PANZELLA. *Night Baseball.* 1992. Glass transfer oil painting.
32¹/₂ x 25¹/₂ in. Gallery 53 Artworks, Cooperstown, New York.

COLORPLATE 125

JEFFREY RUBIN. *David Cone*. 1992.
Oil paint, black and white photo. 41 x 56 in. Collection of the artist.

COLORPLATE 126

THOM ROSS. *Terrific*. 1992. Acrylic on canvas. 30 x 38 in.
Gallery 53 Artworks, Cooperstown, New York.

COLORPLATE 127

JIM DOW. *View of College Park from Behind Home Plate, Charleston, South Carolina, 1991.*
Charleston Rainbows, South Atlantic League A. 4 panel panorama from 8 x 10 in color negative.
Gallery 53 Artworks, Cooperstown, New York.

COLORPLATE 128

RALPH GOINGS. *Baseball*. 1988.
Watercolor on foam core.
5¹/₄ x 5¹/₄ in. The Gladstone
Collection of Baseball Art.

COLORPLATE 129

STEVEN SKOLLAR. *American Icon
(Floater)*. 1992. Oil on board.
10 x 8 in. Gallery 53 Artworks,
Cooperstown, New York.

COLORPLATE 130

ROBERT VALDES. *Baseball #1.* 1992. Watercolor on rag paper. 20 x 28 in.
Collection of the artist.

COLORPLATE 131

LENA GUYOT. *The Love of the Game.* 1988. Mixed media sculpture. 16 x 10 x 8 in.
Cooperstown Bat Company and Gallery 53 Artworks, Cooperstown, New York.

GEORGE HAROLD SISLER
ST. LOUIS - WASHINGTON A.L.
BOSTON, N.L. - 1915 - 1930
HOLDS TWO AMERICAN LEAGUE RECORDS,
MAKING 257 HITS IN 1920 AND BATTING
.41979 IN 1922. RETIRED WITH MAJOR
LEAGUE AVERAGE OF .341. CREDITED WITH
BEING ONE OF BEST TWO FIELDING FIRST
BASEMEN IN HISTORY OF GAME.

ALBERT GOODWILL SPALDING
ORGANIZATIONAL GENIUS OF BASEBALL'S
PIONEER DAYS. STAR PITCHER OF FOREST
CITY CLUB IN LATE 1860'S, 4-YEAR
CHAMPION BOSTONS 1871-1875 AND
MANAGER - PITCHER OF CHAMPION
CHICAGOS IN NATIONAL LEAGUE'S FIRST
YEAR. CHICAGO PRESIDENT FOR 10
YEARS. ORGANIZER OF BASEBALL'S FIRST
ROUND - THE - WORLD TOUR IN 1888.

ROGERS HORNSBY
NATIONAL LEAGUE BATTING CHAMPION
7 YEARS - 1920 TO 1925; 1928. LIFETIME
BATTING AVERAGE .358 HIGHEST IN
NATIONAL LEAGUE HISTORY. HIT .424 IN
1924, 20TH CENTURY MAJOR LEAGUE RECORD.
MANAGER 1926 WORLD CHAMPION ST. LOUIS
CARDINALS. MOST-VALUABLE-PLAYER
1925 AND 1929.

KENESAW MOUNTAIN LANDIS
BASEBALL'S FIRST COMMISSIONER
ELECTED, 1920 — DIED IN OFFICE, 1944
HIS INTEGRITY AND LEADERSHIP
ESTABLISHED BASEBALL IN THE
RESPECT, ESTEEM AND AFFECTION
OF THE AMERICAN PEOPLE.

ROGER BRESNAHAN
BATTERY MATE OF CHRISTY MATHEWSON
WITH THE NEW YORK GIANTS, HE WAS
ONE OF THE GAME'S MOST NATURAL
PLAYERS AND MIGHT HAVE STARRED
AT ANY POSITION, THE "DUKE OF TRALEE"
WAS ONE OF THE FEW MAJOR LEAGUE
CATCHERS FAST ENOUGH TO BE USED
AS A LEADOFF MAN.

DAN BROUTHERS
HARD-HITTING FIRST BASEMAN OF
EIGHT MAJOR LEAGUE CLUBS, HE WAS
PART OF ORIGINAL "BIG FOUR" OF BUFFALO.
TRADED WITH OTHER MEMBERS OF
THAT COMBINATION TO DETROIT, HE HIT
.419 AS CITY WON ITS ONLY NATIONAL
LEAGUE CHAMPIONSHIP IN 1887.

FRED CLARKE
THE FIRST OF THE SUCCESSFUL
"BOY MANAGERS," AT TWENTY-FOUR HE
PILOTED LOUISVILLE'S COLONELS IN
THE NATIONAL LEAGUE. WON 4 PENNANTS
FOR PITTSBURGH AND A WORLD
CHAMPIONSHIP IN 1909. STARRED AS
AN OUTFIELDER FOR 22 SEASONS.

JAMES COLLINS
CONSIDERED BY MANY THE GAME'S
GREATEST THIRD BASEMAN, HE
REVOLUTIONIZED STYLE OF PLAY AT THAT
BAG. LED BOSTON RED SOX TO FIRST
WORLD CHAMPIONSHIP IN 1903. A
CONSISTENT BATTER, HIS DEFENSIVE PLAY
THRILLED FANS OF BOTH MAJOR LEAGUES.

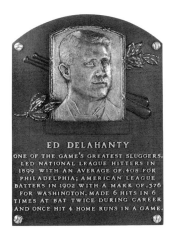

ED DELAHANTY
ONE OF THE GAME'S GREATEST SLUGGERS.
LED NATIONAL LEAGUE HITTERS IN
1899 WITH AN AVERAGE OF .408 FOR
PHILADELPHIA; AMERICAN LEAGUE
BATTERS IN 1902 WITH A MARK OF .376
FOR WASHINGTON. MADE 6 HITS IN 6
TIMES AT BAT TWICE DURING CAREER
AND ONCE HIT 4 HOME RUNS IN A GAME.

HUGH DUFFY
BRILLIANT AS A DEFENSIVE OUTFIELDER
FOR THE BOSTON NATIONALS, HE
COMPILED A BATTING AVERAGE IN 1894
WHICH WAS NOT TO BE CHALLENGED
IN HIS LIFETIME - .438.

HUGHIE JENNINGS
OF BALTIMORE'S FAMOUS OLD ORIOLES,
HE WAS ONE OF THE GAME'S MIGHTY
MITES. A STAR SHORTSTOP HE WAS A
CONSTANT THREAT AT THE PLATE.
ONCE HIT .397. PILOTED DETROIT
TO THREE CHAMPIONSHIPS.

MIKE J. (KING) KELLY
COLORFUL PLAYER AND AUDACIOUS
BASE - RUNNER. IN 1887 FOR BOSTON
HE HIT .394 AND STOLE 84 BASES.
HIS SALE FOR $10,000 WAS ONE OF
THE BIGGEST DEALS OF BASEBALL'S
EARLY HISTORY.

JAMES H. O'ROURKE
"ORATOR JIM" PLAYED BALL UNTIL HE
WAS PAST FIFTY, INCLUDING TWENTY-ONE
MAJOR LEAGUE SEASONS. AN OUTFIELDER
AND CATCHER FOR THE BOSTON RED
STOCKINGS OF 1873, HE LATER WORE
THE UNIFORMS OF THE CHAMPIONSHIP
PROVIDENCE TEAM OF 1879, BUFFALO,
NEW YORK AND WASHINGTON.

WILBERT ROBINSON
"UNCLE ROBBIE"
STAR CATCHER FOR THE FAMOUS
BALTIMORE ORIOLES ON PENNANT CLUBS
OF 1894,'95 AND '96, HE LATER WON FAME
AS MANAGER OF THE BROOKLYN DODGERS
FROM 1914 THROUGH 1931. SET A RECORD OF
7 HITS IN 7 TIMES AT BAT IN SINGLE GAME.

JESSE C. BURKETT
BATTING STAR WHO PLAYED OUTFIELD FOR
THE NEW YORK, CLEVELAND AND ST. LOUIS
N.L. TEAMS AND THE ST. LOUIS AND BOSTON
A.L. TEAMS. SHARES WITH ROGERS HORNSBY
AND TY COBB THE RECORD OF HITTING .400
OR BETTER THE MOST TIMES. ACCOMPLISHED
THIS ON THREE OCCASIONS. TOPPED THE
N.L. IN HITTING THREE TIMES, BATTING
OVER .400 TO GAIN THE CHAMPIONSHIP
IN 1895 AND 1896.

FRANK LEROY CHANCE
FAMOUS LEADER OF CHICAGO CUBS. WON
PENNANT WITH CUBS IN FIRST FULL SEASON
AS MANAGER IN 1906. THAT TEAM COMPILED
116 VICTORIES UNEQUALLED IN MAJOR
LEAGUE HISTORY. ALSO WON PENNANTS
IN 1907, 08 AND 1910 AND WORLD SERIES
WINNER IN 07 AND 08. STARTED WITH
CHICAGO IN 1898. ALSO MANAGER
NEW YORK A.L. AND BOSTON A.L.

CHARLES L. GEHRINGER
SECOND BASEMAN WITH DETROIT A.L. FROM
1925 THROUGH 1941 AND COACH IN 1942.
COMPILED LIFETIME BATTING AVERAGE
OF .321, IN 2323 GAMES, COLLECTED 2839
HITS. NAMED MOST VALUABLE PLAYER IN
A.L. IN 1937. BATTED .321 IN WORLD SERIES
COMPETITION AND HAD A .500 AVERAGE
FOR SIX ALL-STAR GAMES.

CHARLES A. (KID) NICHOLS
RIGHT HANDED PITCHER WHO WON 30 OR
MORE GAMES FOR SEVEN CONSECUTIVE
YEARS (1891-97) AND WON AT LEAST 20
GAMES FOR TEN CONSECUTIVE SEASONS
(1890-99) WITH BOSTON N.L. ALSO PITCHED
FOR ST. LOUIS AND PHILADELPHIA N.L. ONE
OF FEW PITCHERS TO WIN MORE THAN 300
GAMES, HIS MAJOR LEAGUE RECORD BEING
360 VICTORIES, 202 DEFEATS.

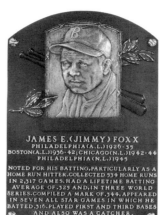

JAMES E. (JIMMY) FOXX
PHILADELPHIA (A.L.) 1926-35
BOSTON (A.L.) 1936-42; CHICAGO (N.L.) 1942-44
PHILADELPHIA (N.L.) 1945
NOTED FOR HIS BATTING, PARTICULARLY AS A
HOME RUN HITTER. COLLECTED 534 HOME RUNS
IN 2,317 GAMES. HAD A LIFETIME BATTING
AVERAGE OF .325 AND IN THREE WORLD
SERIES. COMPILED A MARK OF .344. APPEARED
IN SEVEN ALL STAR GAMES IN WHICH HE
BATTED .316. PLAYED FIRST AND THIRD BASES
AND ALSO WAS A CATCHER.

MELVIN T. (MEL) OTT
NEW YORK (N.L.) 1926-48
ONE OF FEW PLAYERS TO JUMP FROM A HIGH
SCHOOL TEAM INTO MAJORS. PLAYED OUTFIELD
AND THIRD BASE AND MANAGED CLUB FROM
DEC. 1941 THROUGH JULY 1948. HIT 511 HOME
RUNS, N.L. RECORD WHEN HE RETIRED. ALSO
LED IN MOST RUNS SCORED, MOST RUNS BATTED
IN, TOTAL BASES, BASES ON BALLS AND EXTRA
BASES ON LONG HITS. HAD A .304 LIFETIME
BATTING AVERAGE. PLAYED IN ELEVEN ALL STAR
GAMES AND IN THREE WORLD SERIES.

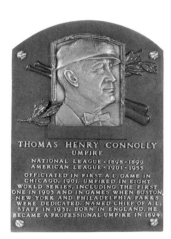

HARRY EDWIN HEILMANN
DETROIT, A.L. - CINCINNATI, N.L.
1916 - 1932
RIGHT HANDED HITTING OUTFIELDER AND
FIRST BASEMAN, WON AMERICAN LEAGUE
BATTING CHAMPIONSHIP FOUR TIMES
1921, '23, '25 AND '27. IN 1923, BATTED .403.
COLLECTED 2660 HITS AND 183 HOME RUNS
IN 2,146 MAJOR LEAGUE GAMES. HAD A
LIFETIME BATTING AVERAGE OF .342 AND
FIELDING MARK OF .975.

PAUL GLEE WANER
(BIG POISON)
PITTSBURGH-BROOKLYN-BOSTON, N.L.
NEW YORK, A.L.
1926 - 1945
LEFT HANDED HITTING OUTFIELDER BATTED
.300 OR BETTER 14 TIMES IN NATIONAL
LEAGUE. ONE OF SEVEN PLAYERS EVER TO
COMPILE 3,000 OR MORE HITS. SET MODERN
N.L. RECORD BY COLLECTING 200 OR MORE
HITS EIGHT SEASONS. MOST VALUABLE PLAYER
IN 1927 AND FOUR TIMES SELECTED FOR
ALL STAR GAME.

EDWARD GRANT BARROW
CLUB EXECUTIVE, MANAGER, LEAGUE
PRESIDENT IN MINORS AND MAJORS FROM
1894 TO 1945. CONVERTED BABE RUTH FROM
PITCHER TO OUTFIELDER AS MANAGER BOSTON
A.L. IN 1918. DISCOVERED HONUS WAGNER
AND MANY OTHER GREAT STARS. WON WORLD
SERIES IN 1918. BUILT NEW YORK YANKEES INTO
OUTSTANDING ORGANIZATION IN BASEBALL
AS BUSINESS MANAGER FROM 1920 TO 1945,
WINNING 14 PENNANTS, 10 WORLD SERIES.

CHARLES ALBERT BENDER
"CHIEF"
PHILADELPHIA A.L. 1903 - 1914
PHILADELPHIA N.L. 1916 - 1917
CHICAGO A.L. 1925
FAMOUS CHIPEWA INDIAN. WON OVER 200
GAMES. PITCHED FOR ATHLETICS IN 1905-
1910 - 1911 - 1913 - 1914 WORLD SERIES.
DEFEATED N.Y. GIANTS 3-0 FOR A'S ONLY
VICTORY IN 1905. FIRST PITCHER IN
WORLD SERIES OF 6 GAMES (1911) TO PITCH
3 COMPLETE GAMES. PITCHED NO-HIT GAME
AGAINST CLEVELAND IN 1910.
HIGHEST A.L. PERCENTAGES IN
1910 - 1911 - 1914.

THOMAS HENRY CONNOLLY
UMPIRE
NATIONAL LEAGUE - 1898-1899
AMERICAN LEAGUE - 1901-1933
OFFICIATED AT FIRST A.L. GAME IN
CHICAGO, 1901. UMPIRED IN EIGHT
WORLD SERIES, INCLUDING THE FIRST
ONE IN 1903 AND IN GAMES WHEN BOSTON,
NEW YORK AND PHILADELPHIA PARKS
WERE DEDICATED. NAMED CHIEF OF A.L.
STAFF IN 1931. BORN IN ENGLAND, HE
BECAME A PROFESSIONAL UMPIRE IN 1894.

JAY HANNA (DIZZY) DEAN
ST. LOUIS (N.L.) 1932 - 1937
CHICAGO (N.L.) 1938 - 1941
ONE OF FOUR N.L. PITCHERS TO WIN 30 OR
MORE GAMES UNDER MODERN REGULATIONS.
PITCHED IN 1934 (ST. L.) 1938 (CHICAGO)
WORLD SERIES. LED LEAGUE IN STRIKEOUTS
1932-33-34-35. SINGLE GAME RECORD WITH
17, JULY 30, 1933. FIRST PITCHER TO MAKE
TWO HITS IN ONE INNING IN WORLD SERIES.
MOST VALUABLE N.L. PLAYER IN 1934.

WILLIAM J. KLEM
UMPIRE
NATIONAL LEAGUE - 1905-1951
KNOWN AS "THE OLD ARBITRATOR." UMPIRED
IN 18 WORLD SERIES. CREDITED WITH
INTRODUCING ARM SIGNALS INDICATING
STRIKES AND FAIR OR FOUL BALLS. FAMOUS
QUOTE: "BASEBALL IS MORE THAN A GAME
TO ME—IT'S A RELIGION." RETIRED AS ACTIVE
UMPIRE IN 1940. NAMED CHIEF OF N.L.
STAFF IN 1941.

ALOYSIUS HARRY SIMMONS
PLAYED WITH 7 MAJOR LEAGUE CLUBS 1924-
1944. STAR WITH PHILA. (A.L.). BATTED
.308 TO .392 FROM 1924 TO 1934. LEADING
BATTER .381 IN 1930, .390 IN 1931. MOST
HITS BY A.L. RIGHT-HANDED BATTER WITH
2831. LED LEAGUE RUNS BATTED IN RUNS
SCORED, HITS AND TOTAL BASES SEVERAL
SEASONS. HIT 3 HOME RUNS, JULY 15, 1932.
LIFETIME BATTING AVERAGE .334.

RODERICK J. WALLACE
CLEVELAND-ST. LOUIS-CINCINNATI N.L.
ST. LOUIS A.L. - 1894 TO 1918
ONE OF LONGEST CAREERS IN MAJOR
LEAGUES. OVER 60 YEARS AS PITCHER,
THIRD BASEMAN, SHORTSTOP, MANAGER,
UMPIRE AND SCOUT. ACTIVE AS PLAYER
FOR 25 YEARS. SET A.L. RECORD FOR
CHANCES IN ONE GAME AT SHORTSTOP, 17,
JUNE 10, 1902. RECOGNIZED AS ONE OF
GREATEST SHORTSTOPS. PITCHED FOR
CLEVELAND IN 1896 TEMPLE CUP SERIES.

HARRY WRIGHT
MANAGER AND CENTERFIELDER OF FAMOUS
CINCINNATI RED STOCKINGS, UNDEFEATED
IN 69 GAMES IN 1869-1870. FIRST MANAGER
TO WIN FOUR STRAIGHT PENNANTS WITH
BOSTON NATIONAL ASSOCIATION 1872-73-74-
75. BROTHER OF GEORGE WRIGHT ALSO IN
HALL OF FAME. SPONSORED FIRST BASEBALL
TOUR TO ENGLAND IN 1876. INTRODUCED
KNICKER UNIFORMS. HIT 7 HOME RUNS IN
GAME AT NEWPORT, KY. IN 1867.

WILLIAM MALCOLM DICKEY
NEW YORK A.L. 1928-1946
SET RECORD BY CATCHING 100 OR MORE
GAMES 13 SUCCESSIVE SEASONS. PLAYED
WITH YANKEES, CHAMPIONS OF 1932-36-37-
38-39-41-42-43, WHEN CLUB WON 7 WORLD
SERIES TITLES. HOLDS NUMEROUS WORLD
SERIES RECORDS FOR CATCHERS, INCLUDING
MOST GAMES, 38. PLAYED ON 8 ALL-STAR
TEAMS FROM 1932 TO 1946. LIFETIME
BATTING AVERAGE OF .313 IN 1789 GAMES.

WALTER J. V. MARANVILLE
"RABBIT"
BOSTON, PITTSBURGH, CHICAGO,
BROOKLYN AND ST. LOUIS,
NATIONAL LEAGUE, 1912 - 1935
PLAYED MORE GAMES, 2153, AT SHORTSTOP
THAN ANY OTHER NATIONAL LEAGUE PLAYER.
AT BAT TOTAL 10078, SURPASSED BY ONLY
ONE NATIONAL LEAGUER, HONUS WAGNER.
MADE 2605 HITS IN 23 SEASONS. MEMBER
OF 1914 BOSTON BRAVES "MIRACLE TEAM"
THAT WON PENNANT, THEN WORLD SERIES
FROM ATHLETICS IN 4 GAMES.

WILLIAM HAROLD TERRY
NEW YORK N.L. 1923 TO 1941
BATTED .401 AND TIED N.L. RECORD FOR
BASE HITS WITH 254 IN 1930. MADE 200 OR
MORE HITS IN SIX SEASONS. RETIRED WITH
LIFETIME BATTING AVERAGE OF .341, A
MODERN N.L. RECORD FOR LEFT-HANDED
BATTERS. MOST VALUABLE PLAYER IN 1930
SUCCEEDED JOHN McGRAW AS MANAGER IN
1932 AND WON PENNANTS IN 1933-36-37.

JOHN FRANKLIN BAKER
PHILADELPHIA A.L. 1908-1914
NEW YORK A.L. 1916-1922
MEMBER OF CONNIE MACK'S FAMOUS
$100,000 INFIELD. LED AMERICAN LEAGUE
IN HOME-RUNS 1911-12-13. HIT 3 IN 1914.
WON TWO WORLD SERIES GAMES FROM
GIANTS IN 1911 WITH HOME-RUNS THUS
GETTING NAME HOME RUN BAKER. PLAYED
IN SIX WORLD SERIES 1910-11-13-14-21-22.

JOSEPH PAUL DI MAGGIO
NEW YORK A.L. 1936 TO 1951
HIT SAFELY IN 56 CONSECUTIVE GAMES
FOR MAJOR LEAGUE RECORD 1941. HIT 2
HOME-RUNS IN ONE INNING 1936. HIT 3
HOME-RUNS IN ONE GAME (3 TIMES). HOLDS
NUMEROUS BATTING RECORDS. PLAYED IN
10 WORLD SERIES (51 GAMES) AND 11 ALL
STAR GAMES. MOST VALUABLE PLAYER
A.L. 1939, 1941, 1947.

CHARLES LEO (GABBY) HARTNETT
CHICAGO N.L. 1922 TO 1940
NEW YORK N.L. 1941
CAUGHT 100 OR MORE GAMES PER SEASON
FOR 12 YEARS EIGHT IN SUCCESSION, 1930
TO 1937 FOR LEAGUE RECORD. SET MARK
FOR CONSECUTIVE CHANCES FOR CATCHER
WITHOUT ERROR, 452 IN 1933-34. HIGHEST
FIELDING AVERAGE FOR CATCHER IN 100 OR
MORE GAMES IN 7 SEASONS. MOST PUTOUTS
N.L. 7292. MOST CHANCES ACCEPTED N.L.
8546. LIFETIME BATTING AVERAGE .297.

THEODORE AMAR LYONS
CHICAGO A.L. 1923 TO 1946
ENTIRE ACTIVE PITCHING CAREER OF 21
SEASONS WITH CHICAGO A.L. WON 260
GAMES, LOST 230. TIED FOR LEAGUE'S MOST
VICTORIES 1925 AND 1927. BEST EARNED RUN
AVERAGE, 2.10 IN 1942 WHEN HE STARTED
AND FINISHED ALL 20 GAMES. PITCHED
NO-HIT GAME, AUG. 21, 1926 AGAINST DETROIT.
PITCHED 21-INNING GAME MAY 24, 1929.

RAYMOND WILLIAM SCHALK
CHICAGO A.L. 1912 TO 1928
NEW YORK N.L. 1929
HOLDER OF MAJOR LEAGUE RECORD FOR
MOST YEARS LEADING CATCHER IN FIELDING,
EIGHT YEARS; MOST PUTOUTS, NINE YEARS;
MOST ASSISTS IN ONE MAJOR LEAGUE (1810);
MOST CHANCES ACCEPTED (8965). CAUGHT
FOUR NO-HIT GAMES INCLUDING PERFECT
GAME IN 1922.

ARTHUR CHARLES (DAZZY) VANCE
BROOKLYN N.L. 1922 TO 1932, 1935
PITTSBURGH N.L. · NEW YORK A.L.
ST. LOUIS N.L. · CINCINNATI N.L.
FIRST PITCHER IN N.L. TO LEAD IN
STRIKEOUTS FOR 7 STRAIGHT YEARS, 1922 TO
1928. LED LEAGUE WITH 28 VICTORIES IN
1924; 22 IN 1929. WON 15 STRAIGHT IN 1924.
PITCHED NO-HIT GAME AGAINST PHILLIES,
1925. MOST VALUABLE PLAYER N.L. 1924.

JOSEPH EDWARD CRONIN
PITTSBURGH N.L. 1926-1927
WASHINGTON A.L. 1928-1934
BOSTON A.L. 1935-1945
NAMED ALL-STAR SHORTSTOP SEVEN
SEASONS. MOST VALUABLE PLAYER A.L.
1930. LED A.L. SHORTSTOPS IN FIELDING
1931-1932. MOST PUTOUTS AND DOUBLE
PLAYS 1930-31-32. LIFETIME BATTING
AVERAGE .302. WON PENNANT IN 1933 IN
FIRST SEASON AS MANAGER WASHINGTON
A.L. AT AGE 26. TRADED TO BOSTON 1934 FOR
REPORTED RECORD PRICE OF $250,000.

HENRY BENJAMIN GREENBERG
DETROIT A.L. 1933 TO 1946
PITTSBURGH N.L. 1947
ONE OF BASEBALL'S GREATEST RIGHT-HANDED
BATTERS. TIED FOR MOST HOME RUNS BY
RIGHT-HANDED BATTER IN 1938-58. MOST
RUNS-BATTED-IN 1935-37-40-46. MOST HOME
RUNS 1938-40-46. WON 1945 PENNANT ON
LAST DAY OF SEASON WITH GRAND SLAM
HOME RUN IN 9TH INNING. PLAYED IN 4
WORLD SERIES, 2 ALL-STAR GAMES. MOST
VALUABLE A.L. PLAYER TWICE-1935, 1940.
LIFETIME BATTING AVERAGE .313.

SAMUEL EARL CRAWFORD
"WAHOO SAM"
CINCINNATI N.L. 1899-1902
DETROIT A.L. 1903-1917
HAD LIFETIME RECORD OF 2964 HITS,
BATTING AVERAGE OF .309. PLAYED 2505
GAMES. HOLDS MAJOR LEAGUE RECORD
FOR MOST TRIPLES, 312. LEAGUE LEADER
ONE OR MORE SEASONS IN DOUBLES, TRIPLES,
RUNS BATTED IN, RUNS SCORED, CHANCES
ACCEPTED, HOME RUNS (N.L. 1901-A.L. 1908)
AND TOTAL BASES (N.L. 1902-A.L. 1913).

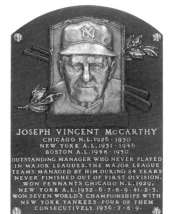

JOSEPH VINCENT McCARTHY
CHICAGO N.L. 1926-1930
NEW YORK A.L. 1931-1946
BOSTON A.L. 1948-1950
OUTSTANDING MANAGER WHO NEVER PLAYED
IN MAJOR LEAGUES. THE MAJOR LEAGUE
TEAMS MANAGED BY HIM DURING 24 YEARS
NEVER FINISHED OUT OF FIRST DIVISION.
WON PENNANTS CHICAGO N.L. 1929,
NEW YORK A.L. 1932-6-7-8-9-41-42-3.
WON SEVEN WORLD'S CHAMPIONSHIPS WITH
NEW YORK YANKEES—FOUR OF THEM
CONSECUTIVELY 1936-7-8-9.

ZACHARIAH (ZACK) DAVIS WHEAT
BROOKLYN N.L. 1909-1926
PHILADELPHIA A.L. 1927
BROOKLYN OUTFIELDER FOR 16 YEARS.
HOLDS BROOKLYN RECORDS FOR: GAMES
PLAYED 2,318, AT BAT 8,859, HITS 2,804,
SINGLES 2,038, DOUBLES 464, TRIPLES 171,
TOTAL BASES 4,003, EXTRA BASE HITS 766,
BATTED .375 (1923) .375 (1924) .359 (1925)
LEAGUE BATTING LEADER .335 (1918)
LIFETIME BATTING AVERAGE .317 WITH
2,884 HITS. PLAYED 2,406 GAMES.

MAX GEORGE CAREY
PITTSBURGH N.L. 1910-1926, 1930
BROOKLYN N.L. 1926-1929, 1932-1933
HOLDS NATIONAL LEAGUE RECORDS FOR OUT-
FIELDERS: GAMES PLAYED, 2421; PUT OUTS,
6363; ASSISTS, 339; TOTAL CHANCES,
6702. MODERN LEAGUE RECORD FOR MOST
STOLEN BASES, 738. MAJOR LEAGUE RECORD
MOST YEARS LEADING LEAGUE IN STOLEN
BASES, 10. BATTING AVERAGE .285 FOR
20 SEASONS. IN 1922 51 STOLEN BASES
IN 53 ATTEMPTS.

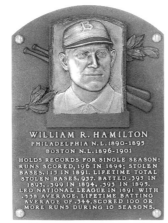

WILLIAM R. HAMILTON
PHILADELPHIA N.L. 1890-1895
BOSTON N.L. 1896-1901
HOLDS RECORDS FOR SINGLE SEASON:
RUNS SCORED, 196 IN 1894; STOLEN
BASES, 115 IN 1891. LIFETIME TOTAL
STOLEN BASES, 937. BATTED .393 IN
1893, .399 IN 1894, .393 IN 1895.
LED NATIONAL LEAGUE IN 1891 WITH
.338 AVERAGE. LIFETIME BATTING
AVERAGE OF .344. SCORED 100 OR
MORE RUNS DURING 10 SEASONS.

ROBERT WILLIAM ANDREW FELLER
CLEVELAND A.L. 1936 TO 1941
1945 TO 1956
PITCHED 3 NO-HIT GAMES IN A.L., 12 ONE HIT
GAMES. SET MODERN STRIKEOUT RECORD
WITH 18 IN GAME, 348 FOR SEASON. LED
A.L. IN VICTORIES 6 (ONE TIE) SEASONS.
LIFE TIME RECORD: WON 266, LOST 162,
P.C. .621, E.R. AVERAGE 3.25, STRUCKOUT 2581.

WILLIAM BOYD McKECHNIE
MANAGER
PITTSBURGH N.L. 1922-1926
ST. LOUIS N.L. 1928-1929
BOSTON N.L. 1930-1937
CINCINNATI N.L. 1938-1946
ONLY N.L. MANAGER TO WIN PENNANTS
WITH THREE DIFFERENT CLUBS-PITTSBURGH
1925; ST. LOUIS, 1928; CINCINNATI, 1939, 1940.
WON WORLD SERIES 1925 AND 1940. NAMED
NO. 1 MAJOR LEAGUE MANAGER 1937 AND
1940. ACTIVE IN BASEBALL AS MANAGER,
COACH, PLAYER, 1906 TO 1953.

JACK ROOSEVELT ROBINSON
BROOKLYN N.L. 1947 TO 1956
LEADING N.L. BATTER IN 1949. HOLDS
FIELDING MARK FOR SECOND BASEMAN
PLAYING IN 150 OR MORE GAMES WITH .992.
LED N.L. IN STOLEN BASES IN 1947 AND
1949. MOST VALUABLE PLAYER IN 1949.
LIFETIME BATTING AVERAGE .311. JOINT
RECORD HOLDER FOR MOST DOUBLE PLAYS
BY SECOND BASEMAN, 137 IN 1951.
LED SECOND BASEMEN IN DOUBLE
PLAYS 1949-50-51-52.

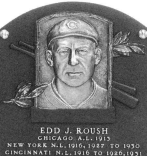

EDD J. ROUSH
CHICAGO A.L. 1913
NEW YORK N.L. 1916, 1927 TO 1930
CINCINNATI N.L. 1916 TO 1926, 1931
LEADING N.L. BATTER IN 1917 AND 1919
BATTED .352 IN 1921, .352 IN 1922, .351
IN 1923, .348 IN 1924. BATTED OVER
.300 -13 SEASONS. LIFETIME BATTING
AVERAGE OF .323. MOST OUTFIELD
PUTOUTS, 410 IN 1920. F.L. 1914-1915.

JOHN GIBSON CLARKSON
WORCESTER, N.L. 1882
CHICAGO, N.L. 1884-87
BOSTON, N.L. 1888-92
CLEVELAND, N.L. 1892-94
PITCHED 4 TO 0 NO-HIT GAME AGAINST
PROVIDENCE IN 1885. WON 328 LOST 175
PCT. 652 LED LEAGUE WITH 53 VICTORIES
IN 1885 (INCLUDING 10 SHUTOUTS) 38 IN
1887, 49 IN 1888 AND 49 IN 1889. HAD
2013 STRIKEOUTS IN 4514 INNINGS.

ELMER HARRISON FLICK
PHILADELPHIA, N.L. 1898-1902
CLEVELAND, A.L. 1902 -1910
OUTFIELDER WHO BATTED .378 FOR
1900 PHILLIES. LEFT LIFETIME MARK
OF .315 FOR 13 SEASONS. A.L. BATTING
CHAMPION IN 1905. LED A.L. IN TRIPLES,
1905-06-07, AND IN STEALS, 1904, TYING
FOR LEADERSHIP AGAIN IN 1906.

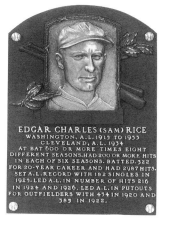

EDGAR CHARLES (SAM) RICE
WASHINGTON, A.L. 1915 TO 1933
CLEVELAND, A.L. 1934
AT BAT 600 OR MORE TIMES EIGHT
DIFFERENT SEASONS. HAD 200 OR MORE HITS
IN EACH OF SIX SEASONS. BATTED .322
FOR 20-YEAR CAREER AND HAD 2987 HITS.
SET A.L. RECORD WITH 182 SINGLES IN
1925. LED A.L. IN NUMBER OF HITS 216
IN 1924 AND 1926. LED A.L. IN PUTOUTS
FOR OUTFIELDERS WITH 454 IN 1920 AND
385 IN 1922.

EPPA RIXEY
PHILADELPHIA, N.L. 1912 TO 1920
CINCINNATI, N.L. 1921 TO 1933
WON 266 LOST 251 PCT. .515 ERA 3.15
SET RECORD FOR MOST VICTORIES BY
LEFT-HANDED PITCHER. LED LEAGUE IN
VICTORIES WITH 25 IN 1922. GAVE ONLY
1082 BASE ON BALLS IN 4494 INNINGS.

LUCIUS BENJAMIN APPLING
CHICAGO A.L. 1930-1950
A.L. BATTING CHAMPION IN 1936 AND 1943.
PLAYED 2,218 GAMES AT SHORTSTOP
FOR MAJOR LEAGUE MARK.
HAD 2,749 HITS.
LIFETIME BATTING AVERAGE OF .310.
LED A.L. IN ASSIST 7 YEARS.
HOLDS A.L. RECORD FOR CHANCES
ACCEPTED BY SHORTSTOP 11,569.

URBAN CLARENCE FABER
CHICAGO A.L. 1914-1933
DURABLE RIGHTHANDER WHO WON 253.
LOST 211. E.R.A. 3.13 GAMES IN TWO DECADES
WITH WHITE SOX. VICTOR IN 3 GAMES
OF 1917 WORLD'S SERIES AGAINST GIANTS.
WON 20 OR MORE GAMES IN SEASON
FOUR TIMES, THREE IN SUCCESSION.

BURLEIGH ARLAND GRIMES
1916 -1934
ONE OF THE GREAT SPITBALL PITCHERS.
WON 270 GAMES, LOST 212 FOR 7 MAJOR
LEAGUE CLUBS, FIVE 20 VICTORY SEASONS.
WON 13 IN ROW FOR GIANTS IN 1927.
MANAGED DODGERS IN 1937 AND 1938.
LIFETIME E.R.A. 3.52.

MILLER JAMES HUGGINS
1904 -1929
MANAGER OF ST. LOUIS CARDINALS
AND NEW YORK YANKEES.
LED YANKEES TO 6 PENNANTS
IN 1921, 1922, 1923, 1926, 1927 AND 1928 AND
3 WORLD SERIES VICTORIES 1923, 1927 AND 1928.
SECOND BASEMAN IN PLAYING DAYS
WITH REDS AND CARDINALS, 1904-1916.

TIMOTHY J. KEEFE
1880 -1893
RIGHTHANDER WHO WON 346 GAMES
FOR TROY, METS, GIANTS AND PHILS
IN ONLY 14 SEASONS.
HIS RECORD STREAK OF 19 STRAIGHT TRIUMPHS
PACED GIANTS TO FLAG IN 1888.
ONE OF FIRST PITCHERS
TO USE A CHANGE OF PACE DELIVERY.

HENRY EMMET MANUSH
1923 -1939
SLUGGING OUTFIELDER
FOR 6 MAJOR LEAGUE CLUBS. BATTING
CHAMPION OF A.L. AT .378 WITH 1926 TIGERS.
LIFETIME AVERAGE OF .330 IN 2,009
MAJOR LEAGUE GAMES. HAD 2,524 HITS.

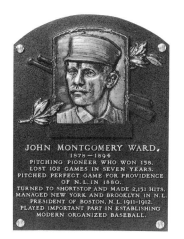

JOHN MONTGOMERY WARD
1878 -1894
PITCHING PIONEER WHO WON 158.
LOST 102 GAMES IN SEVEN YEARS.
PITCHED PERFECT GAME FOR PROVIDENCE
OF N.L. IN 1880.
TURNED TO SHORTSTOP AND MADE 2,151 HITS.
MANAGED NEW YORK AND BROOKLYN IN N.L.
PRESIDENT OF BOSTON, N.L. 1911-1912.
PLAYED IMPORTANT PART IN ESTABLISHING
MODERN ORGANIZED BASEBALL.

JAMES F. (PUD) GALVIN
ST. LOUIS N.A. 1875
BUFFALO N.L. 1879-1885
PITTSBURGH A.A. 1885-1886
PITTSBURGH N.L. 1887-1889 1891-1892
PITTSBURGH P.L. 1890
ST. LOUIS N.L. 1892
WON 365 GAMES. LOST 311.
WHEN ELECTED ONLY FOUR PITCHERS
HAD WON MORE GAMES.
PITCHED NO-HIT GAMES IN 1880 AND 1884.
PITCHED 649 COMPLETE GAMES.

CHARLES DILLON STENGEL
"CASEY"
MANAGED NEW YORK YANKEES 1949-1960.
WON 10 PENNANTS AND 7 WORLD SERIES WITH
NEW YORK YANKEES, ONLY MANAGER TO WIN
5 CONSECUTIVE WORLD SERIES 1949-1953.
PLAYED OUTFIELD 1912-1925 WITH BROOKLYN,
PITTSBURGH, PHILADELPHIA, NEW YORK AND
BOSTON N.L. TEAMS. MANAGED BROOKLYN
1934-1936, BOSTON BRAVES 1938-1943,
NEW YORK METS 1962-1965.

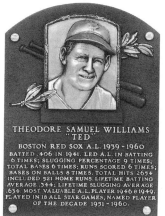

THEODORE SAMUEL WILLIAMS
"TED"
BOSTON RED SOX A.L. 1939-1960
BATTED .406 IN 1941. LED A.L. IN BATTING
6 TIMES; SLUGGING PERCENTAGE 9 TIMES;
TOTAL BASES 6 TIMES; RUNS SCORED 6 TIMES;
BASES ON BALLS 8 TIMES. TOTAL HITS 2654
INCLUDED 521 HOME RUNS. LIFETIME BATTING
AVERAGE .344; LIFETIME SLUGGING AVERAGE
.634. MOST VALUABLE A.L. PLAYER 1946 & 1949.
PLAYED IN 18 ALL STAR GAMES. NAMED PLAYER
OF THE DECADE 1951-1960.

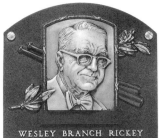

WESLEY BRANCH RICKEY

ST. LOUIS A.L. 1905-1906-1914
NEW YORK A.L. 1907

FOUNDER OF FARM SYSTEM WHICH HE
DEVELOPED FOR ST. LOUIS CARDINALS
AND BROOKLYN DODGERS. COPIED BY ALL
OTHER MAJOR LEAGUE TEAMS.
SERVED AS EXECUTIVE FOR BROWNS,
CARDINALS, DODGERS AND PIRATES.
BROUGHT JACKIE ROBINSON TO BROOKLYN
IN 1947.

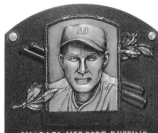

CHARLES HERBERT RUFFING
"RED"

BOSTON, A.L. 1924-1930
NEW YORK, A.L. 1930-1946
CHICAGO, A.L. 1947

WINNER OF 273 GAMES.
WON 20 OR MORE GAMES IN EACH OF FOUR
CONSECUTIVE SEASONS. LED IN COMPLETE
GAMES 1928. TIED IN SHUTOUTS 1938-1939.
WON 7 OUT OF 9 WORLD SERIES DECISIONS.
SELECTED FOR ALL STAR TEAMS
1937-1938-1939

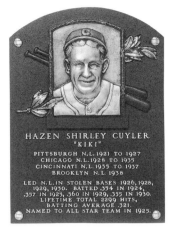

LLOYD JAMES WANER
"LITTLE POISON"

PITTSBURGH N.L., BOSTON N.L.,
CINCINNATI N.L., PHILADELPHIA N.L.,
BROOKLYN N.L. 1927-1945

MADE 223 HITS IN 1927 FIRST YEAR
WITH PITTSBURGH INCLUDING 198 SINGLES,
A MODERN MAJOR LEAGUE RECORD.
LED N.L. IN MOST SINGLES 1927-1928-1929-1931.
LIFE TOTAL 2459 HITS. BATTING AVERAGE .316.
WITH BROTHER PAUL, "BIG POISON"
STARRED IN PITTSBURGH OUTFIELD
1927-1940

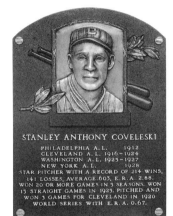

HAZEN SHIRLEY CUYLER
"KIKI"

PITTSBURGH N.L. 1921 TO 1927
CHICAGO N.L. 1928 TO 1935
CINCINNATI N.L. 1935 TO 1937
BROOKLYN N.L. 1938

LED N.L. IN STOLEN BASES 1926, 1928,
1929, 1930. BATTED .354 IN 1924,
.357 IN 1926, .354 IN 1927. LED A.L.
.360 IN 1929, .355 IN 1930.
LIFETIME TOTAL 2299 HITS,
BATTING AVERAGE .321.
NAMED TO ALL STAR TEAM IN 1925.

LEON ALLEN GOSLIN
"GOOSE"

WASHINGTON A.L. 1921 TO 1930, 1933, 1938
ST. LOUIS A.L. 1930 TO 1932
DETROIT A.L. 1934 TO 1937

BATTED .344 IN 1924, .334 IN 1925,
.354 IN 1926, .334 IN 1927. LED A.L.
IN BATTING IN 1928 WITH .379 AVERAGE.
RUNS BATTED IN FOR 1924-129,
HIT .300 OR BETTER 11 YEARS.
LIFETIME TOTAL OF 2735 HITS,
BATTING AVERAGE .316.
MADE 37 HITS IN 5 WORLD SERIES.

JOSEPH MICHAEL MEDWICK
"DUCKY WUCKY"

ST. LOUIS N.L. 1932 TO 1940, 1947, 1948
BROOKLYN N.L. 1940 TO 1943, 1946
NEW YORK N.L. 1943 TO 1945-BOSTON N.L. 1945

LED N.L. IN BATTING IN 1937 WITH .374
AVERAGE, BATTED .353 IN 1935, .351 IN 1936,
.332 IN 1939. LIFETIME TOTAL 2471 HITS,
BATTING AVERAGE .324. NAMED TO ALL STAR
TEAMS 1935-6-7-8-9. MOST VALUABLE PLAYER
N.L. 1937. LED N.L. IN RUNS BATTED IN
AND TWO BASE HITS 1936-7-8.
BATTED .300 OR MORE 15 TIMES.

ROY CAMPANELLA
"CAMPY"

BROOKLYN N.L. 1948 - 1957
MOST VALUABLE PLAYER N.L. 1951-1953-1955
ESTABLISHED RECORDS FOR CATCHERS: MOST
HOME-RUNS IN A SEASON 41, MOST RUNS
BATTED IN 142. SET N.L. RECORD FOR CHANCES
ACCEPTED BY CATCHERS FOR MOST CONSECUTIVE
YEARS 6, TIED RECORD FOR MOST YEARS IN
PUTOUTS 6, CAUGHT 100 OR MORE GAMES FOR
MOST CONSECUTIVE YEARS 9. LED IN FIELDING
AVERAGE FOR CATCHERS 1949-1952-1953-1957.

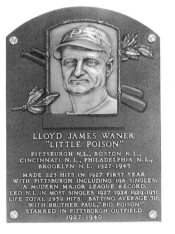

STANLEY ANTHONY COVELESKI

PHILADELPHIA A.L. 1912
CLEVELAND A.L. 1916 - 1924
WASHINGTON A.L. 1925 - 1927
NEW YORK A.L. 1928

STAR PITCHER WITH A RECORD OF 214 WINS,
141 LOSSES, AVERAGE .603, E.R.A. 2.88.
WON 20 OR MORE GAMES IN 5 SEASONS. WON
13 STRAIGHT GAMES IN 1925. PITCHED AND
WON 3 GAMES FOR CLEVELAND IN 1920
WORLD SERIES WITH E.R.A. 0.67.

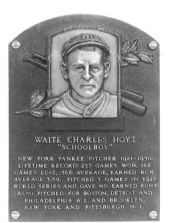

WAITE CHARLES HOYT
"SCHOOLBOY"

NEW YORK YANKEE PITCHER 1921-1930.
LIFETIME RECORD: 237 GAMES WON, 182
GAMES LOST, .566 AVERAGE, EARNED RUN
AVERAGE 3.59. PITCHED 3 GAMES IN 1921
WORLD SERIES AND GAVE NO EARNED RUNS.
ALSO PITCHED FOR BOSTON, DETROIT AND
PHILADELPHIA A.L. AND BROOKLYN,
NEW YORK AND PITTSBURGH N.L.

STANLEY FRANK MUSIAL
"THE MAN"

ST. LOUIS CARDINALS 1941-1963
HOLDS MANY NATIONAL LEAGUE RECORDS,
AMONG THEM: GAMES PLAYED 3026; AT
BAT 10972 TIMES; 3630 HITS; MOST RUNS
SCORED 1949; MOST RUNS BATTED IN 1951;
TOTAL BASES 6134; LED N.L. IN TOTAL
BASES 6 YEARS. SLUGGING PERCENTAGE
6 YEARS. MOST VALUABLE PLAYER 1943-
1946-1948. PLAYED IN 24 ALL-STAR GAMES.
LIFETIME BATTING AVERAGE .331.

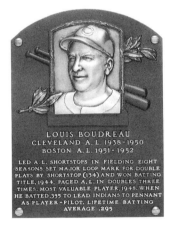

LOUIS BOUDREAU

CLEVELAND A.L. 1938-1950
BOSTON A.L. 1951-1952

LED A.L. SHORTSTOPS IN FIELDING EIGHT
SEASONS. SET MAJOR LOOP MARK FOR DOUBLE
PLAYS BY SHORTSTOP (134) AND WON BATTING
TITLE, 1944. PACED A.L. IN DOUBLES THREE
TIMES. MOST VALUABLE PLAYER, 1948, WHEN
HE BATTED .355 TO LEAD INDIANS TO PENNANT
AS PLAYER-PILOT. LIFETIME BATTING
AVERAGE .295.

EARLE BRYAN COMBS

NEW YORK YANKEES 1924-1935

LEAD-OFF HITTER AND CENTER FIELDER OF
YANKEE CHAMPIONS OF 1926-27-28-32.
LIFETIME BATTING AVERAGE .325. 200 OR
MORE HITS THREE SEASONS. LED LEAGUE
WITH 231 HITS IN 1927 WHILE BATTING .356.
PACED A.L. IN TRIPLES THREE TIMES AND
TWICE LED OUTFIELDERS IN PUTOUTS.
BATTED .350 IN FOUR WORLD SERIES

FORD CHRISTOPHER FRICK

SPORTSWRITER - SPORTSCASTER

FOUNDER OF BASEBALL HALL OF FAME.
PRESIDENT OF NATIONAL LEAGUE 1934-1951.
COMMISSIONER OF BASEBALL 1951-1965.

JESSE JOSEPH (POP) HAINES

CINCINNATI N.L. 1918
ST. LOUIS N.L. 1920-1937

DURABLE RIGHT-HANDER WON 210 GAMES,
LOST 158 - ALL IN HIS 18 YEARS WITH
CARDINALS. GAINED 20-VICTORY CLASS
THREE TIMES. TOSSED 5-0 NO-HITTER
VS. BOSTON, 1924. DEFEATED YANKEES
TWICE IN 1926 WORLD SERIES. LED N.L.
IN COMPLETE GAMES (25), SHUTOUTS (6)
WHILE POSTING 24-10 RECORD, 1927.

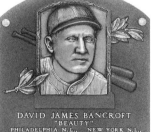

DAVID JAMES BANCROFT
"BEAUTY"

PHILADELPHIA N.L., NEW YORK N.L.,
BOSTON N.L., BROOKLYN N.L.
1915-1930

SET MAJOR LEAGUE RECORD FOR CHANCES
HANDLED BY A SHORTSTOP IN A SEASON - 984
IN 1922. LED LEAGUE IN PUTOUTS FOR SHORT-
STOPS IN 1918-1920-1921-1922. HIT .319 IN 1921,
.321 IN 1922 AND .304 IN 1923 WITH
NEW YORK GIANTS. HIT .319 IN 1925 AND
.311 IN 1926 WITH BOSTON.
PLAYER-MANAGER OF BRAVES, 1924-1927.

JACOB PETER BECKLEY
"OLD EAGLE EYE"
1888 - 1907

FAMED NATIONAL LEAGUE SLUGGER
MADE 2,930 HITS FOR LIFETIME .309 BATTING
AVERAGE. HOLDS RECORD IN MAJORS FOR
FIRST BASE: FOR CHANCES ACCEPTED 25,000
MOST PUTOUTS 23,696, MOST GAMES 2,368.
PLAYED 20 SEASONS WITH PITTSBURGH,
NEW YORK, CINCINNATI AND ST. LOUIS.

CHARLES JAMES HAFEY
"CHICK"

ST. LOUIS N.L. 1924-1931
CINCINNATI N.L. 1932-1937
GREAT OUTFIELDER WHO COMPILED .317
LIFETIME BATTING AVERAGE. LEADING
HITTER OF N.L. WITH .349 IN 1931.
BATTED .329 OR BETTER SIX CONSECUTIVE
YEARS. EQUALLED LEAGUE RECORD OF TEN
HITS IN SUCCESSION, 1929. LIFETIME
FIELDING AVERAGE .971.

HARRY BARTHOLOMEW HOOPER

BOSTON A.L. 1909-1920
CHICAGO A.L. 1921-1925
LEADOFF HITTER AND RIGHT FIELDER OF
1912-15-16-18 WORLD CHAMPION RED SOX.
NOTED FOR SPEED AND STRONG ARM.
COLLECTED 2,466 HITS FOR .281 CAREER
AVERAGE. HAD 3,981 PUTOUTS AND 344
ASSISTS. LIFETIME FIELDING AVERAGE .966.

JOSEPH JAMES KELLEY
1891-1908

STANDOUT HITTER AND LEFT FIELDER OF
CHAMPION 1894-95-96 BALTIMORE ORIOLES
AND 1899-1900 BROOKLYN SUPERBAS. BATTED
OVER .300 FOR 11 CONSECUTIVE YEARS WITH
HIGH OF .391 IN 1894. EQUALLED RECORD
WITH 9 HITS IN 9 AT-BATS IN DOUBLEHEADER.
ALSO PLAYED FOR BOSTON, PITTSBURGH AND
CINCINNATI OF N.L. AND BALTIMORE OF A.L.
MANAGED CINCINNATI 1902 TO 1905 AND
BOSTON N.L. IN 1908.

RICHARD WILLIAM MARQUARD
"RUBE"

NEW YORK N.L.,   BROOKLYN N.L.
CINCINNATI N.L.,   BOSTON N.L.
          1908-1925
THREE-TIME 20-GAME WINNER WITH
GIANT CHAMPIONS OF 1911-12-13. TIED ALL-TIME
RECORD WITH 19 VICTORIES IN A ROW WHILE
WINNING 26 AND LOSING 11 IN 1912. LED
N.L. IN WINNING PERCENTAGE AND
STRIKEOUTS IN 1911. TIED FOR MOST
VICTORIES, 1912. HURLED NO-HIT GAME
AGAINST DODGERS IN 1915.

LEROY ROBERT PAIGE
"SATCHEL"

NEGRO LEAGUES   1926-1947
CLEVELAND A.L.   1948-1949
ST. LOUIS A.L.   1951-1953
KANSAS CITY A.L.   1965
PAIGE WAS ONE OF THE GREATEST STARS
TO PLAY IN THE NEGRO BASEBALL LEAGUES.
THRILLED MILLIONS OF PEOPLE AND WON
HUNDREDS OF GAMES. STRUCK OUT 21 MAJOR
LEAGUERS IN AN EXHIBITION GAME. HELPED
PITCH CLEVELAND INDIANS TO THE 1948
PENNANT IN HIS FIRST BIG LEAGUE YEAR
AT AGE 42. HIS PITCHING WAS A LEGEND
AMONG MAJOR LEAGUE HITTERS.

GEORGE MARTIN WEISS

MASTER BUILDER OF CHAMPIONSHIP TEAMS.
WAS CLUB EXECUTIVE IN MINORS AND
MAJORS FROM 1919 TO 1966.
DEVELOPED BEST MINOR LEAGUE CHAIN
IN GAME AS NEW YORK YANKEE FARM
MANAGER, 1932-1947. GENERAL MANAGER
OF THE YANKEES FROM 1947-1960 WHICH
WON 10 PENNANTS AND 7 WORLD SERIES
DURING THIS PERIOD.
PRESIDENT OF THE NEW YORK METS
1961-1966.

LAWRENCE PETER BERRA
"YOGI"

NEW YORK, A.L. 1946-1963
NEW YORK, N.L. 1965
PLAYED ON MORE PENNANT-WINNERS (14) AND
WORLD CHAMPIONS (10) THAN ANY PLAYER IN
HISTORY. HAD 358 HOME RUNS AND LIFETIME
.285 BATTING AVERAGE. SET MANY RECORDS
FOR CATCHERS, INCLUDING 148 CONSECUTIVE
GAMES WITHOUT AN ERROR. VOTED A.L. MOST
VALUABLE PLAYER 1951-54-55. MANAGED
YANKEES TO PENNANT IN 1964.

JOSHUA (JOSH) GIBSON

NEGRO LEAGUES 1930-1946
CONSIDERED GREATEST SLUGGER IN NEGRO
BASEBALL LEAGUES. POWER-HITTING CATCHER
WHO HIT ALMOST 800 HOME RUNS IN LEAGUE
AND INDEPENDENT BASEBALL DURING HIS
17-YEAR CAREER. CREDITED WITH HAVING
BEEN NEGRO NATIONAL LEAGUE BATTING
CHAMPION IN 1936-38-42-43.

VERNON LOUIS GOMEZ
"LEFTY"

NEW YORK A.L. 1930-1942
WASHINGTON A.L. 1943
WON 20 OR MORE GAMES FOUR TIMES IN
HELPING YANKEES TO WIN SEVEN
PENNANTS. LED A.L. WITH 26-5 RECORD,
2.33 EARNED RUN AVERAGE IN 1934 AND
WITH 21 VICTORIES AND 2.33 ERA IN
1937. PACED A.L. IN WINNING PCT. TWICE,
STRIKEOUTS THREE TIMES. SET WORLD
SERIES MARK BY WINNING 6 GAMES
WITHOUT A LOSS.

WILLIAM HARRIDGE

PRESIDENT OF AMERICAN LEAGUE 1931-1958
AFTER SERVING AS SECRETARY OF
LEAGUE 1927-1931 AND SECRETARY TO
A.L. PRESIDENT 1911-1927.
CHAIRMAN OF AMERICAN LEAGUE
BOARD OF DIRECTORS 1958-1971.

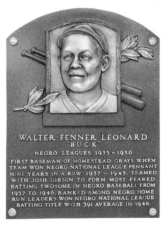

SANFORD KOUFAX
"SANDY"

BROOKLYN N.L. 1955-1957
LOS ANGELES N.L. 1958-1966
SET ALL-TIME RECORDS WITH 4 NO-HITTERS
IN 4 YEARS, CAPPED BY 1965 PERFECT GAME,
AND BY CAPTURING EARNED-RUN TITLE FIVE
SEASONS IN A ROW, 1962-1966. WON 25 OR
MORE GAMES THREE TIMES, HAD 11 SHUTOUTS
IN 1963. STRIKEOUT LEADER FOUR TIMES,
WITH RECORD 382 IN 1965. FANNED 18 IN A
GAME TWICE. MOST VALUABLE PLAYER 1963.
CY YOUNG AWARD WINNER 1963-65-66.

WALTER FENNER LEONARD
"BUCK"

NEGRO LEAGUES 1933-1950
FIRST BASEMAN OF HOMESTEAD GRAYS WHEN
TEAM WON NEGRO NATIONAL LEAGUE PENNANT
NINE YEARS IN A ROW. TEAMED
WITH JOSH GIBSON TO FORM MOST FEARED
BATTING TWOSOME IN NEGRO BASEBALL FROM
1937 TO 1946. RANKED AMONG NEGRO HOME
RUN LEADERS. WON NEGRO NATIONAL LEAGUE
BATTING TITLE WITH .391 AVERAGE IN 1948.

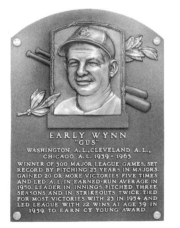

EARLY WYNN
"GUS"

WASHINGTON A.L., CLEVELAND A.L.,
CHICAGO A.L. 1939-1963
WINNER OF 300 MAJOR LEAGUE GAMES, SET
RECORD BY PITCHING 23 YEARS IN MAJORS.
GAINED 20 OR MORE VICTORIES FIVE TIMES
AND LED A.L. IN EARNED-RUN AVERAGE IN
1950. LEADER IN INNINGS PITCHED THREE
SEASONS AND IN STRIKEOUTS TWICE. TIED
FOR MOST VICTORIES WITH 23 IN 1954 AND
LED LEAGUE WITH 22 WINS AT AGE 39 IN
1959 TO EARN CY YOUNG AWARD.

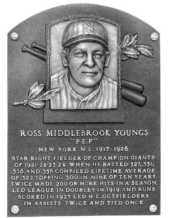

ROSS MIDDLEBROOK YOUNGS
"PEP"

NEW YORK N.L. 1917-1926
STAR RIGHT FIELDER OF CHAMPION GIANTS
OF 1921-22-23-24 WHEN HE BATTED .327, .331,
.336, AND .356. COMPILED LIFETIME AVERAGE
OF .322, TOPPING .300 IN NINE OF TEN YEARS.
TWICE MADE 200 OR MORE HITS IN A SEASON.
LED LEAGUE IN DOUBLES IN 1919 AND RUNS
SCORED IN 1923. LED N.L. OUTFIELDERS
IN ASSISTS TWICE AND TIED ONCE.

ROBERTO WALKER CLEMENTE

PITTSBURGH N.L. 1955-1972
MEMBER OF EXCLUSIVE 3,000-HIT CLUB. LED
NATIONAL LEAGUE IN BATTING FOUR TIMES.
HAD FOUR SEASONS WITH 200 OR MORE HITS
WHILE POSTING LIFETIME .317 AVERAGE AND
240 HOME RUNS. WON MOST VALUABLE PLAYER
AWARD 1966. RIFLE-ARMED DEFENSIVE STAR
SET N.L. MARK BY PACING OUTFIELDERS IN
ASSISTS FIVE YEARS. BATTED .362 IN TWO
WORLD SERIES, HITTING IN ALL 14 GAMES.

WILLIAM GEORGE EVANS

UMPIRE AND EXECUTIVE
EMPLOYED BY AMERICAN LEAGUE IN
1906 AT AGE 22, MAKING HIM YOUNGEST
UMPIRE EVER IN MAJORS. SERVED ON A.L.
STAFF THROUGH 1927. OFFICIATED IN
SIX WORLD SERIES. GENERAL MANAGER
OF CLEVELAND INDIANS, 1927-1935. FARM
DIRECTOR OF BOSTON RED SOX 1936-1940.
PRESIDENT OF SOUTHERN ASSOCIATION,
1942-1946. GENERAL MANAGER OF
DETROIT TIGERS, 1947-1951.

MONFORD (MONTE) IRVIN
NEGRO LEAGUES 1937-1948
NEW YORK N.L., CHICAGO N.L.,
1949-1956
REGARDED AS ONE OF NEGRO LEAGUES' BEST
HITTERS. STAR SLUGGER OF NEWARK EAGLES
WON 1946 NEGRO LEAGUE BATTING TITLE.
LED N.L. IN RUNS BATTED IN AND PACED
"MIRACLE GIANTS" IN HITTING IN 1951
DRIVE TO PENNANT. BATTED .458 AND
STOLE HOME IN 1951 WORLD SERIES.

GEORGE LANGE KELLY
"HIGHPOCKETS"
NEW YORK N.L., PITTSBURGH N.L.
CINCINNATI N.L., CHICAGO N.L.
BROOKLYN, N.L., 1915-1930 AND 1932
ESTABLISHED MAJOR LEAGUE RECORD BY
HITTING SEVEN HOME RUNS IN SIX CONSECUTIVE
GAMES (1924). RAPPED HOMERS IN THREE
SUCCESSIVE INNINGS (1923). DROVE IN MORE THAN
100 RUNS FOUR CONSECUTIVE YEARS, 1921-24.
SET LEAGUE RECORDS FOR CHANCES ACCEPTED
(1,862) AND PUTOUTS (1,759) BY FIRST BASEMAN
IN 1920. ALSO LED IN CHANCES ACCEPTED
1921-22-23.

WARREN EDWARD SPAHN
BOSTON N.L., MILWAUKEE N.L.,
NEW YORK N.L., SAN FRANCISCO N.L.,
1942-1965
BECAME FIFTH BIGGEST WINNER IN MAJORS'
HISTORY WITH 363 VICTORIES. MOST
VICTORIES AND 106 LOSSES BY A LEFT-HANDER. WON 20
OR MORE GAMES 13 SEASONS, SIX IN A ROW.
SET ALL-TIME RECORDS FOR YEARS LEADING
LEAGUE IN VICTORIES (8) AND COMPLETE
GAMES (9). ALSO N.L. CAREER HIGHS WITH
665 GAMES STARTED; 5,264 INNINGS;
2,583 STRIKEOUTS. PITCHED NO-HITTER
IN 1960, ANOTHER IN 1961.

MICHAEL FRANCIS WELCH
"SMILING MICKEY"
TROY N.L. 1880-1882
NEW YORK N.L. 1883-1892
CREDITED WITH MORE THAN 300 VICTORIES
DURING 13 SEASONS IN MAJORS. WON 17
GAMES IN A ROW IN 1885 WHILE COMPILING
44-11 RECORD FOR LEAGUE-LEADING .800
WINNING PERCENTAGE. TOPPED 30-VICTORY
TOTAL IN FOUR YEARS.

JAMES THOMAS BELL
"COOL PAPA"
NEGRO LEAGUES 1922-1950
COMBINED SPEED, DARING AND BATTING
SKILL TO RANK AMONG BEST PLAYERS
IN NEGRO LEAGUES. CONTEMPORARIES
RATED HIM FASTEST MAN ON BASE
PATHS. HIT OVER .300 REGULARLY,
TOPPING .400 ON OCCASION. PLAYED
29 SUMMERS AND 21 WINTERS
OF PROFESSIONAL BASEBALL.

JAMES LE ROY BOTTOMLEY
"SUNNY JIM"
ST. LOUIS N.L., CINCINNATI N.L.,
ST. LOUIS A.L. 1922-1937
SUPERB CLUTCH HITTER. DROVE IN
100 OR MORE RUNS SIX YEARS IN ROW,
1924-1929, LEADING LEAGUE TWICE.
ESTABLISHED RECORD BY BATTING IN
12 RUNS IN ONE GAME. MOST VALUABLE
PLAYER 1928. HIT SEVEN HOMERS
IN SPAN OF FIVE GAMES IN 1929. HAD
LIFETIME .310 BATTING AVERAGE.

JOHN BERTRAND CONLAN
"JOCKO"
UMPIRE
NATIONAL LEAGUE 1941-1965
SUNNY DISPOSITION, ACCURACY AND
HUSTLE EARNED HIM RATING AS STANDOUT
UMPIRE AND HE WON RESPECT OF
PLAYERS AND MANAGERS WITH HIS
FAIRNESS. ONLY ARBITER TO WORK IN
EACH OF FIRST FOUR N.L. PENNANT
PLAYOFFS. CHOSEN FOR SIX WORLD SERIES
AND SIX ALL-STAR GAMES.

EDWARD CHARLES FORD
"WHITEY"
NEW YORK A.L. 1950-1967
POSTED BEST WINNING PERCENTAGE (.690)
AMONG TWENTIETH CENTURY PITCHERS
WITH 200 OR MORE DECISIONS. HAD 236
VICTORIES AND 106 LOSSES. LIFETIME EARNED
RUN AVERAGE 2.74. PACED A.L. IN VICTORIES
AND WINNING PCT. THREE TIMES AND IN
EARNED-RUN AVERAGE AND SHUTOUTS
TWICE. WON CY YOUNG AWARD IN 1961. SET
WORLD SERIES STANDARDS FOR GAMES
PITCHED, 22; INNINGS, 146; WINS, 10. AND
STRIKEOUTS, 94, AND WITH 33⅔ CONSECUTIVE
SCORELESS INNINGS.

MICKEY CHARLES MANTLE
NEW YORK A.L. 1951-1968
HIT 536 HOME RUNS. WON LEAGUE HOMER TITLE
AND SLUGGING CROWN FOUR TIMES. MADE
2415 HITS. BATTED .300 OR OVER IN EACH
OF TEN YEARS WITH TOP OF .365 IN 1957.
TOPPED A.L. IN WALKS FIVE YEARS AND
IN RUNS SCORED SIX SEASONS. VOTED
MOST VALUABLE PLAYER 1956-57-62. NAMED
ON 20 A.L. ALL-STAR TEAMS. SET WORLD
SERIES RECORDS FOR HOMERS, 18; RUNS, 42;
RUNS BATTED IN, 40; TOTAL BASES, 123;
AND BASES ON BALLS, 43.

SAMUEL LUTHER THOMPSON
DETROIT N.L., PHILADELPHIA N.L.
1885-1898; DETROIT A.L. 1906
ONE OF THE FOREMOST SLUGGERS OF
HIS DAY. LIFETIME BATTING AVERAGE
.336. BATTED BETTER THAN .400 TWICE.
GREAT CLUTCH HITTER. COLLECTED
200 OR MORE HITS IN A SEASON THREE
TIMES. TOPPED N.L. IN HOME RUNS AND
RUNS BATTED IN TWICE.

HOWARD EARL AVERILL
"ROCK"
CLEVELAND A.L. DETROIT A.L.
BOSTON N.L. 1929-1941
COMPILED .318 CAREER BATTING AVERAGE
AND HIT 238 HOME RUNS. TWICE MADE
MORE THAN 200 HITS IN SEASON, PACING
LEAGUE WITH 232 IN 1936. DROVE IN
100 OR MORE RUNS FIVE TIMES. RAPPED
FOUR HOMERS, THREE CONSECUTIVELY
IN FIRST GAME AND BATTED IN 11 RUNS
IN 1930 TWIN-BILL.

STANLEY RAYMOND HARRIS
"BUCKY"
SERVED 40 YEARS IN MAJORS AS PLAYER,
MANAGER AND EXECUTIVE, INCLUDING 29 AS
PILOT. SLICK SECOND SACKER EARNED TAG
OF "BOY WONDER" BY GUIDING WASHINGTON
TO 1924 WORLD TITLE AS 27-YEAR-OLD IN
DEBUT AS PLAYER-PILOT. WON A.L. FLAG
AGAIN IN 1925. LED 1947 YANKEES TO
WORLD TITLE. MANAGED DETROIT, BOSTON
RED SOX AND PHILADELPHIA PHILLIES.

WILLIAM JENNINGS HERMAN
CHICAGO, N.L.   BROOKLYN, N.L.
BOSTON, N.L.   PITTSBURGH, N.L.
1931 - 1947
MASTER OF HIT-AND-RUN PLAY. OWNED .304
LIFETIME BATTING AVERAGE. MADE 200 OR
MORE HITS IN SEASON THREE TIMES. LED
N.L. IN HITS (227) AND DOUBLES (57)
IN 1935. SET MAJOR LEAGUE RECORD FOR
SECOND BASEMEN WITH FIVE SEASONS OF
HANDLING 900 OR MORE CHANCES AND N.L.
MARK OF 466 PUTOUTS IN 1933. LED LOOP
KEYSTONERS IN PUTOUTS SEVEN TIMES.

WILLIAM JULIUS JOHNSON
"JUDY"
NEGRO LEAGUES 1923-1937
CONSIDERED BEST THIRD BASEMAN OF HIS
DAY IN NEGRO LEAGUES. OUTSTANDING AS
FIELDER AND EXCELLENT CLUTCH HITTER
WHO BATTED OVER .300 MOST OF CAREER.
HELPED HILLDALE TEAM WIN THREE FLAGS
IN ROW, 1923-24-25. ALSO PLAYED FOR
1935 CHAMPION PITTSBURGH CRAWFORDS.

RALPH McPHERRAN KINER
PITTSBURGH, N.L. CHICAGO, N.L.
CLEVELAND, A.L. 1946-1955
HIT 369 HOME RUNS AND AVERAGED BETTER
THAN 100 RUNS BATTED IN PER SEASON IN
TEN-YEAR CAREER. ONLY PLAYER TO LEAD HIS
LEAGUE OR SHARE LEAD IN HOMERS SEVEN
YEARS IN A ROW, 1946-1952. TWICE HAD
MORE THAN 50 IN SEASON. SET N.L. MARK
OF 101 FOUR-BAGGERS IN TWO SUCCESSIVE
YEARS WITH 54 IN 1949 AND 47 IN 1950.
LED N.L. IN SLUGGING PCT. THREE TIMES.

OSCAR McKINLEY CHARLESTON
NEGRO LEAGUES 1915-1944
RATED AMONG ALL-TIME GREATS OF NEGRO
LEAGUES. VERSATILE STAR BATTED WELL
OVER .300 MOST YEARS. SPEED, STRONG
ARM AND FIELDING INSTINCTS MADE HIM
STANDOUT CENTER FIELDER. LATER MOVED
TO FIRST BASE. ALSO MANAGED SEVERAL
TEAMS DURING 40 YEARS IN NEGRO BASEBALL.

ROGER CONNOR
TROY N.L., NEW YORK N.L.,
NEW YORK P.L., PHILADELPHIA N.L.,
ST. LOUIS N.L. 1880-1897
POWER-HITTING STAR OF DEAD-BALL ERA.
SET CAREER HOME RUN RECORD FOR 19TH
CENTURY PLAYERS. WON LEAGUE BATTING
CHAMPIONSHIP IN 1885 AND HIT .300 OR
BETTER 12 TIMES. HIT THREE HOMERS
IN A GAME IN 1888 AND MADE SIX HITS IN
SIX AT-BATS IN A GAME IN 1895.

ROBERT CAL HUBBARD
UMPIRE
AMERICAN LEAGUE 1936-1951
ONE OF MOST RESPECTED, EFFICIENT AND
AUTHORITATIVE UMPIRES IN HISTORY OF
MAJORS. GENTLE GIANT BOASTED SPECIAL
KNACK FOR DEALING WITH SITUATIONS ON
FIELD. WORKED FOUR WORLD SERIES AND
THREE ALL-STAR GAMES. SERVED AS LEAGUE'S
ASSISTANT UMPIRE SUPERVISOR IN 1952 AND AS
UMPIRE SUPERVISOR FROM 1953 TO 1969.

ROBERT GRANVILLE LEMON
CLEVELAND A.L.,
1941-1942 AND 1946-1958
GAINED COVETED 20-VICTORY CLASS SEVEN
TIMES IN NINE-YEAR SPAN. BECAME ONLY
SIXTH PITCHER IN 20TH CENTURY TO POST
20 OR MORE WINS IN SEVEN SEASONS. HAD
207-128 RECORD FOR CAREER. PACED A.L.
OR TIED FOR LEAD IN VICTORIES THREE
TIMES, SHUTOUTS ONCE, INNINGS PITCHED
FOUR SEASONS AND COMPLETE GAMES FIVE
YEARS. HURLED NO-HITTER IN 1948.

FREDERICK CHARLES LINDSTROM
NEW YORK N.L., PITTSBURGH N.L.,
CHICAGO N.L., BROOKLYN N.L.,
1924-1936
COMPILED LIFETIME .311 BATTING MARK,
INCLUDING SEVEN SEASONS OF .300 OR
BETTER. ONE OF ONLY THREE PLAYERS
TO AMASS 230 OR MORE HITS A YEAR TWICE.
AS YOUNGEST PLAYER (AGE 18) IN WORLD
SERIES HISTORY, HE TIED RECORD WITH
FOUR HITS IN GAME IN 1924. EQUALLED
MAJOR LEAGUE RECORD BY COLLECTING
NINE HITS IN 1928 DOUBLEHEADER.

ROBIN EVAN ROBERTS
PHILADELPHIA N.L., BALTIMORE A.L.,
HOUSTON N.L., CHICAGO N.L.,
1948-1966
WON 286 GAMES THOUGH USUALLY PITCHING
FOR SECOND-DIVISION TEAMS. GAINED 20 OR
MORE VICTORIES SIX YEARS IN A ROW,
1950-1955, AND TOPPED LEAGUE OR TIED
FOR LEAD IN VICTORIES FOUR SUCCESSIVE
SEASONS. LED N.L. FIVE CONSECUTIVE
YEARS IN INNINGS PITCHED, 1951-1955,
AND COMPLETE GAMES, 1952-1956. LED IN
SHUTOUTS AND STRIKEOUTS TWICE EACH.

ERNEST BANKS
"MR. CUB"
CHICAGO N.L., 1953-1971
HIT 512 CAREER HOMERS WITH MORE THAN
40 IN A SEASON FIVE TIMES. HAD RECORD
FIVE GRAND-SLAMS IN 1955. FIRST TO BE
ELECTED N.L. MOST VALUABLE PLAYER TWO
SUCCESSIVE YEARS, 1958-59. LED LEAGUE
IN HOME RUNS AND RUNS BATTED IN TWICE
AND SLUGGING PCT. ONCE. ESTABLISHED
RECORDS FOR MOST HOMERS IN SEASON BY
SHORTSTOP (47 IN 1958) AND FOR FEWEST
ERRORS (12) AND BEST FIELDING AVERAGE
(.985) BY A SHORTSTOP IN 1959.

MARTIN DIHIGO
"EL MAESTRO"
NEGRO LEAGUES 1923-1947
MOST VERSATILE OF NEGRO LEAGUE STARS.
PLAYED IN BOTH SUMMER AND WINTER
BALL MOST OF CAREER, REGISTERED MORE
THAN 260 VICTORIES AS PITCHER. WHEN NOT
ON MOUND HE PLAYED OUTFIELD OR INFIELD.
USUALLY BATTING WELL OVER .300. ALSO
MANAGED DURING AND AFTER PLAYING DAYS.

JOHN HENRY LLOYD
"POP"
NEGRO LEAGUES 1906-1932
REGARDED AS FINEST SHORTSTOP TO PLAY
IN NEGRO BASEBALL. SCIENTIFIC HITTER
BATTED OVER .400 SEVERAL TIMES DURING
HIS 27-YEAR CAREER. PERSONIFIED BEST
QUALITIES OF ATHLETE BOTH ON AND OFF
FIELD. INSTRUMENTAL IN HELPING OPEN
YANKEE STADIUM TO NEGRO BASEBALL IN
1930. MANAGED MORE THAN TEN SEASONS.

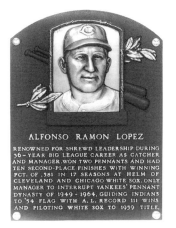

ALFONSO RAMON LOPEZ
RENOWNED FOR SHREWD LEADERSHIP DURING
36-YEAR BIG LEAGUE CAREER AS CATCHER
AND MANAGER. WON TWO PENNANTS AND HAD
TEN SECOND-PLACE FINISHES WITH WINNING
PCT. OF .581 IN 17 SEASONS AT HELM OF
CLEVELAND AND CHICAGO WHITE SOX. ONLY
MANAGER TO INTERRUPT YANKEES' PENNANT
DYNASTY OF 1949-1964, GUIDING INDIANS
TO '54 FLAG WITH A.L. RECORD 111 WINS
AND PILOTING WHITE SOX TO 1959 TITLE.

AMOS WILSON RUSIE
"THE HOOSIER THUNDERBOLT"
INDIANAPOLIS N.L., NEW YORK N.L.,
CINCINNATI N.L., 1889-1895
1897-1898 AND 1901
GENERALLY CONSIDERED FIREBALL KING OF
NINETEENTH-CENTURY MOUNDSMEN. NOTCHED
BETTER THAN 240 VICTORIES IN TEN-YEAR
CAREER. ACHIEVED 30-VICTORY MARK FOUR
YEARS IN ROW AND WON 20 OR MORE GAMES
EIGHT SUCCESSIVE TIMES. LED LEAGUE IN
STRIKEOUTS FIVE YEARS AND LED OR TIED
FOR MOST SHUTOUTS FIVE TIMES.

JOSEPH WHEELER SEWELL
CLEVELAND A.L., NEW YORK A.L.,
1920-1933
POSTED LIFETIME .312 BATTING AVERAGE,
TOPPING .300 IN TEN OF 14 YEARS. MOST
DIFFICULT MAN TO STRIKE OUT IN GAME'S
HISTORY. CREATED RECORDS WITH: FEWEST
CAREER STRIKEOUTS (114), FOUR SEASONS
OF FOUR WHIFFS OR LESS IN 500 AT-BATS
AND 115 GAMES IN ROW WITHOUT FANNING.
LED A.L. SHORTSTOPS IN FIELDING TWICE
AND IN PUTOUTS AND ASSISTS FOUR TIMES.

ADRIAN (ADDIE) JOSS
CLEVELAND A.L., 1902-1910
ONE OF PREMIER PITCHERS OF AMERICAN
LEAGUE'S FIRST DECADE. SPEED, SHARP
CONTROL HELPED HIM TO WIN 20 OR MORE
GAMES FOUR SEASONS IN A ROW. POSTED
LEAGUE-LEADING 27 VICTORIES AND THREE
ONE-HITTERS IN 1907. HURLED PERFECT
GAME IN 1908. HAD ANOTHER NO-HITTER
IN 1910. CREDITED WITH 45 SHUTOUTS
AMONG HIS 160 CAREER VICTORIES.

LELAND STANFORD MacPHAIL
"LARRY"
DYNAMIC, INNOVATIVE EXECUTIVE MADE HIS
MARK AS PROGRESSIVE HEAD OF THREE CLUBS-
CINCINNATI REDS, BROOKLYN DODGERS AND
NEW YORK YANKEES-FROM 1933 TO 1947. WON
CHAMPIONSHIPS IN BOTH LEAGUES--WITH
DODGERS IN 1941 AND YANKEES IN 1947.
PIONEERED NIGHT BALL AT CINCINNATI IN
1935, ALSO INSTALLED LIGHTS AT EBBETS FIELD
AND YANKEE STADIUM. ORIGINATED PLANE
TRAVEL BY PLAYING PERSONNEL AND IDEA
OF STADIUM CLUB. HELPED SET UP EMPLOYEE
AND PLAYER PENSION PLANS.

EDWIN LEE MATHEWS
BOSTON N.L., MILWAUKEE N.L.,
ATLANTA N.L., HOUSTON N.L.,
DETROIT A.L., 1952-1968
BECAME SEVENTH PLAYER IN MAJOR LEAGUE
HISTORY TO HIT 500 HOME RUNS. FINISHED
CAREER WITH 512. HIT 30 OR MORE HOMERS
NINE YEARS IN ROW, 1953-1961, REACHING
40 MARK FOUR TIMES. ESTABLISHED RECORD
FOR HOMERS IN SEASON BY THIRD BASEMAN
WITH 47 IN 1953. LED N.L. IN HOME RUNS
TWICE AND IN WALKS FOUR TIMES. HAD FIVE
SEASONS OF 100 OR MORE RUNS BATTED IN.

WARREN CRANDALL GILES
DEVOTED 50 YEARS TO BASEBALL AS CLUB
AND LEAGUE EXECUTIVE, INCLUDING 33 IN
MAJOR LEAGUES. HEADED CINCINNATI REDS
FROM 1937 TO 1951, CAPTURING PENNANTS
IN 1939-40. NATIONAL LEAGUE PRESIDENT
LONGER THAN ANY OTHER MAN - 18 YEARS
FROM 1951 THROUGH 1969. PRESIDED OVER
FRANCHISE SHIFTS TO PACIFIC COAST AND
EXPANSION TO 12 CLUBS AND INTO CANADA
AS N.L. ENJOYED UNPRECEDENTED
PROSPERITY.

WILLIE HOWARD MAYS, Jr.
"THE SAY HEY KID"
NEW YORK N.L., SAN FRANCISCO N.L.,
NEW YORK N.L., 1951-1973
ONE OF BASEBALL'S MOST COLORFUL AND
EXCITING STARS. EXCELLED IN ALL PHASES OF
THE GAME. THIRD IN HOMERS (660), RUNS (2,062)
AND TOTAL BASES (6,066). SEVENTH IN HITS
(3,283) AND RBI'S (1,903). FIRST IN PUTOUTS
BY OUTFIELDER (7,095). FIRST TO GET BOTH
300 HOMERS AND 300 STEALS. LED LEAGUE IN
BATTING ONCE, SLUGGING FIVE TIMES. HOME
RUNS AND STEALS FOUR SEASONS. VOTED N.L.
MVP IN 1954 AND 1965. PLAYED IN 24
ALL-STAR GAMES - A RECORD.

LEWIS ROBERT WILSON
"HACK"
NEW YORK N.L., CHICAGO N.L.,
BROOKLYN N.L., PHILADELPHIA N.L.,
1923 - 1934
ESTABLISHED MAJOR LEAGUE RECORD OF 190
RUNS BATTED IN AND NATIONAL LEAGUE HIGH
OF 56 HOMERS IN 1930. LED OR TIED FOR N.L.
HOMER TITLE FOUR TIMES. COMPILED LIFETIME
.307 BATTING AVERAGE AND DROVE IN 100 OR
MORE RUNS SIX YEARS. HIT TWO HOMERS IN
INNING IN 1925 AND THREE IN GAME IN 1930.

ALBERT WILLIAM KALINE
DETROIT A.L., 1953 - 1974
TWELFTH PLAYER TO REACH ELITE 3,000-HIT
PLATEAU, SOCKED 399 HOMERS AND ATTAINED
.297 CAREER AVERAGE, WITH NINE YEARS IN
.300 CLASS. FINISHED IN ALL-TIME TOP 15
WITH 2,834 GAMES, 3,007 HITS, 1,583 RUNS
BATTED IN AND 4,852 TOTAL BASES. PLAYED
100 OR MORE GAMES 20 YEARS AND HAD 242
CONSECUTIVE ERRORLESS GAMES IN OUTFIELD,
1970-1972, FOR A.L. RECORD. LED IN HITS
AND WON BATTING TITLE IN 1955 AT AGE 20.

CHARLES HERBERT KLEIN
"CHUCK"
PHILADELPHIA N.L., CHICAGO N.L.,
PITTSBURGH N.L., 1928 - 1944
ONLY PLAYER IN 20TH CENTURY TO COLLECT
200 OR MORE HITS IN EACH OF FIRST FIVE
FULL MAJOR LEAGUE SEASONS. ATTAINED
.320 CAREER AVERAGE AND 300 HOME RUNS.
LED N.L. IN HOMERS AND RUNS BATTED IN
TIMES AND IN RUNS SCORED AND SLUGGING
PCT. THREE EACH. SET LEAGUE RECORD FOR
MOST EXTRA BASE HITS IN SEASON--107 IN 1932.
VOTED MOST VALUABLE PLAYER IN 1932.

EDWIN DONALD SNIDER
"DUKE"
BROOKLYN N.L., LOS ANGELES N.L.,
NEW YORK N.L., SAN FRANCISCO N.L.,
1947 - 1964
HIT 407 CAREER HOME RUNS AND TIED N.L.
RECORD WITH 40 OR MORE ROUND-TRIPPERS
FIVE YEARS IN A ROW, 1953 - 1957. BATTED .300
OR BETTER SEVEN TIMES IN COMPILING .295
LIFETIME AVERAGE. TOPPED LEAGUE IN SLUGG-
ING PCT. TWICE AND TOTAL BASES THREE TIMES.
FIRST TO HIT FOUR HOMERS IN A WORLD SERIES
TWICE -- IN 1952 AND 1955. SET N.L.
RECORD FOR SERIES HOMERS (11).

THOMAS AUSTIN YAWKEY
GAVE BASEBALL MORE THAN FOUR DECADES OF
DEDICATED SERVICE AS OWNER-PRESIDENT OF
BOSTON RED SOX FROM 1933 TO 1976. RATED
ONE OF SPORT'S FINEST BENEFACTORS. SET
PRECEDENT FOR A.L. IN 1936 AS FIRST TO
HAVE TEAM TRAVEL BY PLANE. HIS CLUB WON
PENNANTS IN 1946, 1967 AND 1975 -- AND
NARROWLY MISSED IN 1948, 1949 AND 1972.
VICE-PRESIDENT OF A.L. FROM 1956 TO 1973.

ANDREW (RUBE) FOSTER
RATED FOREMOST MANAGER AND EXECUTIVE IN
HISTORY OF NEGRO LEAGUES. ACCLAIMED TOP
PITCHER IN BLACK BASEBALL FOR NEARLY A
DECADE IN EARLY 1900S. FORMED CHICAGO
AMERICAN GIANTS IN 1911 AND BUILT THEM
INTO MIDWEST'S DOMINANT BLACK TEAM. IN
1920 HE ORGANIZED NEGRO NATIONAL LEAGUE,
HEADED LEAGUE AND MANAGED CHICAGO TEAM
UNTIL RETIREMENT FOLLOWING 1926 SEASON.

ROBERT GIBSON
ST. LOUIS N.L., 1959 - 1975
FIVE-TIME 20-GAME WINNER. HIS 3,117
STRIKEOUTS MADE HIM ONLY 2ND PITCHER TO
REACH 3,000. FIRST TO FAN 200 OR MORE IN
A SEASON 9 TIMES. SET N.L. MARK WITH 1.12
ERA IN 1968, HURLING 13 SHUTOUTS. TWICE
WORLD SERIES MVP, SETTING RECORDS FOR
CONSECUTIVE VICTORIES (7), CONSECUTIVE
COMPLETE GAMES (8), AND STRIKEOUTS IN A
GAME (17) AND A SERIES (35). VOTED N.L.
MVP IN 1968 AND CY YOUNG AWARD WINNER IN
1968 AND 1970. WON NINE GOLD GLOVE AWARDS.

JOHN ROBERT MIZE
"THE BIG CAT"
ST. LOUIS N.L., NEW YORK N.L.,
NEW YORK A.L., 1936 - 1953
KEEN-EYED SLUGGER SMASHED 359 HOME RUNS
AND BATTED .312 IN 15-YEAR CAREER WHILE
TOPPING .300 MARK NINE SEASONS IN A ROW.
SET MAJOR LOOP RECORDS BY HITTING THREE
HOMERS IN A GAME SIX TIMES AND TRIO IN
SUCCESSION ON FOUR OCCASIONS. WON N.L.
BATTING TITLE ONCE, LED OR SHARED LEAD
IN HOMERS AND SLUGGING PCT. FOUR TIMES,
RUNS BATTED IN AND TOTAL BASES THRICE.

HENRY "HANK" L. AARON
MILWAUKEE N.L., ATLANTA N.L.,
MILWAUKEE A.L., 1954 - 1976
HIT 755 HOME RUNS IN 23-YEAR CAREER TO
BECOME MAJORS' ALL-TIME HOME KING. HAD
20 OR MORE FOR 20 CONSECUTIVE YEARS, AT
LEAST 30 IN 15 SEASONS AND 40 OR BETTER
EIGHT TIMES. ALSO SET RECORDS FOR GAME
PLAYED (3,298), AT-BATS (12,364), LONG HITS
(1,477), TOTAL BASES (6,856), RUNS BATTED
IN (2,297). PACED N.L. IN BATTING TWICE
AND HOMERS, RUNS BATTED IN AND SLUGGING
PCT. FOUR TIMES EACH. WON MOST VALUABLE
PLAYER AWARD IN N.L. IN 1957.

ALBERT BENJAMIN CHANDLER
"HAPPY"
BASEBALL'S SECOND COMMISSIONER, 1945 -
1951. UNITED STATES SENATOR (1939 - 1945).
GOVERNOR OF KENTUCKY (1935-39, 1955-59).
IRON-WILLED AND HONEST, HE WAS KNOWN AS
A "PLAYER'S COMMISSIONER" BECAUSE OF HIS
BROAD CONCERN FOR ALL PHASES OF THE GAME.

TRAVIS CALVIN JACKSON
NEW YORK N.L., 1922 - 1936
PREMIER DEFENSIVE SHORTSTOP WHO SWUNG
PRODUCTIVE BAT. KNOWN FOR OUTSTANDING
ARM AND EXCEPTIONAL RANGE AFIELD. LED
N.L. SHORTSTOPS IN ASSISTS FOUR TIMES,
TOTAL CHANCES THREE YEARS AND FIELDING
PCT. AND DOUBLE PLAYS TWICE. ADEPT AS
BUNTER, HE BATTED OVER .300 SIX YEARS
WHILE COMPILING .291 LIFETIME AVERAGE.
DROVE IN MORE THAN 90 RUNS SIX TIMES,
REACHING 101 ON .268 AVERAGE IN 1934.

FRANK ROBINSON
CINCINNATI N.L., BALTIMORE A.L.,
LOS ANGELES N.L., CALIFORNIA A.L.,
CLEVELAND A.L., 1956 - 1976
FIRST TO BE CHOSEN MOST VALUABLE PLAYER
IN BOTH LEAGUES -- N.L. IN 1961 AND A.L.
IN 1966. SET RECORDS BY HITTING HOMERS
IN 32 DIFFERENT PARKS AND WITH PAIR OF
GRAND-SLAMMERS IN SUCCESSIVE INNINGS IN
1970. FOURTH IN HOMERS (586), FIFTH IN
EXTRA BASES ON LONG HITS (2,450), SIXTH
IN TOTAL BASES (5,373). ON RETIRING LED
N.L. IN SLUGGING PCT. IN 1960-61-62 AND
A.L. IN BATTING, HOMERS, RUNS BATTED IN,
TOTAL BASES AND SLUGGING PCT. IN 1966.

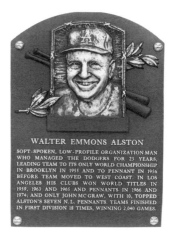

WALTER EMMONS ALSTON
SOFT-SPOKEN, LOW-PROFILE ORGANIZATION MAN
WHO MANAGED THE DODGERS FOR 23 YEARS,
LEADING TEAM TO ITS ONLY WORLD CHAMPIONSHIP
IN BROOKLYN IN 1955 AND TO PENNANT IN 1956
BEFORE TEAM MOVED TO WEST COAST. IN LOS
ANGELES HIS CLUBS WON WORLD TITLES IN
1959, 1963 AND 1965 AND PENNANTS IN 1966
AND 1974; AND ONLY JOHN McGRAW, WITH 10, TOPPED
ALSTON'S SEVEN N.L. PENNANTS. TEAMS FINISHED
IN FIRST DIVISION 18 TIMES, WINNING 2,040 GAMES.

GEORGE CLYDE KELL
PHILADELPHIA A.L. 1943 - 1946
DETROIT A.L. 1946 - 1952
BOSTON A.L. 1952 - 1954
CHICAGO A.L. 1954 - 1956
BALTIMORE A.L. 1956 - 1957
PREMIER A.L. THIRD BASEMAN OF 1940'S AND
1950'S. SOLID HITTER AND SURE-HANDED FIELDER
WITH STRONG, ACCURATE ARM. BATTED OVER
.300 9 TIMES, LEADING LEAGUE WITH .343 IN
1949. LED A.L. THIRD BASEMEN IN FIELDING
PCT. 7 TIMES, ASSISTS 4 TIMES AND PUTOUTS
AND DOUBLE PLAYS TWICE.

JUAN ANTONIO
(SANCHEZ) MARICHAL
SAN FRANCISCO N.L., 1960-1973 BOSTON A.L. 1974
LOS ANGELES N.L., 1975
HIGH-KICKING RIGHT-HANDER FROM DOMINICAN
REPUBLIC WON 243 GAMES AND LOST ONLY 142
OVER 16 SEASONS. WON 20 GAMES SIX TIMES AND
NO-HIT HOUSTON IN 1963. LED N.L. IN COMPLETE
GAMES AND SHUTOUTS TWICE AND IN ERA WITH
2.10 IN 1969. COMPLETED 244 GAMES DURING
CAREER, STRIKING OUT 2,303 AND FINISHING
WITH 2.89 ERA.

BROOKS CALBERT ROBINSON, JR.
BALTIMORE A.L. 1955 - 1977
ESTABLISHED MODERN STANDARD OF EXCELLENCE
FOR THIRD BASEMEN, SETTING MAJOR LEAGUE
RECORDS AT HIS POSITION FOR SEASONS (23),
FIELDING PCT. (.971), GAMES (2,870), PUTOUTS
(2,697), ASSISTS (6,205), AND DOUBLE PLAYS (618).
HIT 268 CAREER HOME RUNS. NAMED TO 18
CONSECUTIVE ALL STAR TEAMS. MVP OF 1970
WORLD SERIES. AMERICAN LEAGUE MVP IN 1964.

LUIS ERNESTO APARICIO
CHICAGO A.L. 1956-1962, 1968-1970
BALTIMORE A.L. 1963-1967
BOSTON A.L. 1971-1973
REGULAR SHORTSTOP FOR ALL OF HIS 18 SEASONS.
SET MAJOR LEAGUE CAREER RECORDS FOR MOST
GAMES (2,581), ASSISTS (8,016), CHANCES ACCEPTED
(12,564) AND DOUBLE PLAYS (1,553) BY A SHORTSTOP;
AND HAS MOST A.L. PUTOUTS (4,548). LED A.L. IN
FIELDING 8 TIMES. TOPPED LEAGUE IN STEALS
HIS FIRST 9 SEASONS, BEGINNING STOLEN BASE
RENAISSANCE. A.L. ROOKIE OF THE YEAR IN 1956.

DONALD SCOTT DRYSDALE
BROOKLYN N.L. 1956-1957
LOS ANGELES N.L. 1958-1969
HARD-THROWING SIDE-ARMER NOTED FOR
INTIMIDATING STYLE AND DURABILITY. HAD 209-166
RECORD WITH 2.95 ERA AND 2,486 STRIKEOUTS.
LED N.L. IN STRIKEOUTS 3 TIMES AND HURLED 49
SHUTOUTS. WAS 25-9 IN 1962 AND WON CY YOUNG
AWARD. THREW 6 SHUTOUTS IN A ROW IN 1968,
SETTING RECORD WITH 58 CONSECUTIVE SCORELESS
INNINGS. PITCHED IN RECORD 8 ALL-STAR GAMES.

RICHARD BENJAMIN FERRELL
ST. LOUIS A.L. 1929-1933, 1941-1943
BOSTON A.L. 1933-1937
WASHINGTON A.L. 1937-1941, 1944-1947
CAUGHT MORE GAMES (1,806) THAN ANY OTHER
AMERICAN LEAGUER. DURABLE DEFENSIVE STAND-OUT
WITH FINE ARM. EXPERT AT HANDLING PITCHERS.
MET CHALLENGE OF 4 KNUCKLE-BALLERS IN SENATORS'
STARTING ROTATION. OFTEN FORMED BATTERY WITH
BROTHER, WES. HIT OVER .300 4 TIMES. SECOND
ONLY TO DICKEY IN A.L. CAREER PUTOUTS AT
RETIREMENT.

HARMON CLAYTON KILLEBREW
WASHINGTON A.L. 1954-1960
MINNESOTA A.L. 1961-1974
KANSAS CITY A.L. 1975
MUSCULAR SLUGGER WITH MONUMENTAL HOME
RUN AND RBI SUCCESS. HIS 573 HOMERS OVER
22 YEARS RANK FIFTH ALL-TIME AND SECOND
ONLY TO RUTH AMONG A.L. HITTERS. TIED OR
LED A.L. IN HOME RUNS 6 TIMES. BELTED OVER
40 ON 8 OCCASIONS AND IS THIRD IN HOME RUN
FREQUENCY. DROVE IN OVER 100 RUNS 9 TIMES.
A.L. MVP IN 1969.

HAROLD HENRY "PEE WEE" REESE
BROOKLYN N.L. 1940-1957
LOS ANGELES N.L. 1958
SHORTSTOP AND CAPTAIN OF GREAT DODGER TEAMS
OF 1940'S AND 50'S. INTANGIBLE QUALITIES OF SUBTLE
LEADERSHIP ON AND OFF FIELD, COMPETITIVE FIRE
AND PROFESSIONAL PRIDE COMPLEMENTED DEPENDABLE
GLOVE. RELIABLE BASE-RUNNING AND CLUTCH-HITTING
AS SIGNIFICANT FACTORS IN 7 DODGER PENNANTS.
INSTRUMENTAL IN EASING ACCEPTANCE OF JACKIE
ROBINSON AS BASEBALL'S FIRST BLACK PERFORMER.

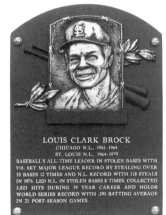

LOUIS CLARK BROCK
CHICAGO N.L. 1961-1964
ST. LOUIS N.L. 1964-1979
BASEBALL'S ALL-TIME LEADER IN STOLEN BASES WITH
938. SET MAJOR LEAGUE RECORD BY STEALING OVER
50 BASES 12 TIMES AND N.L. RECORD WITH 118 STEALS
IN 1974. LED N.L. IN STOLEN BASES 8 TIMES. COLLECTED
3,023 HITS DURING 19 YEAR CAREER AND HOLDS
WORLD SERIES RECORD WITH .391 BATTING AVERAGE
IN 21 POST-SEASON GAMES.

ENOS BRADSHER SLAUGHTER
"COUNTRY"
ST. LOUIS N.L. 1938-1953
NEW YORK A.L. 1954-1955, 1956-1959
KANSAS CITY A.L. 1955-1956 MILWAUKEE N.L. 1959
HARD-NOSED, HUSTLING PERFORMER WHO PLAYED
THE GAME WITH INTENSITY AND DETERMINATION.
FLAT, LEVEL SWING MADE HIM A LIFETIME .300
HITTER WHO INVARIABLY CAME THROUGH IN
CLUTCH SITUATIONS. EXCELLENT OUTFIELDER WITH
STRONG ARM. DARING BASERUNNER FAMOUS FOR
HIS MAD DASH HOME TO WIN 1946 WORLD SERIES
FOR CARDINALS. BATTED .291 IN 5 WORLD SERIES.

JOSEPH FLOYD VAUGHAN
"ARKY"
PITTSBURGH N.L. 1932-1941
BROOKLYN N.L. 1942-1948
AMONG HALL OF FAME SHORTSTOPS, HIS .318
LIFETIME BATTING AVERAGE IS SECOND ONLY TO
HONUS WAGNER'S .329. LED LEAGUE WITH .385 IN
1935. HOMERED TWICE IN 1941 ALL-STAR GAME.
FANNED ONLY 276 TIMES IN 6622 CAREER AT-BATS.
POLISHED FIELDER AND ACCOMPLISHED BASE
RUNNER, LEADING N.L. WITH 20 STOLEN BASES IN
1943.

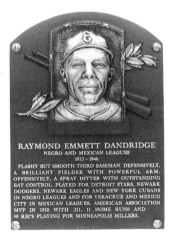

JAMES HOYT WILHELM
NEW YORK N.L. 1952-1956 ST. LOUIS N.L. 1957
CLEVELAND A.L. 1957-1958 BALTIMORE A.L. 1958-1962
CHICAGO A.L. 1963-1968 CALIFORNIA A.L. 1969
ATLANTA N.L. 1969-1970, 1971 CHICAGO N.L. 1970
LOS ANGELES N.L. 1971-1972
BASEBALL'S PREMIER RELIEF PITCHER. USED KNUCKLE
BALL TO WIN 143 GAMES (A RECORD 124 IN RELIEF)
AND AMASSED 227 SAVES OVER 21-YEAR CAREER.
NO-HIT YANKEES ON SEPT. 20, 1958 IN INFREQUENT
START FOR ORIOLES. PITCHED IN RECORD 1070
GAMES WITH LIFETIME ERA OF 2.52.

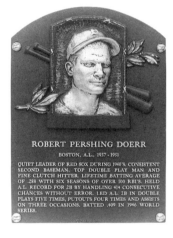

ROBERT PERSHING DOERR
BOSTON, A.L. 1937-1951
QUIET LEADER OF RED SOX DURING 1940'S. CONSISTENT
SECOND BASEMAN, TOP DOUBLE PLAY MAN AND
FINE CLUTCH HITTER. LIFETIME BATTING AVERAGE
OF .288 WITH SIX SEASONS OF OVER 100 RBI'S. HELD
A.L. RECORD FOR 2B BY HANDLING 414 CONSECUTIVE
CHANCES WITHOUT ERROR. LED A.L. 2B IN DOUBLE
PLAYS FIVE TIMES, PUTOUTS FOUR TIMES AND ASSISTS
ON THREE OCCASIONS. BATTED .409 IN 1946 WORLD
SERIES.

ERNEST NATALI LOMBARDI
BROOKLYN, N.L. 1931
CINCINNATI, N.L. 1932 - 1941
BOSTON, N.L. 1942
NEW YORK, N.L. 1943 - 1947
HIT .306 OVER 17 SEASONS DESPITE SLOWNESS AFOOT.
TEN TIMES BATTING OVER .300. WON N.L. BATTING
TITLE WITH .342 IN 1938 AND AGAIN IN 1942 WITH
.330. HELD HANDS LOW, WITH INTERLOCKING GOLF
GRIP AND QUICK STROKE. N.L. MVP IN 1938. SKILLED
RECEIVER AND HANDLER OF PITCHERS. OUTSTANDING
ARM FROM CROUCH POSITION, RIFLING THROWS
WITH SIDE-ARM RELEASE.

WILLIE LEE MC COVEY
"STRETCH"
SAN FRANCISCO, N.L. 1959-1973, 1977-1980
SAN DIEGO, N.L. 1974-1976
OAKLAND, A.L. 1976
TOP LEFT-HANDED HOME RUN HITTER IN N.L.
HISTORY WITH 521. SECOND ONLY TO LOU GEHRIG
WITH 18 CAREER GRAND SLAMS. LED N.L. IN HOMERS
THREE TIMES AND RBI'S TWICE. N.L. ROOKIE OF
YEAR IN 1959, MVP IN 1969 AND COMEBACK PLAYER
OF THE YEAR IN '77. TEAMED WITH WILLIE MAYS
FOR AWESOME 1-2 PUNCH IN GIANTS' LINEUP.

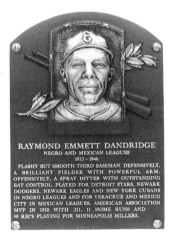

RAYMOND EMMETT DANDRIDGE
NEGRO AND MEXICAN LEAGUES
1933 - 1948
FLASHY BUT SMOOTH THIRD BASEMAN. DEFENSIVELY,
A BRILLIANT FIELDER WITH POWERFUL ARM.
OFFENSIVELY, A SPRAY HITTER WITH OUTSTANDING
BAT CONTROL. PLAYED FOR DETROIT STARS, NEWARK
DODGERS, NEWARK EAGLES AND NEW YORK CUBANS
IN NEGRO LEAGUES AND FOR VERACRUZ AND MEXICO
CITY IN MEXICAN LEAGUES. AMERICAN ASSOCIATION
MVP IN 1950 WITH .311, 11 HOME RUNS AND
80 RBI'S PLAYING FOR MINNEAPOLIS MILLERS.

JAMES AUGUSTUS HUNTER
"CATFISH"
KANSAS CITY, A.L. 1965-1967
OAKLAND, A.L. 1968-1974
NEW YORK, A.L. 1975-1979
THE BIGGER THE GAME, THE BETTER HE PITCHED.
ONE OF BASEBALL'S MOST DOMINANT PITCHERS FROM
1970-76, WINNING OVER 20 FIVE STRAIGHT TIMES. COMPILED
224-166 MARK WITH 3.26 ERA BEFORE ARM TROUBLE
ENDED CAREER AT AGE 33. HURLED PERFECT GAME
VS. TWINS IN 1968. 1974 A.L. CY YOUNG AWARD WINNER.
5-3 IN 12 WORLD SERIES GAMES.

BILLY LEO WILLIAMS
CHICAGO, N.L. 1959-1974
OAKLAND, A.L. 1975-1976
SOFT-SPOKEN, CLUTCH PERFORMER WAS ONE OF
MOST RESPECTED HITTERS OF HIS DAY. BATTED SOLID
.290 OVER 18 SEASONS SOCKING 426 HOME RUNS. HIT 20
OR MORE HOMERS 13 STRAIGHT SEASONS. 1961 N.L.
ROOKIE OF YEAR. 1972 N.L. BATTING CHAMPION WITH
.333. HELD N.L. RECORD FOR CONSECUTIVE GAMES
PLAYED WITH 1117.

WILVER DORNEL STARGELL
"WILLIE"
PITTSBURGH, N.L. 1962 - 1982
INTIMIDATING PRESENCE BETWEEN THE LINES
AND CHARISMATIC PATRIARCH IN CLUBHOUSE
AND DUGOUT. CRUSHED 475 HOMERS, MANY
OF TAPE-MEASURE VARIETY AND HIT MOST
BY ANY PLAYER DURING 1970'S. LIKE HIS
ROUND-TRIPPERS, HIS 1,540 RBI'S ALSO MOST
EVER BY A PIRATE. BATTED .282 OVER 21
SEASONS, ALL WITH PITTSBURGH. SHARED N.L.
MVP HONORS IN 1979, AND NAMED MVP IN '79
N.L. CHAMPIONSHIP SERIES AND WORLD SERIES.

ALBERT JOSEPH BARLICK
UMPIRE
NATIONAL LEAGUE 1940-1971
EARNED RESPECT OF PEERS AND PLAYERS ALIKE WITH
BOOMING, BASSO CALLS, CLEAR AND DECISIVE HAND
SIGNALS, KNOWLEDGE OF RULES, PROFICIENCY ON
BALLS AND STRIKES, ABILITY TO ANTICIPATE AND
THEN HANDLE ROUGH SITUATIONS AND UNCEASING
HUSTLE. PROFESSIONAL UMPIRE FOR FIVE DECADES;
AND AT AGE 25, ONE OF YOUNGEST TO REACH MAJORS,
WHERE HE WORKED 27 FULL SEASONS.

JOHNNY LEE BENCH
CINCINNATI, N.L., 1967-1983
REDEFINED STANDARDS BY WHICH CATCHERS ARE
MEASURED DURING 17 SEASONS WITH "BIG RED
MACHINE"; CONTROLLED GAME ON BOTH SIDES OF PLATE WITH
HIS HITTING (389 HOMERS-RECORD 327 AS A CATCHER,
1,376 RBI'S), THROWING OUT OPPOSING BASE RUNNERS.
CALLING PITCHES AND BLOCKING HOME PLATE. N.L.
MVP, 1970 AND 1972. WON 10 GOLD GLOVES. LAST GAME.
9TH INNING HOMER LED TO 1972 PENNANT.

ALBERT FRED SCHOENDIENST
"RED"
ST. LOUIS, N.L., 1945-1956, 1961-1963
NEW YORK, N.L., 1956-1957
MILWAUKEE, N.L., 1957-1960
ROOMMATE STAN MUSIAL CREDITED HIM WITH "GREATEST
PAIR OF HANDS I'VE EVER SEEN"; SLEEK, FAR-RANGING
SECOND BASEMAN FOR 18 SEASONS. LED N.L. IN FIELDING
AND HIT .300 OR BETTER SEVEN TIMES. WHEN ELECTED
IN 1989 HAD WORN MAJOR LEAGUE UNIFORM 45 CONSECUTIVE
SEASONS AS PLAYER, COACH AND MANAGER, PILOTING
REDBIRDS TO WORLD SERIES IN 1967 AND 1968. 14TH
INNING HOMER WON 1950 ALL-STAR GAME FOR N.L.

CARL MICHAEL YASTRZEMSKI
"YAZ"
BOSTON, A.L., 1961-1983
SUCCEEDED TED WILLIAMS IN FENWAY'S LEFT FIELD
IN 1961 AND RETIRED 23 YEARS LATER AS ALL-TIME
RED SOX LEADER IN 6 CATEGORIES. PLAYED WITH
GRACEFUL INTENSITY IN RECORD 3,308 A.L. GAMES.
ONLY A.L. PLAYER WITH 3,000 HITS AND 400 HOMERS.
3-TIME BATTING CHAMPION. WON MVP AND TRIPLE
CROWN IN 1967 AS HE LED RED SOX TO "IMPOSSIBLE
DREAM" PENNANT.

JOE LEONARD MORGAN
HOUSTON, N.L., 1963-1971, 1980
CINCINNATI, N.L., 1972-1979
SAN FRANCISCO, N.L., 1981-1982
PHILADELPHIA, N.L., 1983
OAKLAND, A.L., 1984
IMPACT PLAYER WHO LIFTED CINCINNATI'S "BIG RED
MACHINE" TO HIGHER LEVEL WITH HIS MULTI-FACETED
SKILLS. TRADEMARK WAS FLAPPING LEFT ARM AS HE
AWAITED PITCH. PACKED UNUSUAL POWER INTO
EXTRAORDINARILY QUICK 150-LB. FIREPLUG FRAME. PLAYED
22 SEASONS AND ALSO HOLDS HOME RUN AND GAMES
PLAYED RECORDS FOR 2B. N.L. MVP, 1975-76.

JAMES ALVIN PALMER
BALTIMORE, A.L., 1965-1984
HIGH-KICKING, SMOOTH-THROWING SYMBOL OF
BALTIMORE'S SIX CHAMPIONSHIP TEAMS OF 1960's,
70's AND 80's. IMPRESSIVE NUMBERS INCLUDE 268
WINS WITH .638 PCT., EIGHT 20-WIN SEASONS, 2.86
ERA AND NO GRAND SLAMS ALLOWED OVER
ENTIRE 19 YEAR CAREER. INTENSITY WAS TRADEMARK
OF 3-TIME CY YOUNG WINNER, WHO COMBINED
STRENGTH, INTELLIGENCE, COMPETITIVENESS AND
CONSISTENCY TO BECOME ORIOLES' ALL-TIME
WINNINGEST HURLER.

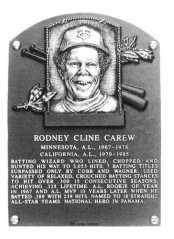

RODNEY CLINE CAREW
MINNESOTA, A.L., 1967-1978
CALIFORNIA, A.L., 1979-1985
BATTING WIZARD WHO LINED, CHOPPED AND
BUNTED HIS WAY TO 3,053 HITS. 7 BATTING TITLES
SURPASSED ONLY BY COBB AND WAGNER. USED
VARIETY OF RELAXED, CROUCHED BATTING STANCES
TO HIT OVER .300 15 CONSECUTIVE SEASONS,
ACHIEVING .328 LIFETIME. A.L. ROOKIE OF YEAR
IN 1967 AND A.L. MVP 10 YEARS LATER WHEN HE
BATTED .388 WITH 239 HITS. NAMED TO 18 STRAIGHT
ALL-STAR TEAMS. NATIONAL HERO IN PANAMA.

FERGUSON ARTHUR JENKINS
PHILADELPHIA, N.L., 1965-1966
CHICAGO, N.L., 1966-1973, 1982-1983
TEXAS, A.L., 1974-1975, 1978-1981
BOSTON, A.L., 1976-1977
CANADA'S FIRST HALL-OF-FAMER. 284-226
LIFETIME WITH 3,192 STRIKEOUTS AND 3.34 ERA
DESPITE PLAYING 12 OF HIS 19 YEAR CAREER IN
HITTERS' BALLPARKS-WRIGLEY FIELD AND FENWAY
PARK. WON 20 GAMES 7 SEASONS, INCLUDING 6
CONSECUTIVE, 1967 - 1972. CY YOUNG AWARD
WINNER, 1971. TRADEMARKS WERE PINPOINT CONTROL
AND CHANGING SPEEDS.

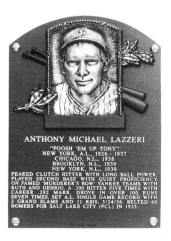

ANTHONY MICHAEL LAZZERI
"POOSH 'EM UP TONY"
NEW YORK, A.L., 1926-1937
CHICAGO, N.L., 1938
BROOKLYN, N.L., 1939
NEW YORK, N.L., 1939
FEARED CLUTCH HITTER WITH LONG BALL POWER.
PLAYED SECOND BASE WITH QUIET PROFICIENCY
ON FAMED MURDERER'S ROW YANKEE TEAMS WITH
RUTH AND GEHRIG. A .300 HITTER FIVE TIMES WITH
CAREER .292 MARK. DROVE IN OVER 100 RUNS
SEVEN TIMES. SET A.L. SINGLE GAME RECORD WITH
2 GRAND SLAMS AND 11 RBIS, 5/24/36. BELTED 60
HOMERS FOR SALT LAKE CITY (PCL) IN 1925.

GAYLORD JACKSON PERRY
SAN FRANCISCO, N.L., 1962-1971
CLEVELAND, A.L., 1972-1975
TEXAS, A.L., 1975-1977, 1980
SAN DIEGO, N.L., 1978-1979
ATLANTA, A.L., 1981
SEATTLE, A.L., 1982-1983
KANSAS CITY, A.L., 1983
ACHIEVED PITCHERS' MAGIC NUMBERS WITH 314 WINS
AND 3,534 STRIKEOUTS. PLAYING MIND GAMES WITH
HITTERS THROUGH ARRAY OF RITUALS ON MOUND WAS
PART OF HIS ARSENAL. 20-GAME WINNER 5 TIMES WITH
LIFETIME ERA OF 3.10. NO-HIT GAMES FOR GIANTS
9/17/68. OUTSTANDING COMPETITOR. ONLY CY YOUNG WINNER
IN BOTH LEAGUES.

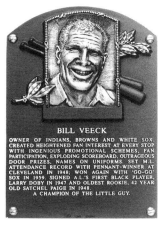

BILL VEECK
OWNER OF INDIANS, BROWNS AND WHITE SOX.
CREATED HEIGHTENED FAN INTEREST AT EVERY STOP
WITH INGENIOUS PROMOTIONAL SCHEMES, FAN
PARTICIPATION, EXPLODING SCOREBOARD, OUTRAGEOUS
DOOR PRIZES, NAMES ON UNIFORMS. SET M.L.
ATTENDANCE RECORD WITH PENNANT-WINNER AT
CLEVELAND IN 1948; WON AGAIN WITH "GO-GO"
SOX IN 1959. SIGNED A.L.'S FIRST BLACK PLAYER,
LARRY DOBY IN 1947 AND OLDEST ROOKIE, 42 YEAR
OLD SATCHEL PAIGE IN 1948.
A CHAMPION OF THE LITTLE GUY.

ROLAND GLEN FINGERS
OAKLAND, A.L., 1968-1976
SAN DIEGO, N.L., 1977-1980
MILWAUKEE, A.L., 1981-1985
CAREER EPITOMIZED EMERGENCE OF MODERN-DAY
RELIEF ACE AS HE APPROACHED LEGENDARY STATUS
WITH CONSISTENT EXCELLENCE COMING OUT OF
BULLPEN. RELIED UPON SINKING FAST BALL TO
BECOME ALL-TIME MAJOR LEAGUE LEADER WITH
341 CAREER SAVES. APPEARED IN 16 WORLD SERIES
GAMES FOR OAKLAND, WINNING 2 AND SAVING 6.
A.L. MVP AND CY YOUNG AWARDEE IN 1981.

WILLIAM ALOYSIUS McGOWAN
(NO. 1)
UMPIRE
AMERICAN LEAGUE 1925-1954
CAME CLOSE TO BEING EXCEPTION TO OLD
ADAGE THAT FANS DON'T PAY TO SEE THE
UMPIRE. INTRODUCED COLORFUL STYLE WITH
VIGOROUS, AGGRESSIVE GESTURES BORDERING
ON THE PUGNACIOUS. ENTHUSIASM NEVER WANED
OVER 30 MAJOR LEAGUE SEASONS WHILE
HUSTLING DEMEANOR COMMANDED PLAYERS'
RESPECT. MOST DURABLE UMPIRE IN HISTORY.
DID NOT MISS AN INNING FOR 16 YEARS
(OVER 2400 CONSECUTIVE GAMES).

HAROLD NEWHOUSER
(PRINCE HAL)
DETROIT, A.L., 1939-1953
CLEVELAND, A.L., 1954-1955
ONLY PITCHER IN MAJOR LEAGUE HISTORY TO
WIN BACK-TO-BACK MVP AWARDS (1944-1945).
STRIKEOUT KING WITH BLAZING FAST BALL.
207-150 OVER 17 CAMPAIGNS. CONSECUTIVE SEASONS
OF 29-9, 25-9 AND 26-9 WITH CORRESPONDING
ERA'S OF 2.22, 1.81 and 1.94 FROM 1944-1946.
HURLED PENNANT-CLINCHER IN 1945 FOLLOWED
BY 2 WORLD SERIES VICTORIES OVER CUBS.

GEORGE THOMAS SEAVER
NEW YORK, N.L., 1967-1977, 1983
CINCINNATI, N.L., 1977-1982
CHICAGO, A.L., 1984-1986
BOSTON, A.L., 1986
FRANCHISE POWER PITCHER WHO TRANSFORMED
METS FROM LOVABLE LOSERS INTO FORMIDABLE
FOES. WON 311 GAMES OVER 20 SEASONS. SET N.L.
CAREER RECORD FOR STRIKEOUTS BY RHP (3,272)
AND MODERN RECORD FOR LOWEST ERA (2.73).
WHIFFED 200 OR MORE N.L. RECORD 10 TIMES
(19 IN A SINGLE GAME). N.L. ROOKIE OF YEAR,
1967 AND 3-TIME CY YOUNG AWARDEE. NO-HIT
CARDS IN 1978.

REGINALD MARTINEZ JACKSON
"MR. OCTOBER"
KANSAS CITY, A.L., 1967
OAKLAND, A.L., 1968-1975, 1987
BALTIMORE, 1976
NEW YORK, A.L., 1977-1981
CALIFORNIA, A.L., 1982-1986
EXCITING PERFORMER WHO PLAYED FOR 11 DIVISION WINNERS AND
FOUND SPECIAL SUCCESS IN WORLD SERIES SPOTLIGHT WITH 10 HOME
RUNS, 24 RBI'S AND .357 BATTING AVERAGE IN 27 GAMES: IN 1977
SERIES, HIT RECORD 5 HOMERS, 4 OF THEM CONSECUTIVE, INCLUDING
3 IN ONE GAME ON 3 FIRST PITCHES OF 3 DIFFERENT HURLERS.
MAMMOTH CLOUT MARKED 1971 ALL-STAR GAME. 563 HOMERS RANK
6TH ON ALL-TIME LIST. A.L. MVP, 1973.

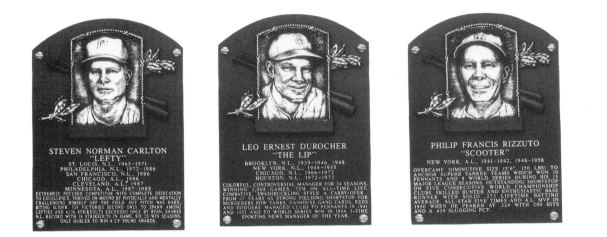

STEVEN NORMAN CARLTON
"LEFTY"
ST. LOUIS, N.L., 1965-1971
PHILADELPHIA, N.L., 1972-1986
SAN FRANCISCO, N.L., 1986
CHICAGO, A.L., 1986
CLEVELAND, A.L., 1987
MINNESOTA, A.L., 1987-1988
EXTREMELY FOCUSED COMPETITOR WITH COMPLETE DEDICATION
TO EXCELLENCE. THRIVED ON MOUND BY PHYSICALLY AND MENTALLY
CHALLENGING HIMSELF OFF THE FIELD. OUT PITCH WAS HARD,
BITING SLIDER. 329 VICTORIES SECOND ONLY TO SPAHN AMONG
LEFTIES AND 4,136 STRIKEOUTS EXCEEDED ONLY BY RYAN. SHARES
N.L. RECORD WITH 19 STRIKEOUTS IN GAME. SIX 20 WIN SEASONS.
ONLY HURLER TO WIN 4 CY YOUNG AWARDS.

LEO ERNEST DUROCHER
"THE LIP"
BROOKLYN, N.L., 1939-1946, 1948
NEW YORK, N.L., 1948-1955
CHICAGO, N.L., 1966-1972
HOUSTON, N.L., 1972-1973
COLORFUL, CONTROVERSIAL MANAGER FOR 24 SEASONS,
WINNING 2,008 GAMES, 7TH ON ALL-TIME LIST.
COMBATIVE, SWASHBUCKLING STYLE A CARRY-OVER
FROM 17 YEARS AS STRONG FIELDING SHORTSTOP FOR
MURDERERS' ROW YANKS, GASHOUSE GANG CARDS, REDS
AND DODGERS. MANAGED CLUBS TO PENNANTS IN 1941
AND 1951 AND TO WORLD SERIES WIN IN 1954. 3-TIME
SPORTING NEWS MANAGER OF THE YEAR.

PHILIP FRANCIS RIZZUTO
"SCOOTER"
NEW YORK, A.L., 1941-1942, 1946-1956
OVERCAME DIMINUTIVE SIZE (5'6", 150 LBS) TO
ANCHOR SUPERB YANKEE TEAMS WHICH WON 10
PENNANTS AND 8 WORLD SERIES DURING HIS 13
MAJOR LEAGUE SEASONS. OUTSTANDING SHORTSTOP
ON FIVE CONSECUTIVE WORLD CHAMPIONSHIP
CLUBS. SKILLED BUNTER AND ENTHUSIASTIC BASE
RUNNER WITH SOLID .273 LIFETIME BATTING
AVERAGE. ALL-STAR FIVE TIMES AND A.L. MVP IN
1950 WHEN HE PEAKED AT .324 WITH 200 HITS
AND A .439 SLUGGING PCT.

INDEX Page numbers in *italics* refer to illustrations.

PHOTOGRAPHY CREDITS

Page 21: *Baseball Players Practicing.* Photograph: Cathy Carver.

Page 25: *Safe at Home.* Courtesy of American Illustrators Gallery/Judy Goffman Fine Art, Inc., New York City.

Page 26: *Gramps and Baseball.* Printed by permission of The Norman Rockwell Family Trust. Copyright © 1992 The Norman Rockwell Family Trust.

Page 93: *Babe Ruth.* Copyright 1933 (renewed 1961) by The Conde Naste Publications, Inc.

Page 96: *Baseball at Night.* Photography courtesy Art Resource, New York.

Page 114: *Ted Williams.* Photograph courtesy ARTCO.

Page 119: *100 Years of Baseball.* Photograph courtesy Curtis Archives. Printed by permission of The Norman Rockwell Family Trust. Copyright © 1992 The Norman Rockwell Family Trust.

Page 124: *Jim Abbott.* Photograph: V. J. Lovero.

Page 137: *A Tough Call.* Printed by permission of The Norman Rockwell Family Trust. Copyright © 1992 The Norman Rockwell Family Trust.

Page 138: *Veteran Bush League Catcher.* Photograph courtesy The New York State Museum, *Diamonds Are Forever* Exhibition.

Page 142: *Shot Heard 'Round the World.* Photograph courtesy ARTCO.

Page 143: *Miracle at Coogan's Bluff.* Photograph courtesy Bill Goff, Inc., Kent, Connecticut.

Page 147: *Thomson Triptych: The Agony of Ralph Branca.* Courtesy of Rick and Jeri DeAngelis, Lexington, Massachusetts.

Page 166: *Yogi Berra.* Copyright © The Curtis Publishing Company.

Page 167: *Stanley Musial.* Copyright © The Curtis Publishing Company.

Page 168: *The Rookie.* Courtesy of American Illustrators Gallery/Judy Goffman Fine Art, Inc., New York City. Printed by permission of The Norman Rockwell Family Trust. Copyright © 1992 The Norman Rockwell Family Trust.

Page 191: *PPF 61.* Photograph copyright © D. James Dee.

Page 210: *World Series.* Courtesy Terry Dintenfass, Inc., New York City.

Page 212: *Ball Park—Boston.* Gift of Mr. and Mrs. Edwin E. Holkin, Highland Park, Illinois. Copyright © ARS, New York/SPADEM, Paris.

Page 216: *Play Ball.* Photo courtesy The New York State Museum, *Diamonds Are Forever* Exhibition.

Page 234: *Baseball.* Gift of the Friends of Art and a Group of Friends of the Gallery. Accession no. F63–16. Copyright © 1993 The Andy Warhol Foundation for the Visual Arts.

Page 235: *Bat Spinning at the Speed of Light.* Acquired 1988.

Page 236: *Spring Training.* Courtesy of the Pucker Gallery, Boston, MA and The New York State Museum, *Diamonds are Forever* Exhibition.

Page 238: *Report from the Fire Zone, Scroll XV.* Photograph courtesy The New York State Museum, *Diamonds are Forever* Exhibition.

Page 239: *Smokey Joe Williams.* Photograph courtesy The New York State Museum, *Diamonds are Forever* Exhibition.

Page 240: *Hats.* Photograph courtesy The Allan Stone Gallery.

Page 260: *Baseball Player (At Bat).* Photograph courtesy The New York State Museum, *Diamonds are Forever* Exhibition.

Page 264: *Take Me Out to the Ballgame.* Copyright © 1990 by James Rizzi, courtesy of John Szoke Graphics, Inc.

Page 271: *Mike's Mask.* Photograph: Franklin Rollins.

Page 282: *Fourth of July Townball at the Farmer's Museum.* Photograph: Richard Walker.

Page 283: *Night Game—Cooperstown, New York.* Photograph: Richard Walker.

Page 286: *Top Step: Shepherd.* Photograph: Joseph Szaszfai.

Page 287: *Bullpen: Pawtucket.* Photograph: Joseph Szaszfai.

Page 293, 294: Ball rotation drawings from *The Physics of Baseball.* Copyright © 1990 by Robert K. Adair. Reprinted by permission of HarperCollins Publisher.

Page 305: *Three and Two.* Photograph courtesy Scott Hull Associates.

Page 306 (left): *Bases Loaded.* Photograph courtesy Jack Dowd Studio.

Page 306 (right): *Third Baseman Fireball Conifer of the Tinkerville Tomcats.* Photograph: Richard Walker.

Page 307: *Stretching II.* Photograph: Richard Walker.

Page 308: *Tiger Stadium.* Photograph courtesy Bill Goff, Inc., Kent, Connecticut.

Page 310: *The Rookie.* Photograph courtesy of the artist.

Page 311: *Contact.* Photograph courtesy ARTCO.

Page 312: *Two–One Count.* Photograph: Richard Walker.

Page 329: *"Whip–O" Fungo Bat.* Copyright © 1984, John Weiss.

Page 330: *Phillies Trainer Jeff Cooper with Jeff Stone.* Copyright © 1984, John Weiss.

Page 331: *Paul Molitor (center).* Copyright © 1988, John Weiss.

Page 332: *Tommy Kelly, son of Twins Manager, Tom Kelly.* Copyright © 1985, John Weiss.

Page 333: *The Phillie Phanatic Kisses Orel Hershiser.* Copyright © 1986, John Weiss.

Page 334: *Oriole Park at Camden Yards.* Photograph copyright © Jeff Goldberg/Esto.

Page 336: *Dennis "Oil Can" Boyd Interview.* Copyright © 1986, John Weiss.

Page 353: *Night Baseball.* Photograph: Richard Walker.

Page 355: *Terrific.* Photograph: Richard Walker.

Page 358 (bottom): *American Icon (Floater).* Photograph: Richard Walker.

Page 359: *Baseball #1.* Photograph courtesy the Allan Stone Gallery. Photograph: David Behl.

Page 360: *The Love of the Game.* Photograph: Richard Walker.